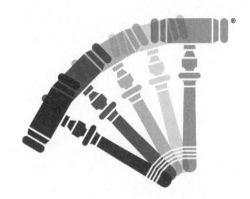

# *Casenote®* *Legal Briefs*

# CONTRACTS

Keyed to Courses Using

**Farnsworth, Sanger, Cohen, Brooks, and Garvin's**
**Contracts: Cases and Materials**

Eighth Edition

Wolters Kluwer

Law & Business

This publication is designed to provide accurate and authoritative information in regard to the subject matter covered. It is sold with the understanding that the publisher is not engaged in rendering legal, accounting, or other professional services. If legal advice or other expert assistance is required, the services of a competent professional person should be sought.

> — From a Declaration of Principles adopted jointly by a Committee of the American Bar Association and a Committee of Publishers and Associates

Copyright © 2014 CCH Incorporated. All Rights Reserved.

Published by Wolters Kluwer Law & Business in New York.

Wolters Kluwer Law & Business serves customers worldwide with CCH, Aspen Publishers, and Kluwer Law International products. (www.wolterskluwerlb.com)

To contact Customer Service, e-mail customer.service@wolterskluwer.com, call 1-800-234-1660, fax 1-800-901-9075, or mail correspondence to:

Wolters Kluwer Law & Business
Attn: Order Department
P.O. Box 990
Frederick, MD 21705

Printed in the United States of America.

1 2 3 4 5 6 7 8 9 0

ISBN 978-1-4548-4074-9

Certified Chain of Custody
Product Line Contains At Least
20% Certified Forest Content
www.sfiprogram.org
SFI-00756

## IMPLIED-IN-FACT CONDITION

Implied-in-fact conditions arise by physical or moral inference from what the parties have expressed (i.e., reasonable expectations of the parties). *Jacob & Youngs, Inc. v. Kent*, 230 N.Y. 239, 129 N.E. 689 (1921).

## IMPLIED-AT-LAW (CONSTRUCTIVE) CONDITION

"Constructive" conditions function to fix the order of performance when the express terms of the bargain are silent in this region.

## DUTY OF PERFORMANCE

Once a condition has been met, a duty of performance arises.

## SATISFACTION OF DUTY

Performance is the most desirable way to "discharge" a duty that arises from a contract. Once a party performs a duty required by a contract, that duty is "discharged."

## DISCHARGE OF DUTY

Duty to perform may be discharged by one of the following methods:

1. Impossibility: As measured by the objective standard, the impossibility must arise after the contract was entered into. The destruction of the subject matter of the contract gives rise to an impossibility, as does the subsequent passing of a law that renders the contract matter illegal. And if the services required in the contract were unique to one person (such as an artist or performer), then the death of the person will give rise to impossibility and discharge the duty inherent in the contract.
2. Impracticability: Occurs when subsequent factors have rendered the cost of performing a contract grossly in excess of what was foreseen. The key is whether the unreasonable increase in price was foreseeable. If it was foreseeable, the impracticability may NOT be used to discharge the duty.
3. Frustration of purpose: Occurs when a subsequent development not foreseeable at the time of entering the contract completely destroys the purpose of the contract (as understood by both parties).
4. Rescission: Duties to a contract may be rescinded by mutual agreement of both parties.
5. Novation:
   a. Novation substitutes a new party for an original party to the contract.
   b. All parties must assent to the substitution.
   c. Once the substitution occurs, then the original party is released from the contract.
6. Accord and Satisfaction: An accord and satisfaction releases debtor from a disputed debt through a new agreement. A valid accord and satisfaction must have consideration and the amount paid to satisfy the debt must be less than the debtor was originally entitled to.
   a. If the debt is undisputed, there is no accord and satisfaction.
   b. There is no consideration involved in releasing someone from a debt that is agreed upon—the debtor may seek additional payment.
   c. If the debt is disputed, then there is a valid accord and satisfaction.

## EXCUSE OF CONDITIONS

However, there are intervening factors that may prematurely "discharge" a duty, thus relieving a party of fulfilling the earlier promise.

1. Anticipatory Repudiation (applies only to bilateral contracts). *Hochster v. De La Tour*, 2 Ellis. & Bl. 678 (1853).
   a. The anticipatory repudiation must be unequivocal, definite, and communicated before the time of performance (must be more than a mere expression of doubt).
   b. Upon the anticipatory repudiation, the non-repudiating party may:
      i. Suspend own performance and sue other party immediately, OR
      ii. Affirm the contract and await the due date for performance.
2. Waiver: A party may voluntarily relinquish a known contract right, such as a condition or a contract, thus excusing the underlying condition or promise. *Clark v. West*, 193 N.Y. 349, 86 N.E. 1 (1908).
3. Estoppel: If a party who has the protection of a condition precedent or concurrent creates an impression that she will NOT insist upon its satisfaction, and the other party reasonably relies on such, the advantaged party will be estopped from insisting upon satisfaction.
4. Prevention or Failure to Cooperate: If a party wrongfully prevents a condition from occurring, whether by prevention or failure to cooperate, she will no longer be given the benefit of it.
5. Substantial Performance:
   a. Only applies to where implied-at-law (constructive) conditions are involved.
   b. Where a party has almost completely performed her duties, but has breached in a minor way, forfeiture of a return performance may be avoided by this rule.

   [Remember, substantial performance does not apply in the sale of goods (Article 2) context; the "perfect tender" rule applies.]
6. Conditions may also be excused by impossibility, impracticability, or frustration.

## CROSSING OFFERS

If there are two crossing offers that are identical and are mailed at the same time to the other party in such a way that they cross in the mail, a contract is not formed.

## PAROL EVIDENCE RULE

### INTERPRETATION OF TERMS

1. Ignorant party wins against knowing party. Restatement § 201.
2. When both parties knew of the differing intent, there is no contract
3. In order of preference:
   a. Express terms.
   b. Course of performance (negotiations).
   c. Course of dealing (previous contracts).
   d. Usage of trade.

## PAROL EVIDENCE RULE

1. Prior or contemporaneous negotiations and agreements that contradict or modify contractual terms are legally irrelevant if the written contract is intended as a complete and final expression of the parties.
   a. "Merger clause": A clause included in the contract intended to buttress the presumption that the written contract is a complete and final expression of the parties. *ARB Inc. v. E-Systems, Inc.*, 663 F.2d 189 (D.C. Cir. 1980).
   b. Such a contract outlined above is said to be "integrated."
2. Exceptions to the Parol Evidence Rule (evidence of the following may be admitted despite the Parol Evidence Rule):
   a. Subsequent modifications to the contract.
   b. Collateral agreement.
   c. Formation defects.
   d. Ambiguous terms.
   e. Existence of a condition precedent.
   f. Partial integration.

## SUBSEQUENT ASSIGNMENTS

Subsequent assignments automatically revoke the former assignment; an assignment in writing is, however, irrevocable. If the assignments are "equal," then usually one applies the "American Rule": first in line is first in right.

## BREACH OF CONTRACT

### MATERIAL v. MINOR BREACH

1. Material breach: One may suspend performance AND sue for damages. *K & G Contr. Co. v. Harris*, 223 Md. 305, 164 A.2d 451 (1960).
2. Minor breach: One may only sue for damages (which may be nominal). It is important to remember that this does NOT suspend the duty to perform. *Walker & Co. v. Harrison*, 347 Mich. 630, 81 N.W.2d 352 (1957).
3. The test for materiality for a breach weighs several factors:
   a. The benefit received by the injured (non-breaching) party.
   b. Adequacy of compensation for the injured party.
   c. The extent to which the non-injured (breaching) party has partly performed.
   d. Hardship to the non-injured party.
   e. Negligence or willful behavior of the breaching party.
   f. The likelihood that the breaching party will perform the remainder of contract.

### LATE PERFORMANCE

1. Usually a minor breach.
2. May become a material breach only where:
   a. Contract requires timely performance (usually UCC).
   b. Contract contains language such as "time is of the essence."

# ELEMENTS OF CONTRACTS

## ELEMENTS OF A CONTRACT

A contract, to be properly formed, needs an offer and an acceptance with consideration.

## TYPES OF CONTRACTS

1. Express contracts are formed when the offer and acceptance are manifested by oral or written words.
2. Implied contracts are formed if the mutual assent of the parties is manifested by conduct. *Wood v. Lucy, Lady Duff-Gordon*, 222 N.Y. 88, 118 N.E. 214 (1917).
3. Quasi-contracts ("implied-at-law") are not technically contracts, but devices created to avoid unjust enrichment.

# DEFENSES TO FORMATION

## STATUTE OF FRAUDS

The following types of contracts require the contract to be in writing in order to be valid:
1. Marriage.
2. Contract cannot be performed within a year.
3. Executor/administrator.
4. Surety.
5. Interest in land.
6. Contract for the sale of goods at a price of $500 or more.

## 5. PART PERFORMANCE FOR A LAND SALE CONTRACT

- Part performance on a land sale contract will waive the Statue of Frauds and allow a land sale to be performed without fulfilling the written requirements of the Statute of Frauds.
- Part performance will be satisfied for a land sale contract if buyer does TWO of the following three:
  1. Part payment.
  2. Possession.
  3. Improvements on the land.
  *Winternitz v. Summit Hills Joint Venture*, 312 Md. 127, 538 A.2d 778 (1988).

## 6. SALE OF GOODS FOR $500 OR MORE

In order to be valid, a contract for a sale of goods requires the following elements:
1. Some writing (at least the quantity); and
2. Be signed by the party to be charged.

To qualify under the Statute of Frauds, the writing presented can be informal in nature (e.g., a scribbled note that contains the quantity amount or a check), and may be spread out over many documents. *Crabtree v. Elizabeth Arden*, 305 N.Y. 48, 110 N.E.2d 551 (1953).

## EXCEPTIONS TO THE STATUTE OF FRAUDS

1. Confirmatory Memo Rule (Between Merchants).
   a. This rule applies only between merchants.
   b. There is a written confirmation sent (within a reasonable time) after the two merchants have come to an oral agreement. If the recipient of the memo does not object to the contents of the memo, then the contract is valid (despite the requirements of the Statute of Frauds). UCC § 2-201(2)
2. Goods are specifically made for the buyer (the goods must only be usable by the buyer).
3. An ADMISSION by one of the parties that a contract was made.
4. The contract has already been performed (the goods have been received and accepted or paid for). *Buffaloe v. Hart*, 114 N.C. App. 52, 441 S.E.2d 172 (1994).

## INCAPACITY, MINORITY

1. Incapacity: Insane persons lack the capacity to enter into a valid contract. Intoxicated people as well.
2. Minority (under the age of 18):
   a. A contract made during one's legal minority may be disaffirmed at any time before or after the attainment of a legal majority. Unless and until the contract is disaffirmed, it remains binding.
   b. Other considerations for minority:
      i. If the contract involves necessities (food, clothes, or medical attention), the minor is still liable for the reasonable market value of the items.
      ii. Once the minor reaches the age of legal majority, the contract may be ratified, and thus be made binding.

## DUTY TO MITIGATE

In most cases, the suing party has a duty to mitigate damages. If the duty has been breached, it merely serves to reduce (does not bar) recovery.

## DURESS

1. Physical Duress: Coercive acts (can be to others beside the victim, i.e., family members) may be a valid personal defense to avoid the obligations of a contract or the forced rescission of a contract.
2. Economic Duress: No defense when one of the parties is in dire need of the subject matter and the other takes advantage of the circumstances to drive an overly harsh bargain.

## MISTAKE

1. Unilateral Mistake: A unilateral mistake of a material fact will not be a defense to contract formation. The contract will be enforceable despite the mistake of one of the parties. *Exception:* The non-mistaken party had reason to know of the mistake by the other party. Only then, does a unilateral mistake become a defense to contract formation. *Market St. Associates v. Frey*, 941 F.2d 588 (7th Cir.1991).
2. Mutual Mistake: If there is a mutual mistake of a material fact concerning the bargain, the parties may engage in a rescission of the contract. *Sherwood v. Walker*, 66 Mich. 568, 33 N.W. 919 (1887).
3. Mistake in Transmission: "Scrivener's error." If there is an error in transmission differing from the parties' original intent, then they may reform the contract to reflect the original terms of the intended bargain.
If one party is aware of the mistake (to an essential term) or should have known of the mistake in transmission, then the other party may use the mistake as a defense to formation.

## UNCONSCIONABILITY

If a contract is deemed "unconscionable," a court will attempt to strike the offending clause(s) from the contract and enforce the rest of the contract.

## ILLEGALITY

If the subject matter of the bargain is illegal, the contract is void. *R.R. v. M.H. & Another*, 426 Mass. 501, 689 N.E.2d 790 (1998). However, a few things should be considered:
1. If the subject matter or participation of parties is declared illegal when the offer is made, the offer is revoked as a matter of law.
2. If the subject matter or participation of the parties is declared illegal AFTER formation, BUT BEFORE performance, then the duties of both parties are discharged under the doctrine of impossibility.

## FRAUD

Misrepresentation of a fact or promise of future performance at the time the contract was made which induces party to enter into the contract.

# PERFORMANCE

## CONDITIONS

1. Promise v. Condition: A promise is a commitment to do or not to do an act that is at the heart of the contract. A condition is an event which will modify the underlying promise (such as when and if the promise must be performed).
2. Effects of Condition v. Promise:
   Failure of a promise = Breach.
   Failure of a condition = Relief from the obligation to perform.

## TYPES OF CONDITIONS

1. Categorized by timing: condition precedent, conditions concurrent, condition subsequent.
2. Categorized by source: express conditions, implied-in-fact, implied-at-law conditions.

## CONDITION PRECEDENT

Condition must occur before performance is due. Once condition occurs, then performance must happen. *Oppenheimer & Co. v. Oppenheim, Appel, Dixon & Co.*, 86 N.Y.2d 685, 660 N.E.2d 415 (1995).

## CONDITIONS CONCURRENT

Conditions to occur at the same time. If one condition has occurred, then the other must occur as well.

## CONDITION SUBSEQUENT

Condition cuts off already existing duty. Once this occurs, duty to perform is excused.

*Example:* In a contract, a clause containing a condition subsequent will state: "I am liable to perform this promise until (the occurrence)."

Performance continues on page 3 ▶

# CONTRACTS

## FORMATION

### IN GENERAL

The parties must form an agreement by consenting to the same terms at the same time. They accomplish this by the process of offer and acceptance. *Lonergan v. Scolnick*, 129 Cal. App. 2d 179, 276 P.2d 8 (1954).

Once there is an offer and an acceptance, the parties have arrived at mutual assent.

### OFFER

An offer is the manifestation of willingness to enter into a bargain, so made as to justify a reasonable person in the position of the offeree in understanding that her assent to that bargain is invited and will conclude it.

### INTENT

Intent must be manifested through such words or acts that a reasonable person would believe an offer is being made. *Lucy v. Zehmer*, 196 Va. 493, 84 S.E.2d 516 (1954).

### ESSENTIAL TERMS OF AN OFFER (COMMON LAW)

1. Identification of the parties.
2. Description of the subject matter.
3. Time for performance.
4. Price.

   *Note:* Silence on some of the terms above may be interpreted to mean that reasonable terms may be determined at a later date.

   (Article 2 of the UCC, which governs the sale of goods, only requires that quantity be an essential term of the contract—all other terms will be filled in appropriately.)

### DURATION OF THE OFFER

1. Merchant's Firm Offer (UCC § 2-205): Usually irrevocable.
2. Option Contract:
   a. Money is paid to keep the offer open for a certain period of time.
   b. Counteroffer does not terminate the power to accept, unless the buyer detrimentally relies on it.

### "INVITATION TO DEAL"

Do not confuse an offer with an "invitation to deal." The latter is more of the type that would be found in catalogs.

*Note:* Crossing offers in the mail that are identical are void and do NOT form a contract.

### OFFER TERMINATION

1. An offeree's power of acceptance may be terminated by:
   a. Rejection or counter-offer by the offeree.
   b. Lapse of time.
   c. Revocation by the offeror.
   d. Death or incapacity of the offeror or offeree.
   e. Non-occurrence of any condition of acceptance under the terms of the offer.
2. Detrimental reliance makes an offer irrevocable for a reasonable time (modern view).
   a. Common Law: No such thing (must go to the UCC—merchant firm offer).
3. Termination by operation of law:
   a. Incapacitation of the offeror.
   b. Destruction of the subject matter prior to an effective acceptance.

### CONSIDERATION

A contract is enforceable only if it is supported by consideration. *Kirksey v. Kirksey*, 8 Ala. 131 (1845). Consideration must be a bargained-for exchange and of legal value.

1. Bargained-for exchange:
   a. Parties must exchange something, even if it is a peppercorn.
   b. Gifts are not "bargained for" and thus do not qualify as consideration (see promissory estoppel).
   c. Forbearance will be sufficient if it benefits the promisor.
   d. Past or moral consideration is not valid.
2. Legal value.
   a. A party must bear a detriment.
   b. A pre-existing legal duty is not consideration.
3. Substitutes for consideration.
   a. Promissory estoppel.
   b. Detrimental reliance.
   c. Modification under the UCC.

### ACCEPTANCE

1. Unilateral:
   a. Acceptance can be done only through performance. *Ragosta v. Wilder*, 156 Vt. 390, 592 A.2d 367 (1991).
   b. Once performance has started, offeror may not revoke the offer.
   c. Offeree must be aware that the offer exists.

2. Bilateral (see Mailbox Rule Chart below):
   a. Requires an exchange of promises.
   b. A valid acceptance (for a bilateral contract) requires that there be an offeree with the power to accept, unequivocal terms of acceptance, and communication of acceptance.

### POWER TO ACCEPT

Generally, the entity to whom the offer has been addressed has the power of acceptance.

### UNEQUIVOCAL TERMS OF ACCEPTANCE

Acceptance must mirror the offeror's terms exactly. Otherwise, the "new" offer with additional or modified terms becomes a new offer.

(Under the UCC, the rule is different. An acceptance need not be an exact mirror of the original offer.)

### COMMUNICATION OF ACCEPTANCE

1. Mailbox Rule: A contract is formed upon the moment of dispatch of the acceptance. This assumes that it is properly sent (i.e., properly addressed, stamped, and deposited in a mailbox). If the acceptance has not been properly sent, then acceptance is effective upon receipt.
   *Note:* The Mailbox Rule only applies to acceptances. Other acts (e.g., rejection) are only effective upon receipt.
2. Exceptions to the Mailbox Rule:
   a. If the offer stipulates that the acceptance is not effective until received. (The parties may contract out of the Mailbox Rule.)
   b. Option contracts are immune to the Rule.
   c. If the offeree sends a rejection and then sends an acceptance, whichever arrives first is effective.
   d. If the offeree sends an acceptance and then a rejection, the Mailbox Rule would normally apply. If the rejection arrived first and the offeror detrimentally relies on it, the Rule would be inapplicable.

### THE MAILBOX RULE

| Timeline | ACCEPTANCE MAILED | REJECTION MAILED | REJECTION RECEIVED | ACCEPTANCE RECEIVED |
| --- | --- | --- | --- | --- |

Contract is formed unless offeror detrimentally relies on rejection before acceptance arrives.

### VARIATIONS OF THE MAILBOX RULE

**Scenario 1.** Rejection arrives first = rejection controls and no contract is formed.

| Timeline | REJECTION MAILED | ACCEPTANCE MAILED | REJECTION RECEIVED | ACCEPTANCE RECEIVED |
| --- | --- | --- | --- | --- |

**Scenario 2.** Acceptance arrives first = acceptance controls and contract is formed.

| Timeline | REJECTION MAILED | ACCEPTANCE MAILED | ACCEPTANCE RECEIVED | REJECTION RECEIVED |
| --- | --- | --- | --- | --- |

## THIRD-PARTY RIGHTS

### THIRD-PARTY BENEFICIARIES

The third party must have been present at the formation of the contract. If third party was added later, look into assignment or delegation.

### THIRD-PARTY BENEFICIARIES

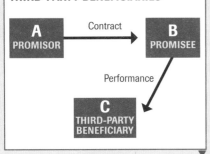

### ENFORCEMENT

- A creditor beneficiary may sue the promisor OR the promisee (not both). *Lawrence v. Fox*, 20 N.Y. 268 (1859).
- A donee beneficiary may sue the promisor but may NOT sue the promisee unless there was detrimental reliance.

### INTENDED BENEFICIARIES

Only intended beneficiaries have contractual rights. Incidental beneficiaries do not. Intended beneficiaries are usually:
1. Identified in the contract; OR
2. There is some indication by the original parties to intend a benefit.

### VESTING

A third-party beneficiary may only enforce a contract if her rights have vested.
1. Three ways a third party vests her rights:
   a. Detrimental reliance.
   b. Filing of a lawsuit (can only assert rights at time of suit).
   c. Third party accepts in a manner expressly invited by the original contracting parties
2. If not vested, original parties may freely modify.
3. Third-party beneficiary has no greater rights than original contracting parties.

## ASSIGNMENT OF RIGHTS

### IN GENERAL

1. Assignor must adequately describe rights to be assigned and manifest an intention to presently vest those rights in the assignee.
2. Certain tasks may NOT be assigned:
   a. Rights in a future contract are generally not assignable.
   b. Assignment of rights is banned if it will substantially change the obligor's duty.
   Common Law: Requirements contracts are not assignable, substantially changes the obligor's duty.
   UCC: Assignment is permissible if reasonable.

---

3. Consideration is not needed; a gratuitous assignment is effective. *Speelman v. Pascal*, 10 N.Y.2d 313, 178 N.E.2d 723 (1961).
4. Subsequent assignments revoke the former assignment. However, an assignment becomes irrevocable if there is one of the following:
   a. Consideration.
   b. Writing.
5. A valid assignment creates privity of contract between the obligor and the assignee while extinguishing privity between the obligor and the assignor.

### ENFORCEMENT

Assignee may sue the obligor. Obligor cannot raise any defenses that the assignor may have against the assignee.

### ASSIGNMENT

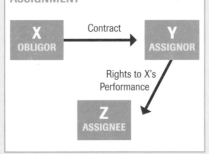

## DELEGATION OF DUTIES

### IN GENERAL

1. Most duties may be delegated with the following exceptions:
   a. Duties involving personal judgment and skill.
   b. Changes the obligee's expectancy (such as requirements and output contracts).
   c. There is a contractual prohibition on delegation.
2. Generally, a delegator remains liable on the contract, even if delegate has expressly assumed the duty.
3. When obligee consents (expressly) to a transfer of duties, then this is an offer of novation, and the original delegator is relieved of any liability.

*Note:* This is different from a novation.

### DELEGATION

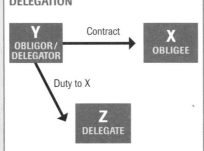

---

## DAMAGES

### MEASURE OF DAMAGES

1. Contracts for the Sale of Land

   Contract price
   − Fair market value

   Damages

   Specific performance may be requested, since land is unique. *Parker v. Twentieth Century-Fox Film Corp.*, 89 Cal. Rptr. 737, 474 P.2d 689 (1970).
2. Employment Contracts
   a. Employer breach:

      Full contract price
      − Wages earned elsewhere after breach

      Damages
   b. Employee breach:

      Cost of replacement
      (to find another employee)
      − Wages due to the employee

      Damages
3. Construction Contracts: *Jacob & Youngs v. Kent*, 230 N.Y. 239, 129 N.E. 889 (1921).
   a. Builder breach:
      i. Non-performance: owner recovers cost of completion.
      ii. Deficient performance: diminution in market value is the measure of damages. (Cost of completion would unjustly enrich the owner.)
   b. Owner breach:

      Cost
      + Expected profit

      Damages

### OTHER DAMAGES

1. Consequential Damages: Damages must have been foreseeable at the time of entering the contract. *Hadley v. Baxendale*, 9 Exch. 341, 156 Eng. Rep 145 (1854).
2. Punitive Damages: Usually reserved for tort and are unusual in a commercial contract case, but have been applied in cases by insureds against their insurance companies for failure to settle or defend in good faith (*Comunale v. Traders & General Ins. Co.*, 50 Cal.2d 654, 328 P.2d 198 (1958)), and in other limited contexts. *Nicholson v. United Pacific Ins. Co.*, 219 Mont. 32, 710 P.2d 1342 (1985).
3. Specific Performance: Available for land and unique goods, but not for services.

## About Wolters Kluwer Law & Business

Wolters Kluwer Law & Business is a leading global provider of intelligent information and digital solutions for legal and business professionals in key specialty areas, and respected educational resources for professors and law students. Wolters Kluwer Law & Business connects legal and business professionals as well as those in the education market with timely, specialized authoritative content and information-enabled solutions to support success through productivity, accuracy and mobility.

Serving customers worldwide, Wolters Kluwer Law & Business products include those under the Aspen Publishers, CCH, Kluwer Law International, Loislaw, ftwilliam.com and MediRegs family of products.

**CCH** products have been a trusted resource since 1913, and are highly regarded resources for legal, securities, antitrust and trade regulation, government contracting, banking, pension, payroll, employment and labor, and healthcare reimbursement and compliance professionals.

**Aspen Publishers** products provide essential information to attorneys, business professionals and law students. Written by preeminent authorities, the product line offers analytical and practical information in a range of specialty practice areas from securities law and intellectual property to mergers and acquisitions and pension/benefits. Aspen's trusted legal education resources provide professors and students with high-quality, up-to-date and effective resources for successful instruction and study in all areas of the law.

**Kluwer Law International** products provide the global business community with reliable international legal information in English. Legal practitioners, corporate counsel and business executives around the world rely on Kluwer Law journals, looseleafs, books, and electronic products for comprehensive information in many areas of international legal practice.

**Loislaw** is a comprehensive online legal research product providing legal content to law firm practitioners of various specializations. Loislaw provides attorneys with the ability to quickly and efficiently find the necessary legal information they need, when and where they need it, by facilitating access to primary law as well as state-specific law, records, forms and treatises.

**ftwilliam.com** offers employee benefits professionals the highest quality plan documents (retirement, welfare and non-qualified) and government forms (5500/PBGC, 1099 and IRS) software at highly competitive prices.

**MediRegs** products provide integrated health care compliance content and software solutions for professionals in healthcare, higher education and life sciences, including professionals in accounting, law and consulting.

Wolters Kluwer Law & Business, a division of Wolters Kluwer, is headquartered in New York. Wolters Kluwer is a market-leading global information services company focused on professionals.

# Format for the Casenote® Legal Brief

**Nature of Case:** This section identifies the form of action (e.g., breach of contract, negligence, battery), the type of proceeding (e.g., demurrer, appeal from trial court's jury instructions), or the relief sought (e.g., damages, injunction, criminal sanctions).

**Fact Summary:** This is included to refresh your memory and can be used as a quick reminder of the facts.

**Rule of Law:** Summarizes the general principle of law that the case illustrates. It may be used for instant recall of the court's holding and for classroom discussion or home review.

**Facts:** This section contains all relevant facts of the case, including the contentions of the parties and the lower court holdings. It is written in a logical order to give the student a clear understanding of the case. The plaintiff and defendant are identified by their proper names throughout and are always labeled with a (P) or (D).

## Palsgraf v. Long Island R.R. Co.

Injured bystander (P) v. Railroad company (D)

N.Y. Ct. App., 248 N.Y. 339, 162 N.E. 99 (1928).

**NATURE OF CASE:** Appeal from judgment affirming verdict for plaintiff seeking damages for personal injury.

**FACT SUMMARY:** Helen Palsgraf (P) was injured on R.R.'s (D) train platform when R.R.'s (D) guard helped a passenger aboard a moving train, causing his package to fall on the tracks. The package contained fireworks which exploded, creating a shock that tipped a scale onto Palsgraf (P).

### 🏛 RULE OF LAW
The risk reasonably to be perceived defines the duty to be obeyed.

**FACTS:** Helen Palsgraf (P) purchased a ticket to Rockaway Beach from R.R. (D) and was waiting on the train platform. As she waited, two men ran to catch a train that was pulling out from the platform. The first man jumped aboard, but the second man, who appeared as if he might fall, was helped aboard by the guard on the train who had kept the door open so they could jump aboard. A guard on the platform also helped by pushing him onto the train. The man was carrying a package wrapped in newspaper. In the process, the man dropped his package, which fell on the tracks. The package contained fireworks and exploded. The shock of the explosion was apparently of great enough strength to tip over some scales at the other end of the platform, which fell on Palsgraf (P) and injured her. A jury awarded her damages, and R.R. (D) appealed.

**ISSUE:** Does the risk reasonably to be perceived define the duty to be obeyed?

**HOLDING AND DECISION:** (Cardozo, C.J.) Yes. The risk reasonably to be perceived defines the duty to be obeyed. If there is no foreseeable hazard to the injured party as the result of a seemingly innocent act, the act does not become a tort because it happened to be a wrong as to another. If the wrong was not willful, the plaintiff must show that the act as to her had such great and apparent possibilities of danger as to entitle her to protection. Negligence in the abstract is not enough upon which to base liability. Negligence is a relative concept, evolving out of the common law doctrine of trespass on the case. To establish liability, the defendant must owe a legal duty of reasonable care to the injured party. A cause of action in tort will lie where harm,

though unintended, could have been averted or avoided by observance of such a duty. The scope of the duty is limited by the range of danger that a reasonable person could foresee. In this case, there was nothing to suggest from the appearance of the parcel or otherwise that the parcel contained fireworks. The guard could not reasonably have had any warning of a threat to Palsgraf (P), and R.R. (D) therefore cannot be held liable. Judgment is reversed in favor of R.R. (D).

**DISSENT:** (Andrews, J.) The concept that there is no negligence unless R.R. (D) owes a legal duty to take care as to Palsgraf (P) herself is too narrow. Everyone owes to the world at large the duty of refraining from those acts that may unreasonably threaten the safety of others. If the guard's action was negligent as to those nearby, it was also negligent as to those outside what might be termed the "danger zone." For Palsgraf (P) to recover, R.R.'s (D) negligence must have been the proximate cause of her injury, a question of fact for the jury.

### ▸ ANALYSIS

The majority defined the limit of the defendant's liability in terms of the danger that a reasonable person in defendant's situation would have perceived. The dissent argued that the limitation should not be placed on liability, but rather on damages. Judge Andrews suggested that only injuries that would not have happened but for R.R.'s (D) negligence should be compensable. Both the majority and dissent recognized the policy-driven need to limit liability for negligent acts, seeking, in the words of Judge Andrews, to define a framework "that will be practical and in keeping with the general understanding of mankind." The Restatement (Second) of Torts has accepted Judge Cardozo's view.

---

### Quicknotes

**FORESEEABILITY** A reasonable expectation that change is the probable result of certain acts or omissions.

**NEGLIGENCE** Conduct falling below the standard of care that a reasonable person would demonstrate under similar conditions.

**PROXIMATE CAUSE** The natural sequence of events without which an injury would not have been sustained.

---

**Party ID:** Quick identification of the relationship between the parties.

**Concurrence/Dissent:** All concurrences and dissents are briefed whenever they are included by the casebook editor.

**Analysis:** This last paragraph gives you a broad understanding of where the case "fits in" with other cases in the section of the book and with the entire course. It is a hornbook-style discussion indicating whether the case is a majority or minority opinion and comparing the principal case with other cases in the casebook. It may also provide analysis from restatements, uniform codes, and law review articles. The analysis will prove to be invaluable to classroom discussion.

**Issue:** The issue is a concise question that brings out the essence of the opinion as it relates to the section of the casebook in which the case appears. Both substantive and procedural issues are included if relevant to the decision.

**Holding and Decision:** This section offers a clear and in-depth discussion of the rule of the case and the court's rationale. It is written in easy-to-understand language and answers the issue presented by applying the law to the facts of the case. When relevant, it includes a thorough discussion of the exceptions to the case as listed by the court, any major cites to the other cases on point, and the names of the judges who wrote the decisions.

**Quicknotes:** Conveniently defines legal terms found in the case and summarizes the nature of any statutes, codes, or rules referred to in the text.

Wolters Kluwer Law & Business is proud to offer *Casenote® Legal Briefs*—continuing thirty years of publishing America's best-selling legal briefs.

*Casenote® Legal Briefs* are designed to help you save time when briefing assigned cases. Organized under convenient headings, they show you how to abstract the basic facts and holdings from the text of the actual opinions handed down by the courts. Used as part of a rigorous study regimen, they can help you spend more time analyzing and critiquing points of law than on copying bits and pieces of judicial opinions into your notebook or outline.

*Casenote® Legal Briefs* should never be used as a substitute for assigned casebook readings. They work best when read as a follow-up to reviewing the underlying opinions themselves. Students who try to avoid reading and digesting the judicial opinions in their casebooks or online sources will end up shortchanging themselves in the long run. The ability to absorb, critique, and restate the dynamic and complex elements of case law decisions is crucial to your success in law school and beyond. It cannot be developed vicariously.

*Casenote® Legal Briefs* represents but one of the many offerings in Legal Education's Study Aid Timeline, which includes:

- *Casenote® Legal Briefs*
- *Emanuel® Law Outlines*
- Emanuel® *Law in a Flash* Flash Cards
- Emanuel® *CrunchTime®* Series
- *Siegel's Essay and Multiple-Choice Questions and Answers Series*

Each of these series is designed to provide you with easy-to-understand explanations of complex points of law. Each volume offers guidance on the principles of legal analysis and, consulted regularly, will hone your ability to spot relevant issues. We have titles that will help you prepare for class, prepare for your exams, and enhance your general comprehension of the law along the way.

To find out more about Wolters Kluwer Law & Business' study aid publications, visit us online at *www.wolterskluwerlb.com* or email us at *legaledu@wolterskluwer.com*. We'll be happy to assist you.

## A. Decide on a Format and Stick to It

Structure is essential to a good brief. It enables you to arrange systematically the related parts that are scattered throughout most cases, thus making manageable and understandable what might otherwise seem to be an endless and unfathomable sea of information. There are, of course, an unlimited number of formats that can be utilized. However, it is best to find one that suits your needs and stick to it. Consistency breeds both efficiency and the security that when called upon you will know where to look in your brief for the information you are asked to give.

Any format, as long as it presents the essential elements of a case in an organized fashion, can be used. Experience, however, has led *Casenote® Legal Briefs* to develop and utilize the following format because of its logical flow and universal applicability.

**NATURE OF CASE:** This is a brief statement of the legal character and procedural status of the case (e.g., "Appeal of a burglary conviction").

There are many different alternatives open to a litigant dissatisfied with a court ruling. The key to determining which one has been used is to discover *who is asking this court for what.*

This first entry in the brief should be kept as *short as possible*. Use the court's terminology if you understand it. But since jurisdictions vary as to the titles of pleadings, the best entry is the one that addresses who wants what in this proceeding, not the one that sounds most like the court's language.

**RULE OF LAW:** A statement of the general principle of law that the case illustrates (e.g., "An acceptance that varies any term of the offer is considered a rejection and counteroffer").

Determining the rule of law of a case is a procedure similar to determining the issue of the case. Avoid being fooled by red herrings; there may be a few rules of law mentioned in the case excerpt, but usually only one is *the* rule with which the casebook editor is concerned. The techniques used to locate the issue, described below, may also be utilized to find the rule of law. Generally, your best guide is simply the chapter heading. It is a clue to the point the casebook editor seeks to make and should be kept in mind when reading every case in the respective section.

**FACTS:** A synopsis of only the essential facts of the case, i.e., those bearing upon or leading up to the issue.

The facts entry should be a short statement of the events and transactions that led one party to initiate legal proceedings against another in the first place. While some cases conveniently state the salient facts at the beginning of the decision, in other instances they will have to be culled from hiding places throughout the text, even from concurring and dissenting opinions. Some of the "facts" will often be in dispute and should be so noted. Conflicting evidence may be briefly pointed up. "Hard" facts must be included. Both must be *relevant* in order to be listed in the facts entry. It is impossible to tell what is relevant until the entire case is read, as the ultimate determination of the rights and liabilities of the parties may turn on something buried deep in the opinion.

Generally, the facts entry should not be longer than three to five *short* sentences.

It is often helpful to identify the role played by a party in a given context. For example, in a construction contract case the identification of a party as the "contractor" or "builder" alleviates the need to tell that that party was the one who was supposed to have built the house.

It is always helpful, and a good general practice, to identify the "plaintiff" and the "defendant." This may seem elementary and uncomplicated, but, especially in view of the creative editing practiced by some casebook editors, it is sometimes a difficult or even impossible task. Bear in mind that the *party presently* seeking something from this court may not be the plaintiff, and that sometimes only the cross-claim of a defendant is treated in the excerpt. Confusing or misaligning the parties can ruin your analysis and understanding of the case.

**ISSUE:** A statement of the general legal question answered by or illustrated in the case. For clarity, the issue is best put in the form of a question capable of a "yes" or "no" answer. In reality, the issue is simply the Rule of Law put in the form of a question (e.g., "May an offer be accepted by performance?").

The major problem presented in discerning what is *the* issue in the case is that an opinion usually purports to raise and answer several questions. However, except for rare cases, only one such question is really the issue in the case. Collateral issues not necessary to the resolution of the matter in controversy are handled by the court by language known as *"obiter dictum"* or merely *"dictum."* While dicta may be included later in the brief, they have no place under the issue heading.

To find the issue, ask *who wants what* and then go on to ask *why did that party succeed or fail in getting it.* Once this is determined, the "why" should be turned into a question.

The complexity of the issues in the cases will vary, but in all cases a single-sentence question should sum up the issue. *In a few cases,* there will be two, or even more rarely, three issues of equal importance to the resolution of the case. Each should be expressed in a single-sentence question.

Since many issues are resolved by a court in coming to a final disposition of a case, the casebook editor will reproduce the portion of the opinion containing the issue or issues most relevant to the area of law under scrutiny. A noted law professor gave this advice: "Close the book; look at the title on the cover." Chances are, if it is Property, you need not concern yourself with whether, for example, the federal government's treatment of the plaintiff's land really raises a federal question sufficient to support jurisdiction on this ground in federal court.

The same rule applies to chapter headings designating sub-areas within the subjects. They tip you off as to what the text is designed to teach. The cases are arranged in a casebook to show a progression or development of the law, so that the preceding cases may also help.

It is also most important to remember to *read the notes and questions* at the end of a case to determine what the editors wanted you to have gleaned from it.

**HOLDING AND DECISION:** This section should succinctly explain the rationale of the court in arriving at its decision. In capsulizing the "reasoning" of the court, it should always include an application of the general rule or rules of law to the specific facts of the case. Hidden justifications come to light in this entry: the reasons for the state of the law, the public policies, the biases and prejudices, those considerations that influence the justices' thinking and, ultimately, the outcome of the case. At the end, there should be a short indication of the disposition or procedural resolution of the case (e.g., "Decision of the trial court for Mr. Smith (P) reversed").

The foregoing format is designed to help you "digest" the reams of case material with which you will be faced in your law school career. Once mastered by practice, it will place at your fingertips the information the authors of your casebooks have sought to impart to you in case-by-case illustration and analysis.

## B. Be as Economical as Possible in Briefing Cases

Once armed with a format that encourages succinctness, it is as important to be economical with regard to the time spent on the actual reading of the case as it is to be economical in the writing of the brief itself. This does not mean "skimming" a case. Rather, it means reading the case with an "eye" trained to recognize into which "section" of your brief a particular passage or line fits and having a system for quickly and precisely marking the case so that the passages fitting any one particular part of

the brief can be easily identified and brought together in a concise and accurate manner when the brief is actually written.

It is of no use to simply repeat everything in the opinion of the court; record only enough information to trigger your recollection of what the court said. Nevertheless, an accurate statement of the "law of the case," i.e., the legal principle applied to the facts, is absolutely essential to class preparation and to learning the law under the case method.

To that end, it is important to develop a "shorthand" that you can use to make marginal notations. These notations will tell you at a glance in which section of the brief you will be placing that particular passage or portion of the opinion.

Some students prefer to underline all the salient portions of the opinion (with a pencil or colored underliner marker), making marginal notations as they go along. Others prefer the color-coded method of underlining, utilizing different colors of markers to underline the salient portions of the case, each separate color being used to represent a different section of the brief. For example, blue underlining could be used for passages relating to the rule of law, yellow for those relating to the issue, and green for those relating to the holding and decision, etc. While it has its advocates, the color-coded method can be confusing and time-consuming (all that time spent on changing colored markers). Furthermore, it can interfere with the continuity and concentration many students deem essential to the reading of a case for maximum comprehension. In the end, however, it is a matter of personal preference and style. Just remember, whatever method you use, underlining must be used sparingly or its value is lost.

If you take the marginal notation route, an efficient and easy method is to go along underlining the key portions of the case and placing in the margin alongside them the following "markers" to indicate where a particular passage or line "belongs" in the brief you will write:

N       (NATURE OF CASE)
RL     (RULE OF LAW)
I        (ISSUE)
HL     (HOLDING AND DECISION, relates to
         the RULE OF LAW behind the decision)
HR     (HOLDING AND DECISION, gives the
         RATIONALE or reasoning behind the
         decision)
HA     (HOLDING AND DECISION, applies the
         general principle(s) of law to the facts of
         the case to arrive at the decision)

Remember that a particular passage may well contain information necessary to more than one part of your brief, in which case you simply note that in the margin. If you are using the color-coded underlining method instead of marginal notation, simply make asterisks or checks in the margin next to the passage in question in the colors that indicate the additional sections of the brief where it might be utilized.

The economy of utilizing "shorthand" in marking cases for briefing can be maintained in the actual brief writing process itself by utilizing "law student shorthand" within the brief. There are many commonly used words and phrases for which abbreviations can be substituted in your briefs (and in your class notes also). You can develop abbreviations that are personal to you and which will save you a lot of time. A reference list of briefing abbreviations can be found on page x of this book.

## C. Use Both the Briefing Process and the Brief as a Learning Tool

Now that you have a format and the tools for briefing cases efficiently, the most important thing is to make the time spent in briefing profitable to you and to make the most advantageous use of the briefs you create. Of course, the briefs are invaluable for classroom reference when you are called upon to explain or analyze a particular case. However, they are also useful in reviewing for exams. A quick glance at the fact summary should bring the case to mind, and a rereading of the rule of law should enable you to go over the underlying legal concept in your mind, how it was applied in that particular case, and how it might apply in other factual settings.

As to the value to be derived from engaging in the briefing process itself, there is an immediate benefit that arises from being forced to sift through the essential facts and reasoning from the court's opinion and to succinctly express them in your own words in your brief. The process ensures that you understand the case and the point that it illustrates, and that means you will be ready to absorb further analysis and information brought forth in class. It also ensures you will have something to say when called upon in class. The briefing process helps develop a mental agility for getting to the *gist* of a case and for identifying, expounding on, and applying the legal concepts and issues found there. The briefing process is the mental process on which you must rely in taking law school examinations; it is also the mental process upon which a lawyer relies in serving his clients and in making his living.

# Abbreviations for Briefs

| | | | | |
|---|---|---|---|---|
| acceptance | acp | offer | O |
| affirmed | aff | offeree | OE |
| answer | ans | offeror | OR |
| assumption of risk | a/r | ordinance | ord |
| attorney | atty | pain and suffering | p/s |
| beyond a reasonable doubt | b/r/d | parol evidence | p/e |
| bona fide purchaser | BFP | plaintiff | P |
| breach of contract | br/k | prima facie | p/f |
| cause of action | c/a | probable cause | p/c |
| common law | c/l | proximate cause | px/c |
| Constitution | Con | real property | r/p |
| constitutional | con | reasonable doubt | r/d |
| contract | K | reasonable man | r/m |
| contributory negligence | c/n | rebuttable presumption | rb/p |
| cross | x | remanded | rem |
| cross-complaint | x/c | res ipsa loquitur | RIL |
| cross-examination | x/ex | respondeat superior | r/s |
| cruel and unusual punishment | c/u/p | Restatement | RS |
| defendant | D | reversed | rev |
| dismissed | dis | Rule Against Perpetuities | RAP |
| double jeopardy | d/j | search and seizure | s/s |
| due process | d/p | search warrant | s/w |
| equal protection | e/p | self-defense | s/d |
| equity | eq | specific performance | s/p |
| evidence | ev | statute | S |
| exclude | exc | statute of frauds | S/F |
| exclusionary rule | exc/r | statute of limitations | S/L |
| felony | f/n | summary judgment | s/j |
| freedom of speech | f/s | tenancy at will | t/w |
| good faith | g/f | tenancy in common | t/c |
| habeas corpus | h/c | tenant | t |
| hearsay | hr | third party | TP |
| husband | H | third party beneficiary | TPB |
| injunction | inj | transferred intent | TI |
| in loco parentis | ILP | unconscionable | uncon |
| inter vivos | I/v | unconstitutional | unconst |
| joint tenancy | j/t | undue influence | u/e |
| judgment | judgt | Uniform Commercial Code | UCC |
| jurisdiction | jur | unilateral | uni |
| last clear chance | LCC | vendee | VE |
| long-arm statute | LAS | vendor | VR |
| majority view | maj | versus | v |
| meeting of minds | MOM | void for vagueness | VFV |
| minority view | min | weight of authority | w/a |
| Miranda rule | Mir/r | weight of the evidence | w/e |
| Miranda warnings | Mir/w | wife | W |
| negligence | neg | with | w/ |
| notice | ntc | within | w/i |
| nuisance | nus | without | w/o |
| obligation | ob | without prejudice | w/o/p |
| obscene | obs | wrongful death | wr/d |

# Table of Cases

# Bases for Enforcing Promises

## *Quick Reference Rules of Law*

# Hawkins v. McGee

## Patient (P) v. Physician (D)

N.H. Sup. Ct., 84 N.H. 114, 146 A. 641 (1929).

**NATURE OF CASE:** Appeal from decision to set aside verdict for breach of warranty of success of an operation.

**FACT SUMMARY:** Hawkins (P) sued McGee (D) for not making his hand perfect after McGee (D) operated on it.

## 🏛 RULE OF LAW
The true measure of a buyer's damages is the difference between the value of the goods as they would have been if the warranty as to the quality had been true and the actual value at the time of sale, including any incidental consequences within the contemplation of the parties when they made their contract.

**FACTS:** Dr. McGee (D) was to remove scar tissue from the right palm of Hawkins (P) and then graft skin from the chest of Hawkins (P) and place it on his palm. McGee (D) stated that the hospital stay should be three to four days, and a few days after that Hawkins (P) could return to work with a 100 percent perfect hand. At trial, McGee (D) argued that even if this statement was made, no reasonable man would understand this as an intention to enter into a contractual relationship. The trial court allowed the jury to consider pain and suffering due to the surgery and the positive ill effects of the surgery. The verdict was in favor of Hawkins (P), but McGee (D) moved to set aside the verdict, because the damages were excessive. The trial court found the damages to be excessive and set aside the verdict, unless Hawkins (P) remitted all sums over $500. When Hawkins (P) refused, the verdict was set aside. Hawkins (P) appealed.

**ISSUE:** Is the true measure of a buyer's damages the difference between the value of the goods as they would have been if the warranty as to the quality had been true and the actual value at the time of the sale?

**HOLDING AND DECISION:** (Branch, J.) Yes. The true measure of damage is the difference between the value of the goods as they would have been if the warranty as to the quality had been true and the actual value at the time of the sale, including any incidental consequences within the contemplation of the parties when they made their contract. Therefore, the true measure of damages in the present case is the difference between the value to Hawkins (P) of a perfect hand, such as promised by McGee (D), and the value of the hand in its present condition. Included are any incidental consequences fairly within the contemplation of the parties when they made

the contract. Any other damages are not to be given. Suffering does not measure this difference in value. Pain is incident to a serious operation. Submitting to the jury as a separate element of damage any change for the worse in the condition of the hand was erroneous and misleading. Instead, damages might properly be determined for McGee's (D) failure to improve the condition of the hand. It is unnecessary to consider whether the evidence justified the trial court's finding that damages greater than $500 were excessive. New trial ordered.

## ▶ ANALYSIS

Prior to a third trial over damages, McGee (D) notified his malpractice insurer, United States Fidelity and Guaranty Co., that he wanted to pay $1,400 to Hawkins (P) to settle the case. He was going to look to them for payment. When the company refused, McGee (D) brought suit, but the court found in favor of the insurance company, having concluded that its policy did not cover special contracts to cure. *McGee v. United States Fidelity & Guaranty Co.*, 53 F.2d 953 (1st Cir. 1931). The insurance company denied coverage as the verdict was for breach of contract and not the tort of malpractice, and its defense was sustained.

◼▬◼

## Quicknotes

**BREACH OF WARRANTY** The breach of a promise made by one party to a contract on which the other party may rely, relieving that party from the obligation of determining whether the fact is true and indemnifying the other party from liability if that fact is shown to be false.

**CONSEQUENTIAL DAMAGES** Monetary compensation that may be recovered in order to compensate for injuries or losses sustained as a result of damages that are not the direct or foreseeable result of the act of a party, but that nevertheless are the consequence of such act and which must be specifically pleaded and demonstrated.

**CURE** In a commercial transaction, the seller has a right to correct a delivery of defective goods within the time originally provided for performance as specified in the contract.

◼▬◼

# Bayliner Marine Corp. v. Crow

Boat manufacturer (D) v. Boat purchaser (P)

Va. Sup. Ct., 257 Va. 121, 509 S.E.2d 499 (1999).

**NATURE OF CASE:** Boat manufacturer's appeal from a judgment against it in a breach of warranty suit.

**FACT SUMMARY:** In the summer of 1989, John Crow (P) was invited by a sales representative for Tidewater Yacht Agency, Inc. (Tidewater) to ride on a new model sport fishing boat manufactured by Bayliner Marine Corp. (D). Crow (P) was most interested in the speed of the boat, and after being given copies of "prop matrixes" and other promotion material, Crow (P) entered into a written contract for the purchase of the 3486 Trophy Convertible in which he had ridden. He took delivery in September 1989, and, in 1992, filed suit for breached express warranties, implied warranties of merchantability, and fitness for a particular purpose (alleging lack of attainment of maximum speed).

---

🏛 **RULE OF LAW**
In assessing the merchantability of goods, the UCC § 2-314(2)(a), (c) requirement that goods must be such as would "pass without objection in the trade" concerns whether a significant segment of the buying public would object to buying the goods, while the requirement that goods "are fit for the ordinary purposes for which such goods are used" concerns whether the goods are reasonably capable of performing their ordinary functions.

---

**FACTS:** John Crow (P) sought to purchase a fishing boat. When he asked the manufacturer, Bayliner Marine Corp. (Bayliner) (D), about the maximum speed, Bayliner's (D) representative explained that he had no personal experience with the boat. Therefore, the representative consulted two documents described as "prop matrixes," which were included by Bayliner (D) in its dealer's manual. The representative gave Crow (P) copies of the "prop matrixes" which listed the boat models offered by Bayliner (D) and stated the recommended propeller sizes, gear ratios, and engine sizes for each model. The "prop matrixes" also listed the maximum speed for each model. The 3486 Trophy Convertible (the boat ultimately purchased) was listed as having a maximum speed of 30 miles per hour when equipped with a size "20 × 20" or "20 × 19" propeller. The boat Crow (P) purchased did not have either size propeller but, instead, had a size "20 × 17" propeller. At the bottom of one of the "prop matrixes" was the following disclaimer: "This data is intended for comparative purposes only, and is available without reference to weather conditions or other variables. All testing was done at or near sea level, with full fuel and water tanks, and approximately 600 lb. passenger and gear weight." Crow

(P) purchased the boat. During the next 12 to 14 months, Crow (P) made numerous repairs and adjustments to the boat in an attempt to increase its speed capability. Despite these efforts, the boat consistently achieved a maximum speed of only 17 miles per hour, except for one brief period. Crow (P) sued the manufacturer Bayliner (D), arguing it had breached express warranties and implied warranties of merchantability and fitness for a particular purpose. Judgment was rendered for Crow (P), and Bayliner (D) appealed.

**ISSUE:** In assessing the merchantability of goods, does the UCC § 2-314(2)(a),(c) requirement that goods must be such as would "pass without objection in the trade" concern whether a significant segment of the buying public would object to buying the goods, while the requirement that goods, "are fit for the ordinary purposes for which such goods are used" concern whether the goods are reasonably capable of performing their ordinary functions?

**HOLDING AND DECISION:** (Keenan, J.) Yes. UCC § 2-314 provides that in all contracts for the sale of goods by a merchant, a warranty is implied that the goods will be merchantable. Under UCC § 2-314(2)(a),(c) to be merchantable, the goods must be such as would "pass without objection in the trade" and as "are fit for the ordinary purposes for which such goods are used." The first phrase concerns whether a "significant segment of the buying public" would object to buying the goods, while the second phrase concerns whether the goods are "reasonably capable of performing their ordinary functions." In order to prove that a product is not merchantable, the complaining party must first establish the standard of merchantability in the trade. Here, Bayliner (D) correctly noted that the record contained no evidence of the standard of merchantability in the offshore fishing boat trade. Nor did the record contain any evidence supporting a conclusion that a significant portion of the boat-buying public would object to purchasing an offshore fishing boat with the speed capability of the 3486 Trophy Convertible (the boat at issue). Crow (P), nevertheless, relied on his own testimony that the boat's speed was inadequate for his intended use, and another witness's opinion testimony that the boat took "a long time" to reach certain fishing grounds in the Gulf Stream off the coast of Virginia. However, this evidence failed to address the standard of merchantability in the trade or whether Crow's (P) boat failed to meet that standard. Thus, Crow (P) failed to prove that the boat would not "pass without objection in the trade" as required by the UCC As to whether the record

*Continued on next page.*

supported a conclusion that Crow's (P) boat was not fit for its ordinary purpose as an offshore sport fishing boat, the evidence was uncontroverted that Crow (P) used the boat for offshore fishing, at least during the first few years after purchasing it, and that the boat's engines were used for 850 hours. While Crow (P) stated that many of those hours were incurred during various repair or modification attempts and that the boat was of little value to him, this testimony did not support a conclusion that a boat with this speed capability is generally unacceptable as an off-shore fishing boat. Finally, the statement in the sales brochure that the model of boat bought by Crow (P) "delivers the kind of performance you need to get to the prime offshore fishing grounds" merely expressed Bayli-ner's (D) opinion concerning the quality of the boat's performance and did not create an express warranty that the boat was capable of attaining a speed of 30 miles per hour. Reversed.

## ▶ ANALYSIS

In Bayliner, Crow (P) contended that the "particular pur-pose" for which the boat was intended was as an offshore fishing boat capable of traveling at a maximum speed of 30 miles per hour. However, to establish an implied warranty of fitness for a particular purpose, the buyer must prove as a threshold matter that he made known to the seller the particular purpose for which the goods were required. In this regard, the *Bayliner* court noted that the record did not support a conclusion that Crow (P) had informed the manufacturer or the seller of this precise requirement. Although Crow (P) had informed them that he intended to use the boat for offshore fishing and discussed the boat's speed in this context, these facts did not establish that the seller actually knew on the date of sale that a boat incapable of travelling at 30 miles per hour was unaccept-able to Crow (P). Accordingly, the *Bayliner* court concluded that the evidence failed to support the trial court's ruling that Bayliner (D) had breached an implied warranty of fitness for a particular purpose.

■■■■

## Quicknotes

**EXPRESS WARRANTY** An express promise made by one party to a contract that the other party may rely on a fact, relieving that party from the obligation of determining whether the fact is true and indemnifying the other party from liability if that fact is shown to be false.

■■■■

# United States Naval Institute v. Charter Communications, Inc.

Author's assignee (P) v. Publisher (D)

936 F.2d 692 (2d Cir. 1991).

**NATURE OF CASE:** Appeal and cross-appeal from a judgment on remand awarding damages and profits in an action for breach of contract.

**FACT SUMMARY:** When Charter Communications (Charter) (D), the exclusive licensee for a paperback edition of a book, for which the United States Naval Institution (Naval) (P) was the author's assignee, shipped the paperback edition to retail stores prior to the date set in the contract, Naval (P) filed suit for damages and Charter's (D) profits on the hardback edition of the book.

**RULE OF LAW**
Damages for breach of contract are generally measured by a plaintiff's actual loss.

**FACTS:** The United States Naval Institute (Naval) (P), as the assignee of the author's copyright in *The Hunt for Red October*, granted Charter Communications (D) and Berkley Publishing Group (collectively, Berkley) (D) an exclusive license to publish a paperback edition of the book "not sooner than October 1985." However, Berkley (D) shipped the paperbacks to retailers earlier than October, so that the paperback went on sale September 15, 1985. Naval (P) sued for breach of the licensing agreement. The court awarded damages to Naval (P), calculating actual damages as the profits Naval (P) would have earned from hardcover sales in September if the competing paperback edition had not been released. The court also awarded Berkley's (D) profit on the displacing copies to Naval (P). Naval (P) appealed as to the profits award, and Berkley (D) cross-appealed.

**ISSUE:** Are damages for breach of contract generally measured by a plaintiff's actual loss?

**HOLDING AND DECISION:** (Kearse, J.) Yes. Damages for breach of contract are generally measured by a plaintiff's actual loss. While on occasion a defendant's profits are used as the measure of damages, this generally occurs when those profits tend to define the plaintiff's loss. Here, Berkley's (D) alleged profits did not define Naval's (P) loss because those who bought the paperback would not have bought the hardcover version in any event. However, the court correctly calculated Naval's (P) actual damages by relying on August sales rather than the lower September sales of the hardcover version. Although there was a declining trend of hardcover sales from March through August, Naval (P) continued to average sales of some 3,000 copies a month in the latter period. Nothing in the record foreclosed the possibility that, absent Berkley's (D) breach, sales of hardcover copies in the latter part of

September would have outpaced sales of those copies in the early part of the month. Thus, it was within the prerogative of the court as finder of fact to look to Naval's (P) August sales to quantify Naval's (P) loss. Reversed as to the award of profits but affirmed in all other respects.

**ANALYSIS**

In its analysis, the court of appeals looked to § 347 and § 356 of the Restatement (Second) of Contracts. An award of a defendant's profits where they greatly exceed the plaintiff's loss and where there has been no tortious conduct on the part of the defendant would tend to be punitive, and punitive awards are not part of the law of contract damages. However, it is proper to lay the normal uncertainty in hypothesizing possible sales at the door of the wrongdoer who altered the proper course of events.

## Quicknotes

**BREACH OF CONTRACT** Unlawful failure by a party to perform its obligations pursuant to contract.

# Sullivan v. O'Connor

Patient (P) v. Plastic surgeon (D)

Mass. Sup. Jud. Ct., 363 Mass. 579, 296 N.E.2d 183 (1973).

**NATURE OF CASE:** Action for damages for breach of contract.

**FACT SUMMARY:** Sullivan (P) claimed that O'Connor (D), a surgeon, had failed to fulfill his promise to enhance her appearance by the plastic surgery he performed on her nose.

## 🏛 RULE OF LAW
Where the proof is clear, a patient can maintain an action for breach of a doctor's agreement or promise to cure or bring about a given result.

**FACTS:** Sullivan (P), an entertainer, was awarded $13,500 for the alleged breach of contract which occurred when the plastic surgery performed on her nose by O'Connor (D), a surgeon, failed to produce the desired result. Sullivan (P) maintained that O'Connor (D) had promised the surgery would improve her appearance and enhance her beauty, but the evidence showed that her appearance had actually been worsened. Although the jury did not find negligence, it found that O'Connor (D) had breached his contract by failing to provide the promised result. However, O'Connor (D) appealed, arguing that agreements by which a physician undertakes to affect a cure or bring about a given result should be declared unenforceable on grounds of public policy.

**ISSUE:** Can a patient sue for breach of a doctor's promise to cure or bring about a given result?

**HOLDING AND DECISION:** (Kaplan, J.) Yes. Whenever there is clear proof that such an agreement existed, a patient is free to sue for his doctor's breach of his promise to cure or bring about a given result. Although some courts have held such agreements unenforceable on public policy grounds, there are many decisions which take the better view that such agreements can be sued upon as long as they can be adequately proven. That has been done in this case. Therefore, recovery was proper. Affirmed.

## ▶ ANALYSIS

The emphasis on proving that an actual agreement to cure or achieve a specific result arose reflects the general concern that patients who are desirous of change will transform a doctor's optimistic opinion into firm promises in their own minds. Thus, the courts that will enforce this type of promise require that there be clear proof of the presence of the assent necessary for an agreement to arise. So wary are some jurisdictions that they statutorily require such promises to be in writing and signed by the physician to be charged to be enforceable.

■━■

## Quicknotes

**BREACH OF CONTRACT** Unlawful failure by a party to perform its obligations pursuant to contract.

■━■

# White v. Benkowski

## Neighbor (P) v. Neighbor (D)

Wis. Sup. Ct., 37 Wis. 2d 285, 155 N.W.2d 74 (1967).

**NATURE OF CASE:** Action in damages for breach of contract.

**FACT SUMMARY:** The Whites (P) contracted with the Benkowskis (D) to supply water for their house.

## 🏛 RULE OF LAW
(1) A jury may take inconvenience into account in awarding exemplary damages.
(2) Punitive damages may not be awarded for breach of contract.

**FACTS:** The Whites (P) purchased a home which had no water supply. The Whites (P) entered into a contract with their next-door neighbors, the Benkowskis (D), to use their well for water. A contract for 10 years was entered into by the parties. After a few years, the relationship between the parties deteriorated. The Benkowskis (D) shut off the water several times allegedly to clear the pipes and to remind the Whites (P) that they were using too much water. The Whites (P), during these periods, had to bathe their children elsewhere and put up with bathroom odors. The Whites (P) filed suit for exemplary and punitive damages. The jury awarded the Whites (P) $10 in exemplary damages, no pecuniary loss being proved or pleaded, and $2,000 in punitive damages. The court reduced the exemplary damages to $1 since no pecuniary loss was proved and disallowed all punitive damages.

**ISSUE:**
(1) May a jury take into account inconvenience in awarding exemplary damages?
(2) May punitive damages be awarded for breach of contract?

**HOLDING AND DECISION:** (Wilkie, J.)
(1) Yes. A jury may take inconvenience into account in awarding exemplary damages.
(2) No. Punitive damages may not be awarded for breach of contract. A nominal award may be rendered for personal inconvenience due to a breach of contract. $10 is such a nominal amount and is clearly sustainable under the evidence. Punitive damages are never authorized in breach of contract actions. It is immaterial whether the breach was either intentional and/or malicious. No moral penalties may be assessed for mere breach of contract. Reversed in part and affirmed in part.

▶ **ANALYSIS**

Some breach of contract actions include tortious conduct for which punitive damages may be awarded. To recover such damages, a tort must be separately pleaded and proved. Every breach of contract is actionable. Trivial breaches or breaches that cause no pecuniary loss will normally result in an award of minimal damages as herein. Damages for breach of contract are meant only to place the injured party in the same position he would have been in if the breach had not occurred.

■━■

## Quicknotes

**PUNITIVE DAMAGES** Damages exceeding the actual injury suffered for the purposes of punishment, deterrence and comfort to plaintiff. Also called "exemplary damages."

■━■

# Hamer v. Sidway

## Assignee (P) v. Estate executor (D)

N.Y. Ct. App., 124 N.Y. 538, 27 N.E. 256 (1891).

**NATURE OF CASE:** Action on appeal to recover upon a contract which is supported by forbearance of a right as consideration.

**FACT SUMMARY:** William E. Story, Sr., promised to pay $5,000 to William E. Story, 2d, if he would forbear in the use of liquor, tobacco, swearing, and playing cards or billiards for money until he became twenty-one years of age.

 **RULE OF LAW**
Forbearance is valuable consideration.

**FACTS:** William E. Story, Sr., agreed with his nephew William E. Story, 2d, that if William E. Story, 2d, would refrain from drinking liquor, using tobacco, swearing, and playing cards or billiards for money until he became twenty-one years of age, he (William E. Story, Sr.) would pay him $5,000. Upon becoming twenty-one years of age, William E. Story, 2d, received a letter from his uncle stating he had earned the $5,000 and it would be kept at interest for him. Twelve years later William E. Story, Sr., died and this action was brought by the assignees of William E. Story, 2d, against the executor of the estate of William E. Story, Sr. Judgment was entered in favor of Hamer (P), the assignee, at the trial at Special Term and was reversed at General Term of the Supreme Court. Hamer (P) appealed.

**ISSUE:** Is forbearance on the part of a promisee sufficient consideration to support a contract?

**HOLDING AND DECISION:** (Parker, J.) Yes. Forbearance on the part of a promise is sufficient consideration to support a contract. Valuable consideration may consist either of some right, interest, profit, or benefit accruing to the one party, or some forbearance, detriment, loss, or responsibility given, suffered, or undertaken by the other. William Story's promise is enforceable. Reversed.

▶ **ANALYSIS**

The surrendering or forgoing of a legal right constitutes a sufficient consideration for a contract if the minds of the parties meet on the relinquishment of the right as a consideration. Consideration may be forbearance to sue on a claim, extension of time, or any other giving up of a legal right in consideration of a promise.

*Quicknotes*

**CONSIDERATION** Value given by one party in exchange for performance, or a promise to perform, by another party.

**FORBEARANCE** Refraining from doing something that one has the legal right to do.

# Dyer v. National By-Products, Inc.

## Employee (P) v. Employer (D)

Iowa. Sup. Ct., 380 N.W.2d 732 (1986).

**NATURE OF CASE:** Appeal for summary judgment dismissing a breach of contract action.

**FACT SUMMARY:** Dyer (P) sued National By-Products, Inc. (D) for breach of a settlement agreement regarding a job-related accident.

## 🏛 RULE OF LAW
Settlement of an unfounded claim asserted in good faith constitutes valuable consideration for settlement agreements.

**FACTS:** Dyer (P) was employed as a foreman for National By-Products, Inc. (National) (D). On October 29, 1981, Dyer (P) lost his right foot in a job-related accident. Dyer (P) returned to work as a foreman for National (D) on August 16, 1982 after a fully paid leave of absence. On March 11, 1983, National (D) indefinitely laid off Dyer (P). Dyer (P) sued National (D) for breach of a settlement agreement alleging that in exchange for Dyer (P) foregoing a lawsuit against National (D), National (D) agreed to employ Dyer (P) for life. National (D) denied making such a deal since Dyer (P) was barred from a civil lawsuit by Workers' Compensation. National (D) maintained that even if a settlement agreement existed, Dyer's (P) forbearance of an invalid claim did not constitute valuable consideration for the agreement. The trial court granted summary judgment, and Dyer (P) appealed.

**ISSUE:** Does settlement of an unfounded claim asserted in good faith constitute valuable consideration for a settlement agreement?

**HOLDING AND DECISION:** (Schultz, J.) Yes. Settlement of an unfounded claim asserted in good faith constitutes valuable consideration for a settlement agreement. It is in the best interests of the legal system to encourage settlement and negotiation. Thus, circumstances may arise where forbearance of an invalid claim can constitute sufficient consideration. So long as the forbearing party has a good faith belief that he is forbearing the pursuit of a legitimate claim, such forbearance will be valid consideration. Summary judgment was inappropriate in the instant case because a material question of fact existed as to whether or not Dyer (P) had a good faith belief that his civil claim was valid. Reversed and remanded.

## ▌ ANALYSIS

This case highlights the significance of valuable consideration in the context of contractual obligations. Often, the issue of consideration can be manipulated to rectify social justice concerns. When one party has more power than another, valuable consideration in contractual obligations can be used to level the playing field.

■══■

## Quicknotes

**FORBEARANCE** Refraining from doing something that one has the legal right to do.

**VALUABLE CONSIDERATION** Value given by one party in exchange for performance, or a promise to perform, by another party.

■══■

# Feinberg v. Pfeiffer Co.

Retired employee (P) v. Employer (D)

Mo. Ct. App., 322 S.W.2d 163 (1959).

**NATURE OF CASE:** Action on appeal by defendant to show failure of contract due to lack of consideration.

**FACT SUMMARY:** Anna Feinberg (P) was given a pension for life by Pfeiffer Co. (D) based upon her past service to Pfeiffer Co. (D). Pfeiffer Co. (D) subsequently refused to pay the pension claiming lack of consideration for its promise to do so.

 **RULE OF LAW**
Past services are not a valid consideration for a promise.

**FACTS:** Anna Feinberg (P) had been a bookkeeper for Pfeiffer Co. (D) for 37 years. The board of Pfeiffer Co. (D) voted to give her a lifetime pension at any time she chose to retire. The pension was based upon Mrs. Feinberg's (P) past service to the company and not upon her continued service. A year and a half after learning of the pension, Mrs. Feinberg (P) retired and began receiving the pension. Six years after her retirement, Pfeiffer Co. (D) refused to continue paying Mrs. Feinberg (P) her pension upon the advice of their attorney and accountants that there existed no valid consideration for the promise to pay. Mrs. Feinberg (P) brought an action to compel payment of her pension by the Pfeiffer Co. (D), and the lower court held for her. Pfeiffer Co. (D) appealed.

**ISSUE:** Are past services valid consideration for a promise?

**HOLDING AND DECISION:** (Doerner, Commn.) No. Past services are not a valid consideration for a promise. Since Mrs. Feinberg (P) made no promise or agreement to continue in the employment of the Pfeiffer Co. (D) in return for its promise to pay her a pension, there existed no mutuality of obligation which is essential to the validity of a contract. Affirmed on other grounds.

▎ *ANALYSIS*

Note that, in the present case, if Feinberg (P) were still healthy and able to work, the decision would have been different. In that situation, it would not be the case that injustice could be avoided only by enforcement of the promise. Note additionally that if Feinberg (P) had continued to work for Pfeiffer (D) until she became physically unable to continue and was forced to retire, she could probably not recover on Pfeiffer's (D) promise. Her retire-

ment would not have been in reliance on Pfeiffer's (D) promise as the doctrine of promissory estoppel requires.

---

## Quicknotes

**PROMISSORY ESTOPPEL** A promise that is enforceable if the promisor should reasonably expect that it will induce action or forbearance on the part of the promisee, and does in fact cause such action or forbearance, and it is the only means of avoiding injustice.

# Mills v. Wyman

Nurse-caretaker (P) v. Parent (D)

Mass. Sup. Jud. Ct., 20 Mass. (3 Pick.) 207 (1825).

**NATURE OF CASE:** Action on appeal to recover on alleged promise.

**FACT SUMMARY:** Mills (P) took care of Wyman's (D) son without being requested to do so and for so doing was promised compensation for expenses arising out of the rendered care by Wyman (D). Wyman (D) later refused to compensate Mills (P).

### 🏛 RULE OF LAW
A moral obligation is insufficient as consideration for a promise.

**FACTS:** Mills (P) nursed and cared for Levi Wyman, the son of Wyman (D). Upon learning of Mills's (P) acts of kindness toward his son, Wyman (D) promised to repay Mills (P) his expenses incurred in caring for Levi Wyman. Later, Wyman (D) refused to compensate Mills (P) for his expenses. Mills (P) filed an action in the Court of Common Pleas where Wyman (D) was successful in obtaining a nonsuit against Mills (P). Mills (P) appealed.

**ISSUE:** Is a moral obligation sufficient consideration for a promise?

**HOLDING AND DECISION:** (Parker, C.J.) No. A moral obligation is not sufficient consideration to support an express promise. However, the universality of the rule cannot be supported. Therefore, there must be some other preexisting obligation which will suffice as consideration. Affirmed.

## ▶ ANALYSIS

In cases such as this one, the nearly universal holding is that the existing moral obligation is not a sufficient basis for the enforcement of an express promise to render the performance that it requires. The general statement is that it is not sufficient consideration for the express promise. The difficulties and differences of opinion involved in the determination of what is a moral obligation are probably much greater than those involved in determining the existence of a legal obligation. This tends to explain the attitude of the majority of courts on the subject and justifies the generally stated rule.

■═■

## Quicknotes

**CONSIDERATION** Value given by one party in exchange for performance, or a promise to perform, by another party.

**EXPRESS PROMISE** The expression of an intention to act, or to forbear from acting, granting a right to the promisee to expect and enforce its performance.

■═■

# Webb v. McGowin

Conscientious worker (P) v. Grateful pedestrian (D)

Ala. Ct. App., 27 Ala. App. 82, 168 So. 196 (1935).

**NATURE OF CASE:** Action on appeal to collect on a promise.

**FACT SUMMARY:** Webb (P) saved the now deceased J. McGowin from grave bodily injury or death by placing himself in grave danger and subsequently suffering grave bodily harm. J. McGowin, in return, promised Webb (P) compensation. McGowin's executors (D) now refuse to pay the promised compensation.

> ### RULE OF LAW
> A moral obligation is a sufficient consideration to support a subsequent promise to pay where the promisor has received a material benefit.

**FACTS:** Webb (P), while in the scope of his duties for the W. T. Smith Lumber Co., was clearing the floor, which required him to drop a 75-lb. pine block from the upper floor of the mill to the ground. Just as Webb (P) was releasing the block, he noticed J. McGowin below and directly under where the block would have fallen. In order to divert the fall of the block, Webb (P) fell with it, breaking an arm and leg and ripping his heel off. The fall left Webb (P) a cripple and incapable of either mental or physical labor. In return for Webb's (P) act, J. McGowin promised to pay Webb (P) $15 every two weeks for the rest of Webb's (P) life. J. McGowin paid the promised payments until his death eight years later. Shortly after J. McGowin's death, the payments were stopped and Webb (P) brought an action against N. McGowin (D) and J. F. McGowin (D) as executors of J. McGowin's estate for payments due him. The executors (D) of the estate were successful in obtaining a nonsuit against Webb (P) in the lower court. Webb (P) appeals.

**ISSUE:** Was the moral obligation to compensate as promised sufficient consideration?

**HOLDING AND DECISION:** (Bricken, J.) Yes. It is well settled that a moral obligation is a sufficient consideration to support a subsequent promise to pay where the promisor has received a material benefit, although there was no original duty or liability resting on the promisor. Reversed and remanded.

**CONCURRENCE:** (Samford, J.) If the benefit is material and substantial, and if was to the person of the promisor rather than to his estate, it is within the class of material benefits which he has the privilege of recognizing and compensating either by an executed payment or an executed promise to pay.

**PETITION FOR REHEARING:** (Foster, J.) If the benefit was material and substantial, and if was to the person of the promisor rather than to his estate, it is within the class of material benefits which he has the privilege of recognizing and compensating either by an executed payment or an executed promise to pay. When the compensation is not only for the benefits which the promisor received, but also for the injuries either to the property or person of the promisee by reason of the services rendered, it fits within the above general rule recognizing that more than a moral benefit is involved. The rehearing is denied.

## ANALYSIS

In most cases where the moral obligation is asserted, the court feels that the promise ought not to be enforced; instead of going into the uncertain field of morality the court chooses to rely upon the rule that moral obligation is not a sufficient consideration. On the other hand, in cases where the promise is one which would have been kept by most citizens and the court feels that enforcement is just, a few courts will enforce the promise using the *Webb v. McGowin* rule. In general, the *Webb v. McGowin* rule is the minority rule and the *Mills v. Wyman* (Mass. 1825), the majority rule.

## Quicknotes

**EXECUTORY PROMISE** A promise to perform an action that has not yet been performed.

**MATERIAL BENEFIT** An advantage gained by entering into a contract that is essential to the performance of the agreement and without which the contract would not have been entered into.

**MORAL CONSIDERATION** An inducement to enter a contract that is not enforceable at law, but is made based on a moral obligation and may be enforceable in order to prevent unjust enrichment on the part of the promisor.

# Harrington v. Taylor

Injured rescuer promisee (P) v. Rescued promisor (D)

N.C. Sup. Ct., 225 N.C. 690, 36 S.E.2d 227 (1945).

**NATURE OF CASE:** Appeal in action to enforce a contract.

**FACT SUMMARY:** In gratitude for Harrington's (P) efforts in saving his life, Taylor (D) promised to pay her for her injuries.

## 🏛 RULE OF LAW
Gratitude for a gratuitous act is insufficient consideration to enforce a promise.

**FACTS:** Harrington (P) prevented Taylor (D) from being killed by his wife. Harrington (P) was severely injured. The next day, Taylor (D) promised to pay Harrington (P) for her injuries. Taylor (D) paid a small amount and then refused to make further payments. Harrington (P) sued for breach of contract, and Taylor (D) alleged that the contract was unenforceable for lack of consideration. The trial court found for Taylor (D) and Harrington (P) appealed.

**ISSUE:** Is gratitude for a gratuitous act sufficient consideration to enforce a contract?

**HOLDING AND DECISION:** (Per curiam) No. Gratitude or moral obligations arising from a gratuitous, humanitarian act are not sufficient considerations to enforce a contract. No matter how much we personally find Taylor's (D) refusal to pay improper, as a matter of law, the promise to pay for Harrington's (P) injuries is unenforceable. Affirmed.

## ▶ ANALYSIS

If the original act was not intended to be gratuitous, an implied contract may be found. For example, if an unconscious person is brought to a hospital and is given care for his injuries, there is an implied promise to pay for these services. In cases of rescue, the act is gratuitous. The rescuer is not presumed to have expected payment for his actions. Therefore, there is no, present consideration to support the subsequent promise to pay.

■══■

## Quicknotes

**CONSIDERATION** Value given by one party in exchange for performance, or a promise to perform, by another party.

**IMPLIED CONTRACT** An agreement between parties that may be inferred from their general course of conduct.

■══■

# Kirksey v. Kirksey

### Widow (P) v. Brother-in-law (D)

Ala. Sup. Ct., 8 Ala. 131 (1845).

**NATURE OF CASE:** Action to recover damages for breach of a promise.

**FACT SUMMARY:** Kirksey (D) promised "Sister Antillico" (P) a place to raise her family "if you come down and see me."

## 🏛 RULE OF LAW
To be legally enforceable, an executory promise must be supported by sufficient, bargained-for consideration.

**FACTS:** Kirksey (D) wrote to his widowed sister-in-law, "Sister Antillico" (P), a letter containing the following clause: "If you will come down and see me, I will let you have a place to raise your family." "Sister Antillico" (P) moved sixty miles to Kirksey's (D) residence, where she remained for over two years. Kirksey (D) then required her to leave although her family was not yet "raised." "Sister Antillico" (P) contended that the loss which she sustained in moving was sufficient consideration to support Kirksey's (D) promise to furnish her with "a place" until she could raise her family. She was awarded $200, and Kirksey (D) appealed.

**ISSUE:** To be legally enforceable, must an executory promise be supported by sufficient, bargained-for consideration?

**HOLDING AND DECISION:** (Ormond, J.) Yes. To be legally enforceable, an executory promise must be supported by sufficient, bargained-for consideration. In this case, a promise on the condition, "if you will come down and see me," is a promise to make a gift. Any expenses incurred by the promisee in "coming down and seeing" are merely conditions necessary to acceptance of the gift. In this case, Kirksey (D) did not appear to be bargaining either for "Sister Antillico's" (P) presence or for her sixty-mile move. Instead, Kirksey (D) merely wished to assist her out of what he perceived as a grievous and difficult situation. Reversed.

## ▌ *ANALYSIS*

This well-known case demonstrates the court's insistence on finding a bargained-for exchange before it will enforce an executory promise. A promise to make a gift is generally not legally binding until it is executed. Compare Williston's famous hypothetical in which a benevolent man says to a tramp: "If you go around the corner to the clothing shop there, you may purchase an overcoat on my credit." This hypothetical highlights the conceptual problem of the present case in that it is unreasonable to construe the walk around the corner as the price of the promise, yet it is a legal detriment to the tramp to make the walk. Perhaps a reasonable (though not conclusive) guideline is the extent to which the happening of the condition will benefit the promisor. The present case might be decided differently today under the doctrine of promissory estoppel, which had not yet been developed in 1845.

---

## Quicknotes

**BREACH OF CONTRACT** Unlawful failure by a party to perform its obligations pursuant to contract.

**CONSIDERATION** Value given by one party in exchange for performance, or a promise to perform, by another party.

**EXECUTORY PROMISE** A promise to perform an action that has not yet been performed.

---

# Lake Land Employment Group of Akron, LLC v. Columber

Former employer (P) v. Former employee (D)

Ohio Sup. Ct., 101 Ohio St. 3d 242, 804 N.E.2d 27 (2004).

**NATURE OF CASE:** Suit for breach of covenant not to compete.

**FACT SUMMARY:** After Columber's (D) job ended, he started a company that competed with his former employer, Lake Land Employment Group of Akron, LLC (Lake Land) (P), in violation of his non-competition agreement. Columber (D) resisted Lake Land's (P) suit by arguing that the agreement was void for lack of consideration.

## 🏛 RULE OF LAW
Continued employment alone satisfies the contractual requirement of consideration in a covenant not to compete entered into by an at-will employee who is already employed by the employer.

**FACTS:** Columber (D) was an at-will employee of Lake Land Employment Group of Akron, LLC (Lake Land) (P) from 1988 to 2001. Lake Land (P) asked him to sign a covenant not to compete in 1991, and Columber (D) signed the agreement. The noncompetition agreement prohibited Columber (D) from being employed by a competitor of Lake Land (P) within a 50-mile radius of Akron, Ohio, for three years after his employment with Lake Land (P) ended. Columber (D) started a business similar to Lake Land's (P) after he stopped working for Lake Land (P). Lake Land (P) sued. Columber (D) answered by pleading that the noncompetition agreement was void for lack of consideration. The trial judge granted Columber's (D) motion for summary judgment, agreeing that no consideration supported the agreement because nothing material to Columber's (D) employment relationship changed after he signed the agreement. The court of appeals affirmed, but it also asked the Ohio Supreme Court to resolve a conflict between its rationale and the rationale used in a similar case by another of the state's intermediate appellate courts. The Ohio Supreme Court accepted jurisdiction over the case.

**ISSUE:** Does continued employment alone satisfy the contractual requirement of consideration in a covenant not to compete entered into by an at-will employee who is already employed by the employer?

**HOLDING AND DECISION:** (Moyer, C.J.) Yes. Continued employment alone satisfies the contractual requirement of consideration in a covenant not to compete entered into by an at-will employee who is already employed by the employer. Although disfavored, covenants not to compete are appropriate where they impose reasonable temporal and geographic limitations. States are split

on the particular issue in this appeal, but, consistent with Ohio law, an at-will employer's forbearance from discharging an employee is sufficient consideration to support a noncompetition agreement. In Ohio, consideration can take either of two forms: a detriment to the promisee or a benefit to the promisor. Since at-will employment is an essentially contractual relationship, either side in the relationship can propose different terms for the relationship at any time. Viewed in this context, a request for an at-will employee to sign a noncompetition agreement is in effect a proposal to renegotiate the employment relationship. When the employee agrees to such different terms, the consideration lies in the employer's forbearance from ending the employer's employment. Reversed and remanded.

**DISSENT:** (Resnick, J.) No consideration supports the agreement here because, contrary to the majority's creative euphemisms, nothing changed in the underlying employment relationship in this case. Lake Land (P) gave up nothing: after the agreement was executed, the company had the same right to fire Columber (D), for any reason or no reason at all, whenever it wanted. Likewise, Columber (D) received nothing, either. Any "forbearance" by the employer in such circumstances consists solely in not firing the employee until after he signs the agreement.

**DISSENT:** (Pfeifer, J.) What the majority finds to be consideration is instead coercion. Even so, the employee's execution of the noncompetition agreement and the employer's promise of continued employment alter the at-will employment relationship, because the employer must continue to employ the employee who executes the agreement for an unspecified period of time. It must be left to the courts to determine the reasonableness of that period.

## ▶ ANALYSIS

Judge Resnick's dissent has much merit; compared to her arguments, the majority's rationale reads as an exercise in legal fiction. The potential weakness in Judge Resnick's own reasoning, though, appears in her statement: "[t]he only actual 'forbearance,' 'proposal,' or 'promise' made by the employer in this situation is declining to fire the employee until he executes the noncompetition agreement." Her reasonably reductive definition of "forbearance" focuses on the precise instant at which the employee signs the agreement. That reductive sense of "forbearance" could be substantially more vital, though, if specific facts showed

*Continued on next page.*

that an at-will employer was indeed ready to fire an employee unless he signed a noncompetition agreement.

∎▬∎

## Quicknotes

**AT-WILL EMPLOYMENT** The rule that an employment relationship is subject to termination at any time, or for any cause, by an employee or an employer in the absence of a specific agreement otherwise.

**CONSIDERATION** Value given by one party in exchange for performance, or a promise to perform, by another party.

**FORBEARANCE** Refraining from doing something that one has the legal right to do.

∎▬∎

# Strong v. Sheffield

Creditor (P) v. Endorser of note (D)

N.Y. Ct. App., 144 N.Y. 392, 39 N.E. 330 (1895).

**NATURE OF CASE:** Action to enforce payment on a promissory note.

**FACT SUMMARY:** Sheffield (D), payer, gave a note to Strong (P), payee, for an antecedent debt which was past due. The only consideration was that Strong (P) would forbear in his demand for payment, though no time period was set. Two years later, Strong (P) demanded payment and Sheffield (D) failed to pay.

## 🏛 RULE OF LAW
A purported promise is illusory and not consideration if by its terms the performance of the promise is entirely optional with the promisor.

**FACTS:** The demand note upon which the action was brought was made by the husband of Sheffield (D), endorsed by her at his request, and delivered to Strong (P), the payee, as security for an antecedent debt owing by the husband to Strong (P). The only consideration was Sheffield's (D) endorsement for Strong's (P) promise to forbear on demand for payment for an unspecified period of time. Strong (P) forbeared on demanding payment for a two-year period, at which time Sheffield (D) was unable to pay the note. The trial court found in favor of Strong (P), but the General Term reversed, and he appealed.

**ISSUE:** Is a promise illusory and not consideration if by its terms the performance of the promise is entirely optional with the promisor?

**HOLDING AND DECISION:** (Andrews, C. J.) Yes. A purported promise is illusory and not consideration if by its terms the performance of the promise is entirely optional with the promisor. A contract between the endorser of a promissory note and the payee is not an exception to the rule that a promise not supported by a consideration cannot support a contract. While an agreement to forbear the collection of a debt presently due is good consideration for an absolute or conditional promise of a third person to pay the debt without the creditor or payee binding himself at the time to forbear collection or to give time, his acquiescence in the request and actual forbearance is also good consideration. But here the note did not in law extend the payment of the debt for it was payable on demand. Strong (P) kept the note and held it personally till such time as he would make a demand. Had Strong (P) made a demand immediately upon receiving the note, his promise to forbear would have been satisfied. While Sheffield (D) may have hoped for a long period of forbearance, there was no agreement to forbear for a fixed or reasonable period of time, but for only as long as Strong

(P) should elect. The consideration is to be tested by the agreement, and not by what was done under it. As there actually was no promise by Strong (P), there was no consideration, and, consequently, no enforceable contract. Affirmed.

## ▌ ANALYSIS

Strong's (P) promise to hold the note only as long as he did not want the money did not commit him to anything. Because of this, he did not appear to have accepted the guarantor's (D) offer, nor was he supplied consideration for guarantor Sheffield's (D) promise to back the note. If a promise is entirely optional with the promisor, it is illusory. The modern trend is away from being overly literal as to whether the promise is illusory. The courts will tend more to consider the intent of the parties and the potential detriment to the party against whom cancellation of the contract is sought. Restatement (Second) of Contracts § 79 defines illusory promises as promises or apparent promises not being consideration if the terms allow the promisor to reserve a choice of alternate performances. UCC § 3-408 has reversed the precise rule of this case. Under that section, no consideration is required to back an obligation guaranteeing an antecedent debt of any kind. Under Restatement (Second) of Contracts § 89(c), if it were shown than it should have reasonably been foreseen by Sheffield (D) that there would be forbearance of a substantial nature and the promise did induce such action or reliance, the case would have gone the other way.

## Quicknotes

**COMMERCIAL PAPER** A negotiable instrument; a written promise, signed by the promisee, to pay a specified sum of money to the promisor either on demand or on a specified date.

**ILLUSORY PROMISE** A promise that is not legally enforceable because performance of the obligation by the promisor is completely within his discretion.

**NUDUM PACTUM** A promise that is unenforceable due to lack of consideration.

**PROMISSORY NOTE** A written promise to tender a stated amount of money at a designated time and to a designated person.

# Mattei v. Hopper

Developer (P) v. Property owner (D)

Cal. Sup. Ct., 51 Cal. 2d 119, 330 P.2d 625 (1958).

**NATURE OF CASE:** Action for breach of contract.

**FACT SUMMARY:** Mattei (P) purchased property from Hopper (D)—the sale to be completed in 120 days if satisfactory leases could be obtained.

## 🏛 RULE OF LAW
"Satisfaction" clauses do not render a contract illusory or raise problems of mutuality of performance.

**FACTS:** After lengthy negotiations, Mattei (P) and Hopper (D) entered into a contract whereby Mattei (P) would purchase property owned by Hopper (D) to develop as a shopping center. Mattei (P) was to pay $1,000 down and the balance in 120 days, assuming that satisfactory leases for the center could be obtained. A contract was signed and the deposit was placed in escrow. Hopper (D) thereafter refused to perform even after being notified that satisfactory leases had been found and the balance of the purchase price had been tendered. Mattei (P) brought suit, and Hopper (D) alleged that the presence of the "obtaining satisfactory leases" clause rendered the contract illusory and was also void for lack of mutuality of performance since Mattei (P) could arbitrarily refuse to perform. The court agreed and dismissed the complaint. Mattei (P) appealed.

**ISSUE:** Does the presence of a "satisfaction" clause render a contract illusory or void it for lack of mutuality?

**HOLDING AND DECISION:** (Spence, J.) No. Depending on the nature of the "satisfaction," the court reads into the contract an obligation to act in good faith or as a reasonable man. Where satisfaction can be objectively ascertained (e.g., the performance of a product or equipment), the reasonable man standard is employed to determine the reasonableness of the rejection. Where, as here, no objective standards can be applied, it becomes a matter of taste, fancy, or judgment. In such cases, the rejecting party is subject to a requirement that he act in good faith. In either case, the mere presence of the "satisfaction" clause does not render the contract illusory or void for lack of mutuality since the validity of any rejection can be tested. Reversed.

## ▶ ANALYSIS

An illusory contract is one under which the promises of one or more of the parties is not binding. It is totally discretionary on his part as to whether he will perform. Illusory contracts may, however, be enforced under quantum meruit for the reasonable value of services or materials actually rendered or under the doctrine of promissory estoppel, where a party relies to his detriment on the promises. These, however, are exceptions and, normally, neither party can enforce an illusory contract which is still executory.

---

## Quicknotes

**BREACH OF CONTRACT** Unlawful failure by a party to perform its obligations pursuant to contract.

**ILLUSORY CONTRACT** A contract that is unenforceable for lack of consideration because a promise by one of the parties to perform is completely within his discretion.

**MUTUALITY OF PERFORMANCE** The requirement for a valid contract that the parties be required to perform.

**PROMISSORY ESTOPPEL** A promise that is enforceable if the promisor should reasonably expect that it will induce action or forbearance on the part of the promisee, and does in fact cause such action or forbearance, and it is the only means of avoiding injustice.

**QUANTUM MERUIT** Equitable doctrine allowing recovery for labor and materials provided by one party, even though no contract was entered into, in order to avoid unjust enrichment by the benefited party.

**REASONABLE MAN STANDARD** A hypothetical person whose judgment represents the standard to which society requires its members to act in their private affairs and in their dealings with others.

# Structural Polymer Group, Ltd. v. Zoltek Corp.

Buyer (P) v. Seller (D)

543 F.3d 987 (8th Cir. 2008).

**NATURE OF CASE:** Appeal by defendant from denial of motions for new trial and for judgment as a matter of law, and cross-appeal by plaintiff from the vacation of a damages award, in an action for breach of a requirements contract.

**FACT SUMMARY:** Structural Polymer Group and Structural Polymer Systems (together SP) (P) sued Zoltek Corp. (D) for breach of a requirements contract for carbon fiber, and a jury returned a verdict for SP (P), which the district court reduced. Zoltek (D) contended, inter alia, that the contract was void for lack of mutuality of obligation. SP (P) contended that the district court erred in reducing the award on the grounds that it was duplicative.

## RULE OF LAW

(1) As a matter of law, there is mutuality of obligations in a requirements contract, and, therefore, sufficient consideration to support the contract, where the purchaser's requirements are not entirely determinable by the purchaser's subjective preferences but are determinable by objective criteria outside of the purchaser's control.

(2) Where a jury awards damages under a requirements contract for lost profits from two products, but the contract limits the quantity the purchaser may obtain of either product, but not both additively, a court does not abuse its discretion in limiting the award so it is not duplicative.

**FACTS:** Structural Polymer Group and Structural Polymer Systems (together SP) (P) and Zoltek Corp. (D) entered into a requirements contract for large-tow (as opposed to small-tow) carbon fiber in 2000. Under the agreement, Zoltek (D) promised to manufacture and sell to SP (P) all of SP's (P) requirements between November 6, 2000, and December 31, 2010, for "Large Filament Count Carbon Fibers (Carbon Fibers) as defined by PANEX 33 specifications," at "then-current market price." SP (P), in turn, promised to "obtain their total requirements for suitable quality, in the reasonable opinion of [SP], Carbon Fibers from [Zoltek]," the volume not to exceed "the amount actually purchased by [SP] in the preceding Contract Year plus one million . . . pounds." Around April 2002, Zoltek (D), which had produced a large-tow carbon fiber product called Panex 33, stopped Panex 33 production and began manufacturing a substitute product called Panex 35. SP (P) ordered no Panex 33 or 35 in 2003, and it

ordered and received 548,935 pounds of Panex 35 in 2004. Two orders for Panex 35 that SP (P) placed with Zoltek (D) in 2005 and 2006 never filled, and SP (P) sued Zoltek (D) for breach of contract alleging lost profits through December 31, 2006, and future lost profits through December 31, 2010. Because the parties disputed whether the agreement entitled SP (P) to both Panex 33 and Panex 35, SP's (P) damages expert made alternative lost profit calculations: $21,138,518 in then-current lost profits under Count I corresponding to 3,960,276 pounds of Panex 35, and $14,906,377 in then-current lost profits under Count II corresponding to 3,000,000 pounds of Panex 33. SP (P) argued that the contract was effectively modified to substitute Panex 35 for Panex 33. A jury awarded SP (P) lost profits under both counts through December 31, 2006, but declined to award SP (P) future lost profits. The district court vacated the lesser award under Count II as duplicative, giving SP (P) a final sum of $21,138,518. Zoltek (D) moved for a new trial, and for judgment as a matter of law, but the district court denied both motions. Zoltek (D) appealed the district court's denial of those motions, contending, inter alia, that the district court erred by refusing to allow it to raise the argument to the jury that the agreement was void for lack of mutuality of obligation. SP (P) cross-appealed the district court's vacation of the jury's award under Count II of the complaint. The court of appeals granted review.

**ISSUE:**

(1) As a matter of law, is there mutuality of obligations in a requirements contract, and, therefore, sufficient consideration to support the contract, where the purchaser's requirements are not entirely determinable by the purchaser's subjective preferences but are determinable by objective criteria outside of the purchaser's control?

(2) Where a jury awards damages under a requirements contract for lost profits from two products, but the contract limits the quantity the purchaser may obtain of either product, but not both additively, does a court abuse its discretion in limiting the award so it is not duplicative?

**HOLDING AND DECISION:** (Colloton, J.)

(1) Yes. As a matter of law, there is mutuality of obligations in a requirements contract, and, therefore, sufficient consideration to support the contract, where the purchaser's requirements are not entirely determinable by the purchaser's subjective preferences but are determinable by objective criteria outside of the purchaser's control. Whether a contract is supported by sufficient

*Continued on next page.*

consideration is determined by a court as a matter of law. Here, Zoltek (D) argues that SP (P) could at all times order or not order Zoltek (D) fiber as it subjectively wanted because (1) SP had zero requirements for large-tow fiber when the contract was formed, (2) the price protection clause gave SP (P) the option to buy carbon fibers from other producers whenever SP (P) wanted to, and (3) SP (P) was free to buy small-tow fiber, which, according to Zoltek (D), was interchangeable with large-tow fiber, in place of large-tow whenever it pleased. All three of Zoletk's (D) arguments are rejected. As to its first argument, the duty of good faith that is implied into requirements contracts by state law renders SP's (P) obligation under the agreement non-illusory. Because of SP's (P) duty of good faith, if SP (P) failed to purchase anything from Zoltek (D) during the term of the agreement, Zoltek (D) could have claimed that SP (P) acted in bad faith by failing to make purchases, and that SP (P) had breached the agreement. As to Zoltek's (D) second argument, the price protection clause in the contract did not render SP's (P) obligation illusory. The price protection clause gave Zoltek (D) a right of first refusal to sell large-tow carbon fiber to SP (P) for the same price as offered by a third party seller. If Zoltek (D) offered to match the price offered by another supplier, then SP (P) was obligated to purchase from Zoltek (D). Instead, only if SP (P) had an unfettered option to purchase from another supplier during the term of the contract, then this option would destroy the exclusivity of the arrangement, and demonstrate lack of consideration. Here, Zoltek's (D) right of first refusal was sufficient to create mutuality of obligation and consideration. Finally, as to Zoltek's (D) third argument, even if small-tow and large-tow fibers are in fact interchangeable, as Zoltek (D) contends, this fact does not negate mutuality of obligation. Instead, when a buyer contracts to purchase its requirements for a product from a particular seller, but then, absent good faith, purchases an interchangeable product from a third party, the buyer may have breached the requirements contract. Thus, here, SP's (P) obligation to purchase in good faith all of its requirements for large-tow fiber exclusively from Zoltek (D) was sufficient consideration to make the contract valid. For all these reasons, the district court did not err in concluding that there was mutuality of obligation and, therefore, consideration. Affirmed as to this issue.

(2) No. Where a jury awards damages under a requirements contract for lost profits from two products, but the contract limits the quantity the purchaser may obtain of either product, but not both additively, a court does not abuse its discretion in limiting the award so it is not duplicative. The verdict form submitted to the jury included alternative damages calculations corresponding to 3,000,000 pounds of Panex 33 and 3,960,276 pounds of Panex 35. The jury awarded SP (P) damages under both calculations. The district court concluded that the agreement entitled SP (P) to either Panex 33 or Panex 35, but not to both—which is why it vacated the lesser of the two awards as duplicative. Despite the alternative damages calculations presented to the jury by SP's (P) expert, the contract did not provide that SP (P) could order the maximum quantity of both Panex 33 and Panex 35. SP (P) instead was entitled to order the quantity of carbon fiber ordered in the immediately preceding year, plus one million pounds. Thus, between 2004 and 2005, it was entitled either to 3,960,276 pounds of Panex 35, or 3,000,000 pounds of Panex 33, but not both. The jury's award under both Count I and Count II gave SP (P) profit corresponding to 6,960,276 pounds of large-tow carbon fiber when at most SP (P) was entitled to 3,960,276 pounds. Accordingly, the district court did not abuse its discretion when it determined that the jury's award under both counts was duplicative and altered the judgment accordingly. Affirmed as to this issue.

## ▶ ANALYSIS

Here, the district court concluded that Zoltek's (D) claim of lack of mutuality was an affirmative defense that Zoltek (D) had failed to raise, and, therefore, had forfeited. The district court's ruling on Zoltek's (D) proposed defense, however, did not foreclose Zoltek (D) from arguing to the jury that SP (P) breached the agreement. If Zoltek (D) had asserted that SP (P) acted in bad faith, that would be an argument that SP (P) had breached the agreement, not that the agreement lacked mutuality or consideration in the first place. Similarly, Zoltek (D) was free to argue that SP's (P) purchase of small-tow fiber from parties other than Zoltek (D) was a breach of the agreement to purchase large-tow fiber exclusively from Zoltek (D). In any event, even if Zoltek (D) had pursued such claims, the jury found that SP (P) performed its obligations under the contract, so that Zoltek (D) would not have prevailed on a breach of contract theory.

## Quicknotes

**MUTUALITY OF OBLIGATION** Requires that both parties to a contract be bound or else neither is bound.

**REQUIREMENTS CONTRACT** An agreement pursuant to which one party agrees to purchase all his required goods or services from the other party exclusively for a specified time period.

# Wood v. Lucy, Lady Duff-Gordon

Agent (P) v. Designer (D)

N.Y. Ct. App., 222 N.Y. 88, 118 N.E. 214 (1917).

**NATURE OF CASE:** Action for damages for breach of a contract for an exclusive right.

**FACT SUMMARY:** Wood (P), in a complicated agreement, received the exclusive right for one year, renewable on a year-to-year basis if not terminated by 90-day notice, to endorse designs with Lucy's (D) name and to market all her fashion designs for which she would receive one half the profits derived. Lucy (D) broke the contract by placing her endorsement on designs without Wood's (P) knowledge.

## 🏛 RULE OF LAW
While an express promise may be lacking, the whole writing may be instinct with an obligation—an implied promise—imperfectly expressed so as to form a valid contract.

**FACTS:** Lucy (D), a famous-name fashion designer, contracted with Wood (P) that for her granting to him an exclusive right to endorse designs with her name and to market and license all of her designs, they were to split the profits derived by Wood (P) in half. The exclusive right was for a period of one year, renewable on a year-to-year basis, and terminable upon a 90-day notice. Lucy (D) placed her endorsement on fabrics, dresses, and millinery without Wood's (P) knowledge and in violation of the contract. Lucy (D) claimed that the agreement lacked the elements of a contract as Wood (P) allegedly was not bound to do anything. The appellate division agreed and dismissed the complaint. Wood (P) appealed.

**ISSUE:** If a promise may be implied from the writing even though it is imperfectly expressed, is there a valid contract?

**HOLDING AND DECISION:** (Cardozo, J.) Yes. While the contract did not precisely state that Wood (P) had promised to use reasonable efforts to place Lucy's (D) endorsement and market her designs, such a promise can be implied. The implication arises from the circumstances. Lucy (D) gave an exclusive privilege, and the acceptance of the exclusive agency was an acceptance of its duties. Lucy's (D) sole compensation was to be one-half the profits resulting from Wood's (P) efforts. Unless he gave his efforts, she could never receive anything. Without an implied promise, the transaction could not have had such business efficacy as they must have intended it to have. Wood's (P) promise to make monthly accountings and to acquire patents and copyrights as necessary showed the intention of the parties that the promise has value by showing that Wood (P) had some duties. The promise to pay Lucy (D) half the profits and make monthly accountings was a promise to use reasonable efforts to bring profits and revenues into existence. Reversed.

## ▶ ANALYSIS

A bilateral contract can be express, implied in fact, or a little of each. The finding of an implied promise for the purpose of finding sufficient consideration to support an express promise is an important technique of the courts in order to uphold agreements which seem to be illusory and to avoid problems of mutuality of obligation. This case is the leading case on the subject. It is codified in UCC § 2-306(2) where an agreement for exclusive dealing in goods imposes, unless otherwise agreed, an obligation to use best efforts by both parties. The broadest acceptance of the principle of this case has been in exclusive agency contracts but has been applied in many other contexts such as output contracts, contracts subject to obtaining a mortgage loan, and an implied promise to use best efforts in securing the loan. Basically, the court is interpreting the intentions and conduct of the parties.

■═■

## Quicknotes

**BILATERAL CONTRACT** An agreement pursuant to which each party promises to undertake an obligation, or to forbear from acting, at some time in the future.

**BREACH OF CONTRACT** Unlawful failure by a party to perform its obligations pursuant to contract.

**IMPLIED PROMISE** A promise inferred by law from a document as a whole and the circumstances surrounding its implementation.

**MUTUALITY OF OBLIGATION** Requires that both parties to a contract are bound or else neither is bound.

■═■

# Ricketts v. Scothorn

Executor (D) v. Promisee (P)

Neb. Sup. Ct., 57 Neb. 51, 77 N.W. 365 (1898).

**NATURE OF CASE:** Action to compel payment on a promissory note given without consideration.

**FACT SUMMARY:** In reliance on her grandfather's promise to pay money, Scothorn (P) quit her employment.

## 🏛 RULE OF LAW
A promise may be legally binding without consideration if it reasonably induced action or forbearance and if injustice can be avoided by its enforcement.

**FACTS:** J.C. Ricketts gave his granddaughter, Scothorn (P), a promissory note for $2,000 on demand. Ricketts indicated that the note was for the purpose of freeing Scothorn (P) from the necessity of working. Scothorn (P) immediately quit her employment. J.C. Ricketts thereafter died and Scothorn (P) then sued A.D. Ricketts (D), executor of the estate, for the amount due on the note.

**ISSUE:** Is the abandonment, induced by a promise of a job, sufficient reliance to estop the promisor from refuting that promise on the ground that it was given without consideration?

**HOLDING AND DECISION:** (Sullivan, J.) Yes. When a promisee is induced by a promise to change his position in accordance with the real or apparent intention of the promisor, the doctrine of estoppel precludes the promisor from later claiming that the promise was not supported by consideration. This remedy is equitable in nature and is designed to prevent the gross injustice which would otherwise result. Affirmed.

## ▶ ANALYSIS

In this leading case the court recognizes that Scothorn's (P) abandoning her job was not consideration for the note. Rather the note was a pure gift and thus, absent reliance, would ordinarily not be enforced because of lack of a bargained-for consideration. Traditionally, the estoppel doctrine had been limited to cases where one party had represented a fact to another party who then relied on the fact as represented. In the present case, the court for the first time extended the estoppel doctrine to promissory expressions (hence "promissory estoppel"). (Cf. Restatement (Second) § 90, which states the most recent version of the doctrine.) (Caveat: Courts have often confused and blended the doctrine of estoppel with the doctrine of consideration resulting in such statements as: "The reliance on the promise serves as the consideration for that promise." This is conceptually misleading since the prom-issory estoppel doctrine is basically a twentieth-century exception to the general rule which requires every enforceable promise to be supported by a bargained-for consideration.)

◼═◼

## Quicknotes

**CONSIDERATION** Value given by one party in exchange for performance, or a promise to perform, by another party.

**PROMISSORY ESTOPPEL** A promise that is enforceable if the promisor should reasonably expect that it will induce action or forbearance on the part of the promisee, and does in fact cause such action or forbearance, and it is the only means of avoiding injustice.

**PROMISSORY NOTE** A written promise to tender a stated amount of money at a designated time and to a designated person.

**RELIANCE** Dependence on a fact that causes a party to act or refrain from acting.

◼═◼

# Feinberg v. Pfeiffer Co.

Retired employee (P) v. Employer (D)

Mo. Ct. App., 322 S.W.2d 163 (1959).

**NATURE OF CASE:** Action on appeal by defendant to show failure of contract due to lack of consideration.

**FACT SUMMARY:** Anna Feinberg (P) was given a pension for life by Pfeiffer Co. (D) based upon her past service to Pfeiffer Co. (D). Pfeiffer Co. (D) subsequently refused to pay the pension claiming lack of consideration for its promise to do so.

## 🏛 RULE OF LAW
Where one acts in reliance on a promise, there is an enforceable contract under the doctrine of promissory estoppel.

**FACTS:** Anna Feinberg (P) had been a bookkeeper for Pfeiffer Co. (D) for 37 years. The board of Pfeiffer Co. (D) voted to give her a lifetime pension anytime she chose to retire. The pension was based upon Mrs. Feinberg's (P) past service to the company and not upon her continued service. A year and a half after learning of the pension, Mrs. Feinberg (P) retired and began receiving the pension. Six years after her retirement, Pfeiffer Co. (D) refused to continue paying Mrs. Feinberg (P) her pension upon the advice of their attorney and accountants that there existed no valid consideration for the promise to pay. Mrs. Feinberg (P) brought an action to compel payment of her pension by the Pfeiffer Co. (D), and the lower court held for her. Pfeiffer Co. (D) appealed.

**ISSUE:** Where one acts in reliance on a promise, is there an enforceable contract under the doctrine of promissory estoppel?

**HOLDING AND DECISION:** (Doerner, Commn.) Yes. Where one acts in reliance on a promise, there is an enforceable contract under the doctrine of promissory estoppel. Plaintiff retired from a lucrative position in reliance upon defendant's promise to pay her an annuity or pension. Judgment for plaintiff is affirmed per curiam.

## ▶ *ANALYSIS*

Note that, in the present case, if Feinberg (P) were still healthy and able to work, the decision would have been different. In that situation, it would not be the case that injustice could be avoided only by enforcement of the promise. Note additionally that if Feinberg (P) had continued to work for Pfeiffer (D) until she became physically unable to continue and was forced to retire, she could probably not recover on Pfeiffer's (D) promise. Her retirement would not have been in reliance on Pfeiffer's (D) promise as the doctrine of promissory estoppel requires.

## *Quicknotes*

**PROMISSORY ESTOPPEL** A promise that is enforceable if the promisor should reasonably expect that it will induce action or forbearance on the part of the promisee, and does in fact cause such action or forbearance, and it is the only means of avoiding injustice.

# Wright v. Newman

Child's non-biological father (D) v. Child's biological mother (P)

Ga. Sup. Ct., 266 Ga. 519, 467 S.E.2d 533 (1996).

**NATURE OF CASE:** Appeal from order of child support based on promissory estoppel.

**FACT SUMMARY:** Wright (D), who had had a relationship with Newman (P), contended that he should not be held liable for child support of Newman's (P) son because the son was not his biological child and he never formally contracted to provide such support. Wright (D) urged that, notwithstanding that for 10 years he had held himself out to others to be the son's father and allowed the child to consider him to be the natural father, such conduct was insufficient to require him to pay child support based on promissory estoppel.

## RULE OF LAW

An obligation to support a child may arise by contract through promissory estoppel where an individual who is not the child's biological parent lists himself on the child's birth certificate as the father, even though he knows he is not; holds himself out as the child's father; and allows the child to believe that he is the child's natural father, and where the child's mother relies on the individual's conduct to her and the child's detriment by refraining from identifying and seeking support from the child's natural father.

**FACTS:** When Newman's (P) son was born, Wright (D) listed himself as the father on the child's birth certificate and gave the child his last name, even though Wright (D) knew he was not the child's biological father. For ten years, Wright (D) held himself out to others as the child's father, and allowed the child to consider him to be the natural father. Newman (P) severed the relationship and all ties with Wright (D) when the child was approximately three years old. For approximately the next five years, Newman (P) and Wright (D) did not communicate. Then over the following two years, Wright (D) visited with the child. However, Wright (D) did not support the child after the child was three. Newman (P) brought suit against Wright (D) for child support, asserting that his liability for such support could be based on promissory estoppel. She asserted that Wright (D) promised to support the child when he asserted he was the child's parent, and that she and the child relied upon Wright's (D) promise to their detriment. Specifically, she refrained from identifying and seeking support from the child's natural father. The trial court ordered Wright (D) to pay child support for Newman's (P) son, and the state's highest court granted review.

**ISSUE:** May an obligation to support a child arise by contract through promissory estoppel where an individual

who is not the child's biological parent lists himself on the child's birth certificate as the father, even though he knows he is not; holds himself out as the child's father; and allows the child to believe that he is the child's natural father, and where the child's mother relies on the individual's conduct to her and the child's detriment by refraining from identifying and seeking support from the child's natural father?

**HOLDING AND DECISION:** (Carley, J.) Yes. An obligation to support a child may arise by contract through promissory estoppel where an individual who is not the child's biological parent lists himself on the child's birth certificate as the father, even though he knows he is not; holds himself out as the child's father; and allows the child to believe that he is the child's natural father, and where the child's mother relies on the individual's conduct to her and the child's detriment by refraining from identifying and seeking support from the child's natural father. Notwithstanding that Wright (D) is neither the child's natural father nor an adoptive father, as a matter of law Wright (D) may still be liable for child support as a matter of contract. Here, there was no formal written contract, but Wright's (D) actions, when taken together, constitute a promise by Wright (D) to Newman (P) and her son that he would assume all of the obligations and responsibilities of fatherhood, including that of providing support. He undertook his commitment knowingly and voluntarily, and continued to do so for some 10 years. The facts can also support the inference that Newman (P) relied to her and her son's detriment by refraining from identifying and seeking support from the child's natural father. If she had not refrained from doing so, she might now have a source of financial support for the child and the child might now have a natural father who provided emotional, as well as financial, support. Thus, the elements of promissory estoppel are met. Those elements are: a promise that the promisor should reasonably expect to induce action or forbearance on the part of the promisee or a third person and which does induce such action or forbearance is binding if injustice can be avoided only by enforcement of the promise. Affirmed as to this issue.

**CONCURRENCE:** (Sears, J.) It should be emphasized that Newman (P) did, in fact, rely upon Wright's (D) promise to her detriment. Wright (D) would have known that Newman (P) refrained from seeking to identify and obtain support from the child's biological father while Wright (D) was fulfilling his commitment to her. Promissory estoppel requires only that the reliance by the injured party be reasonable, and does not require the promisee to

*Continued on next page.*

exhaust all other possible means of obtaining the benefit of the promise from any and all sources before being able to enforce the promise against the promisor. Contrary to the dissent's position, it would not be simple—if at all possible—for Newman (P) to identify the child's biological father and collect support from him. Because it likely will be impossible for Newman (P) to establish the identity of the child's biological father, bring a successful paternity action, and obtain support from that individual, an injustice will result if Wright (D) is allowed to renege on his obligation, since Newman (P) likely will not receive any support to assist in the cost of raising her son, despite having been promised the receipt of such by Wright (D). An even greater injustice will be inflicted upon the boy himself, because a child who has been told by any adult, regardless of the existence of a biological relationship, that he will always be able to depend upon the adult for parenting and sustenance, will suffer a great deal when that commitment is broken.

**DISSENT:** (Benham, C.J.) Here, Newman (P) cannot satisfy a key element of promissory estoppel, namely, that she suffered a detriment by relying on Wright's (D) actions. She has not alleged, nor does the record reveal, that she does not know the identity of the natural father, nor does she show that the natural father is dead or unable to be found. Consequently, she has failed to prove that she is unable to seek support from the natural father. Further, any prejudice incurred by Newman (P) because of the passage of ten years is not due to Wright's (D) actions, since, at least for the past seven years, Newman (P) has been in the same situation, i.e., receiving no support payments from Wright (D). Thus, Wright (D) is not legally obligated to support the child because Newman (P) has failed to show that she or the child incurred any detriment by Wright's (D) failure to fulfill his promise made ten years ago.

## ▶ *ANALYSIS*

The doctrine of promissory estoppel prevents a promisor from reneging on a promise, when the promisor should have expected that the promisee would rely upon the promise, and the promisee does in fact rely upon the promise to her detriment. Sufficient consideration to enforce a contractual promise pursuant to promissory estoppel may be found in any benefit accruing to the promisor, or any reliance, loss, trouble, disadvantage, or charge imposed upon the promisee. Here, the majority focuses on the detriment to Newman (P) and her child, rather than on any benefit accruing to Wright (D).

does in fact cause such action or forbearance, and it is the only means of avoiding injustice.

## *Quicknotes*

**PROMISSORY ESTOPPEL** A promise that is enforceable if the promisor should reasonably expect that it will induce action or forbearance on the part of the promisee, and

# D&G Stout, Inc. v. Bacardi Imports, Inc.

Liquor distributor (P) v. Liquor company (D)

923 F.2d 566 (7th Cir. 1991).

**NATURE OF CASE:** Appeal from summary judgment dismissing a complaint for damages based on reliance on a promise.

**FACT SUMMARY:** When Bacardi Imports, Inc. (Bacardi) (D), after promising to retain General Liquors (General) (P) as its wholesale distributor in northern Indiana, withdrew its product line from General (P), General (P) was forced to sell itself at liquidation prices, after which it sought to recover damages from Bacardi (D).

### RULE OF LAW
A promise which the promisor should reasonably expect to induce action or forbearance on the part of the promisee and a third person and which does induce such action or forbearance is binding if injustice can be avoided only by the enforcement of the promise.

**FACTS:** D&G Stout (P), operating as General Liquors, Inc. (General) (P), was Bacardi Import's (Bacardi) (D) wholesale liquor distributor in northern Indiana. After General (P) survived an industry shake-up and consolidation, it began negotiations with National Wine & Spirits (National) for a possible sale. Bacardi (D), knowing of the negotiations, promised that General (P) would remain its distributor for northern Indiana. Confident that it could continue operating, General (P) then rejected National's offer. But Bacardi (D) reneged on its promise and withdrew its line from General (P). Hiram Walker, General's (P) other major client, also withdrew. Its negotiating leverage destroyed, General (P) was forced to sell to National for $550,000 below the original offer. General (P) sued Bacardi (D) on promissory estoppel grounds for the $550,000 price differential. The district court granted Bacardi's (D) motion for summary judgment. General (P) appealed.

**ISSUE:** Is a promise which the promisor should reasonably expect to induce action or forbearance on the part of the promisee and a third person and which does induce such action or forbearance binding if injustice can be avoided only by the enforcement of the promise?

**HOLDING AND DECISION:** (Cudahy, J.) Yes. A promise which the promisor should reasonably expect to induce action or forbearance on the part of the promisee and a third person and which does induce such action or forbearance is binding if injustice can be avoided only by the enforcement of the promise. Through its repudiation, Bacardi (D) destroyed General's (P) negotiating leverage since General (P) no longer had the alternative of continuing as an independent concern. General (P) was left with

one choice: sell at any price. Under these facts, General (P) had a reliance interest in Bacardi's (D) promise, given in full knowledge that General (P) planned to reject National's offer. While General's (P) allegations must still be proven at trial, Bacardi's (D) promise was of a sort on which General (P) might rely, with the possibility of damages for breach. Reversed and remanded.

### ANALYSIS

Judge Cudahy emphasized that the lost future income expected from an at-will relationship, whether from wages or from profits, is not recoverable on a theory of promissory estoppel. Although an aspiring employee could not sue for lost wages on an employer's unfulfilled promise of at-will employment, he could sue for moving expenses because moving expenses are reliance costs resulting from a forgone opportunity. In summary, reliance costs are recoverable on a promissory estoppel theory, but expectancy damages are not. As a practical matter, the cost that General (P) incurred when it rejected National's offer was a reliance injury and therefore redressable.

---

### Quicknotes

**ANTICIPATORY REPUDIATION** Breach of a contract subsequent to formation but prior to the time performance is due.

**AT-WILL EMPLOYMENT** The rule that an employment relationship is subject to termination at any time, or for any cause, by an employee or an employer in the absence of a specific agreement otherwise.

**EXPECTANCY** The expectation or contingency of obtaining possession of a right or interest in the future.

**FORBEARANCE** Refraining from doing something that one has the legal right to do.

**PROMISSORY ESTOPPEL** A promise that is enforceable if the promisor should reasonably expect that it will induce action or forbearance on the part of the promisee, and does in fact cause such action or forbearance, and it is the only means of avoiding injustice.

**RELIANCE** Dependence on a fact that causes a party to act or refrain from acting.

**REPUDIATION** The actions or statements of a party to a contract that evidence his intent not to perform, or to continue performance, of his duties or obligations hereunder.

*Continued on next page.*

**SUMMARY JUDGMENT** Judgment rendered by a court in response to a motion by one of the parties, claiming that the lack of a question of material fact in respect to an issue warrants disposition of the issue without consideration by the jury.

# Cotnam v. Wisdom

Estate administrator (D) v. Surgeon (P)

Ark. Sup. Ct., 83 Ark. 601, 104 S.W. 164 (1907).

**NATURE OF CASE:** Action to recover damages in quasi-contract for professional medical services.

**FACT SUMMARY:** Wisdom (P) rendered emergency professional medical services to Cotnam (D) after a streetcar accident.

## 🏛 RULE OF LAW
A physician may recover in quasi-contract a reasonable compensation for emergency services rendered on the spot to an unconscious accident victim.

**FACTS:** Harrison was rendered unconscious in a streetcar accident. Wisdom (P), a physician, was summoned to the scene by a passerby and thereafter performed a difficult and unsuccessful operation to save Harrison's life. Harrison died without regaining consciousness. Wisdom (P) sued Cotnam (D), administrator of Harrison's estate, in quasi-contract for the services rendered to Harrison. Judgment at trial was for Wisdom (P). Cotnam (D) appealed.

**ISSUE:** May a physician who renders necessary emergency medical services to an unconscious accident victim recover in quasi-contract even though the victim did not request the service, the victim clearly could not consent to the service, and the victim died a short time later?

**HOLDING AND DECISION:** (Hill, C.J.) Yes. One bereft of all sense and reason may be held liable for "necessaries" furnished to him in good faith. The fact that there was no request for, or consent to, the services is irrelevant since recovery rests on the legal fiction of quasi-contract, a mythical creation of the courts to do justice where there otherwise would be no remedy. Furthermore, the success or failure of an operation is not the measure of a physician's services. Although it is customary for physicians to graduate their charges according to a patient's ability to pay, this custom should not apply where a physician is summoned by a passerby to attend an unconscious and previously unknown victim. The quasi-contract fiction merely requires reasonable compensation and "the services are the same be the patient prince or pauper." The victim's marital status is not relevant to the case, and knowledge of his bachelorhood might well have affected the amount of recovery allowed by the jury. For these reasons, judgment must be reversed and the cause remanded.

**CONCURRENCE:** (Battle, J.) To allow the jury to consider that the estate would go to collateral heirs was a mistake.

## ▶ ANALYSIS

This case should be compared with *Callano v. Oakwood Park Homes Corp.*, 219 A. 2d 332 (1966), where plaintiff, under contract to a third person, planted shrubbery on and enhanced the value of defendant's property, in which quasi-contractual recovery was not allowed. *Cotnam v. Wisdom* may be distinguished in several important ways: (1) Here the services rendered were "necessities" (i.e., a matter of life and death) and extremely emergent in nature. (2) Here the physician had no other remedy. And (3) here there was an obvious "direct relation" between doctor and patient. Underlying this decision is a fundamental public policy consideration. If the court does not allow recovery, doctors will be discouraged from acting in emergency situations (since they would be spending time and effort, not to mention risking malpractice suits, with no possibility of reward). Society, however, wishes to encourage professional action in such circumstances. The standard measure of damages in quasi-contract is the reasonable value of the benefit received. Since it is somewhat confusing to speak of "benefit received" by a patient who died without regaining consciousness (in fact Cotnam (D) tried to make an argument out of this!), the court chooses to speak in terms of "reasonable compensation" for the service.

## Quicknotes

**PUBLIC POLICY** Policy administered by the state with respect to the health, safety and morals of its people in accordance with common notions of fairness and decency.

**QUASI-CONTRACT** An implied contract created by law to prevent unjust enrichment.

# Callano v. Oakwood Park Homes Corp.

Plant nursery operators (P) v. Real estate developer (D)

N.J. Super. Ct., 91 N.J. Super. 105, 219 A.2d 332 (1966).

**NATURE OF CASE:** Action to recover damages in quasi-contract.

**FACT SUMMARY:** The Callanos (P), under contract to a third party, planted shrubbery on and enhanced the value of Oakwood Park's (D) property.

## RULE OF LAW
Where one party receives benefit from a second party, the first party is not unjustly enriched if there was no direct relationship between the parties and the second party did not expect remuneration from the first at the time the benefit was conferred.

**FACTS:** Pendergast contracted to buy a lot from Oakwood Park Homes Corp. (Oakwood Park) (D). The Callanos (P), under separate contract with Pendergast, planted shrubbery on the lot. Thereafter Pendergast died without having paid the Callanos (P), and Pendergast's estate canceled the Oakwood Park (D) contract. Oakwood Park (D), not knowing of Pendergast's failure to pay the Callanos (P), then resold the property the value of which was enhanced by the presence of the shrubs. The Callanos (P) contended that Oakwood Park (D) was unjustly enriched, and were awarded $475 at trial. Oakwood (D) appealed.

**ISSUE:** Is one party with no direct relationship to another necessarily obligated to pay for any benefit received from that latter party on the theory of quasi-contractual liability?

**HOLDING AND DECISION:** (Collester, J.) No. To recover in quasi-contract, a plaintiff must prove that the defendant was unjustly enriched. In the present case, both parties conceded that Oakwood Park (D) was enriched. However, that enrichment was not unjust since the Callanos (P) expected payment from Pendergast and there was no other direct relationship between the Callanos (P) and Oakwood Park (D). Nor did the Callanos (P) perform under any mistake. Recovery on a theory of quasi-contract was designed to provide a remedy where none existed. Here, a remedy exists; the Callanos (P) may sue Pendergast's estate. Reversed.

## ANALYSIS

A quasi-contract is a contract "implied-in-law" (and should be carefully distinguished from an actual contract "implied-in-fact"). A quasi-contract is not a contract at all but is rather an obligation imposed by law to do justice (even though it is clear that no promise was ever made and no meeting of the minds was ever consummated). It is,

in a sense, a noncontractual obligation treated procedurally as if it were a contract (a legal fiction). When allowed, a quasi-contractual recovery (for the reasonable value of benefit received by the defendant) is the court's way of protecting the plaintiff's restitution interest (by putting the defendant back in the position in which he would have been had the benefit never been recovered). Compare a protection of plaintiff's reliance interest (which would attempt to put plaintiff back in the position in which he would have been had he never conferred the benefit). Courts will look hard and long before granting this rather extraordinary remedy in light of the obvious problem of distinguishing between the "officious intermeddler" and the "deserving claimant." Note the court's emphasis in the present case on the Callanos' (P) remedy against Pendergast's estate.

---

## Quicknotes

**QUASI-CONTRACT** An implied contract created by law to prevent unjust enrichment.

**UNJUST ENRICHMENT** The unlawful acquisition of money or property of another for which both law and equity require restitution to be made.

# Creating Contractual Obligations

## Quick Reference Rules of Law

# Lucy v. Zehmer

## Farm purchaser (P) v. Joking seller (D)

Va. Sup. Ct. App., 196 Va. 493, 84 S.E.2d 516 (1954).

**NATURE OF CASE:** Appeal from dismissal of action for specific performance of a land sale contract.

**FACT SUMMARY:** Zehmer (D) claimed his offer to sell his farm to Lucy (P) was made in jest.

## 🏛 RULE OF LAW
If a person's words and acts, judged by a reasonable standard, manifest a certain intent, it is immaterial what may be the real but unexpressed state of that person's mind.

**FACTS:** Zehmer (D) and his wife (D) contracted to sell their 471-acre farm to Lucy (P) for $50,000. Zehmer (D) contends that his offer was made in jest while the three of them were drinking, and that Zehmer (D) only desired to bluff Lucy (P) into admitting he did not have $50,000. Lucy (P) appears to have taken the offer seriously by discussing its terms with Zehmer (D), rewriting it to enable Mrs. Zehmer (D) to sign, by providing for title examination, and by taking possession of the agreement. Lucy (P) offered $5 to bind the deal and the next day sold a one-half interest to his brother (P) in order to raise money. When Zehmer (D) refused to perform the contract, Lucy (P) sued to enforce it, but the court dismissed the action. Lucy. (P) appealed.

**ISSUE:** Does the law impute to a person an intention corresponding to the reasonable meaning of his words and acts?

**HOLDING AND DECISION:** (Buchanan, J.) Yes. The existence of an offer depends upon the reasonable meaning to be given the offeror's acts and words. For the formation of a contract, the mental assent of the parties is not required. If the words and acts of one of the parties have but one reasonable meaning, his undisclosed intention is immaterial except when an unreasonable meaning which he attaches to his manifestations is known to the other party. Accordingly, one cannot say he was merely jesting when his conduct and words would warrant reasonable belief that a real agreement was intended. Reversed and remanded.

## ▶ ANALYSIS

Note that it is not what is said, but how it is heard and reasonably understood. Mutual assent of the parties is required for the formation of a contract, but mental assent is not. Where one party can reasonably believe from the other party's acts and words that a real agreement is intended, the other party's real but unexpressed intention is immaterial. Mutual assent is an objective determination based upon what a reasonable man would believe. An offer is an expression of will or intention creating a power of acceptance upon the offeree. If the offer to sell the farm had been for a price of $50, the court could judge the ridiculousness of the offer in determining whether a reasonable man would believe it to be serious.

■══■

## Quicknotes

**MUTUAL ASSENT** A requirement of a valid contract that the parties possess a mutuality of assent as manifested by the terms of the agreement and not by a hidden intent.

**SPECIFIC PERFORMANCE** An equitable remedy whereby the court requires the parties to perform their obligations pursuant to a contract.

■══■

# Specht v. Netscape Communications Corp.

## User (P) v. Software program provider (D)

306 F.3d 17 (2d Cir. 2002).

**NATURE OF CASE:** Motion to compel arbitration.

**FACT SUMMARY:** Specht (P) downloaded from the Internet free software from Netscape Communications Corp. (Netscape) (D). When an issue arose as to Specht's (P) use of the software, Netscape (D) moved to compel arbitration.

🏛 **RULE OF LAW**
Where consumers are urged to download free software, mere reference to the existence of license terms on a submerged screen does not place consumers on inquiry notice or constructive notice of terms.

**FACTS:** Specht (P) downloaded from the Internet free software from Netscape Communications Corp. (Netscape) (D). Specht (P) then brought suit against Netscape (D), alleging that usage of the software transmitted to Netscape (D) private information about the user's file transfer activity on the Internet in violation of federal statute. Netscape (D) moved to compel arbitration, arguing that Specht's (P) downloading of the Netscape (D) software constituted acceptance of the compulsory arbitration provision contained in the online licensing agreement.

**ISSUE:** Where consumers are urged to download free software, does mere reference to the existence of license terms on a submerged screen place consumers on inquiry notice or constructive notice of terms?

**HOLDING AND DECISION:** (Sotomayor, J.) No. Mere reference to the existence of license terms on a submerged screen does not place consumers on inquiry notice or constructive notice of terms. The download web-page screen was printed in such a manner that it tended to conceal the fact that it was an express acceptance of Netscape's (D) rules and regulations. There is no reason to assume that viewers will scroll down to subsequent screens simply because screens are there. Netscape (D) relies on cases that involve shrinkwrap licensing that placed consumers on inquiry notice. Those cases, *Hill v. Gateway 2000, Inc.*, 105 F.3d 1147 (7th Cir. 1997) and *ProCD, Inc. v. Zeidenberg*, 86 F.3d 1447 (7th Cir. 1996) do not help Netscape (D) because the licensing in those cases was conspicuous. Specht (P) was responding to an offer that did not carry an immediate visible notice of the existence of license terms or require unambiguous manifestations of assent to those terms. The uncontested evidence revealed that Specht (P) was unaware that Netscape (D) intended to attach license terms to the use of the downloaded software.

The district court's denial of the motion to compel arbitration is affirmed.

▶ **ANALYSIS**

As noted by the court in *Specht*, when products are "free" and users are invited to download them in the absence of reasonably conspicuous notice that they are about to bind themselves to contract terms, the transactional circumstances cannot be fully analogized to those "in the paper world" of arm's-length bargaining.

■▬■

## Quicknotes

**CONSTRUCTIVE NOTICE** Knowledge of a fact that is imputed to an individual who was under a duty to inquire and who could have learned of the fact through the exercise of reasonable prudence.

**INQUIRY NOTICE** The communication of information that would cause an ordinary person of average prudence to inquire as to its truth.

■▬■

# Owen v. Tunison

Would-be property buyer (P) v. Owner (D)

Me. Sup. Jud. Ct., 131 Me. 42, 158 A. 926 (1932).

**NATURE OF CASE:** Action for damages for breach of contract for sale of real property.

**FACT SUMMARY:** Tunison (D) replied by letter to Owen's (P) offer to buy Tunison's (D) lot and buildings thereon for $6,000, saying that he could not sell for less than $16,000.

## RULE OF LAW
There can be no contract, no meeting of the minds, between the parties unless there is an offer.

**FACTS:** Owen (P) desired to purchase Tunison's (D) lot and buildings thereon in Bucksport, Maine. Owen (P) wrote Tunison (D) in this regard and offered a purchase price of $6,000. Several weeks later, Tunison (D) replied by letter that he could not sell "unless I was to receive $16,000 cash." Owen (P) replied that he accepted Tunison's (D) offer to sell for $16,000. Tunison (D) refused to go through with the sale, and Owen (P) sued for breach of contract.

**ISSUE:** Is the statement of a minimum sale price to be construed as an offer to sell at that price?

**HOLDING AND DECISION:** (Barnes, J.) No. It cannot be successfully argued that a potential seller's statement of the minimum price he would be willing to accept is an offer to sell at that price. Rather, it is to be construed as an invitation to the potential buyer to make further offers or to enter into negotiations that might lead to a sale. Tunison's (D) letter was most likely written with the intent to open negotiations. It was not a proposal to sell. Judgment for Tunison (D).

## ▶ ANALYSIS

When the potential seller states a price which would be the minimum price acceptable to him, he is not offering to sell at that price. Instead, he is indicating the level at which he may be willing to accept a new offer. The potential seller thereby invites new offers or indicates nothing more than a willingness to enter into negotiations. In construing the potential seller's language, it may be helpful to redraft his response, i.e., "I will sell for $X," or "I will not consider an offer of less than $X," and then determine which response appears to come closer to the meaning of the actual language used.

**OFFER** A proposed promise to undertake performance of an action, or to refrain from acting, that is to become binding upon acceptance by the offeree.

**■═■**

---

## *Quicknotes*

**BREACH OF CONTRACT** Unlawful failure by a party to perform its obligations pursuant to contract.

# Fairmount Glass Works v. Crunden-Martin Woodenware Company

Glass company (D) v. Jar buyer (P)

Ky. Ct. App., 106 Ky. 659, 51 S.W. 196 (1899).

**NATURE OF CASE:** Appeal from judgment for plaintiff in action to recover damages for breach of contract for sale of goods.

**FACT SUMMARY:** Crunden-Martin Woodenware Company (Crunden) (P) requested by letter of Fairmount Glass Works (Fairmont) (D) the lowest price it could give on Crunden's (P) order for Mason jars, which prices Fairmount (D) gave to Crunden (P) but whose order Fairmount (D) then refused to fill.

## ⛪ RULE OF LAW
Where prices are requested on an order and the vendor quotes those prices to the vendee, the vendor has offered to fill the order and is obligated to fill the order upon receipt within a reasonable time of vendee's acceptance.

**FACTS:** Crunden-Martin Woodenware Company (Crunden) (P) requested of Fairmount Glass Works (Fairmont) (D) by letter dated April 20, 1895, the lowest price at which Fairmount (D) could fill Crunden's (P) order for ten carloads of Mason jars. Fairmount (D) answered by letter dated April 23, 1895, with its prices for different sizes of jars with terms and conditions "for immediate acceptance." Crunden (P) telegraphed a reply on April 24, 1895, to "enter order ten carloads as per your quotation. Specifications mailed." The same day, Fairmount (D) telegraphed back it could not fill the order, its output was sold out. Fairmount (D) then received by mail Crunden's (P) specifications calling for "strictly first-quality goods," which Fairmount (D) contends was not an acceptance of their offer (if the court finds an offer) as made. The lower court found for Crunden (P), and Fairmount (D) appealed.

**ISSUE:** Is the quotation of prices by the vendor upon vendee's request for such quotation as part of its order an offer by the vendor to the vendee for goods at the quoted prices, terms, and conditions for vendee to accept or reject?

**HOLDING AND DECISION:** (Hobson, J.) Yes. Where prices are requested on an order and the vendor quotes those prices to the vendee, the vendor has offered to fill the order and is obligated to fill the order upon receipt within a reasonable time of vendee's acceptance. In this case, the quotation of prices "for immediate acceptance" upon Crunden's (P) order was more than a simple quotation of prices, it was an offer. The true meaning of the correspondence is determined by reading it as a whole. After Crunden (P) had accepted the terms, Fairmount (D) could not withdraw its offer. Fairmount's (D) use of the term "for immediate acceptance" when considered with

previous communication indicates an intent to make an offer to Crunden (P) who could then accept or reject within a reasonable time. Fairmount's (D) claim that Crunden's (P) specifications which were received after Fairmount (D) withdrew its offer, were not within the terms of Crunden's (P) telegraphed acceptance fails as Fairmount (D) did not state this objection in its withdrawal of its offer. Affirmed.

## ▶ ANALYSIS

Ordinarily, the mere quotation of prices is not an offer to sell at those prices but rather an invitation to make an offer. Where the evidence shows the intent of the parties to be otherwise, that is, an offer was intended, the general rule will not be followed. The existence of an offer is determined by considering what a reasonable man would believe from his consideration of the words and acts of the other party. It is also suggested that the court is holding the vendee's price inquiry upon an order as a strong basis for vendee's reliance on the vendor's price quotation. Where the price quotation is unsolicited or in response to the general question of what the vendor's lowest price would be, the vendee lacks the reliance seen in this case.

━━

## Quicknotes

**ACCEPTANCE** Assent to the specified terms of an offer, resulting in the formation of a binding agreement.

**BREACH OF CONTRACT** Unlawful failure by a party to perform its obligations pursuant to contract.

**OFFER** A proposed promise to undertake performance of an action, or to refrain from acting, that is to become binding upon acceptance by the offeree.

**RELIANCE** Dependence on a fact that causes a party to act or refrain from acting.

━━

# International Filter Co. v. Conroe Gin, Ice & Light Co.

Water purifier manufacturer (P) v. Ice manufacturer (D)

Tex. Comm. App., 277 S.W. 631 (1925).

**NATURE OF CASE:** Appeal from defense judgment in action for damages for breach of contract.

**FACT SUMMARY:** International Filter Co. (Filter) (P) offered a water purifier to Conroe Gin, Ice & Light Co. (Conroe) (D) by letter, stating that there would be a contract when Conroe's (D) acceptance was approved by Filter's (P) executive officer at its Chicago office. This was done, but Conroe (D) revoked its order claiming no contract existed.

## 🏛 RULE OF LAW
As the offeror is in control of his offer, he may specify the type of acceptance which is required and can dispense with the requirement of its communication.

**FACTS:** International Filter Co. (Filter) (P), through its traveling salesman, submitted to Conroe Gin, Ice & Light Co. (Conroe) (D) a letter offering a water purification system and stating that a contract for purchase would arise when Conroe's (D) order was received and approved by an executive officer of Filter (P) in its Chicago office. On the same day, Conroe (D) communicated its order, which was approved by Engel, Filter's (P) President and Vice President. Filter (P) then sent an acknowledgment of Conroe's (D) order and requested Conroe (D) to send a water sample so the purifier could be properly adjusted before shipment. Two weeks later, Conroe (D) revoked its order, and Filter (P) sued, but the judge found in favor of Conroe (D). The appeals court affirmed, and Filter (P) appealed.

**ISSUE:** May an offeror specify the type of acceptance required?

**HOLDING AND DECISION:** (Nickels, J.) Yes. As the offeror is in control of his offer, he may specify the type of acceptance which is required and can dispense with the requirement of its communication. In this case, notice of acceptance of Conroe's (D) order was not required to be communicated by Filter (P) to Conroe (D). Engel's endorsement of the order was an approval by an executive officer at Filter's (P) Chicago office. The paper then became a contract as notice of acceptance was not required under the terms of the offer. A prompt order was required, and it was expressly stated that a contract would arise upon approval by Filter's (P) executive officer in Chicago. Even though notice of acceptance was not required, Filter's (P) letter of acknowledgment and request for a water sample sufficiently communicated acceptance anyway. The form of the notice of acceptance can be quite different from the acceptance itself. It was quite clear that Filter (P) intended to ship the system and would not have so intended unless it had accepted the order. Reversed and remanded by Cureton, C.J., as recommended.

## ▶ ANALYSIS

Generally, when an offer looks to a bilateral contract, the offeree's promise must be communicated to the offeror. But as the offeror is the "master" of his offer, he can specify the type of acceptance required, and can dispense with the requirement of a communication altogether. Restatement (Second) of Contracts, § 57(a), does not follow this case and requires that the offeree exercise "reasonable diligence to notify the offeror of acceptance or that the offeror will receive an acceptance seasonally." Usually, however, notification of acceptance does not explicitly have to be given if it is made clear by the course of events that it has been given implicitly.

━■━

## Quicknotes

**ACCEPTANCE** Assent to the specified terms of an offer, resulting in the formation of a binding agreement.

**BILATERAL CONTRACT** An agreement pursuant to which each party promises to undertake an obligation, or to forbear from acting, at some time in the future.

**BREACH OF CONTRACT** Unlawful failure by a party to perform its obligations pursuant to contract.

**REVOCATION** The cancellation or withdrawal of some authority conferred or an instrument drafted, such as the withdrawal of a revocable contract offer prior to the offeree's acceptance.

━■━

# White v. Corlies & Tift

## Builder (P) v. Merchant (D)

N.Y. Ct. App., 46 N.Y. 467 (1871).

**NATURE OF CASE:** Appeal from plaintiff's verdict in action for damages for breach of contract.

**FACT SUMMARY:** White (P) attempted to accept an offer by Corlies & Tift (D) by beginning performance of "fitting up" a suite of offices, without indicating to Corlies & Tift (D) his intention to accept.

## RULE OF LAW
Acceptance of an offer must be manifested in such a way as to be communicated to the offeror.

**FACTS:** Corlies & Tift (D) requested White (P) to make an estimate for the fitting up of a suite of offices. The day following White's (P) submission of his estimate, Corlies & Tift's (D) bookkeeper wrote to White (P): "Upon an agreement to finish the fitting up of offices at 57 Broadway in two weeks from date, you can begin at once. The writer will call again, probably between 5 and 6 this p.m." Without replying to the note, White (P) immediately commenced performance by purchasing lumber and beginning work thereon. The following day, Corlies & Tift (D) countermanded their offer, and White (P) successfully brought this action for damages for breach of contract, and Corlies (D) appealed.

**ISSUE:** Can an offeree accept an offer by merely beginning performance without indicating his intention to accept to the offeror?

**HOLDING AND DECISION:** (Folger, J.) No. Where the offeree's act of beginning performance is no indication in itself that he intends to accept the offer, he must manifest his intent to accept by some appropriate act. The only overt act which White (P) claims as indicating his acceptance of the offer was the purchase of those materials necessary for the work and commencing work. Such action was "as well referable to one state of facts as another," and such action did not, in itself, indicate acceptance of the offer. White (P), as offeree, had the duty to manifest his intention to accept in the proper way, to be in the usual course of events, in some reasonable time communicated to Corlies & Tift (D). It is not necessary that such manifestation actually reach the offeror before he is bound by the offeree's acceptance. It is enough that the offeree set in motion an indication of his acceptance of the offer, which would normally result in his communication to the offeror. Reversed; new trial ordered.

## ANALYSIS
The problem in this case is the ambiguous meaning of the bookkeeper's note to White (P). Did the offer invite acceptance by return promise or by performance? Was the agreement yet to be accepted by White's (P) promise, or had a contract already been concluded, allowing immediate performance by White (P)? The lower court determined that White (P) had a right to act on the note that Corlies & Tift's (D) offer looked toward performance rather than toward a return promise, or a unilateral contract. However, this appraisal was reversed by the court of appeals which concluded that the offer was not one that could be accepted by mere performance, but looked toward and must be expressly assented to by a return promise or a bilateral contract.

## Quicknotes

**ACCEPTANCE** Assent to the specified terms of an offer, resulting in the formation of a binding agreement.

**BILATERAL CONTRACT** An agreement pursuant to which each party promises to undertake an obligation, or to forbear from acting, at some time in the future.

**BREACH OF CONTRACT** Unlawful failure by a party to perform its obligations pursuant to contract.

# Allied Steel and Conveyors, Inc. v. Ford Motor Co.

Machinery manufacturer (D) v. Car company (P)

277 F.2d 907 (6th Cir. 1960).

**NATURE OF CASE:** Action for indemnification against damages awarded for personal injuries in a prior suit.

**FACT SUMMARY:** Hankins, an employee of Allied Steel and Conveyors, Inc. (Allied) (D), was injured during performance of Allied's (D) contract with Ford Motor Co. (Ford) (P) before Allied (D) had formally accepted the contract as per terms of Ford's (P) offer.

## 🏛 RULE OF LAW
Where the offeror merely suggests a permitted method of acceptance, other methods of acceptance are not precluded.

**FACTS:** Ford Motor Co. (Ford) (P) submitted to Allied Steel and Conveyors, Inc. (Allied) (D) an agreement for the purchase of machinery which provided: "This purchase order agreement is not binding until accepted. Acceptance should be executed on acknowledgment copy which should be returned to buyer." Accompanying this agreement was a separate form requiring Allied (D) to assume full responsibility for the negligence of both its own and Ford's (P) employees in connection with Allied's (D) installation of the machinery. Allied (D) began installation prior to executing and returning the agreement in November, and in September its employee Hankins had sustained injuries as a result of the negligence of a Ford (P) employee. Hankins sued Ford (P), which in turn impleaded Allied (D). The trial resulted in a verdict for Hankins against Ford (P) and for Ford (P) against Allied (D). Allied (D) appealed. Allied (D) contended that it was not bound by the indemnification provision at the time of Hankins's injury since the contract was not in effect prior to its formal acceptance of Ford's (P) offer in November.

**ISSUE:** If an offeror requests acceptance by return promise, may the offeree accept instead by undertaking performance?

**HOLDING AND DECISION:** (Miller, J.) Yes. An offeree may accept by undertaking performance if the offeror was merely suggesting a permitted method of acceptance. In this case, the words "should be" executed and returned were such a suggestion, and Ford (P) was not prescribing an exclusive manner of acceptance. If it had, an attempt by Allied (D) to accept by undertaking performance would not create a contract. But where acceptance by return promise is only a suggested rather than an exclusive method, the offeree may also accept by undertaking the performance called for by the contract with the offeror's knowledge and consent. In such a case, the undertaking of performance operates as a promise to render a complete performance. Affirmed.

## ▶ ANALYSIS

This holding may at first seem contrary to *White v. Corlies and Tift,* 46 N.Y. 467 (1871), in that it permits acceptance by performance even where a return promise is requested, while the *White* holding required a return promise despite omission of any required method of acceptance. The crucial factor, however, is notification of acceptance to the offeror. In *White v. Corlies & Tift,* the court was concerned lest the offeror find himself indebted for a performance without any means of learning whether his offer had been accepted. In *Allied v. Ford,* the court is careful to limit acceptance by performing, stating that it must be undertaken with the offeror's "knowledge, consent and acquiescence." In addition, it felt that the offeree who had performed with the offeror's consent, leading the offeror to believe a contract had been formed, "should not be allowed to assert an actual intent at variance with the meaning of his acts."

━━

## Quicknotes

**ACCEPTANCE** Assent to the specified terms of an offer, resulting in the formation of a binding agreement.

**IMPLEADER** Procedure by which a third party, who may be liable for all or part of liability, is joined to an action so that all issues may be resolved in a single suit.

**INDEMNIFICATION** The payment by a corporation of expenses incurred by its officers or directors as a result of litigation involving the corporation.

━━

# Corinthian Pharmaceutical Systems, Inc. v. Lederle Laboratories

## Distributor (P) v. Manufacturer (D)

### 724 F. Supp. 605 (S.D. Ind. 1989).

**NATURE OF CASE:** Motion for specific performance of sales contract.

**FACT SUMMARY:** Corinthian Pharmaceutical Systems, Inc. (Corinthian) (P), distributor of DTP vaccine, placed an order with Lederle Laboratories (Lederle) (D), manufacturer, for 1,000 vials of vaccine, but when only part of the order was delivered and the remainder was to be shipped later at a higher price, Corinthian (P) brought an action for breach of contract.

---

**RULE OF LAW**
A seller's price list is not an offer to the buyer, and a subsequent partial shipment of the buyer's order is not an acceptance sufficient to form a contract.

---

**FACTS:** Corinthian Pharmaceutical Systems, Inc. (Corinthian) (P) distributed DTP vaccines, which were purchased from Lederle Laboratories (Lederle) (D) on a regular basis. As a routine business practice, Lederle (D) issued price lists to its customers. The list stated that the prices were subject to change without notice and that any changes take effect at the time of shipment. In an internal memo to its representatives, Lederle (D) indicated that the price for the vaccine would be increased to $171 per vial due to the high cost of insurance and product liability lawsuits. The content of the memo was leaked to Corinthian (P) before the price increase was to be announced to the other customers. Corinthian (P) immediately placed an order for 1,000 vials through Lederle's (D) computer ordering system. The order stated that $64.32 would be the payable price for each vial. Lederle (D) made a partial shipment of 50 vials at the price indicated in Corinthian's (P) order, which was accepted. At the same time, Lederle (D) sent a letter to Corinthian (P) indicating that the partial shipment was to accommodate him and the remainder would be shipped for the price of $171 per vial. Subsequently, Corinthian (P) brought an action for breach of contract, seeking specific performance of the order. Lederle (D) moved for summary judgment.

**ISSUE:** Is a seller's price quote and a partial shipment of the buyer's order a valid offer and acceptance to form an enforceable contract?

**HOLDING AND DECISION:** (McKinney, J.) No. A contract is formed when the offer is properly accepted and supported by consideration. An offer is a manifestation of one's willingness to enter into a bargain. Thus, price quotations are not offers but only invitations for the recipient to make an offer. As a result, Lederle's (D) price lists sent to Corinthian (P) did not constitute an offer. The offer was actually made by Corinthian (P) when it placed an order via the computer ordering system. Since the parties were merchants and the offer was for a sale of goods, UCC § 2-206 governed the mode of acceptance. The Code allows for acceptance to be in any reasonable form and manner. In addition, it provides that shipment of nonconforming goods by the seller who gives notice that the shipment is merely an accommodation is not an acceptance but a counteroffer. Here, Lederle's (D) partial shipment, although nonconforming, was a counteroffer, since it was followed by a notification that the shipment is only an accommodation. Thus, there was no contract formed between the parties. Motion for summary judgment granted.

---

**ANALYSIS**

This case involved the manner by which the offeree must indicate his commitment or promise. UCC § 2-206 no longer requires that an acceptance be the mirror image of the offer, which was required by common law. Furthermore, the commitment may either be demonstrated by promissory language or a promissory act.

---

## Quicknotes

**BREACH OF CONTRACT** Unlawful failure by a party to perform its obligations pursuant to contract.

**CONSIDERATION** Value given by one party in exchange for performance, or a promise to perform, by another party.

**COUNTEROFFER** A statement by the offeree which has the legal effect of rejecting the offer and of proposing a new offer to the offeror.

**OFFER** A proposed promise to undertake performance of an action, or to refrain from acting, that is to become binding upon acceptance by the offeree.

**SPECIFIC PERFORMANCE** An equitable remedy whereby the court requires the parties to perform their obligations pursuant to a contract.

**SUMMARY JUDGMENT** Judgment rendered by a court in response to a motion by one of the parties, claiming that the lack of a question of material fact in respect to an issue warrants disposition of the issue without consideration by the jury.

# Dickinson v. Dodds

Land buyer (P) v. Land seller (D)

C.A., Ch.D., L.R. 2 Ch. D. 463 (1876).

**NATURE OF CASE:** Appeal from decree of specific performance of a land sale contract.

**FACT SUMMARY:** Dodds (D) attempted to revoke an offer to sell land to Dickinson (P), but Dickinson (P) agreed to purchase prior to communication of the revocation to him.

## 🏛 RULE OF LAW
An offeree may not bind an offeror by accepting a revoked offer, even if the revocation had not been communicated to him prior to acceptance.

**FACTS:** Dodds (D) offered in writing to sell certain real estate to Dickinson (P). Dodds (D) later sought to revoke the offer, but the note of revocation was not delivered to Dickinson (P). Dickinson (P) communicated acceptance to Dodds (D), who informed him that he had sold the land to another. Dickinson (P) sued for specific performance. The chancellor issued a decree of specific performance, and Dodds (D) appealed.

**ISSUE:** Can an offeree bind an offeror by accepting a revoked offer, even if the revocation had not been communicated to him prior to acceptance?

**HOLDING AND DECISION:** (Lord James, J.) No. An offeree may not bind an offeror by accepting a revoked offer, even if the revocation had not been communicated to him prior to acceptance. A binding contract requires a "meeting of the minds." When an offeror withdraws his offer and the offeree accepts, no meeting has occurred. Even if the offer is still open to the knowledge of the offeree, the fact is that the offeror is no longer of a mind to form the contract, so acceptance does not bind him. Here, even though it was not communicated to Dickinson (P), Dodds (D) did revoke the offer, so no contract was formed. Reversed.

**CONCURRENCE:** (Lord Mellish, J.) If an offeror is no longer of a mind to offer for sale a property, he cannot be compelled to do so.

## ▶ ANALYSIS

A traditional requirement for a contract was a "meeting of the minds," as described by the court here. The term used today is "mutual assent," as stated in § 17 of the Restatement (Second) of Contracts. The concept is the same.

## Quicknotes

**ACCEPTANCE** Assent to the specified terms of an offer, resulting in the formation of a binding agreement.

**MEETING OF THE MINDS** A requirement of a valid contract that the parties possess a mutuality of assent as manifested by the terms of the agreement and not by a hidden intent; enforceability of the contract is limited to those terms to which the parties assented.

**REVOCATION** The cancellation or withdrawal of some authority conferred or an instrument drafted, such as the withdrawal of a revocable contract offer prior to the offeree's acceptance.

**SPECIFIC PERFORMANCE** An equitable remedy whereby the court requires the parties to perform their obligations pursuant to a contract.

■━■

# Drennan v. Star Paving Co.

## General contractor (P) v. Paving subcontractor (D)

Cal. Sup. Ct., 51 Cal. 2d 409, 333 P.2d 757, en banc (1958).

**NATURE OF CASE:** Appeal from award of damages for failure to perform according to a bid.

**FACT SUMMARY:** Drennan (P), a contractor, in preparing his bid on a public construction project, used the bid for paving work by subcontractor Star Paving Co. (Star) (D), but after Drennan (P) was awarded the contract, Star (D) informed Drennan (P) that its paving bid was in error.

### 🏛 RULE OF LAW
A promise which the promisor should reasonably expect to induce action or forbearance of a definite and substantial character on the part of a promisee and which does induce such action or forbearance is binding if injustice can be avoided only by enforcement of the promise.

**FACTS:** Drennan (P) was preparing a bid on a public school construction project. On the day the bid was to be submitted, Star Paving Co. (Star) (D) phoned in its bid of $7,131.60 for paving. That bid was recorded and posted on a master sheet by Drennan (P). It was customary in the area for bids to be phoned in on the day set for bidding and for general contractors to rely on them in computing their own bids. Star's (D) bid for paving was low and used by Drennan (P) in preparing his bid, which was low. The contract was awarded to Drennan (P) that same evening. The next day, Star (D) informed Drennan (P) of an error in its paving bid and refused to do the paving for less than $15,000. Drennan (P), after several months of searching, engaged another company to do the paving for $10,948.60 and sued for the cost difference. From adverse judgment in the lower courts, Star (D) appealed.

**ISSUE:** Is a promise which the promisor should reasonably expect to induce action or forbearance of a definite and substantial character on the part of a promisee and which does induce such action or forbearance binding if injustice can be avoided only by enforcement of the promise?

**HOLDING AND DECISION:** (Traynor, J.) Yes. A promise which the promisor should reasonably expect to induce action or forbearance of a definite and substantial character on the part of a promisee and which does induce such action or forbearance is binding if injustice can be avoided only by enforcement of the promise. Star (D) had reason to expect that if its bid was low it would be used by Drennan (P) and so induced "action . . . of a definite and substantial character on the part of the promisee." Star's (D) bid did not state or clearly imply revocability at any time before acceptance. Where there is an offer for a unilateral contract, the theory that the offer is revocable at any time before complete performance is obsolete. When any part of the consideration requested in the offer is given or tendered by the offeree, the offeror is bound. That is, the main offer includes a subsidiary promise, which is implied, that if part of the requested performance is given, the offeror will not revoke his offer, and if tender is made, it will be accepted. See Restatement § 45. In more extreme cases, merely acting in justifiable reliance of an offer may serve as sufficient reason to make the promise binding. See Restatement § 90. Section 90's purpose is to make a promise binding even though consideration is lacking; its absence is not fatal to the enforcement of the subsidiary promise. Reasonable reliance acts in lieu of ordinary consideration. Star (D) had a stake in Drennan's (P) reliance on its bid. This interest plus Drennan's (P) being bound by his own bid, make it only fair that Drennan (P) should have the chance to accept Star's (D) bid after the general contract was awarded to Drennan (P). While Star's (D) bid was the result of mistake, it was not such a mistake that Drennan (P) knew or should have known it was in error. A 160 percent variance in paving bids was not unusual in the area. Because the mistake misled Drennan (P) as to the paving cost under the circumstances, Star's (D) bid should be enforced. Affirmed.

## ▶ ANALYSIS

The case greatly broadened the view of promissory estoppel, Restatement § 90, as interpreted by Hand in *James Baird Co. v. Gimbel Bros.*, 64 F. 2d 344 (2d Cir. 1933), to extend beyond the area of charitable or donative promises to general business use. This view was adopted in Restatement (Second) § 90, which was written after this case. Note a subcontractor's bid must be more than a mere estimate, and, of course, if it reasonably appears to be based upon a mistake, reliance cannot be justified. The cases that apply promissory estoppel show the subcontractor to be bound by his bid, but the general contractor is not bound to accept the bid. Note that Justice Traynor works into Restatement § 90 through § 45 (the Brooklyn Bridge hypothetical), expanding the view that giving or tendering consideration will bind the promise to include justifiable reliance to have the same effect. In the *Drennan* case, circumstances and business practices peculiar to the area were important. Telephoned bids were a common practice. Wide variances in paving costs were expected, thereby adding strength to Drennan's (P) position, as an

*Continued on next page.*

error in a paving bid would not be reasonably noticed. Also see Restatement (Second) § 89B(2) for this viewpoint as extended to option contracts.

━━■

## Quicknotes

**PROMISSORY ESTOPPEL** A promise that is enforceable if the promisor should reasonably expect that it will induce action or forbearance on the part of the promisee, and does in fact cause such action or forbearance, and it is the only means of avoiding injustice.

━━■

# Dorton v. Collins & Aikman Corp.

Carpet retailer (P) v. Carpet manufacturer (D)

453 F.2d 1161 (6th Cir. 1972).

**NATURE OF CASE:** Action to compel arbitration.

**FACT SUMMARY:** Collins & Aikman's (D) acceptance form contained a compulsory arbitration clause, while Dorton's (P) order form did not.

## RULE OF LAW

An arbitration provision may be deemed a nonmaterial alteration of the contract in certain circumstances.

**FACTS:** Dorton (P) orally ordered carpeting from Collins & Aikman (D). Collins & Aikman's (D) acceptance form contained a compulsory arbitration clause. Acceptance of an order, according to Collins & Aikman's (D) form, was subject to all terms and conditions of the form. Dorton (P) sued Collins & Aikman (D), and it attempted to obtain a stay of the proceedings pending arbitration as required under its form. The district court held that the language of the form did not make acceptance of all its provisions a condition precedent to the formation of a contract. It, therefore, found that the contract was controlled by UCC § 2-207(3), where the conduct of the parties is such as to indicate that a contract has been formed. The court found, as a matter of law, that terms on an acceptance could not force arbitration on a party.

**ISSUE:** May an arbitration provision be deemed a non-material alteration of the contract in certain circumstances?

**HOLDING AND DECISION:** (Celebreezze, J.) Yes. An arbitration provision may be deemed a nonmaterial alteration of the contract in certain circumstances. UCC § 2-207 was adopted to prevent the operation of the common law mirror image rule. An acceptance and offer need not exactly match to find the existence of a valid contract. Traditionally, written offers and acceptances contain numerous provisions favorable to the drafter. In recognition of this fact, a contract is found where essential terms are present or inferable. Inconsistent terms do not become a part of the contract. If specific acceptance of the buyer's or seller's terms is made a condition precedent to the formation of the contract, no contract is formed absent an assent. Even in such cases, a contract may be formed by the actions if the parties and terms which materially alter the contract are deleted. We do not find that Collins & Aikman's (D) form requires acceptance of all terms as a condition precedent to formation of a contract. This must be specifically and unequivocally stated. Therefore, the question is whether the arbitration clause materially alters the contract as formed under UCC § 2-207(3). Arbitration clauses have gained wide acceptance, and we do not find

that they constitute a per se material alteration. We remand for such a finding. Also, there was no evidence adduced to indicate that the oral offer did not contain an arbitration provision. This should also be determined on remand.

## ANALYSIS

Under the common law, silence is not deemed to be consent. The UCC alters this approach and would allow nonmaterial terms to become part of the contract unless they are objected to by the other party within 10 days of receipt. UCC § 2-207(2). Prior to *Dorton*, an arbitration provision was specifically found to constitute an unreasonable additional term which does not become a part of the contract unless specifically consented to by the other party. Thus, there is a split in the courts.

## Quicknotes

**ACCEPTANCE** Assent to the specified terms of an offer, resulting in the formation of a binding agreement.

**ARBITRATION CLAUSE** Provision contained in a contract pursuant to which both parties agree that any disputes arising thereunder will be resolved through arbitration.

**CONDITION PRECEDENT** The happening of an uncertain occurrence, which is necessary before a particular right or interest may be obtained or an action performed.

**MIRROR-IMAGE RULE** The common law rule that for acceptance to be effective the offeree must accept each and every term of the offer.

**OFFER** A proposed promise to undertake performance of an action, or to refrain from acting, that is to become binding upon acceptance by the offeree.

**UCC § 2-207** Additional terms contained in a response to an offer that do not materially alter the original bargain will be incorporated unless notice of objection is given within a reasonable time.

# Bayway Refining Co. v. Oxygenated Marketing & Trading A.G.

## Seller (P) v. Buyer (D)

215 F.3d 219 (2d Cir. 2000).

**NATURE OF CASE:** Appeal from summary judgment for plaintiff in an action for breach of contract between merchants.

**FACT SUMMARY:** Oxygenated Marketing and Trading A.G. (OMT) (D), as a merchant buyer, contended that it had created a genuine issue of material fact that a contract term in a contract it had entered with Bayway Refining Co. (Bayway) (P), which allocated liability to the buyer for an excise tax, constituted a material alteration under UCC § 2-207(2)(b), and, therefore, was presumed to have been rejected by OMT (D). Bayway (P) contended that the term constituted an additional term that was presumed to have been accepted under § 2-207(2)(b).

## 🏛 RULE OF LAW
A merchant who asserts that a proposed additional term to a contract constitutes a material alteration under UCC § 2-207(2)(b) will not prevail on his claim where he fails to raise a factual issue as to whether the term results in surprise or hardship to him.

**FACTS:** Oxygenated Marketing and Trading A.G. (OMT) (D), a merchant in the petroleum industry, made an offer to buy MTBE from Bayway Refining Co. (Bayway) (P), another merchant in the industry. Bayway's (P) response, which acted as an acceptance, contained a "Tax Clause," which provided that "Buyer shall pay seller the amount of any federal, state and local excise, gross receipts, import, motor fuel, superfund and spill taxes and all other federal, state and local taxes however designated, other than taxes on income, paid or incurred by seller directly or indirectly with respect to the oil or product sold hereunder and/or on the value thereof." OMT (D) did not object to the term, and accepted delivery of MTBE. The transaction created a tax liability, covered under the Tax Clause, of around $464,000. Bayway (P) paid the tax, and then demanded reimbursement from OMT (D), which refused to pay, contending it had never agreed to the Tax Clause. Bayway (P) sued OMT (D) for payment of the tax liability, and the district court held that the Tax Clause had properly been incorporated into the contract. The court of appeals granted review.

**ISSUE:** Will a merchant who asserts that a proposed additional term to a contract constitutes a material alteration under UCC § 2-207(2)(b) prevail on his claim where he fails to raise a factual issue as to whether the term results in surprise or hardship to him?

**HOLDING AND DECISION:** (Jacobs, J.) No. A merchant who asserts that a proposed additional term to a contract constitutes a material alteration under UCC § 2-207(2)(b) will not prevail on his claim where he fails to raise a factual issue as to whether the term results in surprise or hardship to him. OMT (D) bears the burden of proving that the Tax Clause constitutes a material alteration. Section 2-207(2)(b) is an exception to the general rule of § 2-207(2) that additional terms become part of a contract between merchants. That general rule is in the nature of a presumption concerning the intent of the contracting parties. Thus, if neither party introduced any evidence, the Tax Clause would, by the plain language of § 2-207(2), become part of the contract. To implement that presumption, the burden of proving the materiality of the alteration must fall on the party that opposes inclusion—here, OMT (D). A material alteration is one that would "result in surprise or hardship if incorporated without express awareness by the other party." Some types of terms are per se material alterations, but the Tax Clause at issue is not one of them because, in part, it is limited, discrete and the subject of no special protection. Accordingly, OMT (D) must prove that in this case the Tax Clause resulted in surprise or hardship. Surprise, within the meaning of the material alteration exception, has both the subjective element of what a party actually knew and the objective element of what a party should have known. To carry the burden of showing surprise, a party must establish that, under the circumstances, it cannot be presumed that a reasonable merchant would have consented to the additional term. Although OMT (D) has adduced evidence that the term came as an amazement to its executives—and thus has shown that subjectively it was surprised—it has failed to show that, as a matter of objective surprise, a reasonable merchant in the industry would be surprised by the Tax Clause. On the other hand, Bayway (P) introduced evidence that the Tax Clause reflects custom and practice in the industry. The evidence was compelling that shifting tax liability to a buyer is the custom and practice in the petroleum industry. Moreover, common sense supports Bayway's (P) evidence of custom and practice, since the federal excise tax is imposed when taxable fuels are sold to any person who is not registered under a specified federal statute. The buyer thereby controls whether any tax liability is incurred in a transaction. A trade practice that reflects a rational allocation of incentives would place the burden of the tax on the party that is in the position to obviate it—here, on OMT (D) as the buyer. Because shifting tax

*Continued on next page.*

liability to a buyer is the custom and practice in the petroleum industry, OMT (D) could not have been objectively surprised by the Tax Clause. OMT (D) has also failed to raise a genuine issue as to hardship. It has only shown that it is a small business dependent on precarious profit margins, and that it would suffer a loss it cannot afford. That showing does not amount to hardship, which is typically found, if at all, when an additional term is one that creates or allocates an open-ended and prolonged liability. Here, the Tax Clause places on a buyer a contractual responsibility that bears on a specific sale of goods, that is not uncommon in the industry, and that the buyer could avoid by registration. Any loss that the Tax Clause imposed on OMT (D) is thus limited, routine and self-inflicted. For these reasons, the district court did not err in granting summary judgment to Bayway (P). [Affirmed.]

# ▶ ANALYSIS

As the court notes, certain additional terms are deemed material as a matter of law. For example, an arbitration clause is per se a material alteration in those states that require an express agreement to commit disputes to arbitration, given that arbitration clauses waive a range of rights that are solicitously protected. Another example of additional terms that are deemed per se material alterations are waivers of warranties of merchantability or fitness for a particular purpose and clauses granting the seller the power to cancel upon the buyer's failure to meet any invoice.

---

# Quicknotes

**CUSTOM AND USAGE** A customary practice that is so widespread that it has become mandatory and has the force of law.

**PRESUMPTION** A rule of law requiring the court to presume certain facts to be true based on the existence of other facts, thereby shifting the burden of proof to the party against whom the presumption is asserted to rebut.

**UCC § 2-207** Provides that a definite expression of acceptance sent within a reasonable time operates as an acceptance even though it states terms additional to or different from those offered, unless acceptance is expressly made conditional on assent to the additional terms.

---

# Step-Saver Data Systems, Inc. v. Wyse Technology

Software purchaser (P) v. Software designer (D)

939 F.2d 91 (3d Cir. 1991).

**NATURE OF CASE:** Appeal from a directed verdict for the defendant in an action for breach of warranty.

**FACT SUMMARY:** When software programs that Step-Saver Data Systems, Inc. (Step-Saver) (P) purchased from Wyse Technology (D) and TSL (D) for resale failed to operate properly, Step-Saver (P) brought suit for breach of warranty, but the trial court held that a box-top warranty disclaimer was incorporated into the parties' contract agreement.

## 🏛 RULE OF LAW
An additional term will not be incorporated into a contract if the term's addition to the contract would materially alter the parties' agreement.

**FACTS:** Step-Saver Data Systems, Inc. (Step-Saver) (P) purchased and resold copies of a Wyse Technology (Wyse) (D) program which was produced by The Software Link, Inc. (TSL) (D). Step-Saver (P) would telephone TSL (D) to place an order and then send a purchase order detailing the terms. TSL (D) would ship the order promptly, along with an invoice containing essentially identical terms. No reference was made during the telephone calls, or on either the purchase orders or the invoices, to a disclaimer of any warranties. However, TSL (D) printed such a disclaimer on the software's box-top. When the program failed to operate properly, Step-Saver (P) filed suit against TSL (D) and Wyse (D). Wyse (D) was later exonerated. The district court, holding that the terms of the "box-top license" governed the purchase, granted a directed verdict for TSL (D). Step-Saver (P) appealed, arguing that the box-top disclaimer never became a part of their agreement.

**ISSUE:** Will an additional term be incorporated into a contract if the term's addition to the contract would materially alter the parties' agreement?

**HOLDING AND DECISION:** (Wisdom, J.) No. An additional term will not be incorporated into a contract if the term's addition to the contract would materially alter the parties' agreement. This is the provision stated in § 2(b) of UCC § 2-207, which governs the analysis here. The contract between the parties was sufficiently definite without the terms provided by the box-top license. From a review of the parties' course of dealing or performance, it appears that they have not incorporated the warranty disclaimer into their agreement. Thus, the box-top license should have been treated as a written confirmation containing additional terms. Because the warranty disclaimer and limitation of remedies terms would materially alter the agreement between Step-Saver (P) and TSL (D), these terms did not become a part of the contract. Reversed and remanded for further consideration on the warranty claims.

## ▶ ANALYSIS

Under the common law of sales, and to some extent still for contracts outside the UCC, an acceptance that varied any term of the offer operated as a rejection of the offer and simultaneously made a counteroffer. The terms of the party who sent the last form, typically the seller, would become the terms of the parties' contract. This result was known as the "last shot rule." The UCC rejected this approach.

---

## *Quicknotes*

**BREACH OF WARRANTY** The breach of a promise made by one party to a contract that the other party may rely on a fact, relieving that party from the obligation of determining whether the fact is true and indemnifying the other party from liability if that fact is shown to be false.

**COUNTEROFFER** A statement by the offeree which has the legal effect of rejecting the offer and of proposing a new offer to the offeror.

**DIRECTED VERDICT** A verdict ordered by the court in a jury trial.

**UCC § 2-207** Provides that a definite expression of acceptance sent within a reasonable time operates as an acceptance even though it states terms additional to or different from those offered, unless acceptance is expressly made conditional on assent to the additional terms.

---

# ProCD, Inc. v. Zeidenberg

Software manufacturer (P) v. Purchaser (D)

86 F.3d 1447 (7th Cir. 1996).

**NATURE OF CASE:** Appeal from an order in favor of defendant in a case alleging breach of the terms of a shrinkwrap or end-user license.

**FACT SUMMARY:** When Zeidenberg (D), a customer, bought and then resold the data compiled on its CD-ROM software disk, ProCD (P) sued for breach of contract.

## 🏛 RULE OF LAW
A buyer accepts goods when, after an opportunity to inspect, he fails to make an effective rejection.

**FACTS:** ProCD (P) compiled information from over 3,000 telephone directories into a computer database which it sold on CD-ROM disks. Every box containing the disks declared that the software came with restrictions stated in an enclosed license. This license, which was encoded on the CD-ROM disks as well as printed in the manual, and which appeared on a user's screen every time the software ran, limited use of the application program and listings to non-commercial purposes. Zeidenberg (D) bought a ProCD (P) software package but decided to ignore the license and to resell the information in the database. Zeidenberg (D) also made the information from ProCD's (P) database available over the Internet for a price, through his corporation. ProCD (P) sued for breach of contract. The district court found that placing the package of software on the shelf was an "offer," which the customer "accepted" by paying the asking price and leaving the store with the goods. A contract includes only those terms which the parties have agreed to and one cannot agree to secret terms. Thus, the district court held that buyers of computer software need not obey the terms of shrinkwrap licenses. Such licenses were found to be ineffectual because their terms did not appear on the outsides of the packages. ProCD (P) appealed.

**ISSUE:** Does a buyer accept goods when, after an opportunity to inspect, he fails to make an effective rejection?

**HOLDING AND DECISION:** (Easterbrook, J.) Yes. A buyer accepts goods when, after an opportunity to inspect, he fails to make an effective rejection under § 2-602 of the Uniform Commercial Code. A vendor, as master of the offer, may invite acceptance by conduct, and may propose limitations on the kind of conduct that constitutes acceptance. ProCD (P) proposed a contract that a buyer would accept by using the software after having an opportunity to read the license at leisure. Zeidenberg (D) did this, since he had no choice when the software splashed the license across his computer screen and would not let him

proceed without indicating acceptance. The license was an ordinary contract accompanying the sale of products and was therefore governed by the common law of contracts and the Uniform Commercial Code. Transactions in which the exchange of money precedes the communication of detailed terms are common. Buying insurance or buying a plane ticket are two such common examples. ProCD (P) extended an opportunity to reject if a buyer should find the license terms unsatisfactory. Zeidenberg (D) inspected the package, tried out the software, learned of the license, and did not reject the goods. Reversed and remanded.

## ▶ ANALYSIS

The sale of information contained in computer databases presented new challenges to courts. Some courts found that the sale of software was the sale of services, rather than of goods. This case treated the sale of software as a sale of goods governed by Article 2 of the UCC.

∎▭∎

## Quicknotes

**CD-ROM** Compact disc read-only memory.

**INSPECTION OF GOODS** The examination of goods, which are the subject matter of a contract for sale, for the purpose of determining whether they are satisfactory.

**REJECTION** The refusal to accept the terms of an offer.

**SHRINKWRAP LICENSE** Terms of restriction packaged inside a product.

**UCC § 2-602** Provides that a rejection after an opportunity to inspect may be effective unless the buyer manifests acceptance in the manner invited by the offeror.

∎▭∎

# Hill v. Gateway 2000, Inc.

## Consumer (P) v. Company (D)

105 F.3d 1147 (7th Cir. 1997).

**NATURE OF CASE:** Appeal of denial of a motion to compel arbitration.

**FACT SUMMARY:** Hill (P) brought a RICO suit against Gateway (D) after purchasing a mail order computer. Gateway (D) moved to compel arbitration. The request was denied, and Gateway (D) appealed.

### RULE OF LAW
Terms sent in the box with a product that state that they govern the sale unless the product is returned within 30 days are binding on a buyer who does not return the product.

**FACTS:** Hill (P) purchased a computer from Gateway 2000, Inc. (Gateway) (D) through a telephone order and subsequently brought suit against Gateway (D), in which a civil Racketeer Influenced and Corrupt Organizations Act (RICO) claim and other claims were asserted. Gateway (D) thereupon sought enforcement of an arbitration clause which had been included in the terms sent to Hill (P) in the box in which the computer was shipped. The federal district court denied the arbitration request, and Gateway (D) appealed.

**ISSUE:** Are terms sent in the box with a product that state that they govern the sale unless the product is returned within 30 days binding on a buyer who does not return the product?

**HOLDING AND DECISION:** (Easterbrook, J.) Yes. Terms sent in the box with a product that state that they govern the sale unless the product is returned within 30 days are binding on a buyer who does not return the product. The Hills (P) conceded noticing the statement of terms but denied reading it closely enough to discover the agreement to arbitrate. An agreement to arbitrate must be enforced except upon such grounds as exist at law or in equity for the revocation of any contract. A contract need not be read to be effective. People who accept products take the risk that the unread terms may in retrospect prove unwelcome. Terms inside Gateway's (D) box stand or fall together. If they constitute the parties' contract because the Hills (P) had an opportunity to return the computer after reading them, then all must be enforced. The court rejects Hills's (P) argument that the provision in the box should be limited to executory contracts and to licenses in particular. Both parties' performance of this contract was complete when the box arrived at their home. The case does not depend on the fact that the seller characterized the transaction as a license rather than as a contract, but rather treated it as a contract for the sale of goods and reserved

the question whether for other purposes a "license" characterization might be preferable. All debates about characterization to one side, the transaction here was not executory. Vacated and remanded for arbitration.

## ANALYSIS

While observing that the federal Magnuson-Moss Warranty Act requires firms to distribute their warranty terms on request, the court noted that the Hills (P) did not contend that Gateway (D) would have refused to enclose the remaining terms also. Concealment would be bad for business, scaring some customers away and leading to excessive returns from others. Second, said the court, shoppers can consult public sources (computer magazines, the web sites of vendors) that may contain this information. Third, they may inspect the documents after the product's delivery. In this case, the Hills (P) took the third option. By keeping the computer beyond 30 days, the Hills (P) accepted Gateway's (D) offer, including the arbitration clause.

---

## Quicknotes

**ARBITRATION** An agreement to have a dispute heard and decided by a neutral third party, rather than through legal proceedings.

**ARBITRATION CLAUSE** Provision contained in a contract pursuant to which both parties agree that any disputes arising thereunder will be resolved through arbitration.

**RICO** Racketeer Influenced and Corrupt Organization laws; federal and state statutes enacted for the purpose of prosecuting organized crime.

# Hoffman v. Red Owl Stores

## Would-be franchisee (P) v. Supermarket chain operator (D)

Wis. Sup. Ct., 26 Wis. 2d 683, 133 N.W.2d 267 (1965).

**NATURE OF CASE:** Action for damages grounded on promissory estoppel.

**FACT SUMMARY:** Hoffman (P), who desired to obtain a Red Owl Stores (Red Owl) (D) franchise, was assured that he had the necessary capital required. On the basis of the statements and conduct of Red Owl's (D) representative, Lukowitz, Hoffman (P) took certain steps including selling his bakery and moving to another city in order to acquire the franchise. Negotiations collapsed when it was clear Red Owl (D) had misrepresented the actual amount of capital required, which was nearly double the original figure.

## RULE OF LAW

It is not necessary for the promise needed to sustain a cause of action to embrace all essential details of a proposed transaction between promisor and promisee so as to be the equivalent of an offer that would result in a binding contract between the parties if the promisee were to accept the same.

**FACTS:** In November 1959, Hoffman (P), owner and operator of a bakery, contacted Red Owl Stores (Red Owl) (D), which operated a supermarket chain, seeking to obtain a Red Owl Store (D) franchise. Having only $18,000 to invest, Hoffman (P) was assured by Red Owl (D) that that was sufficient. In February 1961, upon Red Owl's (D) advice, Hoffman (P) acquired a grocery store which, three months later, Red Owl (D) told him to sell, assuring him they would find him a larger store. He was again assured that $18,000 was sufficient capital to invest. In September 1961, upon Red Owl's (D) advice, Hoffman (P) put $1,000 down on a lot in another town and was told, "Everything is ready to go. Get your money together and we are set." Red Owl (D) then told Hoffman (P) to sell his bakery, which he did for $10,000, a $2,000 loss. Hoffman (P) paid $125 rent on a house near the lot and spent $140 moving to another town to gain experience working in a grocery store, but that job never materialized and he went to work on the nightshift at a bakery. Negotiations on the contract faltered as Red Owl (D) considered several arrangements when, by February 1962, $34,000 was required by Red Owl (D) for Hoffman (P) to acquire the franchise. Hoffman (P) then sued Red Owl (D) and was awarded the following damages: $2,000 for the sale of the bakery, $1,000 for the option on the lot, $140 moving expenses, and $125 rent. The trial court ordered a new trial on the jury's award of $16,735 for the sale of the grocery store.

**ISSUE:** Must the promise necessary to sustain an action for promissory estoppel embrace all essential details of a proposed transaction between promisor and promisee so as to be the equivalent of an offer that would result in a binding contract if accepted?

**HOLDING AND DECISION:** (Currie, C.J.) No. An action grounded upon promissory estoppel is not the equivalent of a breach of contract action. Originally, the doctrine of promissory estoppel was used as a substitute for consideration with the acts of detrimental reliance corresponding to consideration. To so limit the doctrine of promissory estoppel to the essentials of a contract—a promise supported by consideration—would be to expose any party who detrimentally relies during complicated negotiations to the grave risk of being taken advantage of without remedy. Restatement § 90 does not require the equivalent of a promise supported by consideration. To do so would be to hold a breach of contract action and an action grounded on promissory estoppel to be one and the same. All items of damage are sustained except on the sale of the grocery store, where damages should be limited to the difference between the sale price received and fair market value of the assets sold, giving consideration to any goodwill attaching. Affirmed.

## ⏵ ANALYSIS

This case, in broadening the doctrine of promissory estoppel, makes clear for the first time it is a separate action and not a breach of contract action. At the time Red Owl (D) could foresee Hoffman's (P) detrimental reliance, there arose the consideration sufficient to uphold Red Owl's (D) promise. The court's so finding enables it to utilize Restatement § 90. Promissory estoppel has become the basis of an action that is neither contract, quasi-contract, nor tort. Note that loss of profit is not awarded because under the doctrine, damages to be awarded should only be in the amount the court deems necessary to prevent injustice, that is, to return the injured to the status quo. This is very similar to the theory of *culpa in contrahendo* (fault in negotiating), recognized by many European courts, which awards damages to the party injured when the other party at fault during negotiations prevents a contract's perfection by his conduct.

## Quicknotes

**PROMISSORY ESTOPPEL** A promise that is enforceable if the promisor should reasonably expect that it will induce action or forbearance on the part of the promisee, and does in fact cause such action or forbearance, and it is the only means of avoiding injustice.

# Dixon v. Wells Fargo Bank, N.A.

## Mortgagor (P) v. Mortgagee (D)

798 F. Supp. 2d 336 (D. Mass. 2011).

**NATURE OF CASE:** Motion to dismiss in action for injunction; specific performance of an oral contract; and damages arising from a mortgagee's impending foreclosure on a mortgaged property.

**FACT SUMMARY:** The Dixons (P) contended that Wells Fargo Bank, N.A. (Wells Fargo) (D) was promissorily estopped from foreclosing on their house because Wells Fargo (D) had orally agreed to enter into a mortgage loan modification, and caused them, in reliance on its representations, to default on their payments.

### 🏛 RULE OF LAW
A mortgagor states a claim for promissory estoppel where the mortgagor, in reliance on the mortgagee's oral promise to consider the mortgagor for a mortgage loan modification, has taken steps, including stopping payments on the loan, that render the mortgagor worse off by subjecting the mortgagor to foreclosure.

**FACTS:** The Dixons (P) had a mortgage with Wells Fargo Bank, N.A. (Wells Fargo) (D). The Dixons (P) orally agreed with Wells Fargo (D) to take the steps necessary to be considered for a mortgage loan modification. As part of this agreement, Wells Fargo (D) instructed the Dixons (P) to stop making payments on their loan, i.e., to default, and it was contemplated that the unpaid payments would be added to the note as modified. In addition, Wells Fargo (D) requested certain financial information, which the Dixons (P) promptly supplied. Despite the Dixons' (P) compliance with Wells Fargo's (D) demands, Wells Fargo (D) refused to abide by the oral agreement to consider the Dixons (P) for a loan modification and instead sought to foreclose on the Dixon's (P) house, the fair market value of which exceeded the mortgage loan balance and any arrearage. The Dixons (P) filed suit against Wells Fargo (D), seeking (1) an injunction prohibiting Wells Fargo (D) from foreclosing on their home; (2) specific performance of the oral agreement to enter into a loan modification; and (3) damages. They argued that Wells Fargo (D) should have anticipated their compliance with the terms of its promise to consider them for a loan modification. They contended not only was it reasonable they would rely on the promise, but also that their reliance left them considerably worse off, for by entering into default they became vulnerable to foreclosure. Wells Fargo (D), having removed the action from state court to federal district court, moved for dismissal of the Dixons' (P) complaint, arguing that the allegations were insufficient to invoke the doctrine of promissory estoppel.

**ISSUE:** Does a mortgagor state a claim for promissory estoppel where the mortgagor, in reliance on the mort-

gagee's oral promise to consider the mortgagor for a mortgage loan modification, has taken steps, including stopping payments on the loan, that render the mortgagor worse off by subjecting the mortgagor to foreclosure?

**HOLDING AND DECISION:** (Young, J.) Yes. A mortgagor states a claim for promissory estoppel where the mortgagor, in reliance on the mortgagee's oral promise to consider the mortgagor for a mortgage loan modification, has taken steps, including stopping payments on the loan, that render the mortgagor worse off by subjecting the mortgagor to foreclosure. This state (Massachusetts) has not used the term "promissory estoppel," but instead has used "detrimental reliance." An action based on reliance is equivalent to a contract action, and the party bringing such an action must prove all the necessary elements of a contract other than consideration, which is supplied by the detrimental reliance. However, even where detrimental reliance acts as a substitute for consideration, the promise on which a claim for promissory estoppel is based must be interchangeable with an offer, and must demonstrate an intention to act or refrain from acting in a specified way, so as to justify a promisee in understanding that a commitment has been made. The putative promise, like any offer, must be sufficiently definite and certain in its terms to be enforceable. Where an agreement to enter into a contract leaves the terms of that contract for future negotiation, it is too indefinite to be enforced, and the courts generally will not enforce such open-ended "agreements to agree." Moreover, it is believed that parties should be able to walk away from the transaction if they are unable to reach a deal. Because the complaint alleges that the parties had an "agreement to enter into a loan modification agreement," it appears that they had an unenforceable "agreement to agree," and that, therefore, Wells Fargo (D) is correct that the complaint fails to state a claim. The Dixons (P) reply that they are not seeking specific performance of a promised loan modification, but that Wells Fargo (D) is held to its promise to consider them for a loan modification. Thus, if the court were to uphold the promissory estoppel claim, it would not be "trapping" Wells Fargo (D) into a vague, indefinite, and unintended loan modification masquerading as an agreement to agree. Furthermore, because the parties had not even begun to negotiate the terms of a loan modification, Wells Fargo's (D) promise is more like an agreement to negotiate, rather than an agreement to agree, but even such agreements to negotiate tend not to be enforced, since judicial enforcement of vague agreements to negotiate would risk imposing on parties contractual obligations they had not taken on themselves. Nevertheless, Wells Fargo (D) made a specific promise to

*Continued on next page.*

consider the Dixons' (P) eligibility for a loan modification if they defaulted on their payments and submitted certain financial information. This promise was not made in exchange for a bargained-for legal detriment, as there was no bargain between the parties; instead, the legal detriment that the Dixons (P) claim to have suffered was a direct consequence of their reliance on Wells Fargo's (D) promise. Promissory estoppel has evolved into an equitable remedy that seeks to avoid injustice worked by a negotiating party that has made a promise during negotiations on which the other party has relied to its detriment. It is no longer merely a consideration substitute. This is reflected in § 90 of the Restatement (Second) of Contracts, which Massachusetts has adopted. While the courts of Massachusetts have yet to formally embrace promissory estoppel as more than a consideration substitute, the state's continued insistence that a promise be definite is arguably in tension with its adoption of § 90. This tension is not irreconcilable, however, as the case law reveals a willingness on courts' part to enforce even an indefinite promise made during preliminary negotiations where the facts suggest that the promisor's words or conduct were designed to take advantage of the promisee, even where the promisor did not act fraudulently. Here, Wells Fargo (D) convinced the Dixons (P) that to be eligible for a loan modification they had to default on their payments, and it was only because they relied on this representation and stopped making their payments that Wells Fargo (D) was able to initiate foreclosure proceedings, thus gaining the upper hand by inducing the Dixons (P) to open themselves up to a foreclosure action. In specifically telling the Dixons (P) that stopping their payments and submitting financial information were the "steps necessary to enter into a mortgage modification," Wells Fargo (D) not only should have known that the Dixons (P) would take these steps believing their fulfillment would lead to a loan modification, but also must have intended that the Dixons (P) do so. Accordingly, as a matter of fair dealing, Wells Fargo (D) should not have attempted to foreclose on the Dixon's (P) home based on a situation created solely by Wells Fargo's (D) promise. Such conduct is what permits application of the promissory estoppel doctrine here. A remaining concern is that by imposing precontractual liability for specific promises made to induce reliance during preliminary negotiations, courts will restrict parties' freedom to negotiate by reading in a duty to bargain in good faith not recognized at common law. This concern can be minimized by limiting the promisee's recovery to reliance expenditures. Furthermore, the foreseeability and injustice requirements of § 90 render inquiry into whether the promisor acted in bad faith unnecessary, which, in turn, obviates any need to impose a precontractual duty to negotiate in good faith. Finally, contrary to the conventional wisdom that precontractual liability unduly restricts the freedom to negotiate, a default rule allowing recovery but limiting it to reliance expenditures may in fact promote more efficient bargaining. Thus, if the Dixons (P) can prove their allegations by a prepon-

derance of the evidence, they will be entitled to the value of their expenditures in reliance on Wells Fargo's (D) promise. In sum, foreclosure is a powerful act with significant consequences, and where a bank has obtained the opportunity to foreclose by representing an intention to do the exact opposite—i.e., to negotiate a loan modification that would give the homeowner the right to stay in his or her home—the doctrine of promissory estoppel is properly invoked to provide at least reliance-based recovery. Motion to dismiss is denied.

## ▶ *ANALYSIS*

As with this case, other cases reveal that where the promisor opportunistically has strung along the promisee, the imposition of liability despite the preliminary stage of the negotiations produces the most equitable result. This balancing of the harms is explicitly made an element of recovery under the doctrine of promissory estoppel by the last words of § 90 of the Restatement, which make the promise binding only if injustice can be avoided by its enforcement. Binding the promisor to a promise made to take advantage of the promisee is also the most efficient result, since, in cases of opportunism, the "willingness to impose a liability rule can be justified as efficient since such intervention may be the most cost-effective means of controlling opportunistic behavior, which both parties would seek to control ex ante as a means of maximizing joint gains. Because private control arrangements may be costly, the law-supplied rule may be the most effective means of controlling opportunism and maximizing joint gain." See Juliet P. Kostritsky, "The Rise and Fall of Promissory Estoppel or Is Promissory Estoppel Really as Unsuccessful as Scholars Say It Is: A New Look at the Data," 37 *Wake Forest L. Rev.* 531, 574 (2002).

■■■

## *Quicknotes*

**DETRIMENTAL RELIANCE** Action by one party, resulting in loss, which is based on the conduct or promises of another.

**PROMISSORY ESTOPPEL** A promise that is enforceable if the promisor should reasonably expect that it will induce action or forbearance on the part of the promisee, and does in fact cause such action or forbearance, and it is the only means of avoiding injustice.

■■■

# Cyberchron Corp. v. Calldata Systems Development, Inc.

Computer manufacturer (P) v. Contractor (D)

47 F.3d 39 (2d Cir. 1995).

**NATURE OF CASE:** Appeal from promissory estoppel award.

**FACT SUMMARY:** Grumman procured computer equipment from Cyberchron Corp. (P) in order to fill a government contract, but later purchased the equipment at a lower cost elsewhere.

## 🏛 RULE OF LAW
Promissory estoppel has three elements: (1) a clear and unambiguous promise; (2) a reasonable and foreseeable reliance by the party to whom the promise is made; and (3) an injury sustained by the party asserting the estoppel by reason of the reliance.

**FACTS:** Calldata Systems Development, Inc. (Calldata) (D), a subsidiary of Grumman, was under contract to provide customized computer equipment to the government. Cyberchron Corp. (P) attempted to produce some of this equipment, but none was ever delivered. A purchase order was delivered by Grumman to Cyberchron (P); however, Cyberchron (P) never agreed to its terms. The district court concluded no enforceable agreement existed, but awarded reliance damages to Cyberchron (P) for materials and labor costs under a theory of promissory estoppel.

**ISSUE:** Does promissory estoppel have three elements: (1) a clear and unambiguous promise; (2) a reasonable and foreseeable reliance by the party to whom the promise is made; and (3) an injury sustained by the party asserting the estoppel by reason of the reliance?

**HOLDING AND DECISION:** (Mahoney, J.) Yes. Promissory estoppel has three elements: (1) a clear and unambiguous promise; (2) a reasonable and foreseeable reliance by the party to whom the promise is made; and (3) an injury sustained by the party asserting the estoppel by reason of the reliance. An unconscionable injury is sometimes required to satisfy the third element. Grumman's conduct by pressuring Cyberchron (P) to produce equipment at a great expense and then purchasing it cheaper elsewhere was unconscionable. Affirmed.

## ▶ ANALYSIS

Though the court awarded reliance damages, it declined to award damages for administrative or engineering overhead because these were not specifically proven. The court states that the award of such damages is allowable where "there is a demonstrable past history of ongoing business operations, without requiring proof that a specific alternative project would have absorbed the overhead costs at issue." The case was remanded for a redetermination of damages on this issue.

■==■

## *Quicknotes*

**OVERHEAD** The necessary costs associated with the operation of a business that are constant and are unrelated to the costs of production.

**PROMISSORY ESTOPPEL** A promise that is enforceable if the promisor should reasonably expect that it will induce action or forbearance on the part of the promisee, and does in fact cause such action or forbearance, and it is the only means of avoiding injustice.

**RELIANCE** Dependence on a fact that causes a party to act or refrain from acting.

**UNCONSCIONABILITY** Rule of law whereby a court may excuse performance of a contract, or of a particular contract term, if it determines that such term(s) are unduly oppressive or unfair to one party to the contract.

■==■

# Channel Home Centers, Division of Grace Retail Corp. v. Grossman

Prospective tenant (P) v. Mall owner (D)

795 F.2d 291 (3d Cir. 1986).

**NATURE OF CASE:** Appeal of dismissal of action for damages for breach of contract.

**FACT SUMMARY:** Grossman (D) used a letter of intent to rent, executed by Channel Home Centers (P), to obtain financing, but then rented to a competitor.

## RULE OF LAW
A letter of intent to rent providing that the lessor will take the unit off the market is enforceable if the lessor uses the latter to help obtain financing.

**FACTS:** Grossman (D) obtained a controlling interest in a retail mall and sought tenants. Grossman (D) intended to upgrade the facilities. Channel Home Centers (Channel Home) (P) expressed an interest in leasing space. Channel Home (P) executed a letter of intent to rent that provided that Grossman (D) would take the space off the market. Grossman (D) used the letter in his efforts to obtain upgrade financing, which was consummated. Grossman (D) subsequently rented to a competitor of Channel Home (P), which sued for breach. The district court found that no contract had been formed and dismissed. Channel Home (P) appealed.

**ISSUE:** Is a letter of intent to rent providing that the lessor will take the unit off the market enforceable if the lessor uses the letter to help obtain financing?

**HOLDING AND DECISION:** (Becker, J.) Yes. A letter of intent to rent providing that the lessor will take the unit off the market is enforceable if the lessor uses the letter to help obtain financing. Such a document may be seen as an agreement to negotiate in good faith. This is more than an unenforceable "agreement to agree." It will be a binding contract if, like other contracts, both parties manifest an intention to be bound, the terms are sufficiently definite to be enforced, and consideration was exchanged. Here, the actions of the parties, both in terms of the agreement and subsequent activities, manifested such an intention. The terms were detailed, including the agreement that the space would be taken off the market. Finally, consideration was received by Grossman (D) in that the letter helped him obtain financing. The agreement had sufficient specificity to make it an enforceable contract if the parties so intended. Whether the parties intended to be bound must be determined at trial. Reversed and remanded.

## ▶ ANALYSIS

Grossman (D) argued that no money was paid, and therefore no consideration was exchanged. This was an unduly narrow view of consideration. If a benefit is conferred upon a promisor, consideration is passed. Here, the value of the letter in obtaining financing was such a benefit.

## Quicknotes

**BREACH OF CONTRACT** Unlawful failure by a party to perform its obligations pursuant to contract.

**LETTER OF INTENT** A written draft embodying the proposed intent of the parties and which is not enforceable or binding.

# Toys, Inc. v. F.M. Burlington Company

## Tenant (P) v. Landlord (D)

Vt. Sup. Ct., 582 A.2d 123 (1990).

**NATURE OF CASE:** Appeal from summary judgment for plaintiff in action for breach of a lease renewal option.

**FACT SUMMARY:** F.M. Burlington Co. (Burlington) (D), the owner of a mall, contended that an option in its lease with Toys, Inc. (P) was too indefinite to be binding where it provided that the "the fixed minimum rental shall be renegotiated to the then prevailing rate within the mall."

## 🏛 RULE OF LAW
An option agreement is binding where it sets forth a definite, ascertainable method of determining the price term and all other essential terms.

**FACTS:** Toys, Inc. (P), entered into a five-year lease with F.M. Burlington Co. (Burlington) (D), the owner of a mall. The lease, which Burlington (D) had drafted, gave Toys (P) an option to renew for five additional years. The option provided, inter alia, that "the fixed minimum rental shall be renegotiated to the then prevailing rate within the mall." Toys (P) gave Burlington (D) timely notice of its intent to renew, and Burlington (D) confirmed that Toys (P) was exercising its option to renew and then stated the prevailing rate per square foot in the mall. Toys (P) responded that its understanding of the prevailing rate was different from that stated by Burlington (D). The parties attempted to come to agreement on a rent structure for the renewal period, but could not. Eventually, Burlington (D) informed Toys (P) that it would lease the space to another party, and Toys (P) secured another space and left the mall. Toys (P) sued Burlington (D) for breach of the lease's renewal option. Burlington (D) argued that Toys' (P) failure to accept Burlington's (D) stated prevailing rate, the renewal option had lapsed. Toys (P) claimed that the lease had created a binding option. The trial court granted summary judgment for Toys (P), finding that the lease had created a valid option for Toys (P) to renew for an additional five years, and the court rejected Burlington's (D) argument that the option was merely an unenforceable agreement to agree. The state's highest court granted review.

**ISSUE:** Is an option agreement binding where it sets forth a definite, ascertainable method of determining the price term and all other essential terms?

**HOLDING AND DECISION:** (Dooley, J.) Yes. An option agreement is binding where it sets forth a definite, ascertainable method of determining the price term and all other essential terms. The test is whether the option agreement contains all material and essential terms to be incorporated in the subsequent document. It is not necessary that the option agreement contain all the terms of the contract as long as it contains a practicable, objective method of determining the essential terms. Here, Burlington (D) drafted the option provision, so that any ambiguity in it must be construed against Burlington (D). The language in the option clause, that "the fixed minimum rental shall be renegotiated to the then prevailing rate within the mall," sets forth a definite, ascertainable method of determining the price term for the lease extension. Burlington (D) argues that the term "renegotiate" in the renewal clause shows an intent to reach a future agreement. While the choice of wording could have been more precise, Toys (P) is correct that the term means that the then-existing "prevailing rate" would be determined by agreement, and does not mean that the parties would start from a clean slate in renegotiating a rent term. Even if Burlington (D) is given the benefit of all inferences and reasonable doubt, there is no genuine issue of fact as to whether there was an enforceable option to renew. Therefore, as a matter of law, a valid option existed.

## ▶ ANALYSIS

The determination that an option is binding, as was made in this case, does not necessarily end the inquiry as to whether the parties formed a contract. An option is merely an agreement to hold open a specific offer to a specific party for a stated time, and the essence of the option must be accepted according to its terms in order to generate a binding contract. Thus, there may also be the issue of whether the option was properly accepted. Such a determination may be based upon consideration of the overall course of dealings between the parties, their evident purposes, and the inferences to be drawn from the facts.

■=■

## Quicknotes

**INTER ALIA** Among other things.

**SUMMARY JUDGMENT** Judgment rendered by a court in response to a motion made by one of the parties, claiming that the lack of a question of material fact in respect to an issue warrants disposition of the issue without consideration by the jury.

■=■

# Oglebay Norton Co. v. Armco, Inc.

## Shipping company (P) v. Mining company (D)

Ohio Sup. Ct., 52 Ohio St. 3d 232, 556 N.E.2d 515 (1990).

**NATURE OF CASE:** Appeal from a judgment ordering specific performance of a long-term shipping contract.

**FACT SUMMARY:** When Oglebay Norton Co. (Oglebay) (P) and Armco, Inc. (D) could not agree on a shipping rate under their long-term contract, Oglebay (P) sought a declaratory judgment from the court that the contract rate was the correct rate, or, alternatively, that the court would set a reasonable rate.

### 🏛 RULE OF LAW
If the parties intend to conclude a contract for the sale of goods where the price is not settled, the price is a reasonable price at the time of delivery if the price is to be fixed in terms of an agreed standard set by a third person or agency and is not so set.

**FACTS:** Oglebay Norton Co. (Oglebay) (P) and Armco (D) had a long-term contract for Oglebay (P) to ship iron ore for Armco (D). The price was established by reference to the regular rates as published in *Skillings Mining Review*. The contract was modified four times during the next 23 years, requiring substantial capital investment by Oglebay (P). When the parties were not able to agree on a rate after *Skillings* ceased publishing, Oglebay (P) sought a declaratory judgment that the contract rate was the correct rate or, alternatively, for the court to declare a reasonable rate. The court set the rate for that season at $6.25 per gross ton, requiring notification of the court if the parties could not agree on a future rate. A court-appointed mediator would then help them reach a mutual agreement. The court of appeals affirmed. Armco (D) appealed.

**ISSUE:** If the parties intend to conclude a contract for the sale of goods and the price is not settled, is the price a reasonable price at the time of delivery if the price is to be fixed in terms of an agreed standard set by a third person or agency and is not so set?

**HOLDING AND DECISION:** (Per curiam) Yes. If the parties intend to conclude a contract for the sale of goods and the price is not settled, the price is a reasonable price at the time of delivery if the price is to be fixed in terms of an agreed standard set by a third person or agency and is not so set. In this case, the undisputed dramatic changes in the market prices of Great Lakes shipping rates and the length of the contract would make it impossible for a court to award Oglebay (P) accurate damages due to Armco's (D) breach. Thus, specific performance of the contract is necessary. Moreover, ordering the parties to mediate for the duration of the contract is proper, given their unique business relationship, and their intent to be bound. Affirmed.

## ▶ ANALYSIS

The fourth modification, in 1980, of the contract at issue here extended it to the year 2010. To meet Armco's (D) requirements, Oglebay (P) then began a $95 million capital improvement program. The parties were unable to agree on a rate after a serious downturn in the iron and steel industry in 1984. In the face of those changed circumstances, Armco (D) had argued that the complete breakdown of the primary and secondary contract pricing mechanisms rendered the 1957 contract unenforceable.

━━■

### Quicknotes

**DECLARATORY JUDGMENT** A judgment of the rights between opposing parties that is binding, although consequential relief is not awarded (i.e., damages).

**SPECIFIC PERFORMANCE** An equitable remedy whereby the court requires the parties to perform their obligations pursuant to a contract.

━━■

# Statutes of Frauds

## Quick Reference Rules of Law

# C.R. Klewin, Inc. v. Flagship Properties, Inc.

Construction manager (P) v. Contractor (D)

Conn. Sup. Ct., 220 Conn. 569, 600 A.2d 772 (1991).

**NATURE OF CASE:** Certified appeal in action for breach of contract.

**FACT SUMMARY:** Flagship Properties, Inc. (D) orally agreed to use C.R. Klewin Properties, Inc. (Klewin) (P) as a construction manager on a project likely to take more than one year to complete, but contracted with another contractor after becoming dissatisfied with Klewin's (P) work.

## 🏛 RULE OF LAW
The Statute of Frauds, requiring a writing for an agreement that is not to be performed within one year from the making thereof, will not render unenforceable an oral contract that fails to specify explicitly the time for performance, even when performance will likely take more than one year.

**FACTS:** Flagship Properties, Inc. (Flagship) (D) representatives held a dinner with C.R. Klewin, Inc. (Klewin) (P) representatives. During the meeting, Klewin (P) suggested what fee it would require to serve as a construction manager. At the end of the meeting, the Flagship (D) agent said that they had a deal and the agents from both parties shook hands. No other terms or conditions were conclusively established. The agreement was publicized and a press conference was held. Construction began on May 4, 1987, on the first phase of the project. In March 1988, Flagship (D) retained another contractor for the next phase. Klewin (P) filed suit in district court for breach of an oral contract. Flagship's (D) motion for summary judgment was granted. Klewin (P) appealed. The Second Circuit Court of Appeals certified questions to the Connecticut Supreme Court on issues not addressed in Connecticut case law.

**ISSUE:** Will the Statute of Frauds, requiring a writing for an agreement that is not to be performed within one year from the making thereof, render unenforceable an oral contract that fails to specify explicitly the time for performance when performance of that contract within one year of its making is very unlikely?

**HOLDING AND DECISION:** (Peters, C.J.) No. The Statute of Frauds, requiring a writing for an agreement that is not to be performed within one year from the making thereof, will not render unenforceable an oral contract that fails to specify explicitly the time for performance, even when performance will likely take more than one year. The Statute of Frauds excludes contracts except those whose performance cannot possibly be completed within one year. Connecticut case law has narrowly construed the statute of frauds in this area. In this case, the oral agreement did not specify a time for completion. When an oral contract does not expressly dictate that performance will last beyond one year, the contract will be construed as a matter of law to be a contract of indefinite duration for purposes of the Statute of Frauds. Given this narrow interpretation of the Statute of Frauds, it is enough that the agreement left open the possibility of completion within one year. The contract is enforceable.

## ▶ ANALYSIS

Historians are unclear as to the reason for including the one-year category in the Statute of Frauds. Commentators, however, agree the Statute does not accomplish any of its possible purposes very well. Most jurisdictions construe the one-year provision as narrowly as possible to minimize the number of contracts voided by its operation.

■▬■

## Quicknotes

**STATUTE OF FRAUDS** A statute that requires specified types of contracts to be in writing in order to be binding.

■▬■

# Central Ceilings, Inc. v. National Amusements, Inc.

## Subcontractor (P) v. Property owner (D)

Mass. App. Ct., 70 Mass. App. Ct. 172, 873 N.E.2d 754 (2007).

**NATURE OF CASE:** Appeal from verdict and judgment against defendant in breach of contract action.

**FACT SUMMARY:** National Amusements, Inc. (National) (D) contended that its oral promise to pay Central Ceilings, Inc. (Central) (P), a subcontractor on the building of a theater complex owned by National (D), what the general contractor, Old Colony Construction Corp. (Old Colony), owed to Central (P), was unenforceable under the Statute of Frauds and that the exception to the Statute of Frauds known as the "leading object" or "main purpose" exception was inapplicable because the alleged agreement did not constitute a novation.

### 🏛 RULE OF LAW

Under the "leading object" or "main purpose" exception to the Statute of Frauds, an oral promise that is not a novation may be enforced where the promisor has made the promise to secure the promisee's performance and the satisfaction of any obligation of a third party that is made as a part of that promise is merely incidental to the promise.

**FACTS:** Central Ceilings, Inc. (Central) (P), a carpentry subcontractor, was hired by Old Colony Construction Corp. (Old Colony), to do work on a theater complex owned by National Amusements, Inc. (National) (D). When the initial due date for completion had passed, and it became clear that Old Colony was having difficulty paying its bills, Central's (P) agent obtained an oral guaranty from National's (D) agent that National (D) would pay to Central (P) what Old Colony would owe to Central (P). National (D) was interested in completing the project on an expedited basis to outstrip its competitors. Based on National's (D) promise, Central (P) continued working on the project. Months later, when National (D) had finished its payments to Old Colony, it refused to pay Central (P), which sued for breach of contract and won a $600,000 verdict. National (D) appealed, claiming, inter alia, that the oral promise was, at best, a promise to pay for another's debt, and, therefore, had to be in writing. It also argued that no exception to this requirement applied, since the promise did not constitute a novation. The state's intermediate appellate court granted review.

**ISSUE:** Under the "leading object" or "main purpose" exception to the Statute of Frauds, may an oral promise that is not a novation be enforced where the promisor has made the promise to secure the promisee's performance and the satisfaction of any obligation of a third party that is made as a part of that promise is merely incidental to the promise?

**HOLDING AND DECISION:** (Peretta, J.) Yes. Under the "leading object" or "main purpose" exception to the Statute of Frauds, an oral promise that is not a novation may be enforced where the promisor has made the promise to secure the promisee's performance and the satisfaction of any obligation of a third party that is made as a part of that promise is merely incidental to the promise. The "leading object" or "main purpose" exception to the Statute of Frauds provides that a promise does not have to be in writing where the fair inference is that the leading object (main purpose) of the promise is to obtain a benefit for the promisor from the promisee, so that the debt thus incurred may fairly be deemed to be that of the promisor. National (D) argues that the only way in which the oral agreement here could be excepted from the Statute of Frauds is if it were a novation, i.e., it released Old Colony from it's obligation to Central (P), and substituted National (D) for Old Colony as the obligor. This argument is rejected, because novation is only one way to remove an agreement from the Statute of Frauds. The "leading object" exception addresses a different situation, such as occurred here, whereby (1) a third party is indebted; (2) there is no novation; and (3) the third party's duty to the creditor will be terminated by the performance promised by the defendant. In such a situation, the "leading object" exception applies because the promise was given primarily or solely to serve the promisor's own interests. Case law recognizes that a property owner's promise to pay subcontractors or suppliers may, in appropriate circumstances, come within the "leading object" exception. Here, there was enough evidence to bring the agreement within this exception, because National (D) wanted the project completed by a certain date so it could profit thereby and beat out its competitors; Central (P) was a key subcontractor; Central (P) was one of the few that could deliver the requested performance. Therefore, based on this evidence and under these circumstances, National's (D) promise was given to secure Central's (P) continued and expedited performance; any satisfaction of Old Colony's debt was merely incidental to this promise. Affirmed.

### ▌ *ANALYSIS*

The issue of whether the promisor's "main purpose" or "leading object" is to secure a benefit for itself is typically a fact question for the jury. Thus, when asserting this

*Continued on next page.*

exception, the plaintiff must plead sufficient facts from which such a "main purpose" can be inferred or ascertained. A few factors that could be probative include whether the third party has been in default or has repudiated its obligations, whether the value of the benefit is equal to the amount promised to be paid for it, and whether the promisor has initiated the agreement on its own without involving the third-party obligor.

## Quicknotes

**INTER ALIA** Among other things.

**NOVATION** The substitution of one party for another in a contract with the approval of the remaining party and discharging the obligations of the released party.

**PROMISOR** Party who promises to render an obligation to another in the future.

# Crabtree v. Elizabeth Arden Sales Corp.

## Employee (P) v. Employer (D)

N.Y. Ct. App., 305 N.Y. 48, 110 N.E.2d 551 (1953).

**NATURE OF CASE:** Appeal from affirmance of award of damages in action for breach of an employment contract.

**FACT SUMMARY:** Crabtree (P) was hired by Elizabeth Arden Sales Corp. (D) to be the latter's sales manager. No formal contract was signed, but separate writings pieced together showed Crabtree (P) to have been hired for a two-year term with pay raises after the first and second six months. When he did not receive his second pay raise, Crabtree (P) sued for damages for breach.

### RULE OF LAW
To satisfy the statute of frauds, the memorandum expressing the contract may be pieced together out of separate writings, connected with one another either expressly or by the internal evidence of subject matter and occasion, rather than being contained in a single document.

**FACTS:** In September 1947, Crabtree (P) began negotiating with Elizabeth Arden Sales Corp. (Arden) (D) for the position of the latter's sales manager. Being unfamiliar with the cosmetics business and giving up a well-paying, secure job, Crabtree (P) insisted upon an agreement for a definite term. He asked for three years at $25,000 per year. But Arden (D) offered two years, with $20,000 per year the first six months, $25,000 per year the second six months, and $30,000 per year the second year. This was written down by Arden's (D) personal secretary with the notation "2 years to make good." A few days later, Crabtree (P) telephoned to Mr. Johns, Arden's (D) executive vice president, his acceptance. Crabtree (P) received a "welcome" wire from Miss Arden (D). When he reported for work, a "payroll change" card was made up and initialed by Mr. Johns showing the above pay arrangement with a salary increase noted "as per contractual agreement." Crabtree (P) received his first pay raise as scheduled but not his second one. Miss Arden (D) allegedly refused to approve the second increase, denying Crabtree (P) had been hired for any specific period. The trial court entered judgment for Crabtree (P), the state's intermediate appellate court affirmed, and the state's highest court granted review.

**ISSUE:** To satisfy the statute of frauds may the memorandum expressing the contract be pieced together out of separate writings, connected with one another either expressly or by the internal evidence of subject matter and occasion, rather than being contained in a single document?

**HOLDING AND DECISION:** (Fuld, J.) Yes. To satisfy the statute of frauds, the memorandum expressing the contract may be pieced together out of separate writings, connected with one another either expressly or by the internal evidence of subject matter and occasion, rather than being contained in a single document. First, as it is alleged that the contract is for a period of two years, there must be written evidence of its terms to be enforceable, as the two-year performance places it within the statute of frauds. The payroll cards, one initialed by Arden's (D) executive vice president and the other by its controller, unquestionably constituted a memorandum under the statute. It is enough that they were signed with the intent to authenticate the information contained therein and that such information evidences the terms of the contract. The cards had all essential terms except for duration. But as the memorandum can be pieced together from more than one document, all that is required between the papers is a connection established simply by reference to the same subject matter or transaction. Parol evidence is permissible in order to establish the connection. As the note prepared by Arden's (D) personal secretary shows it was made in Miss Arden's (D) presence as well as that of Johns and of Crabtree (P), the dangers of parol evidence are at a minimum. All of the terms must be set out in writing and cannot be shown by parol. That memo, the paper signed by Johns, and the paper signed by the controller all refer on their faces to the Crabtree (P) transaction. The controller's paper shows that it was prepared for the purpose of a "salary increase per contractual arrangements with Miss Arden" (D). That is a reference to more comprehensive evidence, and parol evidence can so explain. "2 years to make good" probably had no other purpose than to denote the duration of the arrangement, and parol evidence may explain its meaning. Affirmed.

### ▶ ANALYSIS

When there is more than one writing and all are signed by the party to be charged, and it is clear by their contents that they relate to the same transaction, there is little problem. When not all the documents are signed, difficulties obviously crop up. It becomes difficult to say the memorandum has been authenticated to the party to be charged. When the unsigned document is physically attached to the signed writing, the statute of frauds is satisfied. And, as illustrated by this case, this is true when the signed document by its terms expressly refers

*Continued on next page.*

to the unsigned document. The cases conflict where the papers are not attached or fail to refer to the other. The minority holds that is a failure to show sufficient authentication. The better view is that if the signed document does not expressly refer to the unsigned, it is sufficient if internal evidence refers to the same subject matter or transaction. If so, extrinsic evidence is admissible to help show the connection between the documents.

■━■

## Quicknotes

**BREACH OF CONTRACT** Unlawful failure by a party to perform its obligations pursuant to contract.

**PAROL EVIDENCE** Evidence given verbally; extraneous evidence.

■━■

# Beaver v. Brumlow

Seller of land (P) v. Buyer of land (D)

N.M. Ct. App., 148 N.M. 172, 231 P.3d 628 (2010).

**NATURE OF CASE:** Appeal from judgment for defendants/counterclaim plaintiffs in action for ejectment.

**FACT SUMMARY:** The Beavers (P), who orally agreed to sell land to the Brumlows (D), but then reneged on the agreement, contended that the statute of frauds barred specific performance of the agreement because the Brumlows' (D) part performance was not "unequivocally referable" to the verbal agreement, and the verbal agreement was not certain as to the purchase price and time of performance.

## 🏛 RULE OF LAW
Specific performance of an oral contract for the sale of land is not barred by the statute of frauds where the terms of the contract other than the purchase price have been proved, there has been part performance by both parties to the agreement, the part performance refers unequivocally to the sale of land through possession and the making of improvements, and a remedy at law would be inadequate.

**FACTS:** The Beavers (P) agreed verbally to sell property to the Brumlows (D) on which the Brumlows (D) would site a house. Mr. Brumlow worked for the Beavers (P) at the time the agreement was made. In reliance on the Beavers' (P) promise, and with the Beavers' (P) permission, the Brumlows (D) cashed out their retirement plans and bought and installed a mobile home on the property and then added permanent improvements to it. The cost to the Brumlows (D) of purchasing the house and making improvements was around $85,000. The Beavers (P) supported the Brumlows' (D) efforts and helped them obtain necessary permits and applications. Throughout this time, the Brumlows (D) requested that the Beavers (P) formalize the parties' agreement, but the Beavers (P) never did, although they promised to and consulted an attorney about drafting the necessary documents. The parties also never agreed on a price or a date of closing. The Beavers (P) let the Brumlows (D) quietly enjoy possession of the land for several years. Then, all that changed. Mr. Brumlow (D) terminated his employment with the Beavers (P), as he was going to work for their competitor. Hurt and angry, the Beavers (P) decided not to sell the agreed upon tract of land to the Brumlows (D). Instead, they attempted to restructure the agreement as a "lease" by having the Brumlows (D) sign an agreement under which the Brumlows (D) would pay the Beavers (P) $400 per month, though the agreement used no language of a lease, so that the Brumlows (D) believed the agreement was for payment for the land. When the Brumlows (D) began writing "Land Pay-

ment" on the checks, the Beavers (P) stopped cashing the checks and alleged that the "agreement" was for rental. The Brumlows (D) attempted to amicably resolve the dispute by offering to pay cash in the amount of the fair market value for the property and to have the property surveyed at their expense. The Beavers (P) refused, and then filed an ejectment action, alleging that the Brumlows (D) were in violation of their "rental" agreement. The Brumlows (D) denied the existence of a rental agreement and affirmatively alleged that their occupancy was pursuant to an agreement to purchase the property. The Brumlows (D) also filed counterclaims that included claims for breach of contract, fraud, and prima facie tort. The Beavers (P) pleaded the statute of frauds as a defense, arguing that the Brumlows' (D) part performance was not "unequivocally referable" to the verbal agreement, and the verbal agreement was not certain as to the purchase price and time of performance. The trial court held that the parties had entered into an agreement for the sale of land, and that by reneging on that agreement, the Beavers (P) injured the Brumlows (D), so that they committed a prima facie tort, which they knew would harm the Brumlows (D). The court rejected the statute of frauds defense on the grounds that part performance of the contract by both parties was sufficient to remove the contract from the statute of frauds. The court gave the Brumlows (D) a choice between money damages for the tort and specific performance of the contract, with the purchase price to be determined by an independent appraisal of the fair market value of the property, payable in cash within 30 days; the Brumlows (D) chose specific performance. The state's intermediate appellate court granted review.

**ISSUE:** Is specific performance of an oral contract for the sale of land barred by the statute of frauds where the terms of the contract other than the purchase price have been proved, there has been part performance by both parties to the agreement, the part performance refers unequivocally to the sale of land through possession and the making of improvements, and a remedy at law would be inadequate?

**HOLDING AND DECISION:** (Vigil, J.) No. Specific performance of an oral contract for the sale of land is not barred by the statute of frauds where the terms of the contract other than the purchase price have been proved, there has been part performance by both parties to the agreement, the part performance refers unequivocally to the sale of land through possession and the making of improvements, and a remedy at law would be inadequate.

*Continued on next page.*

The statute of frauds generally bars actions on contracts for the sale of land or interests in land where there has been no written agreement for the sale, signed by the party to be charged or the party's representative. However, a judicially created exception to this rule known as the doctrine of part performance—effected to overcome the harshness and injustice that might result from a literal and mechanical application of the rule—provides that where an oral contract not enforceable under the statute of frauds has been performed to such extent as to make it inequitable to deny effect thereto, equity may consider the contract as removed from operation of the statute of frauds and decree specific performance. Here, it is uncontested that the agreement was made, or even that the parties partially performed. The key objection by the Beavers (P) to application of the part performance doctrine is that the character of the Brumlows' (D) performance was not sufficiently indicative of an oral agreement to sell land to qualify as partial performance. To satisfy the part performance doctrine, part performance must be referrable to the contract. In other words, it must be shown that there was no other reason for the performance than performance under the contract. Here, the Beavers (P) argue that the Brumlows' (D) conduct was consistent with those taken by a person who needs a place to live and who is given an opportunity to reside on another person's property. The Beavers (P) argue that if there is an alternative explanation for the actions taken in reliance of the oral contract, those actions are not "unequivocally referable" to the contract, and application of the part performance doctrine is improper. This argument is rejected. First, the "unequivocally referable" concept does not mean that outside of the contract, there can be no other plausible explanation for the part performance. Instead, it means that an outsider, knowing all of the circumstances of a case except for the claimed oral agreement, would naturally and reasonably conclude that a contract existed regarding the land, of the same general nature as that alleged by the claimant. In other words, the performance must lead an outsider to "naturally and reasonably" conclude that the contract alleged actually exists. Two indicators of such performance are taking possession of the property, and making valuable, permanent, and substantial improvements to the property. Here, the Brumlows (D) did both. In sum, the Brumlows' (D) reliance on the agreement and their part performance were sufficient to take the oral agreement outside of the statute of frauds. The Brumlows (D) also argue that the trial court impermissibly imposed on them a purchase price to which they had never agreed when the court ordered that the purchase price would be established by an appraisal and that the terms of the payment would be in cash payable within 30 days. Precedent provides that a claim for specific performance of a contract involving land will not fail for failure to specify a price where the contract is otherwise complete, and there has been part performance of the contract by a transfer of possession. In such situations, equity may imply a reasonable price to avoid inequity. Here, the contract was

otherwise complete, and the Brumlows (D) relied on it to their detriment by taking possession and making improvements. Therefore, the trial court, in the exercise of its equitable powers, did not err in ordering that the purchase price be determined by an independent appraisal at fair market value. Significantly, the Beavers (P) do not challenge the fairness of the purchase price established by the trial court. Similarly, where a closing date has not been agreed to, equity may supply a reasonable time for performance. Finally, because it is well settled that land is unique and is assumed to have special value not replaceable in money, the Brumlows (D) did not have an adequate remedy at law. Affirmed.

## ▶ ANALYSIS

As did the court in this case, the majority of courts, in deciding whether a promisee's performance is "unequivocally referable" to the contract, look for two key factors: (1) whether the party seeking enforcement has obtained possession of the property, and (2) whether that party has made valuable improvements to the property. If these two factors are present, the majority of courts will apply the part performance exception. For these courts, mere payment of money usually is not enough. The Restatement (Second) of Contracts does not use the "unequivocally referable" standard, but, instead, focuses on whether the party seeking enforcement has, in reliance on the contract, so changed his position that only specific performance can avoid injustice.

══════

## Quicknotes

**BREACH OF CONTRACT** Unlawful failure by a party to perform its obligations pursuant to contract.

**COUNTERCLAIM** An independent cause of action brought by a defendant to a lawsuit in order to oppose or deduct from the plaintiff's claim.

**EJECTMENT** An action to oust someone in unlawful possession of real property and to restore possession to the party lawfully entitled to it.

**FAIR MARKET VALUE** The price of particular property or goods that a buyer would offer and a seller would accept in the open market following full disclosure.

**FRAUD** A false representation of facts with the intent that another will rely on the misrepresentation to his detriment.

**PART PERFORMANCE** Partial performance of a contract, promise or obligation.

**PRIMA FACIE CASE** An action where the plaintiff introduces sufficient evidence to submit the issue to the judge or jury for determination.

*Continued on next page.*

**REMEDY AT LAW** Compensation for violation of a right or injuries sustained that is available in a court of law, as opposed to a court of equity.

**SPECIFIC PERFORMANCE** An equitable remedy whereby the court requires the parties to perform their obligations pursuant to a contract.

**STATUTE OF FRAUDS** A statute that requires specified types of contracts to be in writing in order to be binding.

**TORT DAMAGES** Monetary compensation awarded by the court to a party injured as the result of the tortious act of another.

# Monarco v. Lo Greco

Devisee (P) v. Stepson (D)

Cal. Sup. Ct., 35 Cal. 2d 621, 220 P.2d 737 (1950).

**NATURE OF CASE:** Action for partition of property and an accounting.

**FACT SUMMARY:** Christie (D) had been promised the family farm by his stepfather, Castiglia, now deceased, if he would abandon his plans to leave home and would, instead, work the farm. Christie (D) worked the farm for 20 years, increasing its value 25 times, but Castiglia secretly changed his will and left the farm to his grandson, Monarco (P).

🏛 **RULE OF LAW**
The doctrine of estoppel may be used to assert the Statute of Frauds to prevent fraud that would result from refusal to enforce oral contracts in certain circumstances.

**FACTS:** In 1926, Carmela and Natale Castiglia promised Christie Lo Greco (D), Carmela's son by a prior marriage, that if he would abandon his plans to leave home and work their farm instead, they would leave him the farm when they died. Christie (D) worked for room and board for twenty years, and the value of the farm rose from $4,000 to $100,000. Natale, shortly before his death, secretly changed his will to leave his interest in the farm to his grandson, Monarco (P). The will was probated and the property was distributed to Monarco (P), who brought an action for partition of the properties and an accounting. Christie (D) cross-claimed to have Monarco (P) declared a constructive trustee of the property. The trial court found in his favor, and Monarco (P) appealed.

**ISSUE:** May the doctrine of estoppel be used to assert the Statute of Frauds to prevent fraud that would result from refusal to enforce oral contracts in certain circumstances?

**HOLDING AND DECISION:** (Traynor, J.) Yes. The use of the doctrine of estoppel to assert the Statute of Frauds to prevent fraud that would result from the refusal to enforce oral contracts under certain circumstances is permissible where an unconscionable injury would result from denying enforcement after one party has been induced by the other seriously to change his position in reliance on the contract or where unjust enrichment would result if a party who has received the benefits of the other party's performance were allowed to rely on the Statute. Both occurred here. Christie (D) relied on Natale's continued assurances, thus giving up the opportunity to accumulate property of his own, to make the family venture a success instead. Natale, meanwhile, reaped the benefits of the contract. He and his devisees would be unjustly enriched if the Statute could be invoked to relieve them of their contractual obligations. Where either unconscionable injury or unjust enrichment would result from refusal to enforce the contract, the doctrine of estoppel has been applied whether or not there was reliance upon representations going to the Statute requirements itself. It is not the representation that the contract will be put into writing or that the Statute will not be induced, but the promise that the contract a party relies upon will be performed. Affirmed.

▶ **ANALYSIS**

Cases which hold that part performance takes a case out of the Statute of Frauds can be explained on grounds of promissory estoppel in the sense that relief is granted because of detrimental reliance by a party on a promise. Note that the doctrine of part performance antedated the general concept of promissory estoppel and has its own particularized rules. Many jurisdictions have departed from the narrower path of part performance to base their decisions on grounds of estoppel whenever the equities are so great as to make a contrary decision unconscionable.

■▬■

## Quicknotes

**CONSTRUCTIVE TRUST** A trust that arises by operation of law whereby the court imposes a trust upon property lawfully held by one party for the benefit of another, as a result of some wrongdoing by the party in possession so as to avoid unjust enrichment.

**DOCTRINE OF ESTOPPEL** An equitable doctrine precluding a party from asserting a right to the detriment of another who justifiably relied on the conduct.

**RELIANCE** Dependence on a fact that causes a party to act or refrain from acting.

**STATUTE OF FRAUDS** A statute that requires specified types of contracts to be in writing in order to be binding.

■▬■

# St. Ansgar Mills, Inc. v. Streit

## Grain dealer (P) v. Hog farmer (D)

Iowa Sup. Ct., 613 N.W.2d 289 (2000).

**NATURE OF CASE:** Appeal from summary judgment for defendant in action to enforce an oral contract for the sale of corn.

**FACT SUMMARY:** St. Ansgar Mills, Inc. (P), a corn grain dealer, contended that its written confirmation of an oral contract entered into on July 1 with Streit (D), a hog farmer, was not unreasonably delivered on August 10 as a matter of law since other factors, including volatile market conditions, large sale price, custom and practice of the parties in the delivery of confirmations, a long-time amicable business relationship, and Streit's (D) father's practice of regularly coming to St. Ansgar Mills (P) to pay Streit's (D) open account and retrieve written confirmations, all affected the reasonableness of the delivery under the circumstances.

## RULE OF LAW

Factors of volatile market conditions, large sale price, custom and practice of parties in the delivery of confirmations, long-time amicable business relationship, and a purchaser's practice of regularly coming to a seller's business may be indicative of the reasonableness of the delivery of the written confirmation of a sale pursuant to an oral contract in determining whether the delivery constitutes an exception to the Statute of Frauds.

**FACTS:** Streit (D), a hog farmer, regularly purchased corn feed from St. Ansgar Mills, Inc. (P). The price of the corn was established on the Chicago Board of Trade and was hedged by St. Ansgar Mills (P) by futures position on that exchange. Sales were typically made when a farmer called St. Ansgar Mills (P) and accepted a cash price for future delivery, which price St. Ansgar Mills (P) hedged through its broker and which obligated it to purchase the corn at that price at the time of the future delivery. Over many years, Streit (D) entered into numerous contracts with St. Ansgar Mills (P). The parties' practice was that after Streit (D) accepted a price orally, St. Ansgar Mills (P) would prepare a written confirmation of the sale and either mail it to him to sign and return, or wait for his father to sign the confirmation when he would stop into the business, usually on a regular monthly basis during the first ten days of the month, and pay the amount of Streit's (D) open account. If the confirmation was mailed to Streit (D), typically he would fail to sign the confirmation for a long period of time, and he also failed to return contracts sent to him. Nevertheless, he never refused delivery of grain he purchased by telephone. Breaking with this long-standing practice, on July 1, Streit (D) ordered corn from St. Ansgar

Mills (P) as he usually did, and St. Ansgar Mills (P) set aside the confirmation anticipating his father would come to their offices within ten days. But the father did not stop by until August 10, at which time he was given the written confirmation. Streit (D) later refused delivery of the corn he had ordered because the price of corn had plummeted below the quoted price shortly after the agreement was made. St. Ansgar Mills (P) sued him for breach of contract, seeking damages of about $152,000, which represented the difference between the contract price of the corn and the market price at the time Streit (D) refused delivery. Streit (D) moved for summary judgment on the grounds that the contract was governed by the Uniform Commercial Code (UCC) and was unenforceable as a matter of law under the Statute of Frauds. He claimed the written confirmation delivered on August 10 did not satisfy the Statute of Frauds for two reasons. First, he claimed he was not a merchant (the court determined this was a jury question), and, second, he claimed the written confirmation was not received within a reasonable time after the alleged oral agreement. The trial court agreed on this argument and held that, as a matter of law, the written confirmation had not been delivered within a reasonable time after the oral contract had been entered into, based on the large amount of the sale, volatile market conditions, and lack of an explanation by St. Ansgar Mills (P) for failing to send the written confirmation to Streit (D) after his father failed to stop by their offices as usual. St. Ansgar Mills (P) appealed, claiming the question was one that should have been left to a jury, and the state's highest court granted review.

**ISSUE:** May factors of volatile market conditions, large sale price, custom and practice of parties in the delivery of confirmations, longtime amicable business relationship, and a purchaser's practice of regularly coming to a seller's business be indicative of the reasonableness of the delivery of the written confirmation of a sale pursuant to an oral contract in determining whether the delivery constitutes an exception to the Statute of Frauds?

**HOLDING AND DECISION:** (Cady, J.) Yes. Factors of volatile market conditions, large sale price, custom and practice of parties in the delivery of confirmations, long-time amicable business relationship, and a purchaser's practice of regularly coming to a seller's business may be indicative of the reasonableness of the delivery of the written confirmation of a sale pursuant to an oral contract in determining whether the delivery constitutes an exception to the Statute of Frauds. Under the UCC, which is applicable to sales of goods between

*Continued on next page.*

merchants, the writing requirements of the Statute of Frauds are considered to be satisfied if, within a reasonable time, a written confirmation is received and the merchant receiving it has reason to know of its contents, unless written notice of objection of its contents is given within 10 days after receipt. Thus, a writing is still required, but it does not need to be signed by the party against whom the contract is sought to be enforced. This encourages merchants to send written confirmations of oral agreements. Although 10 days is specified as the time in which the receiving merchant must object, the UCC uses a flexible standard of reasonableness regarding the time in which the confirmation must be received. Also, one of the UCC's purposes is to permit the expansion of commercial practices through the custom and practice of the parties, and course of dealings between parties may be used to determine whether their conduct has been reasonable. Accordingly, all relevant circumstances must be taken into account when determining the reasonableness of the time in which written confirmation has been received by a merchant. Usually, this question is left to the jury. Here, the trial court looked at the large amount of the sale, volatile market conditions, and lack of an explanation by St. Ansgar Mills (P) for failing to send the written confirmation to Streit (D). However, these are not the only factors to consider. Other relevant factors that must also be considered are that the parties had developed a custom or practice to delay delivery of the confirmation, maintained a longtime amicable business relationship and had engaged in many other similar business transactions without incident, and that St. Ansgar Mills (P) did not have reason to suspect that Streit's (D) father's failure to follow his usual and customary practice of stopping by the business was a concern. Therefore, when these factors are also considered, there is a genuine dispute over the reasonableness of the delay in delivering the written confirmation, so that the question should be decided by a jury rather than on summary judgment. Reversed and remanded.

## ▶ ANALYSIS

The Uniform Commercial Code establishes three general exceptions to the writing requirement: (1) goods made specially for the buyer and not suitable for resale to others toward which the seller has made a substantial beginning of their manufacture or commitments for their procurement; (2) where the party against whom enforcement is sought admits the existence of the contract in pleadings, testimony, or before the court; and (3) goods for which payment has been received and goods accepted. UCC § 2-201(3)(a)-(c). Additionally, a contract "may be made in any manner sufficient to show agreement, including conduct by both parties which recognizes the existence of the contract." UCC § 2-204(1). The agreement which creates the contract qualifies even though the exact moment of its making is undetermined or terms are left open, so long as

the parties intended to make a contract. UCC § 2-204(2), (3).

## Quicknotes

**BREACH OF CONTRACT** Unlawful failure by a party to perform its obligations pursuant to contract.

**SUMMARY JUDGMENT** Judgment rendered by a court in response to a motion made by one of the parties, claiming that the lack of a question of material fact in respect to an issue warrants disposition of the issue without consideration by the jury.

# CHAPTER 4

# Policing the Bargaining Process

## Quick Reference Rules of Law

# Douglass v. Pflueger Hawaii, Inc.

Former employee (P) v. Former employer (D)

Hawaii Sup. Ct., 110 Hawaii 520, 135 P.3d 129 (2006).

**NATURE OF CASE:** Appeal from grant of motion to stay action and to compel arbitration in an action for various employment-law claims.

**FACT SUMMARY:** Douglass (P), who was 17 when he went to work at Pflueger Hawaii, Inc. (Pflueger) (D), contended that he was not contractually bound by an arbitration provision set forth in Pflueger's (D) employee handbook because, at the time, he was a minor child who did not have the legal capacity to bind himself as a party to the arbitration agreement.

## 🏛 RULE OF LAW
A minor, who the legislature has determined may contract for employment, is not entitled to disaffirm his employment contract by reason of his minority status.

**FACTS:** Douglass (P) was 17 when he was hired by Pflueger Hawaii, Inc. (Pflueger) (D), a car dealership. Douglass (P) was given an employee handbook, which contained an arbitration provision that provided that any and all claims arising out of the employee's employment with the company would be settled by final binding arbitration. The handbook also included anti-harassment/discrimination policies. Douglass (P) signed an acknowledgment form that he had received the handbook. A few months later, Douglass (P) was seriously injured on the job when his supervisor sprayed him on the buttocks area with an air hose—Douglass's (P) anus, rectum and colon were instantaneously penetrated, inflated, and dilated by the force of the blast. Douglass (P) brought suit for several employment claims: (1) hostile, intimidating and/or offensive working environment; (2) unsafe working environment; (3) sexual assault and sexual discrimination; (4) negligent training (of its supervisor); and (5) negligent supervision. Pflueger (D) moved to stay the action and compel arbitration in accordance with the employee handbook's arbitration provision. The trial court granted the motion, and the state's highest court granted review.

**ISSUE:** Is a minor, who the legislature has determined may contract for employment, entitled to disaffirm his employment contract by reason of his minority status?

**HOLDING AND DECISION:** (Moon, C.J.) No. A minor, who the legislature has determined may contract for employment, is not entitled to disaffirm his employment contract by reason of his minority status. The threshold question is whether Douglass (P), as a minor, has an absolute right to disaffirm his employment contract with Pflueger (D), including the arbitration provision.

Under the common law rule known as "the infancy doctrine" or "the infancy law doctrine," contracts entered into by minors are voidable. Upon reaching the age of majority, the former minor may choose either to ratify or avoid contractual obligations entered into during his or her minority. The underlying purpose of this doctrine is to protect minors from their inexperience and to protect them from unscrupulous adults who might take advantage of them. The rule that a minor's contracts are voidable, however, is not absolute. An exception to the rule is that a minor may not avoid a contract for goods or services necessary for his health and sustenance. The rationale for the exception is that if minors were not able to contract for things absolutely necessary to their existence, they would suffer. The state's legislature has codified this exception by providing statutorily that contracts relating to medical care, hospital care, and drug or alcohol abuse treatment are contracts for "necessaries" and that minors who enter into contracts for such services cannot later disaffirm them by reason of their minority status. Because Douglass's (P) employment was not a "necessary," his employment contract would not be covered by the "necessaries" exception to the infancy doctrine, so that if only the infancy doctrine applied, Douglass (P) would be able to avoid his employment contract. However, the state's child labor laws also must be looked to. Those laws incorporate the policy underpinning the infancy doctrine, and provide that a minor who has attained the age of 16 years but not 18 years may be employed under certain circumstances. Thus, with respect to contracts of employment, it is apparent that, by relaxing the requirements for 16- and 17-year-olds to obtain employment, the legislature clearly viewed minors in this particular age group as capable and competent to contract for gainful employment and, therefore, should be bound by the terms of such contracts. Accordingly, the general rule that contracts entered into by minors are voidable is not applicable in the employment context. While the statute requires a 16- or 17-year-old to obtain an age certificate from the state's department of labor, regardless of whether Douglass (P) obtained such a certificate before going to work at Pflueger's (D) is irrelevant to this issue. For these reasons, the trial court properly rejected Douglass's (P) argument that he was entitled to disaffirm his employment contract, including the arbitration provision, by reason of his minority status. [The court went on to hold that the arbitration provision was unenforceable as a consequence of its placement in the employment handbook, which failed to alert Douglass (P) to its presence or scope, and, therefore Douglass (P) could not assent to it.

*Continued on next page.*

Accordingly, the court held that Douglass (P) could not be compelled to arbitrate his claims.]

## ▶ *ANALYSIS*

It should be emphasized that contracts entered into by minors generally are voidable under the infancy doctrine, but not void ab initio. However, the minor's right to disaffirm a contract may expressly be limited by statute, or it may be lost if the contract has received judicial approval at the time it was entered into. In some states, the right may be lost through parental consent, and it may also be lost through ratification, where upon reaching majority, the former minor affirms the contract, as by continued performance under the contract. As this case demonstrates, it may also be lost through judicial interpretation of legislative intent.

■■■■

## *Quicknotes*

**AB INITIO**  From its inception or beginning.

**INFANCY**  Minority; refers to the state of not having achieved the age of legal majority.

■■■■

# Ortelere v. Teachers' Retirement Bd.

Decedent's husband (P) v. Public retirement system (D)

N.Y. Ct. App., 25 N.Y.2d 196, 250 N.E.2d 460 (1969).

**NATURE OF CASE:** Appeal from dismissal of action to avoid a contract entered into by a mentally infirm person.

**FACT SUMMARY:** Grace Ortelere, deceased, was a schoolteacher in New York City on leave from her work for mental illness after having suffered a mental breakdown. She had a $70,925 reserve in the public retirement system. While on leave, she borrowed the maximum amount possible from the system and made an irrevocable election for maximum retirement benefits of $450 during her lifetime, revoking an earlier election of $375 a month with the unexhausted reserve to be paid to her family. She did not tell her husband (P) of this change which would leave him without her benefits upon her death which occurred two months later.

## RULE OF LAW

A person incurs only voidable contractual duties by entering into a transaction if by reason of mental illness or defect (1) he is unable to understand in a reasonable manner the nature and consequences of the transaction, or (2) he is unable to act in a reasonable manner in relation to the transaction, and the other party has reason to know of his condition.

**FACTS:** Ortelere's (P) wife, Grace, who was a 60-year-old New York City schoolteacher on leave from work due to mental illness, had a retirement system reserve of $70,925. Her psychiatrist believed she also suffered from cerebral arteriosclerosis, and she had suffered a nervous breakdown. Ortelere (P) quit his job to care for his wife. Two months before her death, Grace, without telling her husband (P), made an irrevocable election to take maximum possible retirement benefits of $450 a month, thereby revoking a previous election of $325 per month which would have paid the balance of the $70,925 reserve to her family upon her death. She also borrowed the maximum amount possible from the system, $8,760. Her new plan would not pay the balance of her reserve to her family upon her death (two months later). Ortelere (P) sued to set aside Grace's election on the ground of mental incompetence. Her psychiatrist said in testimony that Grace was incapable of making any kind of rational decision. The appeals court dismissed the complaint, and Ortelere (P) appealed.

**ISSUE:** Does a person incur only voidable contractual duties by entering into a transaction if by reason of mental illness or defect he (1) is unable to understand in a reasonable manner the nature and consequences of the transaction, or (2) he is unable to act in a reasonable manner in relation to the transaction, and the other party has reason to know of his condition?

**HOLDING AND DECISION:** (Breitel, J.) Yes. A person incurs only voidable contractual duties by entering into a transaction if by reason of mental illness or defect (1) he is unable to understand in a reasonable manner the nature and consequences of the transaction, or (2) he is unable to act in a reasonable manner in relation to the transaction, and the other party has reason to know of his condition. Earlier, traditional legal standards of competency were developed when psychiatry was in its infancy and should be expanded in light of greater medical knowledge. The old test failed to account for one who by reason of mental illness is unable to control his conduct even though his cognitive ability seems unimpaired. Accordingly, when the other party knows or should know of the mentally ill person's condition, the contract should be voidable, in addition to the earlier rule where the contract is voidable by reason of mental illness or defect if he is unable to understand in a reasonable manner the nature and consequences of the transaction. See Restatement (Second) § 18(c). Forty years of contribution to a retirement system should not be allowed to be forfeited by a brief act by a known mentally ill person. As the trial court's findings were based on the traditional legal standard rather than on the broader, modern rule, the judgment is reversed and a new trial is ordered.

**DISSENT:** (Jasen, J.) Because Grace sent a detailed letter to Retirement Board (D) requesting various explanations as to the benefits of one retirement election over the other, it seems clear that if she had sufficient capacity to ask such questions, she had sufficient capacity to understand the answers. As her entire family income was retirement plan money, the extra $75 a month income was a necessity and a decision to change her retirement plan was rational and necessary. The traditional standard of mental competency, whether the mind was so affected as to render the ill person wholly and absolutely incompetent to comprehend and understand the nature of the transaction, has proved workable over the years and should be retained.

## ANALYSIS

While older cases tend to hold contracts entered into by the mentally incompetent as void, modern authority's overwhelming weight is to hold them voidable. Generally, insanity is considered to exist where a party does not understand the nature and consequences of his act at the time of the transaction. Courts will look to see if the

*Continued on next page.*

transaction was entered into during a "lucid interval" or a period of "insane delusion." While this has been criticized as being unscientific, the lack of psychiatric tests probably makes it easier for the court to reach just results. If the contract is fair and beneficial to the alleged incompetent, the tendency is to uphold it; if not, the tendency is to void the contract. This appears to be a consideration of the court in the instant case due to the loss of a great sum of money as a result of the alleged incompetent's decision.

■▬■

# Cundick v. Broadbent

Sheep rancher (P) v. Property purchaser (D)

383 F.2d 157 (10th Cir. 1967).

**NATURE OF CASE:** Appeal from dismissal of action to set aside an agreement to sell land.

**FACT SUMMARY:** Mrs. Cundick (P) claimed her husband did not have the mental capacity to enter into a contract to sell his land.

## 🏛 RULE OF LAW
Mental capacity to contract depends upon whether the allegedly disabled person possessed sufficient reason to enable him to understand the nature and effect of the act in issue.

**FACTS:** Cundick (P), a sheep rancher, entered into a contract with Broadbent (D) to sell his lands to Broadbent (D). The two men signed a handwritten agreement and later a long form document drafted by Cundick's (P) attorney. A month later the parties agreed to amend the agreement, again with the aid of Cundick's (P) attorney, in order to raise the purchase price. Under the agreement, Broadbent (D) would have purchased the land and Cundick's (P) interest in a development company for less than half of the assets' estimated value. Cundick's wife (P), after being appointed Cundick's (P) guardian ad litem, sought to rescind the contract, claiming that her husband was incompetent to make the contract. Two doctors and a psychologist testified at trial that Mr. Cundick (P) was confused and exhibited poor judgment. The trial court, however, dismissed the action. Mrs. Cundick (P) appealed.

**ISSUE:** Does mental capacity to contract depend upon whether the allegedly disabled person possessed sufficient reason to enable him to understand the nature and effect of the act in issue?

**HOLDING AND DECISION:** (Murrah, C.J.) Yes. Mental capacity to contract depends upon whether the allegedly disabled person possessed sufficient reason to enable him to understand the nature and effect of the act in issue. Weak-mindedness alone does not constitute incompetence requiring a contract to be voidable. Intelligence is not required to form a valid contract. The contracting parties must be able to understand the effect of the actions they are taking but not necessarily the wisdom of the action. Mr. Cundick (P) may be weak-minded, but he was not utterly incapable of transacting his business affairs at the time he made the contract. Furthermore, Broadbent (D) did not defraud Mr. Cundick (P) by taking advantage of his weakness. The initial price, although very low, was subsequently raised when the parties modified the contract. Mrs. Cundick (P) and her attorney both participated in making the deal and did not at that time raise

questions as to Mr. Cundick's (P) capacity to make the deal. Affirmed.

**DISSENT:** (Hill, J.) The medical testimony clearly supports a finding of incompetence. No mentally competent rancher would dispose of his ranch interests for only half their value.

## ▶ ANALYSIS

The early rule for incapacity stated that a contract was void if made by someone incompetent. The rule was subsequently relaxed to the point where an incompetent was allowed to contract, but the contract was voidable at his election. The decision to void the contract is subject to equitable considerations.

---

### Quicknotes

**GUARDIAN AD LITEM** Person designated by the court to represent an infant or ward in a particular legal proceeding.

**RESCISSION** The canceling of an agreement and the return of the parties to their positions prior to the formation of the contract.

---

# Kenai Chrysler Center, Inc. v. Denison

## Car dealer (D) v. Guardian of developmentally disabled adult (P)

Alaska Sup. Ct., 167 P.3d 1240 (2007).

**NATURE OF CASE:** Appeal from summary judgment for plaintiffs in action for declaratory and injunctive relief from a contract entered into by a guardianship's ward.

**FACT SUMMARY:** Kenai Chrysler Center, Inc., (Kenai Chrysler) (D) sold a car to David Denison, not knowing that David was developmentally disabled and subject to the legal guardianship of his parents (P). When the Denisons (P) tried to return the car and insisted that the contract was void, Kenai Chrysler (D) refused to take it back, contending that a valid guardianship order does not automatically void an attempt by the ward to create a binding contract, and that the party contracting with the ward, at the very least, is entitled to restitution.

## RULE OF LAW
As a matter of law, a valid guardianship order voids an attempt by the guardianship's ward to create a binding contract.

**FACTS:** David Denison, a developmentally disabled young adult who lived independently, but was subject to the legal guardianship of his parents (P), used his debit card to buy a car from Kenai Chrysler Center, Inc. (Kenai Chrysler) (D). When the Denisons (P) tried to return the car and insisted that the contract was void, Kenai Chrysler (D) refused to take it back and demanded restitution to rescind the contract. The Denisons (P) sued Kenai Chrysler (D), seeking both a judgment declaring that the sales contract was void because of the guardianship and an injunction to prevent Kenai Chrysler (D) from enforcing the contract. The trial court granted summary judgment to the Denisons (P), and Kenai Chrysler (D) appealed. The state's highest court granted review.

**ISSUE:** As a matter of law, does a valid guardianship order void an attempt by the guardianship's ward to create a binding contract?

**HOLDING AND DECISION:** (Bryner, C.J.) Yes. As a matter of law, a valid guardianship order voids an attempt by the guardianship's ward to create a binding contract. Under the Restatement (Second) of Contracts § 13, the existence of a valid legal guardianship precludes the formation of a valid contract with the guardianship's ward. In keeping with this view, a party who attempts to enter into a contract with a ward is entitled to restitution only in the absence of actual or constructive knowledge of the ward's incompetence. Here, the guardianship order for David gave notice to the public of his incapacity. Thus, because Kenai Chrysler (D) had constructive notice of David's incapacity, it was not entitled to restitution. Also rejected is Kenai Chrysler's (D) argument that factual issues concerning David's state of mind at the time of the sale should have precluded summary judgment.

## ANALYSIS

Comment a to Restatement § 13 provides that guardianship proceedings are treated as giving public notice of the ward's incapacity and establish his status with respect to transactions during guardianship even though the other party to a particular transaction may have no knowledge or reason to know of the guardianship: the guardian is not required to give personal notice to all persons who may deal with the ward. Because the world is on constructive notice of the guardianship, the contract is void ab initio, rather than merely voidable.

---

## Quicknotes

**AB INITIO** From its inception or beginning.

**CONSTRUCTIVE NOTICE** Knowledge of a fact that is imputed to an individual who was under a duty to inquire and who could have learned of the fact through the exercise of reasonable prudence.

**GUARDIANSHIP** A legal relationship whereby one party is responsible for the care and control over another and his property due to some legal incapacity on the part of the ward.

# Alaska Packers' Assn. v. Domenico

Packing employer (D) v. Seamen (P)

117 F. 99 (9th Cir. 1902).

**NATURE OF CASE:** Action in admiralty for breach of contract.

**FACT SUMMARY:** Seamen (P), who had agreed to ship from San Francisco to Alaska at a fixed pay, refused to continue working once they reached Alaska, and demanded a new contract with more compensation.

## 🏛 RULE OF LAW
A promise to pay a man for doing that which he is already under contract to do is without consideration.

**FACTS:** A group of seamen (P) entered into a written contract with Alaska Packers' Association (D) to go from San Francisco to Alaska on the Packers' (D) ships, and to work as sailors and fishermen. Compensation was fixed at $60 for the season, and two cents for each salmon caught. Once they had reached port in Alaska, the seamen (P) refused to continue work and demanded that compensation be increased to $100. A superintendent for Packers' (D), unable to hire a new crew, drew up a new contract, substituted in the sum of $100 and signed it although he expressed doubt at the time that he had the authority to do so. The seamen (P) resumed work, but upon the ship's return to San Francisco, Packers' (D) refused to honor the new contract. The seamen (P) filed an admiralty action for breach of contract.

**ISSUE:** Is a promise to pay a man for performing a duty he is already under contract to perform without consideration?

**HOLDING AND DECISION:** (Ross, J.) Yes. The performance of a pre-existing legal duty guaranteed by contract is not sufficient consideration to support a promise. No astute reasoning can change the plain fact that the party who refuses to perform, and thereby coerces a promise from the other party to pay him an increased compensation for doing that which he is legally bound to do, takes an unjustifiable advantage of the necessities of the other party. The parties in the present case have not voluntarily rescinded or modified their contract. The Packers' (D) second contract with the seamen is unenforceable although the seamen (P) completed their performance in reliance on it. Reversed.

## ▶ ANALYSIS

A few cases have held that the promise to pay additional compensation is enforceable. Consideration is found in the promisee's giving up of his power to breach the first contract. In other words, by refusing to continue work, the promisee has invoked the option to pay money damages rather than to invest his labor in further performance. This view has been questioned on the ground that a promisee may have the power to breach a contract, but certainly not the legal right, and, in any event, he should not be encouraged to do so.

◼▬◼

## Quicknotes

**ADMIRALTY** That area of law pertaining to navigable waters.

**CONSIDERATION** Value given by one party in exchange for performance, or a promise to perform, by another party.

**DETRIMENTAL RELIANCE** Action by one party resulting in loss that is based on the conduct or promises of another.

**PRE-EXISTING DUTY** A common law doctrine that renders unenforceable a promise to perform a duty, which the promisor is already legally obligated to perform, for lack of consideration.

◼▬◼

# Watkins & Son v. Carrig

## Excavator (P) v. Contractor (D)

N.H. Sup. Ct., 91 N.H. 459, 21 A.2d 591 (1941).

**NATURE OF CASE:** Action to recover damages for breach of an alleged contract.

**FACT SUMMARY:** After Watkins & Son (Watkins) (P) encountered solid rock in the course of excavation, Carrig (D) agreed to raise the price in the original excavation contract.

## 🏛 RULE OF LAW
A modification made to meet the reasonable needs of standard and ethical practices of men in their business dealings with each other operates as a partial rescission of a prior contract and is thus enforceable since supported by consideration.

**FACTS:** Watkins & Son (Watkins) (P) contracted to excavate "all material" from Carrig's (D) cellar for a stated price. After work commenced, solid rock was encountered and Carrig (D) orally agreed to pay a much greater price for the excavation. Watkins (P) successfully sought to recover the larger amount due under the later agreement. Carrig (D) appealed.

**ISSUE:** When two contracting parties enter a second agreement providing a higher price for the original work, may that second agreement be enforceable?

**HOLDING AND DECISION:** (Allen, C.J.) Yes. Although promise to pay more for work which is already owing under contract is without consideration, yet if the prior contract is first (or simultaneously) rescinded, the original work is consideration for the new promise in its entirety. But whether the contract was rescinded with a totally new one to take its place, or whether the old contract remained in force with a modification of its terms, is unimportant since a modification (or at least one which meets the reasonable needs of standard and ethical practices of men in their business dealings with each other) involves a partial rescission. Affirmed.

## ▶ ANALYSIS

Note that the court expressly rejects Williston's suggestion to look at the "total effect" of the transaction (which has Carrig (D) paying "more for less") in favor of an examination of the "inherent makeup" of the transaction. This may reflect the fact that the court had already made up its mind in light of "fundamental justice and reasonableness" and was searching for a way to justify its conclusions. A "gift" rationale, which is largely edited out in the casebook, is another example of how courts have stretched to get around the "preexisting duty" rule in their efforts to successfully distinguish coercive modifications from com-

mercially useful ones. The present case anticipates Restatement (Second) of Contracts § 89(d). Note further that the court is not willing to come right out and say that a modification needs no consideration to be binding (see UCC § 2-209) but instead resorts to the old "rescission doctrine" of *Schwartzreich v. Bauman-Basch Inc.*, 231 N.Y. 196 (1921) by calling a modification a "partial rescission." Arguably, however, the court has arrived at the UCC position. (Caveat: Whereas the present case and Restatement (Second) of Contracts § 89(d) are involved with mutually executory contracts, UCC § 2-209 is not restricted to this category. But note the "good faith" limitation in comment 2 therein.)

## Quicknotes

**ASSUMPSIT** An oral or written promise by one party to perform or pay another.

**CONSIDERATION** Value given by one party in exchange for performance, or a promise to perform, by another party.

**MODIFICATION** A change to the terms of a contract without altering its general purpose.

**RESCISSION** The canceling of an agreement and the return of the parties to their positions prior to the formation of the contract.

# Austin Instrument, Inc. v. Loral Corporation

## Components supplier (P) v. Radar manufacturer (D)

### N.Y. Ct. App., 29 N.Y.2d 124, 272 N.E.2d 533 (1971).

**NATURE OF CASE:** Appeal from award of damages for price increases.

**FACT SUMMARY:** Austin Instrument, Inc. (Austin) (P) threatened to withhold delivery of precision parts unless Loral Corporation (D) would raise the contract price.

## 🏛 RULE OF LAW
A contract modification is voidable on the ground of duress when the party claiming duress establishes that its agreement to the modification was obtained by means of a wrongful threat from the other party which precluded the first party's exercise of free will.

**FACTS:** Loral Corporation (D) was under contract to produce radar sets for the government. The contract contained a liquidated damage clause for late delivery and a cancellation clause in case of default by Loral (D). Loral (D), who did a substantial portion of its business with the government, awarded Austin (P) a subcontract to supply some of the precision parts. Subsequently, Austin Instrument, Inc. (Austin) (P) threatened to cease delivery of the parts unless Loral (D) consented to substantial increases in the subcontract price. After contacting 10 manufacturers of precision gears and finding none that could produce the parts in time to meet its commitment to the government, Loral (D) acceded to Austin's (P) demand, and then sued to recover payment. Austin (P) also sued, but its complaint was dismissed. It appealed an award of damages to Loral (D).

**ISSUE:** Is a contract modification acceded to by one party under circumstances amounting to economic duress enforceable against that party?

**HOLDING AND DECISION:** (Fuld, C.J.) No. A contract modification is voidable on the ground of duress when it is established that the party making the claim was forced to agree to it by means of a wrongful threat precluding the exercise of his free will. Loral (D) has made out a classic case of economic duress in that: (1) Austin (P) threatened to withhold delivery of "needful goods" unless Loral (D) agreed; (2) Loral (D) could not obtain the goods from another source of supply; and (3) the ordinary remedy of an action for breach of the original subcontract would not be adequate since so much was riding on Loral's (D) own general contract with the government. Thus, it is manifest that Austin's (P) threat deprived Loral (D) of its free will. Loral (D) actually had no choice. Affirmed as modified.

**DISSENT:** (Bergan, J.) The question of whether or not acts asserted as constituting economic duress produce the damaging effect attributed to them is a routine type of issue of fact. The fact was resolved at trial against Loral (D), and it was affirmed at the appellate division. The question should not have been reopened here.

## ▶ ANALYSIS

Although it has generally been held that a threat to breach a contract does not constitute economic duress, courts have recently begun to hold that various kinds of unethical business compulsion do constitute duress. The present case is an example of this trend. Note that even under the UCC (which recognizes modification without consideration—§ 2-209), the requirement of good faith is ever present.

━━━

## *Quicknotes*

**DEFAULT** Failure to carry out a legal obligation.

**DURESS** Unlawful threats or other coercive behavior by one person that causes another to commit acts that he would not otherwise do.

**GOOD-FAITH REQUIREMENT** An implied warranty that the parties will deal honestly in the satisfaction of their obligations and without an intent to defraud.

**LIQUIDATION** The reduction to cash of all assets for distribution to creditors.

**MODIFICATION** A change to the terms of a contract without altering its general purpose.

━━━

# Odorizzi v. Bloomfield School District

Teacher (P) v. School district (D)

Cal. Dist. Ct. App., 246 Cal. App. 2d 123, 54 Cal. Rptr. 533 (1966).

**NATURE OF CASE:** Appeal from judgment dismissing action to rescind resignation based on undue influence.

**FACT SUMMARY:** Odorizzi (P) was arrested on homosexual charges. Immediately after his release the Bloomfield School District (D) convinced him to resign.

## 🏛 RULE OF LAW
When a party's will has been overborne, so that in effect his actions are not his own, a charge of undue influence may be sustained.

**FACTS:** Odorizzi (P) was arrested for criminal homosexual activities. At the time he was under contract as a teacher for the Bloomfield School District (District) (D). Immediately after he was released on bail, the District (D) convinced him to resign. Odorizzi (P) was subsequently acquitted of the charges, but was refused reemployment by the District (D). He brought suit to rescind his resignation. He charged duress, menace, fraud, and undue influence. He claimed that the superintendent of the District (D) and the principal of his school came to his apartment immediately after his release. He had not slept in nearly 40 hours and was under severe emotional and physical stress. He was told that if he did not immediately resign the District (D) would be forced to suspend him and then dismiss him. This would occasion embarrassing and humiliating publicity. However, if he resigned, the matter would be kept quiet and his chance for future jobs would not be impaired. The trial court found nothing wrong with these actions, no confidential relationship existed, and the District (D) would have been forced by law to suspend Odorizzi (P).

**ISSUE:** When a party's will has been overborne, so that in effect his actions are not his own, may a charge of undue influence be sustained?

**HOLDING AND DECISION:** (Fleming, J.) Yes. When a party's will has been overborne, so that in effect his actions are not his own, a charge of undue influence may be sustained. While none of Odorizzi's (P) allegations has any basis, he has made out a prima facie case of undue influence. In essence the charge involves the use of excessive pressures to persuade one vulnerable to such pressures to decide a matter contra to his judgment. Extreme weakness or susceptibility is an important factor in establishing undue influence. It is normally found in cases of extreme youth or age or sickness. While it normally involves fiduciary or other confidential relationships, they are not necessary to the action. Here, extreme pressures were leveled against Odorizzi (P). He had just gone through an arrest, booking, and interrogation procedure for a crime which, if well publicized, would subject him to public humiliation. He was threatened with such publicity if he did not immediately resign. He was approached at his apartment immediately after his release. He was not given the opportunity to think the matter over or to consult outside advice. He was told that in any event he would be suspended and dismissed. These factors present a jury issue. If Odorizzi (P) can establish that he wouldn't have resigned but for these pressures and the jury finds that they were unreasonable and overbore his will, Odorizzi (P) could rescind his resignation. Reversed.

## ▶ ANALYSIS

Many types of contracts may be rescinded for undue influence. Mortmaine statutes are in effect in some states. These hold that bequests made to churches shortly before death and after a visit by religious leaders are void and unenforceable. Wills may be declared invalid where they were procured through undue influence. Contracts to sell land for far less than its value and transfers made in fear of civil or criminal prosecution are other examples.

■=■

## *Quicknotes*

**RESCISSION** The canceling of an agreement and the return of the parties to their positions prior to the formation of the contract.

**UNDUE INFLUENCE** Improper influence that deprives the individual freedom of choice or substitutes another's choice for the person's own choice.

■=■

# Swinton v. Whitinsville Sav. Bank

House purchaser (P) v. Seller (D)

Mass. Sup. Jud. Ct., 311 Mass. 677, 42 N.E.2d 808 (1942).

**NATURE OF CASE:** Action in tort to recover damages for alleged fraudulent concealment of facts.

**FACT SUMMARY:** Whitinsville Sav. Bank (D) knowingly sold a termite-infested house to Swinton (P) but did not tell Swinton (P) of its condition.

## 🏛 RULE OF LAW
Where both parties to a contract of sale are dealing at arm's length, mere nondisclosure of latent defects in the goods will not render one party liable to the other party.

**FACTS:** Whitinsville Sav. Bank (Whitinsville) (D) sold a termite-infested house to Swinton (P). Although Whitinsville (D) knew the house was infested and Swinton (P) could not readily observe this condition upon inspection, Whitinsville (D) did not make known the true condition before the sale. Swinton (P) was subsequently put to unanticipated expense to control the termites.

**ISSUE:** Is one party to a contract liable to the second party for not revealing latent defects in the object of the contract?

**HOLDING AND DECISION:** (Qua, J.) No. Where there is (1) no false statement uttered, (2) no attempt by the concealor to affirmatively prevent the concealee from acquiring the true facts, and (3) no peculiar duty to speak (based on some unusual relationship between the parties); bare nondisclosure of truth will not render one party to a contract liable to the other. Otherwise a seller would have to disclose every defect unknown to the buyer and presumably a buyer would have to disclose every defect unknown to the seller. The law has not yet reached the point of imposing upon the frailties of human nature a standard so idealistic as this. Judgment for Whitinsville (D).

## ▶ ANALYSIS

This well-known case is a beautiful example of the common law doctrine of caveat emptor (let the buyer beware). The doctrine is founded on the theory that buyers and sellers of goods must look out for themselves and transact at their own risk. Although allowing parties to reap the benefit of superior knowledge admittedly has a certain appeal, a strict application of caveat emptor may lead to economic inefficiency. Consider, for example, that after the present case potential home buyers in Massachusetts will be forced to hire expensive inspection crews simply to discover what the seller already knows and could reveal very cheaply were he required to do so. In today's fast-paced society of adhesion contracts and big merchants, caveat emptor is not heard from too often since so many sales are not bargained at arm's length.

■══■

## Quicknotes

**ADHESION CONTRACT** A contract, usually in standardized form, that is prepared by one party and offered to another, whose terms are so disproportionately in favor of the drafting party that courts tend to question the equality of bargaining power in reaching the agreement.

**CAVEAT EMPTOR** Let the buyer beware; doctrine that a buyer purchases something at his own risk.

■══■

# Kannavos v. Annino

## Apartment building buyer (P) v. Seller (D)

Mass. Sup. Jud. Ct, 356 Mass. 42, 247 N.E.2d 708 (1969).

**NATURE OF CASE:** Action to rescind a contract of sale for alleged fraudulent concealment of facts.

**FACT SUMMARY:** Annino (D) sold her multi-family dwelling to Kannavos (P) without telling him that the use of the house as a multi-family dwelling was illegal.

### 🏛 RULE OF LAW
Where one party to a contract of sale goes beyond "bare nondisclosure" and knowingly misrepresents material facts by telling "half-truths," the other party may rescind the contract even though he could have ascertained the whole truth by checking public records.

**FACTS:** Annino (D) converted her house into a multi-family dwelling in knowing violation of a city zoning ordinance. Kannavos (P) bought the house in response to an advertisement which indicated that a buyer could make money by renting out the eight apartments in the house. Kannavos (P) did not check the zoning ordinances even though they were on public record; and Annino (D), knowing that Kannavos's (P) reason for buying was to rent out the apartments, did not inform him of the zoning regulations. Soon after the sale, the city started legal proceedings to abate the nonconforming use of the house; and then Kannavos (P) sought to rescind the sale.

**ISSUE:** May one party to a contract of sale rescind the contract if statements made by the other party go beyond the "bare nondisclosure" rule of *Swinton v. Whitinsville Sav. Bank*, 311 Mass. 677, (1942)?

**HOLDING AND DECISION:** (Cutter, J.) Yes. One party to a contract of sale may rescind the contract if statements made by the other party go beyond the "bare nondisclosure" rule of *Swinton v. Whitinsville Sav. Bank*, 311 Mass. 677, 42 N.E.2d 808 (1942). Where enough was said and done by the seller so that she was bound to disclose more to avoid deception of the buyer, and yet she did not disclose more, the buyer may rescind the contract for the seller's fraudulent deception. Although there may be no duty imposed upon one party to a transaction to speak for the information of the other if he does speak with reference to a given point of information, voluntarily or at the other's request, he is bound to speak honestly and to divulge all the material facts bearing upon the point that lies within his knowledge. Fragmentary information may be as misleading as active representation, and half-truths may be as actionable as whole lies. In this case, the original advertisement was the half-truth from which rose Annino's (D) duty to tell "all the material

facts." The fact that Kannavos (P) could have checked the public record does not deprive him of his right to rescind. Affirmed in part and reversed in part.

### ▶ ANALYSIS

This case demonstrates judicial reluctance to apply caveat emptor strictly. Perhaps the court was swayed by the fact that the misrepresented circumstance was itself an illegality. The present case, by not requiring the buyer to check through public records merely to discover what the seller already knew, is a step in the direction of economic efficiency.

---

### Quicknotes

**CAVEAT EMPTOR** Let the buyer beware; doctrine that a buyer purchases something at his own risk.

**FRAUD** A false representation of facts with the intent that another will rely on the misrepresentation to his detriment.

**RESCISSION** The canceling of an agreement and the return of the parties to their positions prior to the formation of the contract.

---

# Speakers of Sport v. ProServ

## Sports agency (P) v. Sports agency (D)

178 F.3d 862 (7th Cir. 1999).

**NATURE OF CASE:** Appeal from summary judgment for defendant in action for tortious fraudulent interference with a business relationship

**FACT SUMMARY:** Speakers of Sport (Speakers) (P) contended that ProServ (D) tortiously interfered with the contract Speakers (P) had with Ivan Rodriguez, a professional baseball player, when it promised to get him between $2 and $4 million in endorsements if he signed with ProServ (D)—which he did, terminating his contract (which was terminable at will) with Speakers (P).

---

### 🏛 RULE OF LAW
A promise in the nature of puffing that is not part of a fraudulent scheme cannot be the basis for an action for fraudulent interference with a business relationship.

---

**FACTS:** Ivan Rodriguez, a highly successful catcher with the Texas Rangers baseball team, in 1991 signed the first of several one-year contracts making Speakers of Sport (Speakers) (P) his agent. ProServ (D) wanted to expand its representation of baseball players and to this end, in 1995, invited Rodriguez to its office and there promised that it would get him between $2 and $4 million in endorsements if he signed with ProServ (D)—which he did, terminating his contract (which was terminable at will) with Speakers (P). ProServ (D) failed to obtain significant endorsement for Rodriguez and after just one year he switched to another agent who the following year landed him a five-year $42 million contract with the Rangers. Speakers (P) then brought suit against ProServ (D) charging that the promise of endorsements that ProServ had made to Rodriguez was fraudulent and had induced him to terminate his contract with Speakers (P). The district court granted ProServ's (D) motion for summary judgment. The court of appeals granted review.

**ISSUE:** Can a promise in the nature of puffing that is not part of a fraudulent scheme be the basis for an action for fraudulent interference with a business relationship?

**HOLDING AND DECISION:** (Posner, C.J.) No. A promise in the nature of puffing that is not part of a fraudulent scheme cannot be the basis for an action for fraudulent interference with a business relationship. What ProServ (D) did was in the nature of competition that is protected by the "competitor's privilege," which serves as a defense to the tort of improper interference. If it was a tort for one agent to promise a client to do better than the client's existing agent, not only would the competition that serves as the engine of our economy be stifled, but the agent making the promise would be running a grave legal risk. Of course, an agent cannot promise to do what he knows he cannot fulfill—that is fraud—but the kind of promise made by ProServ (D) here was puffing in the sense of a sales pitch that is intended, and that a reasonable person in the position of the "promisee" would understand, to be aspirational rather than enforceable. ProServ (D) did not guarantee or warranty Rodriguez a minimum amount of endorsements. The only reasonable meaning to attach to ProServ's (D) representations to Rodriguez is that it would try to get as many endorsements as possible for him and that it was optimistic that it could get him at least $2 million worth of them. Thus, ProServ's (D) representations were not a promise at all. However, even if they constituted a promise (or a warranty), they cannot be the basis for a finding of fraud because they were not part of a scheme to defraud evidenced by more than the allegedly fraudulent promise itself. Affirmed.

### ▶ ANALYSIS

Speakers (P) could not sue Rodriguez for breach of contract, because he had not broken their contract, which was terminable at will. Nor, therefore, could it accuse ProServ (D) of inducing a breach of contract. However, Speakers (P) was able to assert its claim against ProServ (D) because it did have a contract with Rodriguez, and inducing the termination of a contract, even when the termination is not a breach because the contract is terminable at will, can still be an actionable tort, either as an interference with prospective economic advantage, or as an interference with the contract at will itself. Here, however, Judge Posner found that ProServ's (D) actions were not actionable under either theory.

■=■

### Quicknotes

**PUFFING** The communication of an opinion not intended as a representation of fact and upon which an action for fraud or misrepresentation cannot be based.

**TERMINABLE AT WILL CONTRACT** Contract for an employment relationship which the employer or employee may end at any time and for any cause.

■=■

# Vokes v. Arthur Murray, Inc.

## Dancer (P) v. Dance instructor (D)

Fla. Dist. Ct. App., 212 So. 2d 906 (1968).

**NATURE OF CASE:** Action for cancellation of contracts.

**FACT SUMMARY:** Vokes (P) was continually cajoled into purchasing thousands of hours of dancing lessons at Arthur Murray, Inc. (D).

### RULE OF LAW
Where one party has superior knowledge, statements made within the area of such knowledge may be treated as statements of fact.

**FACTS:** Vokes (P), at age 51, decided she wished to become an accomplished dancer. Over a period of years, by flattery, cajolery, awards, etc., Vokes (P) was convinced to sign up, under a number of contracts, for $31,000 worth of dancing lessons from Arthur Murray, Inc. (D). Vokes (P) was repeatedly informed that she was a promising student who was quickly becoming sufficiently skilled to pursue a career as a professional dancer. Vokes (P) subsequently brought an action to cancel the unused portion of approximately 2,302 hours of lessons to which she had subscribed. Vokes (P) alleged that she had attained little or no skill as a dancer and obviously had no such aptitude. Vokes (P) alleged that Arthur Murray (D) employees had purposefully misrepresented her skills and had taken unconscionable advantage of her. Vokes (P) alleged that she had relied on Arthur Murray (D) employees' superior knowledge as to her ability and the skills necessary to become a professional dancer.

**ISSUE:** May a party reasonably rely on opinions as assertions of fact when given by a party of superior knowledge on the subject?

**HOLDING AND DECISION:** (Pierce, J.) Yes. Normally, the party to a contract has no reasonable right to rely on opinions expressed by the other party to the contract. Misrepresentations of opinion are normally not actionable. However, a statement made by a party having superior knowledge may be regarded as a statement of fact even though it would be regarded as opinion if the parties were dealing on the basis of equal knowledge. Where a party undertakes to make representations based on its superior knowledge, it is under a duty to act honestly and to disclose the entire truth. Vokes (P) has stated a valid cause of action. Reversed.

### ▶ ANALYSIS

Basically, *Vokes* is concerned with reliance and credibility. One has a right to rely on opinions of attorneys, doctors, etc. *Vokes* extends such reasonable reliance to experts or those highly knowledgeable in a field in which plaintiff is generally unfamiliar. *Ramel v. Chasebrook Construction Company,* 135 So. 2d 876 (1961). To be actionable, the misrepresentation must be material and there must be some overreaching in cases such as *Vokes.*

---

### Quicknotes

**MISREPRESENTATION** A statement or conduct by one party to another that constitutes a false representation of fact.

**RELIANCE** Dependence on a fact that causes a party to act or refrain from acting.

## Quick Reference Rules of Law

# Gianni v. R. Russell & Co., Inc.

## Tenant (P) v. Building owner (D)

Pa. Sup. Ct., 281 Pa. 320, 126 A. 791 (1924).

**NATURE OF CASE:** Appeal from award of damages for breach of an alleged oral contract for an exclusive right.

**FACT SUMMARY:** R. Russell & Co., Inc. (Russell) (D) acquired the office building in which Gianni (P) leased space for selling tobacco, soft drinks, and candy. Russell (D) negotiated a new lease for a three-year period with Gianni (P) on the condition he would not sell tobacco. Gianni (P) alleged he only accepted this because orally Russell (D) gave him the exclusive right to sell soft drinks which was violated when another tenant sold soft drinks, cutting into Gianni's (P) profits.

> ### 🏛 RULE OF LAW
> All preliminary negotiations, conversations, and verbal agreements are merged in and superseded by the subsequent written contract, and unless fraud, accident, or mistake is alleged, the writing constitutes the agreement between the parties, and its terms cannot be added to or subtracted from by parol evidence.

**FACTS:** Gianni (P) had a store in a Pittsburgh office building where he sold tobacco, fruit, candy, and soft drinks. R. Russell & Co. (Russell) (D) acquired the building and negotiated a new lease with Gianni (P) for his space in the building. The new lease expressly prohibited Gianni (P) from selling tobacco. The lease was left with Gianni (P) and read to him by two persons, including his daughter. Gianni (P) said he accepted the lease because orally Russell (D) had given him the exclusive right to sell soft drinks in the building, but this oral promise was not included in the writing. Shortly afterward, Russell (D) leased space to a drug company which moved in next to Gianni (P). The drug company was not limited against the sale of soft drinks and Gianni's (P) profits were greatly reduced. Gianni (P) sued to uphold the purported exclusive right and was granted relief. Russell (D) appealed.

**ISSUE:** When there is a written contract, does this writing constitute the entire agreement between the parties, thus precluding the admission of parol evidence?

**HOLDING AND DECISION:** (Schaffer, J.) Yes. Where parties without any fraud, mistake, or accident have deliberately put an agreement in writing, the law declares the writing to be not only the best but the only evidence of their agreement. Without alleging fraud, accident, or mistake, the writing must be the entire contract and parol evidence must be excluded. When an oral agreement is alleged, the court must also look to see if the oral agreement and the written agreement relate to the same subject matter and are so interrelated that both would be executed at the same time and in the same contract. If so, the scope of the subsidiary oral agreement must be taken to be covered by the writing. Here, both agreements concerned the same subject, the use of the leased space. Since Gianni (P) claimed that his promise was part of the consideration for the exclusive right to sell soft drinks, it would have been the natural thing to have included the promise of the exclusive right in the writing. It was extremely pertinent to that part of the writing. Where the cause of action rests entirely on an alleged oral understanding concerning a subject dealt with in a written contract, it is assumed that the writing was intended to set forth the entire agreement on that particular subject. Reversed.

## ▶ ANALYSIS

This case illustrates the strict view of the parol evidence rule as expounded by Professor Williston. Under this view, any intent of the parties must be shown from the writing itself. Some critics say it is a fiction to call this a showing of intent but that, actually, when the parties have adopted a written contract that gives every appearance of being final and complete, that is the form in which the entire contract must be incorporated. Any omitted terms are considered void. Professor Corbin, oppositely, believes it is absurd to limit proof of intent to the intent appearing in the writing itself. The issue comes down to whether parol evidence should be admitted at the risk of perjury and the possibility that superseded agreements will be treated as operative or whether transaction security requires a formal writing including the entire agreement without exception. There is support for both sides, but the view allowing parol evidence appears to be gaining broader acceptance. Even so, most courts, if it can be shown that the oral agreement was collateral to the written contract, will then open the matter to proof. Otherwise, many courts fear the jury will see the party trying to introduce parol evidence as the underdog and will probably resolve ambiguities in that party's favor.

## Quicknotes

**ORAL CONTRACT** A contract that is not reduced to written form.

**PAROL EVIDENCE RULE** Doctrine precluding parties to an agreement from introducing evidence of prior or contemporaneous agreements in order to repudiate or alter the terms of a written contract.

# Masterson v. Sine

## Grantor (P) v. Grantees (D)

Cal. Sup. Ct., 68 Cal. 2d 222, 436 P.2d 561 (1968).

**NATURE OF CASE:** Action for declaratory relief to establish a right to enforce an option.

**FACT SUMMARY:** Dallas and Rebecca Masterson (P) owned a ranch as tenants in common and conveyed it to Medora and Lu Sine (D) by grant deed reserving an option to purchase the ranch back within 10 years—by February 25, 1968—for the same consideration as was paid for the ranch plus the depreciation value of any improvements the Sines (D) might have added. When Dallas went bankrupt, Rebecca (P) sought to establish her right to enforce the option.

## RULE OF LAW
Evidence of oral collateral agreements should be excluded only when the fact finder (the court) is likely to be misled.

**FACTS:** Dallas Masterson and his wife, Rebecca Masterson (P), owned a ranch as tenants in common. On February 25, 1958, they conveyed by grant deed the ranch to his sister and her husband, Medora and Lu Sine (D), reserving an option to repurchase the ranch within 10 years from the date of conveyance for the consideration paid by the Sines (D) plus depreciation value of any improvements as allowed under U.S. income tax regulations. Dallas Masterson went bankrupt. Rebecca Masterson (P) and Dallas's trustee in bankruptcy (P) sought to establish their right to enforce the option. Parol evidence was admitted to clarify the meaning of the option.

**ISSUE:** Was the option provision too uncertain to be enforced so that parol evidence should not have been admitted as to clarify its meaning?

**HOLDING AND DECISION:** (Traynor, C.J.) No. Parol evidence was necessary to clarify the terms of the option which expressly stated an intention to reserve an option. However, it was the error of the trial court to exclude extrinsic evidence that the option was personal to the grantors and therefore nonassignable. When a written contract is a complete and full embodiment of the agreement's terms, parol evidence cannot be used to add to or vary the terms. When only part of the agreement is complete, the same rule applies to that part, but parol evidence can be shown to prove elements as to the remainder not reduced to writing. It must be determined whether the parties intended the written agreement to be the complete and full embodiment of the terms. However, this rule has not been applied consistently. A parol evidence rule must take into consideration the problems of human memory being less accurate than a writing and the possibility of

fraud. Accordingly, evidence of oral collateral agreements should be excluded only when the fact finder is likely to be misled. Under Restatement (First), § 240(1)(b), parol evidence of a collateral agreement is permitted if such an agreement is shown as might naturally be made as a separate agreement by parties situated as were parties to the written contract. Or from an opposite standpoint which is even more liberal, if the additional terms are such that, if agreed upon, they would certainly have been included, then parol evidence is not admissible, UCC § 2-202. Here, the option clause did not explicitly provide that it contained the complete agreement. The deed does not speak to assignability. Nothing showed that the parties had any warnings as to the disadvantages of failing to put the whole agreement in the deed. Therefore, it appeared that collateral agreements might naturally be made as a separate agreement. The judgment must be reversed to permit parol evidence on the issue of assignability of the option.

**DISSENT:** (Burke, J.) Parol evidence should not be permitted to contradict the terms of this written agreement. To hold that parol evidence is admissible where the collateral oral agreement might naturally have been made as a separate agreement by the parties under the particular agreement is too uncertain and confusing. The holding permits a bankrupt to deceive his creditors by testifying to nonassignability which he failed to state in the writing so as to keep the ranch out of the hands of the trustee. This appears to be evidence which would mislead the fact finder.

## ANALYSIS

In this case, California opts for the more liberal approach to the parol evidence rule as supported by Professor Corbin. Here, the California Court under Chief Justice Traynor found that when any rule of law is riddled with exceptions and decisions about it are difficult to reconcile, litigation is stimulated rather than reduced. The tendency toward liberalizing the admission of parol evidence is based upon the trial court judge's having control over the testimony and his determining when it would appear that proffered testimony is perjured. The more liberal rule is supposed to remove the problems found in the restrictive rule favored by Williston, which finds the intent of the parties in their writing only. In the extreme, this would disallow oral testimony as to intent whenever a writing exists thereby possibly defeating the true intent of the parties.

*Continued on next page.*

## *Quicknotes*

**COLLATERAL AGREEMENT** An agreement that is made prior to or contemporaneous with a written agreement which is admissible in evidence so long as it is consistent with the written document.

**PAROL EVIDENCE** Evidence given verbally; extraneous evidence.

**PAROL EVIDENCE RULE** Doctrine precluding parties to an agreement from introducing evidence of prior or contemporaneous agreements in order to repudiate or alter the terms of a written contract.

# Bollinger v. Central Pennsylvania Quarry Stripping and Construction Co.

Landowner (P) v. Construction firm (D)

Pa. Sup. Ct., 425 Pa. 430, 229 A.2d 741 (1967).

**NATURE OF CASE:** Action to reform and enforce as reformed a contract granting a right to the use of land.

**FACT SUMMARY:** The Bollingers (P) contracted to permit Central Pennsylvania Quarry Stripping and Construction Co. (Central) (D) to deposit its construction waste on the Bollingers' (P) property if Central (D) removed the topsoil and covered the waste with it. This oral condition was not included in the written agreement and was apparently omitted by mistake. Central (D) failed to remove the topsoil and cover the waste.

## 🏛 RULE OF LAW
A court of equity has the power to reform a writing and make it correspond to the understanding of the parties on the ground of mistake so long as that mistake is mutual.

**FACTS:** The Bollingers (P) contracted with Central Pennsylvania Quarry Stripping and Construction Co. (Central) (D) to permit the latter to deposit its construction waste from work on the Pennsylvania Turnpike on the Bollingers' (P) land. There was an oral understanding that Central (D) would remove the topsoil from the land, deposit the waste, and then cover the waste with the topsoil. The Bollingers (P) signed the agreement without reading it, assuming the provision was in the writing. Central (D) removed and replaced the topsoil at first but then ceased to continue the procedure and just dumped the waste. The Bollingers (P) filed an action asking that the contract be reformed to include the missing provision. The court granted the requested relief, and Central (D) appealed.

**ISSUE:** Does a court of equity have the power to reform a writing and make it correspond to the understanding of the parties on the ground of mistake so long as that mistake is mutual?

**HOLDING AND DECISION:** (Musmanno, J.) Yes. A court of equity has the power to reform a writing and make it correspond to the understanding of the parties on the ground of mistake so long as that mistake is mutual. One condition for reforming a contract is alleging and proving mutual mistake of the parties. Just because one party denies having made a mistake, it does not mean the court cannot find there was, in fact, a mutual mistake. When a mistake is real and actual, the court can correct the writing. Where a party simply has not understood what he was signing, the court will not touch the writing. The evidence showed that Central (D) had been fulfilling the oral agreement at first and that it followed the same topsoil procedure with the Bollingers' (P) neighbor. The court could conclude that Central (D) would not have done so if it had not so agreed. Affirmed.

## ▌ ANALYSIS

Reformation of a writing will be decreed when its words do not express the meaning upon which the parties agreed. This must be proved convincingly. Various mistakes can be corrected such as omitting an agreed-upon provision and inserting an incorrect provision or a provision not assented to. A common error is an incorrect description of the subject matter of the writing. Should the legal effect of the words in which a contract or conveyance is expressed, if by reason or mistake of law, be different from the meaning upon which the parties agreed and intended, reformation is a proper remedy. It is improper if to enforce terms to which a party never assented. Usually when a party fails to read the writing he has signed, he is considered negligent and bears the brunt of his error. Here, apparently as it appeared, there was evidence of an agreement; Bollinger (P) was permitted to attempt to show it.

---

## Quicknotes

**COURT OF EQUITY** A court that determines matters before it consistent with principles of fairness and not in strict compliance with rules of law.

**MUTUAL MISTAKE** A mistake by both parties to a contract, who are in agreement as to what the contract terms should be, but the agreement as written fails to reflect that common intent; such contracts are voidable or subject to reformation.

**REFORMATION** A correction of a written instrument ordered by a court to cause it to reflect the true intentions of the parties.

---

# Pacific Gas & Electric Co. v. G.W. Thomas Drayage & Rigging Co.

Electric company (P) v. Turbine repairer (D)

Cal. Sup. Ct., 69 Cal. 2d 33, 442 P.2d 641 (1968).

**NATURE OF CASE:** Appeal from award of injury to property.

**FACT SUMMARY:** G.W. Thomas Drayage & Rigging Co. (Thomas) (D) contracted to repair Pacific Gas & Electric Co.'s (Pacific's) (P) steam turbine and to perform work at its own risk and expense and to indemnify Pacific (P) against all loss and damage. Thomas (D) also agreed not to procure less than $50,000 insurance to cover liability for injury to property. But when the turbine rotor was damaged, Pacific (P) claimed it was covered under that policy while Thomas (D) said it was only to cover injury to third persons.

> ## 🏛 RULE OF LAW
> The test of admissibility of extrinsic evidence to explain the meaning of a written instrument is not whether it appears to the court to be plain and unambiguous on its face but whether the offered evidence is relevant to prove a meaning to which the language of the instrument is reasonably susceptible.

**FACTS:** G.W. Thomas Drayage & Rigging Co. (Thomas) (D) contracted to replace the upper metal cover on Pacific Gas & Electric Co.'s (Pacific's) (P) steam turbine and agreed to perform all work "at [its] own risk and expense" and to "indemnify" Pacific (P) against all loss, damage, expense, and liability resulting from injury to property arising out of or in any way connected with performance of the contract. Thomas (D) agreed to obtain not less than $50,000 insurance to cover liability for injury to property. Pacific (P) was to be an additional named insured, but the policy was to contain a cross-liability clause extending the coverage of Pacific's (P) property. During the work, the cover fell, damaging the exposed rotor in the amount of $25,144.51. Thomas (D) during trial offered to prove under similar contracts entered into by Pacific (P) that the indemnity clause was meant to cover injury to third person's property only, not to Pacific's (P). Having determined that the contract had a plain meaning, the court refused to admit any contradictory evidence and ruled in favor of Pacific (P).

**ISSUE:** Was Thomas's (D) offered evidence relevant to proving a meaning to which the language of the instrument was susceptible?

**HOLDING AND DECISION:** (Traynor, C.J.) Yes. While the trial court admitted that the contract was "the classic language for a third party indemnity provision," it held that the plain language of the contract would give a meaning covering Pacific's (P) damage. How-ever, this admission by the court clearly shows the ambiguous nature of the agreement and the need for extrinsic evidence in order to clarify the intentions of the parties. Extrinsic evidence for the purpose of showing the intent of the parties could be excluded only when it is feasible to determine the meaning of the words from the instrument alone. Rational interpretation requires at least an initial consideration of all credible evidence to prove the intention of the parties. Reversed.

## ▶ ANALYSIS

This case strongly disapproves of the "plain meaning rule" which states that if a writing appears clear and unambiguous on its face, the meaning must be determined from "the four corners" of the writing without considering any extrinsic evidence at all. The trial court applied this rule. However, the rule, while generally accepted but widely condemned, would exclude evidence of trade usage, prior dealings of the parties, and even circumstances surrounding the creation of the agreement. UCC § 2-202 expressly throws out the plain meaning rule. Instead, it allows use of evidence of a course of performance or dealing to explain the writing "unless carefully negated." Here, Chief Justice Traynor greatly expanded the admission of extrinsic evidence to show intent. When he says it should not be admitted only when it is feasible "to determine the meaning the parties gave to the words from the instrument alone," he is saying in all practicality that extrinsic evidence to show intent should be admissible in just about any case, that rarely will the instrument be so exact as to clearly show intent.

---

## Quicknotes

**EXTRINSIC EVIDENCE** Evidence that is not contained within the text of a document or contract but which is derived from the parties' statements or the circumstances under which the agreement was made.

# Greenfield v. Philles Records, Inc.

## Singing group (P) v. Record producer (D)

N.Y. Ct. App., 98 N.Y.2d 562, 780 N.E.2d 166 (2002).

**NATURE OF CASE:** Appeal in contract dispute over redistribution rights.

**FACT SUMMARY:** Greenfield (P) brought suit for breach of contract, and Philles Records, Inc. (D) argued she was barred from receiving damages by virtue of a general release executed in her divorce decree.

## RULE OF LAW

Extrinsic evidence can be admitted to explain the meaning of a general release even if the language of the contract is plain and unambiguous.

**FACTS:** Greenfield (P), formerly known as Veronica Bennett, was part of the 1960s singing group, "The Ronettes." The Ronettes had entered into a recording contract with Philles Records, Inc. (Philles) (D), which was owned by Phil Spector. The contract provided that the artists transferred full ownership rights of their master recordings for redistribution in any technological format. The group disbanded in 1967, and Greenfield married Spector in 1968. Greenfield and Spector divorced in 1974, and as part of their divorce decree they executed a mutual general release agreement resolving all past and future claims and obligations between them. In the 1980s there was a resurgence of interest in 1960s music and Philles (D), by use of a new recording technology called "synchronization," began licensing master recordings of the Ronettes for use in movies and television. Philles (D) also licensed master recordings for domestic redistribution and sold compilation albums of the singing group's music. No royalties were paid to the members of the Ronettes, and the members of the singing group sued alleging breach of contract. Philles (D) initially denied the existence of any contract, but later stipulated to the use of an unexecuted copy of the original Ronettes contract to determine the party's rights. The trial court found that absolute ownership rights had not been conveyed to Philles (D) and awarded damages in favor of the plaintiffs. The court of appeals affirmed.

**ISSUE:** Can extrinsic evidence be admitted to explain the meaning of a general release even if the language of the contract is plain and unambiguous?

**HOLDING AND DECISION:** (Graffeo, J.) Yes. Extrinsic evidence can be admitted to explain the meaning of a general release even if the language of the contract is plain and unambiguous. The plain language of the recording contract provides: "Without limitation of the foregoing, [Philles] shall have the right to make phonographic records, tape recordings or other reproductions of the performances embodied in such recordings by any method now or hereafter known. . . ." Applying the "plain meaning rule," the court finds that absolute ownership rights, without royalties, were granted to Philles (D) in terms of the synchronization licensing—the new media form not in existence at the time of the contract. However, Philles (D) acknowledges that the royalty schedule in the contract encompasses the domestic redistribution of the compilation albums and royalties are owed to plaintiffs on these sales. Philles (D) argues that as to Greenfield (P), the one member of the singing group who married and divorced its owner Phil Spector, all damages are barred as a result of the general release agreement executed in conjunction with their divorce. However, in contrast to New York's "four corners rule" to contract interpretation that applies to the recording contract, the divorce decree was issued in accordance with California law, and California's rules of construction apply. In California, extrinsic evidence is admissible if it is relevant to prove a meaning "to which the language of the instrument is reasonably susceptible." The trial court, applying this rule, determined that the general release in the divorce decree did not apply to the rights of compensation governed under the recording contract. Affirmed as modified.

## ANALYSIS

Conflict of laws issues predominate in contract cases and winning a dispute over which forum's laws of construction apply is frequently determinant of the issues in the case. This case illustrates both the strict application of the plain meaning rule in New York, and the application of California's rule to allow extrinsic evidence for interpreting a contract in conformity with a "reasonably susceptible" meaning of the language employed.

---

## Quicknotes

**EXTRINSIC EVIDENCE** Evidence that is not contained within the text of a document or contract but which is derived from the parties' statements or the circumstances under which the agreement was made.

# Trident Center v. Connecticut General Life Ins. Co.

## Commercial group (P) v. Lender (D)

### 847 F.2d 564 (9th Cir. 1988).

**NATURE OF CASE:** Appeal from a dismissal of contract action.

**FACT SUMMARY:** The district court dismissed Trident Center's (Trident) (P) declaratory relief action, ruling that the contract was clear and did not allow for prepayment of a loan, which Trident (P) sought to establish by parol evidence.

## 🏛 RULE OF LAW
Parol evidence is admissible to raise an ambiguity in a contract even where the writing itself contains no ambiguity.

**FACTS:** Trident Center (Trident) (P), an enterprise consisting of an insurance company and two large, sophisticated law firms, entered into a loan agreement with Connecticut General Life Ins. Co. (Connecticut) (D). The written agreement provided Trident (P) would borrow $56 million to construct an office building. The loan was to be paid off over a period of time; however, the contract precluded full repayment within the first 12 years. Because of a drop in interest rates, Trident (P) sought to repay the loan in full after four years. It claimed, despite the clear language of the contract, that the parties intended to allow prepayment at any time if a penalty was paid. Trident (P) brought a declaratory relief action requesting a court interpretation of the contract. Trident (P) unsuccessfully sought to present parol evidence of the meaning of the contract while admitting the language was unambiguous. The court dismissed the action, and Trident (P) appealed.

**ISSUE:** Is parol evidence admissible to show an ambiguity in an otherwise unambiguous contract?

**HOLDING AND DECISION:** (Kozinski, J.) Yes. Parol evidence is admissible to show an ambiguity in an otherwise unambiguous contract. Because language cannot infallibly communicate the true meaning or intent of parties to a contract, parol evidence must be allowed where such intent is in issue. Thus, it was error to deny use of such evidence and to dismiss the action. Reversed and remanded.

## ▶ ANALYSIS

This case does not represent the traditional common law view of the parol evidence rule. The opinion is very critical of the outcome which is mandated by the law of California, where the case arose. The opinion foresees considerable litigation invited by this decision and a breakdown in the finality of a written agreement.

■▬■

## Quicknotes

**AMBIGUITY** Language that is capable of more than one interpretation.

**PAROL EVIDENCE RULE** Doctrine precluding parties to an agreement from introducing evidence of prior or contemporaneous agreements in order to repudiate or alter the terms of a written contract.

■▬■

# Frigaliment Importing Co. v. B.N.S. International Sales Corp.

Chicken purchaser (P) v. Seller (D)

190 F. Supp. 116 (S.D.N.Y. 1960).

**NATURE OF CASE:** Action for breach of warranty of a contract for the sale of goods.

**FACT SUMMARY:** Frigaliment Importing Co. (Frigaliment) (P) ordered a large quantity of "chicken" from B.N.S. International Sales Corp. (B.N.S.) (D), intending to buy young chicken suitable for broiling and frying, but B.N.S. (D) believed, in considering the weights ordered at the prices fixed by the parties, that the order could be filled with older chicken suitable for stewing only and termed "fowl" by Frigaliment (P).

## RULE OF LAW

The party who seeks to interpret the terms of the contract in a sense narrower than their everyday use bears the burden of persuasion to so show, and if that party fails to support its burden, it faces dismissal of its complaint.

**FACTS:** Frigaliment Importing Co. (Frigaliment) (P), a Swiss corporation, and B.N.S. International Sales Corp. (B.N.S.) (D), a New York corporation, made two almost identical contracts for the sale of chicken by the latter to the former as follows: U.S. fresh frozen chicken, Grade A, government inspected, eviscerated, all wrapped and boxed suitably for export, 75,000 lbs. 2½-3 lbs. at $33 per 100 lbs. and 25,000 lbs. 1½-2 lbs. at $36.50 per 100 lbs. The second contract was the same except for 25,000 lbs. less of the heavier chicken and a price of $37 per 100 lbs. for the lighter birds. B.N.S. (D), being new to the poultry business, believed any kind of chicken could be used to fill the order, including stewing chickens. Most of the order for heavier birds was filled with stewing chickens as that was the only way B.N.S. (D) could make a profit on the contract. Frigaliment (P) sued for breach of warranty.

**ISSUE:** Does the party who seeks a narrow interpretation of the terms of a contract bear the burden of persuasion to so show?

**HOLDING AND DECISION:** (Friendly, J.) Yes. Frigaliment (P) failed to support its burden. While cables leading up to negotiations were predominantly in German, the use of the English word "chicken" as meaning "young chicken" rather than the German word "huhn" meaning broilers and stewers lost its force when B.N.S. (D) asked if any kind of chickens were wanted to which an affirmative answer meaning "huhn" was given. B.N.S. (D), being new to the chicken trade, the other party must show the other's acceptance of the trade use of a term. Frigaliment (P) failed to offer such proof. There was conflicting evidence anyway as to the trade use of the word "chicken." B.N.S.'s (D) price

of $33 per 100 lbs. for the larger birds was $2 to $4 less than for broilers. Frigaliment (P) could not say that the price appeared reasonable because it was closer to the $35 broiler price than the $30 stewer price. B.N.S. (D) could be expected not to sell at a loss. While the evidence is generally conflicting, overall it appeared that B.N.S. (D) believed it could comply by supplying stewing chicken. This did conform with one dictionary meaning, with the definition in the department of animal regulations to which at least there was a contractual reference, and with some trade usage. This evidence must be relied upon as the contract language itself could not settle the question here. Reversed to order the complaint dismissal.

## ANALYSIS

In determining the intent of the parties, the court will turn first to the language of the contract to see whether the meaning of the ambiguous term can be raised. If this is unsuccessful, the court must look to other evidence. Under Restatement (First), § 235, certain guidelines aid in determining meaning. First, the ordinary meaning of language throughout the country is given to words unless circumstances show that a different meaning is applicable. Also, all circumstances surrounding the transaction may be taken into consideration. Also, if after consideration of all factors, it is still uncertain what meaning should be given, a reasonable, lawful, and effective meaning to all manifestations of intention is preferred to an interpretation which leaves a part of such unreasonable, unlawful, or ineffective, Restatement (First), § 236(a). Even so, the principal apparent purpose of the parties should be given greater weight in determining the meaning to be given.

■■■

### Quicknotes

**AMBIGUOUS** Vague; unclear; capable of more than one meaning.

**BREACH OF WARRANTY** The breach of a promise made by one party to a contract that the other party may rely on a fact, relieving that party from the obligation of determining whether the fact is true and indemnifying the other party from liability if that fact is shown to be false.

■■■

# Nanakuli Paving & Rock Co. v. Shell Oil Co.

Paving contractor (P) v. Asphalt supplier (D)

664 F.2d 772 (9th Cir. 1981).

**NATURE OF CASE:** Appeal from order setting aside award of damages for breach of contract.

**FACT SUMMARY:** Shell Oil Co. (D) contended it was not obligated to price protect Nanakuli Paving & Rock Co. (P), and its conduct in the past did not constitute a course of conduct governing the contract.

## 🏛 RULE OF LAW
Trade usage and course of performance will be read into contracts where such are so prevalent the parties would have to have meant to incorporate them in the terms of the contract.

**FACTS:** Nanakuli Paving & Rock Co. (Nanakuli) (P) contracted with Shell Oil Co. (Shell) (D) to purchase its requirements of asphalt under two long-term contracts. The contract contained specific prices for the asphalt. Between 1969 and 1974, Shell (D) kept the price static to Nanakuli (P), while raising it to others. Thereafter, the price steadily increased. Nanakuli (P) sued, contending that an implied element of the contract was Shell's (D) duty to price protect. It argued the duty was such a clearly understood policy in the trade that it was assumed to be a part of the contract. This was strengthened, it argued, by Shell's (D) past performance of the contract. Shell (D) contended such was not part of the trade in which it dealt, and its past performance was a waiver of the price terms for that time. Finally, it argued the specific price terms controlled. The court set aside a jury verdict for Nanakuli (P), and Nanakuli (P) appealed.

**ISSUE:** Will trade usage and course of performance be read into contracts?

**HOLDING AND DECISION:** (Hoffman, J.) Yes. Trade usage and course of conduct will be read into contracts where such are so prevalent that the parties would have meant to incorporate them in the contract terms. Evidence was presented showing the prevalence of price protection in the asphalt trade. This, along with Shell's (D) past performance, was sufficient to allow the jury to find that the terms were incorporated in the contract. As a result, the verdict should have been upheld. Reversed.

**CONCURRENCE:** (Kennedy, J.) This opinion should not be interpreted to permit juries to import price protection from a concept of good faith not based on well-established custom or usage.

## ▶ ANALYSIS

Custom and course of performance are important tools in the interpretation of contracts. Many times they are used to define words which take on a specific meaning within the confines of an industry or trade in which the contract is executed. Often, as in this case, they are used as a general guide to interpret the contract as a whole and to fill gaps created by unexpected contingencies.

## Quicknotes

**JUDGMENT N.O.V.** A judgment entered by the trial judge reversing a jury verdict if the jury's determination has no basis in law or fact.

**TRADE USAGE** A course of dealing or practice commonly used in a particular trade.

# Columbia Nitrogen Corp. v. Royster Co.

Phosphate purchaser (D) v. Phosphate producer (P)

451 F.2d 3 (4th Cir. 1971).

**NATURE OF CASE:** Appeal from judgment for plaintiff in breach of contract action.

**FACT SUMMARY:** Columbia Nitrogen Corp. (D) contended that under the Uniform Commercial Code (UCC) usage of trade and course of dealing could properly be used to explain or supplement the express terms of a written contract it had entered with Royster Co. (P) for the purchase of phosphate where the contract did not expressly preclude such evidence and where default and damages terms were set forth in only general terms.

## 🏛 RULE OF LAW
Under the Uniform Commercial Code (UCC), evidence of usage of trade and course of dealing may be used to explain or supplement the express terms of a written contract where the contract does not expressly preclude such evidence and where the terms to be explained or supplemented are set forth in only general terms.

**FACTS:** Columbia Nitrogen Corp. (Columbia) (D) and Royster Co. (Royster) (P) were both in the fertilizer business, and, for years, Royster (P) had purchased nitrogen from Columbia (D). Then Royster (P) began producing phosphate and Columbia (D) agreed to purchase a minimum of 31,000 tons of phosphate a year for three years. After the agreement was entered into, phosphate prices plunged and Columbia (D) was unable to resell at competitive prices, so it purchased only one-tenth of the agreed-to tonnage during the first year. Royster (P) sold the remaining phosphate at market price and sued Columbia (D) for the difference between that price and the contract price. Columbia (D) adduced evidence that trade practice was that express price and quantity terms in the mixed fertilizer industry were mere projections to be adjusted according to market forces. It also attempted to show that in its dealings with Royster (P) over the years, there was repeated and substantial deviation from stated amount or price. The trial court excluded this evidence on the ground that "custom and usage or course of dealing are not admissible to contradict the express, plain, unambiguous language of a valid written contract, which by virtue of its detail negates the proposition that the contract is open to variances in its terms." The court of appeals granted review.

**ISSUE:** Under the Uniform Commercial Code (UCC), may evidence of usage of trade and course of dealing be used to explain or supplement the express terms of a written contract where the contract does not expressly preclude such evidence and where the terms to be explained or supplemented are set forth in only general terms?

**HOLDING AND DECISION:** (Butzner, J.) Yes. Under the Uniform Commercial Code (UCC), evidence of usage of trade and course of dealing may be used to explain or supplement the express terms of a written contract where the contract does not expressly preclude such evidence and where the terms to be explained or supplemented are set forth in only general terms. Although the UCC provides that evidence of usage of trade and course of dealing should be excluded whenever it cannot be reasonably construed as consistent with the terms of the contract, such evidence, as here, may be admitted even where a contract on its face appears complete, provided the explanatory or supplemental terms are consistent with the contract. Here, the evidence adduced by Columbia (D) is consistent with the written contract. First, the contract does not expressly exclude the use of such evidence. Second, the contract is silent about adjusting prices and quantities to reflect market fluctuations, neither permitting nor prohibiting such adjustments. This silence is a "fitting occasion" for using evidence of trade usage and course of dealing to supplement and explain the contract. Similarly, the contract's use of "Products Supplied Under Contract" in reference to minimum tonnages and additional quantities is a description that permits the use of this extrinsic evidence. Finally, the contract neither specifies what constitutes default nor what damages will be, and, again, extrinsic evidence may be used to supplement and explain terms that would cover these situations. It is insufficient, as Royster (P) urges, to merely fill in these gaps by applying general common law contract principles, since the policy underlying the UCC is to reflect market realities and avoid overly legalistic interpretations. Also rejected is Royster's (P) argument that the contract's merger clause, which provides that "no verbal understanding will be recognized by either party hereto . . . ," also should preclude the evidence. Verbal understanding is not synonymous with trade usage and course of dealing. The outcome would have been different had the merger clause explicitly provided that evidence of trade usage and course of dealing would be excluded in any dispute over the contract's meaning. The UCC supports this position, as its official comment notes that course of dealing and trade usage are admissible unless expressly negated. Vacated and remanded.

## ▶ ANALYSIS

Under the UCC, it is assumed that the parties to a contract take course of dealing and usage of trade into account

*Continued on next page.*

when the contract is negotiated and drafted, and thus these become an element of the meaning of the words used. As this case illustrates, it is only when the contract itself expressly negates the use of course of dealing and usage of trade is this assumption also negated. In any event, the course of actual performance by the parties is considered the best indication of what they intended the contract to mean.

■■■

## Quicknotes

**BREACH OF CONTRACT** Unlawful failure by a party to perform its obligations pursuant to contract.

**COURSE OF DEALING** Previous conduct between two parties to a contract that may be relied upon to interpret their actions.

**USAGE OF TRADE** A course of dealing or practice commonly used in a particular trade.

■■■

# Raffles v. Wichelhaus

Cotton seller (P) v. Cotton buyer (D)

Ct. of Exchequer, 2 H. & C. 906, 159 Eng. Rep. 375 (1864).

**NATURE OF CASE:** Action for damages for breach of a contract for the sale of goods.

**FACT SUMMARY:** Raffles (P) contracted to sell cotton to Wichelhaus (D) to be delivered from Bombay at Liverpool on the ship "Peerless." Unknown to the parties was the existence of two different ships carrying cotton, each named "Peerless" arriving at Liverpool from Bombay, but at different times.

## 🏛 RULE OF LAW
Where neither party knows or has reason to know of the ambiguity, or where both know or have reason to know, the ambiguity is given the meaning that each party intended it to have.

**FACTS:** Raffles (P) contracted to sell Wichelhaus (D) 125 bales of Surat cotton to arrive from Bombay at Liverpool on the ship "Peerless." Wichelhaus (D) was to pay 17¼ pence per pound of cotton within an agreed-upon time after the arrival of the goods in England. Unknown to the parties, there were two ships called "Peerless," each of which was carrying cotton from Bombay to Liverpool. Wichelhaus expected the cotton to be shipped on the "Peerless" which was to sail in October, while Raffles (P) had expected the cotton to be shipped on the "Peerless" set to sail in December. As Wichelhaus (D) could not have the delivery he expected, he refused to accept the later delivery.

**ISSUE:** Did a latent ambiguity arise showing that there had been no meeting of the minds, hence, no contract?

**HOLDING AND DECISION:** (Per curiam) Yes. While the contract did not show which particular "Peerless" was intended, the moment it appeared two ships called "Peerless" were sailing from Bombay to Liverpool with a load of cotton, a latent ambiguity arose, and parol evidence was admissible for the purpose of determining that both parties had intended a different "Peerless" to be subject in the contract. When there is an ambiguity, it is given the meaning that each party intended it to have. However, if different meanings were intended, there is no contract if the ambiguity relates to a material term. Consequently, there was no meeting of the minds, and no binding contract.

## ▶ ANALYSIS

When there is no integration of the contract, the standard for its interpretation is the meaning that the party making the manifestation should reasonably expect the other party to give it, i.e., a standard of reasonable expectation. This case illustrates an exception to this rule. Where there is an ambiguity, if both parties give the same meaning to it, there is a contract. If the parties each give a different meaning to the ambiguity, then there is no contract as occurred here. The ambiguity struck at a material term as payment was to be made within an agreed upon time after delivery. The parties could not even agree on the time of delivery. The other exception occurs when one party has reason to know of the ambiguity and the other does not, so it will bear the meaning given to it by the latter, that is the party who is without fault. Note that under UCC § 2-322, delivery "exship," it would make no difference which ship would be carrier of the goods and the case would have gone the other way. However, Restatement (First) § 71 would appear to follow the general rule of the present case.

## Quicknotes

**AMBIGUITY** Language that is capable of more than one interpretation.

**MATERIAL TERMS OF CONTRACT** A fact without the existence of which a contract would not have been entered.

**MUTUAL ASSENT** A requirement of a valid contract that the parties possess a mutuality of assent as manifested by the terms of the agreement and not by a hidden intent.

# Colfax Envelope Corp. v. Local No. 458-3M

Manufacturer (P) v. Labor union (D)

20 F.3d 750 (7th Cir. 1994).

**NATURE OF CASE:** Appeal from summary judgment for defendant in declaratory judgment action brought under the Taft-Hartley Act, 29 U.S.C. § 185.

**FACT SUMMARY:** Colfax Envelope Corp. (Colfax) (P) contended that an essential term in a collective bargaining agreement was so ambiguous that there was no meeting of the minds between Colfax (P) and Local No. 458-3M (D), and that, therefore, the entire agreement had to be rescinded.

> ### 🏛 RULE OF LAW
> A contract will not be rescinded merely because one or more of its terms is patently ambiguous and the parties have not attempted to clarify the patent ambiguity.

**FACTS:** Colfax Envelope Corp. (Colfax) (P) manufactured envelopes, and a few of its employees, who printed the envelopes, were unionized, belonging to Local No. 458-3M (the "union") (D). Ordinarily, Colfax (P) did not participate in the collective bargaining negotiations between the association of printing companies that it was part of and the union (D). Instead, when a collective bargaining agreement was reached between the association and the union (D), the union (D) would send a copy to Colfax (P), and, at its option, it could subscribe to the agreement or bargain on its own with the union (D) for different terms. When the latest agreement was negotiated between the association and the union (D), the union (D) sent a summary to Colfax (P), which, based on interpretations of its union members familiar with the negotiations, accepted the terms in the summary. A key term, relating to the number of people needed to operate different kinds of printing presses, listed "4C 60 Press-3 Men" and "5C 78 Press-4 Men." Colfax (P) believed this meant that all presses operated as four-color presses would require only three individuals to man them. A copy of the actual agreement contained a typo that supported this interpretation. However, when the corrected agreement was sent to Colfax (P), the manning requirements were different from what Colfax (P) had understood them to be. The agreement provided that four-color presses between 45 and 60 inches required three individuals (the prior agreement was less generous, requiring three individuals for presses between 45 and 50 inches), but that all four-color presses over 60 inches required four. Colfax (P) refused to sign the agreement, but the union (D) claimed that it was bound by its acceptance of the summary. Colfax (P) brought suit under section 301 of the Taft-Hartley Act, 29 U.S.C. § 185, for a declaration that it had no collective bargaining contract

with the union (D) because the parties never agreed on an essential term—the manning requirements for Colfax's (P) printing presses. The union (D) counterclaimed for an order to arbitrate, since the agreement required arbitration of disputes. The district court granted summary judgment for the union (D), and the court of appeals granted review.

**ISSUE:** Will a contract be rescinded merely because one or more of its terms is patently ambiguous and the parties have not attempted to clarify the patent ambiguity?

**HOLDING AND DECISION:** (Posner, C.J.) No. A contract will not be rescinded merely because one or more of its terms is patently ambiguous and the parties have not attempted to clarify the patent ambiguity. The term in dispute is "4C 60 Press-3 Men." Colfax (P) believes it refers to four-color presses 60 inches and over, whereas the union maintains that it refers to four-color presses between 45 and 60 inches. If the disagreement over this term is so deep as to support the conclusion that no agreement was ever entered, then the contract must be rescinded. One way this has been previously expressed is that there has been no "meeting of the minds." This premise, that there must be a meeting of the minds to have a binding contract, is strained, however. Most contract disputes arise because the parties did not foresee and provide for some contingency that has subsequently materialized, over which it can be said there was no meeting of minds. Nonetheless, in most cases, such disputes are treated as disputes over contractual meaning, not as grounds for rescinding the contract. Thus, a literal meeting of the minds is not required to have a binding contract. A better rule is that a contract may be rescinded without liability when there is "no sensible basis for choosing between conflicting understandings" of the contractual language and where neither party is responsible (or both are equally responsible) for the ambiguity. The clearest cases for rescission on the ground that there was "no meeting of the minds" (or, better, that there was a "latent ambiguity" in the sense that neither party knew that the contract was ambiguous) are ones in which an offer is garbled in transmission, which is defined broadly. While the case at bar is superficially similar to such a case, the difference is that here, Colfax (P) should have known that the term 4C 60 Press was unclear and susceptible of different interpretations. Thus, Colfax (P) merely gambled that its interpretation would be the one accepted by a court in the event of a dispute. This case does not present a term that reasonably seems unequivocal to the parties but in reality is not; it is only in those cases of true latent

*Continued on next page.*

ambiguity that rescission is permitted, but not in cases such as the one here where the parties should have realized that the term was ambiguous and could have, but chose not to, clarify the ambiguous term. Having failed to clarify the patently ambiguous term, Colfax (P) must have the meaning of the term arbitrated, and the arbitrator must decide if in fact there was no meeting of the minds. Affirmed.

## ▌ ANALYSIS

In subsequent analysis, Judge Posner indicated that even where neither party may be blamed for the ambiguity, or where both parties are equally to blame, rescission should not be ordered where doing so will provide a windfall to one of the parties.

■■■■

## Quicknotes

**AMBIGUOUS** Vague; unclear; capable of being understood to have more than one meaning

**CONTRACT** An agreement pursuant to which a party agrees to act, or to forbear from acting, in exchange for performance on the part of the other party.

**LATENT AMBIGUITY** Language capable of more than one interpretation that seems clear on its face, but the introduction of extrinsic evidence proves it to have a different meaning.

**MEETING OF THE MINDS** A requirement of a valid contract that the parties possess a mutuality of assent as manifested by the terms of the agreement and not by a hidden intent; enforceability of the contract is limited to those terms to which the parties assented.

■■■■

# Koken v. Black & Veatch Construction, Inc.

Manufacturer or distributor (D) v. General contractor (P)

426 F.3d 39 (1st Cir. 2005).

**NATURE OF CASE:** Appeal from summary judgment for defendant in breach of warranty action.

**FACT SUMMARY:** Black & Veatch Construction, Inc. (B&V) (P) contended that a fire blanket used to protect a welding area was unfit for its ordinary purpose because it failed to protect against fire during a torch-cutting operation, and, therefore, the implied warranty of merchantability was breached.

---

### RULE OF LAW
A breach of the implied warranty of merchantability claim brought under the UCC will not be sustained where the plaintiff has not adduced sufficient objective evidence that goods are not fit for the ordinary purposes for which they are used.

---

**FACTS:** Black & Veatch Construction, Inc. (B&V) (P) was the general contractor on a project during which a fire occurred during a torch-cutting operation. A fire blanket had been used to protect the area where the welding occurred, and although the fire was quickly extinguished, a generator was damaged by the chemicals in the fire extinguisher and $9 million in delay and repair damages occurred as a result. B&V (P) sued the fire blanket's manufacturer (D) and distributor (D) under the theory that under the Uniform Commercial Code (UCC) the blanket was unfit for its ordinary purpose and therefore that the implied warranty of merchantability had been breached. B&V (P) presented no evidence of an ordinary user's reasonable expectations of how the fire blanket should have performed. The district court held that as a matter of law there was no breach of the implied warranty of merchantability since the blanket performed as expected, and it accordingly granted summary judgment to the manufacturer (D) and distributor (D). The court of appeals granted review.

**ISSUE:** Will a breach of the implied warranty of merchantability claim brought under the UCC be sustained where the plaintiff has not adduced sufficient objective evidence that goods are not fit for the ordinary purposes for which they are used?

**HOLDING AND DECISION:** (Dyk, J.) No. A breach of the implied warranty of merchantability claim brought under the UCC will not be sustained where the plaintiff has not adduced sufficient objective evidence that goods are not fit for the ordinary purposes for which they are used. It is not disputed here that the manufacturer (D) and distributor (D) are merchants for UCC purposes, and, therefore, the UCC's implied warranty of merchantability applies to the blanket. To be merchantable, a good must be "fit for the ordinary purposes for which such goods are used." The issue of whether the blanket was being used for

its ordinary purpose was waived below, so the only remaining issue is whether the blanket was "unfit" for this purpose. Where a good performs as expected, it is fit for its intended purpose. The question, therefore, is whether the blanket performed as expected. This question is not a subjective one, but rather must be based on the reasonable expectations of an ordinary user, i.e., the standard is an objective one. B&V (P) bears the burden of proving that the blanket was unfit for its intended purpose, but it did not adduce evidence as to the reasonable expectations of consumers of the fire blanket. It did not, for example, present expert testimony on trade customs or industry standards, or any evidence of consumers' reasonable expectations. It was not enough to present only the testimony of the single user of the fire blanket who believed it did not perform as expected, as this was merely evidence of the subjective expectations of a particular user. Therefore, summary judgment was appropriate. Affirmed.

---

### ANALYSIS

As this case demonstrates, the implied warranty of merchantability applies to the ordinary use to which goods are put, and not to every particular, non-ordinary use that a purchaser may put them to. To cover instances where a purchaser intends to put goods to a non-ordinary use, the UCC provides, in § 2-315, the implied warranty of fitness for a particular purpose. Whether this implied warranty arises is a fact question determined by the circumstances as to whether a seller of goods has reason to know of such particular purpose and that the buyer is relying on the seller to provide goods that will be fit for such a purpose.

---

### Quicknotes

**BREACH OF WARRANTY** The breach of a promise made by one party to a contract on which the other party may rely, relieving that party from the obligation of determining whether the fact is true and indemnifying the other party from liability if that fact is shown to be false.

**IMPLIED WARRANTY** An implied promise made by one party to a contract that the other party may rely on a fact, relieving that party from the obligation of determining whether the fact is true and indemnifying the other party from liability if that fact is shown to be false.

**IMPLIED WARRANTY OF MERCHANTABILITY** An implied promise made by a merchant in a contract for the sale of goods that such goods are suitable for the purpose for which they are purchased.

# Lewis v. Mobil Oil Corporation

Sawmill operator (P) v. Oil company (D)

438 F.2d 500 (8th Cir. 1971).

**NATURE OF CASE:** Appeal from jury verdict for plaintiff in breach of warranty action.

**FACT SUMMARY:** Mobil Oil Corp. (Mobil) (D) contended that there was no implied warranty of fitness for a particular use when it supplied oil for Lewis's (P) hydraulic equipment, even though Lewis (P) had indicated that he needed the lubricant for a hydraulic system for his sawmill operations and that he himself did not know the appropriate type of oil, and, after problems arose, Lewis (P) requested that Mobil (D) ascertain that the oil was the correct type for his operations.

## ⚖ RULE OF LAW
Under the UCC, an implied warranty of fitness for a particular use will be found to exist where there is evidence that the seller of goods has reason to know any particular purpose for which the goods are required and that the buyer is relying on the seller's skill or judgment to select or furnish suitable goods for that particular purpose.

**FACTS:** Lewis (P), a sawmill operator, converted his equipment to a hydraulic system. He had done business for a long time with Mobil Oil Corp. (Mobil) (D) through its local dealer, Rowe. Lewis (P) asked Rowe to determine and supply the correct oil for the new hydraulic system. Rowe, too, did not know what the proper lubricant for Lewis's (P) machinery was, but told Lewis (P) he would find out. The only information given to Rowe by Lewis (P) was that the machinery was operated by a gear-type pump; Rowe did not request any further information. Rowe then sold Lewis (P) a type of oil with no chemical additives. Within days, the equipment began experiencing problems, and in six months the system broke down and had to be replaced. The cause of the breakdown was undetermined, but the oil was suspected, and Lewis (P) asked Rowe to be sure he was supplying the right kind of oil. Rowe continued to supply the same oil. For the next two years, Lewis (P) continued experiencing trouble with the system, and numerous pumps were replaced. Finally, a Mobil (D) representative inspected the equipment and recommended a different type of oil that contained certain anti-foaming additives. Following this change, the system worked satisfactorily. Lewis (P) sued for damages caused by Mobil's (D) oil on the theory that the implied warranty of fitness for a particular purpose had been breached, since the oil was not suitable for such use, and that the improper oil caused the mechanical breakdowns, with consequent damages to his business. A jury returned a verdict and damages for Lewis (P), and the court of appeals granted review.

**ISSUE:** Under the UCC, will an implied warranty of fitness for a particular use be found to exist where there is evidence that the seller of goods has reason to know any particular purpose for which the goods are required and that the buyer is relying on the seller's skill or judgment to select or furnish suitable goods for that particular purpose?

**HOLDING AND DECISION:** (Gibson, J.) Yes. Under the UCC, an implied warranty of fitness for a particular use will be found to exist where there is evidence that the seller of goods has reason to know any particular purpose for which the goods are required and that the buyer is relying on the seller's skill or judgment to select or furnish suitable goods for that particular purpose. Mobil (D) contends there was no warranty of fitness in this case, and that the equipment problems were attributable to improper filtration. It also contends that at most there was a warranty of merchantability, and since the oil provided to Lewis (P) was not unfit for use in hydraulic systems generally, this warranty was not breached. Because there was a warranty of fitness, it is unnecessary to determine whether the warranty of merchantability was breached. Under the UCC, there are two requirements for an implied warranty of fitness: (1) that the seller has "reason to know" of the use for which the goods are purchased, and (2) that the buyer relies on the seller's expertise in supplying the proper product. Both of these requirements were met here. The evidence shows that Rowe (and therefore Mobil (D)) knew that Lewis (P) was purchasing the oil for his particular hydraulic system and not for just a hydraulic system in general. It is also clear that Lewis (P) was relying on Mobil (D) to supply him with the proper oil for the system. Whether there is a warranty of fitness is a question of fact to be determined by all the circumstances. A buyer does not need to provide the seller actual knowledge of the particular purpose for which the goods are intended or of his reliance on the seller's skill and judgment, if the circumstances are such that the seller has reason to realize the purpose intended or that the reliance exists. Here, Lewis (P) made it clear he did not know what kind of oil was necessary and that he was relying on Mobil's (D) expertise to provide the correct oil. If Mobil (D) needed more information to make a proper determination, it was incumbent on Mobil (D) to get the additional information before making its recommendation. As the evidence shows, this could have easily been done in the first place by sending an engineer to the sawmill to inspect the equipment. Mobil (D) argues that even if there was a warranty of fitness, the damages were caused by abnormalities in Lewis's (P) system. First, this argument

*Continued on next page.*

goes to causation, not to the existence of the warranty. Second, even if the system had certain peculiarities, the whole point of an implied warranty of fitness is that a product be suitable for a specific purpose, and that a seller should not supply a product which is not so suited. In any event, there was no evidence here that the system was abnormal, since it functioned properly when the correct oil was used. Affirmed.

## ▌ANALYSIS

As to damages, the UCC provides in § 2-714(2) that the "measure of damages for breach of warranty is the difference at the time and place of acceptance between the value of the goods accepted and the value they would have had if they had been as warranted, unless special circumstances show proximate damages of a different amount." In § 2-714(3) and § 2-715, incidental and consequential damages are permitted, and § 2-715(2)(a) permits consequential damages including "any loss resulting from general or particular requirements and needs of which the seller at the time of contracting had reason to know and which could not reasonably be prevented by cover or otherwise." Thus, in this case, the ordinary measure of damages for breach of warranty was not applicable, since Lewis (P) did not pay a price exceeding the value of the oil delivered. Rather, since the breach was of an implied warranty of fitness for a particular purpose, the "special circumstances" exception was applicable.

## Quicknotes

**IMPLIED WARRANTY** An implied promise made by one party to a contract that the other party may rely on a fact, relieving that party from the obligation of determining whether the fact is true and indemnifying the other party from liability if that fact is shown to be false.

**MEASURE OF DAMAGES** Monetary compensation, that may be awarded by the court to a party who has sustained injury or loss to his person, property or rights due to another party's unlawful act, omission or negligence.

**WARRANTY OF FITNESS** An implied promise made by a merchant in a contract for the sale of goods that such goods are suitable for the purpose for which they are purchased.

**WARRANTY OF MERCHANTABILITY** An implied promise made by a merchant in a contract for the sale of goods that such goods are suitable for the purpose for which they are purchased.

# South Carolina Electric and Gas Co. v. Combustion Engineering, Inc.

## Utility (P) v. Manufacturer (D)

### S.C. Ct. App., 283 S.C. 182, 322 S.E.2d 453 (1984).

**NATURE OF CASE:** Appeal from summary judgment for defendant in action for breach of warranties.

**FACT SUMMARY:** South Carolina Electric and Gas Co. (SCE&G) (P) contended that a disclaimer of implied warranties for a steam generating boiler manufactured by Combustion Engineering, Inc. (Combustion) (D) was ineffective as a matter of law because it did not satisfy statutory requirements for such a disclaimer; Combustion (D) successfully asserted that the disclaimer was effective because the circumstances surrounding the purchase of the boiler by SCE&G (P) were sufficient to put SCE&G (P) on notice that implied warranties were excluded from the transaction.

---

## 🏛 RULE OF LAW

A disclaimer of implied warranties for goods will be upheld even though the disclaimer does not meet statutory requirements for how it must be written and presented in a contract where the parties are commercially sophisticated and the course of dealing indicates that the language of the disclaimer was neither unbargained for nor unexpected by the purchaser.

---

**FACTS:** South Carolina Electric and Gas Co. (SCE&G) (P) purchased a steam generating boiler and all its ancillary equipment, such as hoses, from Combustion Engineering, Inc. (Combustion) (D), the manufacturer, for SCE&G's (P) power generating plant. The contract of sale included an express one-year warranty and also contained a disclaimer of warranties provision that purported to exclude all warranties, whether express or implied, other than the express warranty set forth. The disclaimer did not contain the word "merchantability" as required by statute to exclude an implied warranty of merchantability, and appeared on the 17th page of the 22-page contract in the same type as the rest of the contract. The heading of the provision simply read, "WARRANTY." Nonetheless, the parties had negotiated for seven months over the inclusion of a provision that did not disclaim implied warranties under state law. Eventually, SCE&G (P) acceded to Combustion (D) and agreed to forego state-provided implied warranties and to have only the express warranty in the contract. Two years after the boiler was installed, a flexible metal hose ruptured and sprayed heated fuel oil across the surface of the boiler, and SCE&G (P) sued Combustion (D), among other things, for breach of an implied warranty that the boiler was fit for a particular purpose and breach of an implied warranty that the boiler was merchantable. The trial court granted summary judgment to Combustion (D), finding

that the implied warranties were excluded as a matter of law by the disclaimer. The state's intermediate appellate court granted review.

**ISSUE:** Will a disclaimer of implied warranties for goods be upheld even though the disclaimer does not meet statutory requirements for how it must be written and presented in a contract where the parties are commercially sophisticated and the course of dealing indicates that the language of the disclaimer was neither unbargained for nor unexpected by the purchaser?

**HOLDING AND DECISION:** (Goolsby, J.) Yes. A disclaimer of implied warranties for goods will be upheld even though the disclaimer does not meet statutory requirements for how it must be written and presented in a contract where the parties are commercially sophisticated and the course of dealing indicates that the language of the disclaimer was neither unbargained for nor unexpected by the purchaser. SCE&G (P) is correct that the disclaimer failed to meet statutory requirements to exclude implied warranties of merchantability and fitness for a particular purpose because it failed to mention the word "merchantability" and was not conspicuous, because it appeared toward the end of the contract in the same type size and color as the rest of the contract. The provision containing the disclaimer was also misleading because it suggested "a grant of warranty rather than a disclaimer" because the heading of the item merely read "WARRANTY." Notwithstanding these shortcomings of the disclaimer provision, the question remains whether a genuine issue of material fact existed as to whether the disclaimer came within the statutory exception that provides that a disclaimer will be effective when "the circumstances surrounding the transaction are in themselves sufficient to call the buyer's attention to the fact that no implied warranties are made or that a certain implied warranty is excluded." Evidence of correspondence between the parties shows that the parties bargained over whether Combustion (D) would agree to be bound by implied warranties under state law, and that SCE&G (P) eventually agreed to having only the express warranty that became part of the contract. SCE&G (P), however, contends that this correspondence was not part of the contract, and can only be used to resolve the ambiguity of the disclaimer provision—which is a question that must be left to a jury. The question of whether the correspondence is part of the contract does not need to be reached because the disclaimer provision is unambiguous. The correspondence is not being used to resolve an ambiguity, but is being used to determine whether the language

*Continued on next page.*

of the disclaimer was unbargained for and unexpected by SCE&G (P). If there is no genuine issue of material fact as to this issue, then SCE&G (P) cannot claim as a matter of law that the disclaimer does not exclude the implied warranties of merchantability or of fitness for a particular purpose. The evidence of the correspondence between the parties shows that the language in the disclaimer provision came as no surprise to SCE&G (P), since it had been bargaining with Combustion (D) over that language for several months. Both parties are commercially sophisticated and possess relatively equal bargaining strength, so that it cannot be said that the provision was not bargained for. For these reasons, the disclaimer was effective to disclaim the implied warranties of merchantability and fitness for a particular purpose, even though it did not satisfy statutory requirements for how it should be written or presented in the contract. Accordingly, summary judgment was appropriate. Affirmed.

## ▶ *ANALYSIS*

A clause in a contract may be deemed to be conspicuous when it is so written that a reasonable person against whom it is to operate ought to have noticed it. Language in the body of a form may be found to be "conspicuous" if it is in larger or other contrasting type, such as when it is boldfaced or italicized, or in a different color. Some courts have noted that that actual awareness by a non-consumer buyer (i.e., a sophisticated businessperson) of a disclaimer prior to entering into a sales contract and possession of substantially equivalent bargaining power satisfies the purpose of the "conspicuous" requirement.

## *Quicknotes*

**AMBIGUITY** Language that is capable of being understood to have more than one interpretation.

**EXPRESS WARRANTY** A promise made by one party to a contract that the other party may rely on a fact, relieving that party from the obligation of determining whether the fact is true and indemnifying the other party from liability if that fact is shown to be false.

**IMPLIED WARRANTY** An implied promise made by one party to a contract that the other party may rely on a fact, relieving that party from the obligation of determining whether the fact is true and indemnifying the other party from liability if that fact is shown to be false.

**IMPLIED WARRANTY OF FITNESS** An implied promise made by a merchant in a contract for the sale of goods that such goods are suitable for the purpose for which they are purchased.

**IMPLIED WARRANTY OF MERCHANTABILITY** An implied promise made by a merchant in a contract for the sale of goods that such goods are suitable for the purpose for which they are purchased.

**SUMMARY JUDGMENT** Judgment rendered by a court in response to a motion made by one of the parties, claiming that the lack of a question of material fact in respect to an issue warrants disposition of the issue without consideration by the jury.

# Henningsen v. Bloomfield Motors, Inc.

### Car buyer (P) v. Car dealer (D)

N.J. Sup. Ct., 32 N.J. 358, 161 A.2d 69 (1960).

**NATURE OF CASE:** Appeal from award of damages for breach of an implied warranty.

**FACT SUMMARY:** Henningsen's (P) wife was injured by a steering failure in a new car purchased from Bloomfield Motors, Inc. (D) under a contract in which the dealer purported to disclaim all implied warranties of merchantability.

## RULE OF LAW
An attempt by an automobile dealer (or manufacturer) to disclaim an otherwise implied warranty of merchantability will be declared void as against public policy.

**FACTS:** Henningsen (P) purchased a new car from Bloomfield Motors, Inc. (D). Henningsen's (P) wife was injured when the steering mechanism failed 10 days after the car had been delivered. Bloomfield Motors (D) contended that any implied warranty of merchantability was disclaimed by a provision on the back of the purchase contract (among eight and a half inches of fine print) which limited liability for breach of warranty to replacement of defective parts. Bloomfield (D) appealed from a judgment for Henningsen (P).

**ISSUE:** Is an automobile dealer's (or manufacturer's) disclaimer of all warranties of merchantability (beyond replacement of parts) effective in insulating that automobile dealer from liability for breach of a warranty of merchantability which would otherwise be implied?

**HOLDING AND DECISION:** (Francis, J.) No. An automobile dealer's (or manufacturer's) disclaimer of all warranties of merchantability (beyond replacement of parts) is not effective in insulating that automobile dealer from liability for breach of a warranty of merchantability which would otherwise be implied. Although "freedom of contract" is an important and guiding concept in the law, provisions which clearly tend toward injury of the public will be declared void as against public policy. Because of the gross disparity of bargaining power between the consumer and the giant and essential automobile industry (most of which uses a similar disclaimer clause) there can be no arm's-length bargaining on the subject of warranty. The consumer must take the purchase contract as he finds it or he must forego his car. (Nor can he seek a competitor who offers greater security.) A warranty disclaimer which deprives the consumer of the protection which the "legislative will" has sought to provide through implied warranties, thus clearly tends toward the injury of the public. Affirmed.

## ▶ ANALYSIS

In this landmark case, a court for the first time came out against an exculpatory clause in an "adhesion" contract squarely on the ground that it violated public policy. Courts had previously denied seemingly "unfair" clauses, their intended effects, by various processes of strained interpretation resulting in great confusion and doctrinal inconsistency. This decision has been reinforced by UCC § 2-302 concerning "unconscionable" clauses. (Caveat: the language of and comments to § 2-302 are of little help and this section of the UCC will require considerable judicial fleshing out before its meaning becomes clear.) The present case was a big step in a general movement currently reshaping much of tort (and contract) law. Economic efficiency underlies this movement which attempts to put a loss on the party who can best absorb it as well as adjust subsequent behavior with an eye toward avoiding similar losses in the future.

### Quicknotes

**ADHESION CONTRACT** A contract, usually in standardized form, that is prepared by one party and offered to another, whose terms are so disproportionately in favor of the drafting party that courts tend to question the equality of bargaining power in reaching the agreement.

**ARM'S-LENGTH MERGER** A merger negotiated between two unrelated parties, each acting in his own self-interest.

**IMPLIED WARRANTY** An implied promise made by one party to a contract that the other party may rely on a fact, relieving that party from the obligation of determining whether the fact is true and indemnifying the other party from liability if that fact is shown to be false.

**IMPLIED WARRANTY OF MERCHANTABILITY** An implied promise made by a merchant in a contract for the sale of goods that such goods are suitable for the purpose for which they are purchased.

# Limits on the Bargain and Its Performance

## Quick Reference Rules of Law

# McKinnon v. Benedict

## Homeowner (P) v. Resort owner (D)

Wis. Sup. Ct., 38 Wis. 2d 607, 157 N.W.2d 665 (1968).

**NATURE OF CASE:** Action brought in equity to enjoin property owner from violating contractual restrictions on the use of land.

**FACT SUMMARY:** The Benedicts (D), in order to buy a summer resort, borrowed $5,000 from adjoining property owner, McKinnon (P), who promised to help the Benedicts (D) attract tourists if the Benedicts (D) would not cut trees between the resort and his property nor make certain other improvements for a period of 25 years. When the resort did not prosper and the Benedicts (D) began to add a trailer park and tent camp, McKinnon (P) brought suit to enjoin further improvements.

## RULE OF LAW

Contracts which are oppressive, that is, fail to meet the test of reasonableness, will not be enforced in equity.

**FACTS:** Mr. Benedict (D), a retail jeweler, and his wife (D), in order to purchase a summer resort consisting of a lodge and some cabins on about 80 acres of land adjoining McKinnon's (P) 1,000 acres of land, borrowed $5,000 interest-free from McKinnon (P) who promised also to help attract business. The Benedicts (D), in return, promised not to cut trees between the camp and McKinnon's (P) land and to make no improvements closer to his land than the present buildings. The restrictions were for a term of 25 years. They did not affect all the resort, but did affect all of the most desirable part. When the resort did not prosper, the Benedicts (D), who had repaid the $5,000 loan in seven months, spent $9,000 bulldozing and installing utilities for a trailer park and tent camp. When McKinnon (P), who wintered in Arizona, returned, he filed suit and obtained an injunction enjoining the improvements.

**ISSUE:** Was the restrictive contract reasonable so as to be enforced in action in equity?

**HOLDING AND DECISION:** (Heffernan, J.) No. The contract, being oppressive, cannot be enforced in equity. Coupled with the general equitable principle is the policy that restrictions on the use of land are not favored in the law. The Benedicts (D) are under great hardship. The only monetary consideration was a loan which they repaid on time. The loan was not unsecured as McKinnon (P) took a mortgage on their cottage property. McKinnon's (P) aid in generating business was booking one group, which stayed a week. The Benedicts (D) great need for the loan placed them in an untenable bargaining position that made it impossible for them to deal at arm's length with McKinnon (P). Accordingly, the inadequacy of consideration was so gross as to be unconscionable. The contract, therefore, being unreasonable, will not be enforced by a court of equity. As the improvements to the land are barely visible during summer, the only time McKinnon (P) is on the land, the damage to him is minimal, while the damage of enforcing the restrictions against the Benedicts (D) would be major, it is within the discretion of the court to protect persons from equitable remedies which would cause them harshness or oppression. Reversed.

## ▶ ANALYSIS

This case was brought in equity, that is to say, there was no remedy available to the plaintiff at law. Instead, the Benedicts (D) sought specific performance of the contract, abeyance of the restriction, through injunction enjoining any violation of the contract. Cases in equity are decided by the judge sitting without a jury and such cases are decided on a basis of fair play and common decency. Often the phrase "balancing the equities" is used to describe the weighing of the rights of the parties against each other. The court did not give the Benedicts (D) carte blanche to bulldoze and cut trees as they please. But permission to make improvements that would not harm McKinnon (P), though outside the bounds of this agreement, was given. The contract was oppressive, as the Benedicts (D), being of very weak bargaining power next to McKinnon (P), received inadequate consideration for the severe restriction he promised to uphold.

---

## Quicknotes

**EQUITABLE** Just; fair.

**INJUNCTION** A remedy imposed by the court ordering a party to cease the conduct of a specific activity.

**OPPRESSION** The abuse of one's authority resulting in the infliction of injury on another.

**SPECIFIC PERFORMANCE** An equitable remedy whereby the court requires the parties to perform their obligations pursuant to a contract.

**UNCONSCIONABLE** A situation in which a contract, or a particular contract term, is unenforceable if the court determines that such term(s) are unduly oppressive or unfair to one party to the contract.

# Tuckwiller v. Tuckwiller

Caretaker (P) v. Estate executor (D)

Mo. Sup. Ct., 413 S.W.2d 274 (1967).

**NATURE OF CASE:** Action for specific performance of a contract for the transfer of real property.

**FACT SUMMARY:** Mr. and Mrs. Tuckwiller (P) lived on the Hudson family farm as renters; about half the farm was owned by Mrs. Metta Hudson Morrison, who returned to live on the farm after contracting Parkinson's disease. She asked Mrs. Tuckwiller (P) to care for her during her remaining lifetime and signed a paper promising to give Mrs. Tuckwiller (P) her farm, which was willed for sale, the proceeds of which were to go to the creation of a student loan fund at Davidson College. Mrs. Morrison died before she could change the will.

## 🏛 RULE OF LAW
Whenever a contract concerning real property is in its nature and incidents entirely unobjectionable, it is as much a matter of course for a court of equity to decree specific performance of it, as it is for a court of law to give damages for the breach of it.

**FACTS:** The Tuckwillers (P) were renters on the Hudson family farm, half of which was owned by Metta Hudson Morrison who returned to the farm after contracting Parkinson's disease. Having no immediate relatives and not wanting to live in an impersonal nursing home, she asked Mrs. Tuckwiller (P) to care for her during her life and she signed a paper promising her farm to Mrs. Tuckwiller (P) in return for care. Mrs. Tuckwiller (P) quit her job to provide Mrs. Morrison with three meals a day, "a good bed," and "any possible act of nursing, and . . . her every possible pleasure." The farm was willed to Davidson College for sale, the proceeds of which were to create a student loan fund. Mrs. Morrison made an appointment with her lawyer to change the will; however, she fainted and fell. In the ambulance, she had the attendants witness the paper. She died the next month without having changed the will. The college and Mrs. Morrison's executors (D) resisted giving the farm to the Tuckwillers (P).

**ISSUE:** Is there the requisite essential fairness and adequate consideration necessary for the enforcement in equity of the contract for real estate?

**HOLDING AND DECISION:** (Welborn, Commn.) Yes. While prior services cannot provide the consideration essential to a binding contract, such prior services and the past relations of the parties may properly be considered in connection with the fairness of the contract and adequacy of the consideration. Having no immediate family and not desiring to stay in an impersonal nursing home, Mrs. Morrison felt freer to dispose of the farm without an exact quid pro quo. Her insistence that the contract be witnessed and her unsuccessful attempt to change her will are clear evidence of her satisfaction with the bargain. While Mrs. Tuckwiller's (P) services were but for a short duration with a monetary value unquestionably far less in value to that of the farm, it is not necessary with a contract for real estate to award the monetary value of Mrs. Tuckwiller's (P) services to her. Once essential fairness and adequate consideration are found, the fact that the contract is one for real estate determines the question of the adequacy of the legal remedy of monetary damages. Whenever a contract for real property is entirely unobjectional so that it possesses no features appealing to the discretion of the court, a court of equity (as in this case) will decree specific performance, while a court of law will give damages for breach. Affirmed.

## ▌ ANALYSIS

An action for specific performance is inherently an equitable remedy. It is not a legal remedy. An action in equity cannot be brought if there is an available remedy in law. Courts of equity, which sit without juries, have great discretion in determining the issue. Here, the contract was aleatory, that is, involving risk or hazard. The surrounding circumstances in equity actions become important in guiding the court to its decision. Because of the lack of relatives of Mrs. Morrison, her satisfaction expressed by her actions, plus in some respects the fact Mrs. Tuckwiller (P) quit her job to fulfill her side of the bargain, the court can determine the good intent of the parties and enforce the contract.

---

### Quicknotes

**ALEATORY** A transaction or agreement between parties that is contingent upon the occurrence of an uncertain or fortuitous event.

**EQUITABLE REMEDY** A remedy that is based upon principles of fairness as opposed to rules of law.

**QUID PRO QUO** What for what; in the contract context, used synonymously with consideration to refer to the mutual promises between two parties rendering a contract enforceable.

**SPECIFIC PERFORMANCE** An equitable remedy whereby the court requires the parties to perform their obligations pursuant to a contract.

# Black Industries, Inc. v. Bush

## Middleman (P) v. Manufacturer (D)

110 F. Supp. 801 (D. N.J. 1953).

**NATURE OF CASE:** Action for damages for breach of a contract for the sale of goods.

**FACT SUMMARY:** Bush (D), who was to produce mechanical parts for Black Industries, Inc. (Black) (P) who was reselling them to another company which was selling the equipment to the United States, failed to deliver the parts, claiming Black (P) was receiving excessive profits in violation of public policy when the government was involved in the Korean War. Bush (D) moved for summary judgment.

> ## 🏛 RULE OF LAW
> Differences in the relative values of the consideration in a contract between businessmen dealing at arm's length without fraud will not affect the validity of the contract.

**FACTS:** Black Industries, Inc. (Black) (P) contracted with Bush (D) for the latter to produce and sell to Black (P) 1.3 million anvils at $4.40 per thousand; 750,000 holder primers at $11.50 per thousand; and 700,000 plunger supports at $12 per thousand, all to be made to government specifications. Black (P) was to resell the items to two other companies that were using the parts to satisfy contracts they had with the government. Black (P) was to make a profit of 84.09 percent on anvils, 39.13 percent on holder primers, and 68.33 percent on plunger supports. Bush (D) was to deliver directly to the companies to which Black (P) was reselling the parts but Black (P) was to handle all the billing, and was to be responsible for differences between Bush's (D) quotations and the ultimate price. Bush (D), alleging Black (P) was receiving excessive profits against public policy during time of [the Korean] war because the price was eventually passed on to the U.S. government, failed to deliver. Black (P) alleged it lost about $19,000 on its two resale contracts. Bush (D) moved for summary judgment.

**ISSUE:** Will differences in the relative values of the consideration in a contract between businessmen dealing at arm's length without fraud affect the validity of the contract?

**HOLDING AND DECISION:** (Forman, C.J.) No. Differences in the relative values of the consideration in a contract between businessmen dealing at arm's length without fraud will not affect the validity of the contract. To be void as against public policy without evidence of fraud, the contract must fall into at least one of three categories. It must be a contract by which the defendant pays the plaintiff to induce a public official to act in a certain manner; it must be a contract to do an illegal act; or it must be a contract contemplating collusive bidding on a public contract. The first and third categories are those directly impinging on governmental activities and the ones upon which Bush (D) most heavily relied. But the contract's only effect upon the government was indirect in that the government was to buy machines made by component parts manufactured by Bush (D) and resold by Black (P) to manufacturers who would sell the finished product to the government. Even if it were shown that Black (P) was to have received a far greater profit than Bush (D) for a much smaller contribution, Bush (D) nevertheless would be bound by the familiar rule that relative values of the consideration in a contract between businessmen dealing at arm's length without fraud will not affect the validity of the contract. The court does not believe that it should determine the validity of a contract between ordinary businessmen on the basis of its beliefs as to the adequacy of the consideration. This would lead the court to having to determine the fairness of profits taken by all middlemen. Motion for summary judgment denied.

## ▶ ANALYSIS

First, this is a case brought for damages. Such an action is an action in law. In an action in law, the court will not look to the adequacy of consideration as it will do in an action for specific performance which is an action in equity. The courts' discretion is not as wide in an action in law as in an action in equity. This case appears to be guided by the somewhat old, but strict, rule that the court would be making an unwarranted interference if it were to relieve an adult party from a bad bargain. But, also, courts do not want to prescribe prices because it is thought the administration of the law of contracts would become inefficient. Additionally, the test of enforceability would become clouded by vague rules of "fairness" and "reasonableness." Notice, too, that the middleman generally performs an important function in contracting by bringing together sellers and buyers who would otherwise be ignorant of the business needs of each other. Also, here, Black (P), as middleman, took the risk of the difference in the ultimate price from that of the quoted price, which is perhaps a justification for the high profit.

---

## Quicknotes

**SUMMARY JUDGMENT** Judgment rendered by a court in response to a motion by one of the parties, claiming that the lack of a question of material fact in respect to an issue warrants disposition of the issue without consideration by the jury.

# O'Callaghan v. Waller & Beckwith Realty Co.

Injured tenant (P) v. Landlord (D)

Ill. Sup. Ct., 15 Ill. 2d 436, 155 N.E.2d 545 (1958).

**NATURE OF CASE:** Action to recover damages for negligence.

**FACT SUMMARY:** O'Callaghan (P) was injured by her landlord's negligence under a lease which exculpated the landlord from liability for negligence.

## RULE OF LAW
A lease clause exculpating a landlord from liability for his own negligence should be upheld and is not void as against public policy.

**FACTS:** O'Callaghan (P), a tenant in an apartment building maintained and operated by Waller & Beckwith Realty Co. (Waller) (D), was injured in the apartment's courtyard on defective pavement attributed to Waller's (D) alleged negligence. O'Callaghan's (P) lease contained an exculpatory clause which clearly purported to relieve Waller (D) from liability for negligence. O'Callaghan's (P) jury verdict was reversed by the appeals court, and she appealed.

**ISSUE:** In a residential lease, is an exculpatory clause releasing the landlord from liability for his own negligence void as against public policy?

**HOLDING AND DECISION:** (Schaefer, J.) No. Exculpatory clauses in the landlord-tenant forum (whether business or residential) should be enforced for the following reasons: (1) the lessor-lessee relationship has been considered a matter of private, not public, concern; (2) exculpatory clauses for landlords benefit tenants as well; (3) the landlord-tenant relationship is not possessed of the monopolistic characteristics that have characterized some other relations with respect to which exculpatory clauses have been held invalid; and (4) the subject is appropriate for legislative, rather than judicial, action. Furthermore, any disparity in bargaining power caused by a housing shortage, which may or may not have existed when the lease was drawn, was a sporadic and transitory sort of condition. Judicial determination should rest upon a durable moral basis. Affirmed.

**DISSENT:** (Bristow, J.) In the pervasive arena of the landlord-tenant relationship the important negligence standard which has been developed to protect members of society from one another has been effectively destroyed by the majority opinion. The landlord-tenant relationship is not significantly distinguishable from the employer-employee relationship in which exculpatory clauses have been declared void as against public policy.

## ANALYSIS

The present case was decided before the landmark case of *Henningsen v. Bloomfield Motors*, 32 N.J. 358 (1960), which finally recognized in judicial opinion the doctrine of "contracts of adhesion." Although today the boundaries of "public policy" are in a state of confusion, the trend is definitely away from the majority's decision in the present case. Many courts have made a distinction (in deciding whether or not to allow exculpatory clauses) between commercial and residential leases on grounds of the relative bargaining power of the parties involved. Even where exculpatory clauses are not struck down, they are usually strictly construed.

## Quicknotes

**EXCULPATORY CLAUSE** A clause in a contract relieving one party from liability for certain unlawful conduct.

**NEGLIGENCE** Conduct falling below the standard of care that a reasonable person would demonstrate under similar conditions.

**PUBLIC POLICY** Policy administered by the state with respect to the health, safety and morals of its people in accordance with common notions of fairness and decency.

# Graham v. Scissor-Tail, Inc.

Concert promoter (P) v. Agent (D)

Cal. Sup. Ct., 171 Cal. Rptr. 604, *en banc* (1981).

**NATURE OF CASE:** Appeal from judgment confirming an arbitration award, on grounds that contract requiring arbitration was an unenforceable contract of adhesion and that the arbitration clause therein was unconscionable.

**FACT SUMMARY:** Graham (P), an experienced and sophisticated concert promoter, contended that a union-provided form contract he entered into was an unenforceable contract of adhesion, notwithstanding that the contract fell within his reasonable expectations, and that an arbitration clause in the contract was unconscionable.

> ## RULE OF LAW
> A contract of adhesion is enforceable against the adhering party where the contract falls within the reasonable expectations of that party.

**FACTS:** Bill Graham (P), an experienced and sophisticated contract promoter, entered into several identical contracts with Scissor-Tail, Inc. (D), which represented the well-known recording artist Leon Russell, for a multi-city concert tour. Each contract was a form contract, known in the industry as an American Federation of Musicians (AFM) Form B Contract. All AFM members were prohibited from entering contracts other than those provided by the union, so that Graham (P) was unable to negotiate a separate contract with Russell. The contracts provided that any disputes arising from the contracts would be arbitrated before the AFM's international executive board. Graham (P), who had entered into thousands of AFM contracts, had previously appeared before the AFM's international executive board to resolve disputes arising from other contracts. When a dispute arose regarding the Russell concert tour, Graham (P) brought suit for breach of contract. Scissor-Tail (D) moved successfully to compel arbitration, and, after the union's international executive board ruled in Scissor-Tail's (D) favor, Graham (P) appealed the confirmation of the arbitration award, contending that the Form B Contract was an unenforceable contract of adhesion, and that the arbitration clause therein was unconscionable. The state's highest court granted review.

**ISSUE:** Is a contract of adhesion enforceable against the adhering party where the contract falls within the reasonable expectations of that party?

**HOLDING AND DECISION:** [Judge not listed in casebook excerpt.] Yes. A contract of adhesion is enforceable against the adhering party where the contract falls

within the reasonable expectations of that party. The term "contract of adhesion" signifies "a standardized contract, which, imposed and drafted by the party of superior bargaining strength, relegates to the subscribing party only the opportunity to adhere to the contract or reject it." Here, notwithstanding Graham's (P) stature in the music business, he was forced to enter into the Form B contract, so that he was an "adherent" of the contract, and the contract was a contract of adhesion. Characterizing a contract as one of adhesion, however, does not indicate its legal affect per se. Such contracts are fully enforceable unless other factors are present that make them unenforceable. Generally, there are two judicially imposed limitations on the enforcement of adhesion contracts or provisions thereof. First, if a contract of adhesion or one of its provisions does not fall within the reasonable expectations of the weaker or "adhering" party, the contract or provision will not be enforced against him. Second, a contract or provision, even if consistent with the reasonable expectations of the parties, will be denied enforcement if, considered in its context, it is unduly oppressive or unconscionable. Here, it cannot be said that the contract at issue was in any way contrary to Graham's (P) reasonable expectations, given that he had been a party to thousands of AFM contracts containing a similar arbitration provision. He had been involved in prior proceedings before the AFM regarding disputes with other musical groups arising under prior contracts, and he even indicated he would go before the AFM if the dispute was not settled to his satisfaction. These facts indicate that he was well aware that all disputes arising under the contracts were to be resolved by arbitration before the AFM For all of these reasons it must be concluded that the provisions requiring such arbitration were wholly consistent with Graham's (P) reasonable expectations upon entering into the contract, and the contract is enforceable unless the arbitration provision was unconscionable. [The court went on to conclude that the arbitration provision was unconscionable because it designated as the arbitrator the AFM's international executive board, which the court concluded was presumptively biased in favor of its members.] [The procedural outcome of the case is not indicated in the casebook extract.]

## ANALYSIS

Although the court in this decision concluded that the arbitration provision in the contract at issue was unconscionable, because it designated a biased arbitrator, this conclusion would not necessarily preclude the parties from

*Continued on next page.*

arbitrating their dispute, especially given the strong public policy favoring arbitration. On remand, the parties could be afforded a reasonable opportunity to agree on a suitable, non-biased arbitrator and, failing such agreement, the trial court, on petition of either party, could appoint the arbitrator. Only in the absence of an agreement or petition to appoint would the court proceed to a judicial determination of the controversy.

■=■

## Quicknotes

**ADHESION CONTRACT** A contract that is not negotiated and is usually prepared by the dominant party on a "take it or leave it" basis.

**ARBITRATION CLAUSE** Provision contained in a contract pursuant to which both parties agree that any disputes arising thereunder will be resolved through arbitration.

**UNCONSCIONABILITY** Rule of law whereby a court may excuse performance of a contract, or of a particular contract term, if it determines that such terms are unduly oppressive or unfair to one party to the contract as a result of disparity in bargaining power during the formation of the contract.

■=■

# Doe v. Great Expectations

## Unnamed individuals (P) v. Dating service (D)

N.Y. Civ. Ct., 809 N.Y.S.2d 819 (2005).

**NATURE OF CASE:** Consolidated actions to recover amounts paid under social referral services contracts.

**FACT SUMMARY:** Doe (P) and Roe (P) contended that they were entitled to recover amounts paid under a social referral services contract they had each entered separately with Great Expectations (D) on the grounds that the contract and service violated the state's Dating Service Law.

### 🏛 RULE OF LAW
Where a consumer form contract violates state law that provides for actual damages or a set amount, whichever is greater, a consumer is entitled to a full refund of the contract price paid as restitutionary damages.

**FACTS:** Doe (P) and Roe (P) each separately entered into social referral services contracts with Great Expectations (D), which with some minor variations were identical, boilerplate form contracts. Doe (P) paid $1,000 for six months and Roe (P) paid $3,790 for 36 months, which was later extended to 54 months. Roe (P) was given oral assurances of 12 introductions to be provided over the course of 36 months. Under the form contract, Great Expectations (D) offered to expand a client's social horizons primarily by posting a client's video and profile on an Internet site on which other clients could review them and, thereafter, as desired, approach a selected client for actual social interaction. Great Expectations (D) did not guarantee a match. Under the state's Dating Service Law, where the dating service did not assure it would furnish a client with a specified number of social referrals per month, the service was permitted to charge no more than $25. The service was also required to provide notice of a three-day "cooling off" right to cancel, and was also required to provide each client with a "Dating Service Consumer Bill of Rights." The service was also required to provide each client with several other rights. The law also provided that damages would be actual damages or $50, whichever was greater. Doe (P) and Roe (P) brought suit to recover the amounts they had paid under their respective contracts on the grounds that the contracts violated the state's Dating Service Law.

**ISSUE:** Where a consumer form contract violates state law that provides for actual damages or a set amount, whichever is greater, is a consumer entitled to a full refund of the contract price paid as restitutionary damages?

**HOLDING AND DECISION:** (Lebedeff, J.) Yes. Where a consumer form contract violates state law that

provides for actual damages or a set amount, whichever is greater, a consumer is entitled to a full refund of the contract price paid as restitutionary damages. Here, the contracts fall within the purview of the Dating Service Law, which covers services that match members by creating a location and mechanism for members to assess each other by reviewing another member's video, photograph and profile. It does not matter whether the service actually matches members; it is sufficient if the service makes available the matching of members or supplies the means for matching the members. The service here is not taken out of the law's scope merely because the matching was to be done over the Internet, since the law specifically includes services that utilize computers. Given that the service was subject to the Dating Service Law, there were numerous violations here. The most glaring was massive overcharging, since where the dating service does not ensure it will furnish a client with a specified number of social referrals per month, the service may charge no more than $25—so here the amounts charged were much greater than that (even though Roe (P) was orally assured of 12 introductions to be provided over the course of 36 months, the service failed to commit to any number of introductions in any given month, so it still violated the law in this regard). The form contract also violated every mandate of the Dating Service Law, with the single exception that each contract did contain notice of a three-day "cooling off" right to cancel. The service failed to provide to the clients written notice of a mandatory "Dating Service Consumer Bill of Rights," which also had to be provided to them and was not. Other provisions that were not provided in the contract included various cancellation rights, the right to put the membership on hold, return of a client's private information and materials, and other rights. As to damages, the Dating Service Law states that "[a]ny person who has been injured by reason of a violation of this section may bring . . . an action to recover his or her actual damages or fifty dollars whichever is greater." Here, "actual damages" includes the difference between each contract price and the $25 fee which is the maximum fee permitted under the Dating Service Law for these contracts. Both Roe (P) and Doe (P) seek a return of the full balance paid, which raises the question of whether they establish damages justifying a return of the additional $25 each. Because (based on the credibility of the claimants) neither of them would have entered into these contracts if they had properly been informed of their rights and the contracts contained the appropriate provisions, each claimant is entitled to a refund of the final $25 balance at issue, plus

*Continued on next page.*

interest from the contract date. That is, they are each entitled to a full refund as restitutionary damages. This is supported by the statute's legislative history, which added "actual damages" in addition to authorizing the state's attorney general to bring enforcement actions. This "evened the playing field" by offering a single remedy of restitution to a consumer, which could be achieved by the alternate routes of commencing an individual suit or filing a complaint with the attorney general. It follows, logically, that the legislature, by adding the "actual damage" language to the statute did not intend to erode the state's commitment to protect consumers from price gouging by dating services, so that "actual damage" may include the maximum fee that may be charged by such services.

In addition, Great Expectations (D) should return personal material to each claimant, even though the contracts as written do not require it to do so, so that it will be in compliance with the law. Finally, the court has the judicial discretion to report Great Expectations (D) to the appropriate government authorities. It may do so considering all the circumstances, such as the nature of the offense, the effect of such report on the administration of justice, and, in particular, on the court's truth determining function. Also to be considered is whether a report could be "undesirable" if it "would dissuade witnesses on trial from telling the whole truth or encourage the threat of possible criminal proceedings as a means of pressure, for settlement purposes or otherwise, by one litigant against another," and whether the report is in the public interest. Weighing all these factors, it is determined that Great Expectations (D) should be reported, because, among other things, doing so is in the public interest, given that its acts violated rules governing a regulated industry and appear to reflect a continuing pattern and practice as indicated by, among other things, the use of a printed boiler plate form found not to be in accordance with applicable laws. Also, the court's past and future truth-determining function has not been, and will not be affected by a report since the proceeding is concluded, and a question touching upon the administration of justice and the integrity of a court order may be posed in that a similar course of conduct by Great Expectations (D) or a related entity was previously litigated. Actual damages for the plaintiffs awarded and amendment of the defendant's name ordered.

## ▌ *ANALYSIS*

As this case illustrates, courts may police the use of standard form contracts not only by giving effect to protective legislation by determining whether the contracts adhere to statutory law, but also by reporting violations to various government authorities, such as a state's attorney general or consumer protection agency.

■■■

## *Quicknotes*

**RESTITUTION** The return or restoration to rightful owner to prevent unjust enrichment.

■■■

# Williams v. Walker-Thomas Furniture Co.

## Furniture buyer (D) v. Retailer (P)

### 350 F.2d 445 (D.C. Cir. 1965).

**NATURE OF CASE:** Action to replevy goods for breach of contract.

**FACT SUMMARY:** Walker-Thomas Furniture Co. (P) sold to Williams (D) furniture burdened by a cross-collateral clause and, subsequent to Williams's (D) default, sought to replevy all goods previously purchased by Williams (D).

---

### 🏛 RULE OF LAW
The defense of unconscionability to action on a contract is judicially recognized.

---

**FACTS:** Walker-Thomas Furniture Co. (Walker-Thomas) (P) sold furniture to Williams (D) under a printed form contract containing a cross-collateral clause, the effect of which was to keep a balance due on every item purchased until the balance due on all items, whenever purchased, was liquidated. As a result, Walker-Thomas (P) retained by the terms of the contract the right to repossess all items previously purchased in the event of any default. At the time Williams (D) made her last purchase, she had a balance of $164 still owing from her prior purchases, although she had already paid $1,400 toward clearing her account. Subsequently, Williams (D) defaulted on payment and Walker-Thomas (P) sought to replevy all goods previously sold to Williams (D). This case involves Williams's (D) defense of that action.

**ISSUE:** Does the court have the power to refuse enforcement of contracts found to be unconscionable?

**HOLDING AND DECISION:** (Wright, J.) Yes. "Where the element of unconscionability is present at the time a contract is made, the contract should not be enforced. Unconscionability has generally been recognized to include an absence of meaningful choice on the part of one of the parties together with contract terms which are unreasonably favorable to the other party." Meaningfulness of choice is to be determined in light of all the circumstances—for example, gross disparity of bargaining power. The case should be remanded to the lower court for findings on the issue of unconscionability.

**DISSENT:** (Danaher, J.) Congress should consider corrective legislation to protect the public from exploitative contracts.

---

### ▶ ANALYSIS

The majority opinion, written by J. Skelly Wright, relies heavily on UCC § 2-302 to support its position. But the meaning and effect of § 2-302 has been hotly debated. Comment I to that provision defines "unconscionability" in terms of itself and says its principle is to prevent "oppression and unfair surprise," not to disturb the "allocation of risks because of superior bargaining power." It is not clear whether the present case involves procedural unconscionability (i.e., some sort of "bargaining nastiness" like deliberately concealing the cross-collateral clause in a maze of fine print) or substantive unconscionability (in which case the concern is with the allegedly "unfair" terms themselves, regardless of how they were presented). It is equally unclear whether or not the ambiguous UCC § 2-302 is intended to apply to both kinds of unconscionability. If Judge Wright was concerned with procedural unconscionability (i.e., Walker-Thomas [P], through bargaining nastiness created Williams's [D] "lack of meaningful choice"), there is little about which to quarrel. But if he had substantive unconscionability on his mind many analytical problems arise. For example, UCC § 2-302(2) allows the court to take "commercial setting, purpose, and effect" into account. But isn't it a businessman's "commercial purpose" to make money? And if the cross-collateral clause has that "effect," why should the court strike it down (absent bargaining nastiness)? Consider further what will happen if Walker-Thomas (P) is not allowed to use its clause: either (1) furniture prices will rise correspondingly and more poor people will be unable to afford furniture at all or perhaps (2) Walker-Thomas (P) will be forced to refuse sale outright to risky clients. Unless a less onerous alternative is found, the cross-collateral clause is probably better left as is. This decision is not untypical of other Skelly Wright opinions which are full of good intentions but which contain potentially deeper evils with the opposite effect. (See, for example, *Javins v. First Nat. Realty Corp.*, 428 F. 2d 1071 (D.C. Cir. 1970) in the field of landlord-tenant law.) Note, finally, that any court which declares a contract "substantively" unconscionable is dealing in the dangerous and tenuous business of substituting its own valuation of the contract goods for that of the parties involved. This kind of paternalism should be approached with caution.

---

### Quicknotes

**CROSS-COLLATERAL CLAUSE** Provision contained in a contract pursuant to which both parties provide security that performance will be rendered or that payment will be made.

*Continued on next page.*

**REPLEVIN** An action to recover personal property wrongfully taken.

**UNCONSCIONABLE** A situation in which a contract, or a particular contract term, is unenforceable if the court determines that such term(s) are unduly oppressive or unfair to one party to the contract.

■▬■

# Jones v. Star Credit Corp.

Buyer (P) v. Seller (D)

N.Y. Sup. Ct., 298 N.Y.S.2d 264 (1969).

**NATURE OF CASE:** Action to reform a contract on grounds of unconscionability.

**FACT SUMMARY:** Jones (P) purchased a freezer from Star Credit (D) for $900 plus credit charges, but the actual retail value of the freezer was only $300.

🏛 **RULE OF LAW**
A court may refuse to enforce a contract for the sale of goods on the ground that an excessive price term renders the contract unconscionable.

**FACTS:** Jones (P), a welfare recipient, purchased a freezer from Star Credit (D) for $900 ($1,439.69, including credit charges and $18 sales tax). Jones (P) had already paid $619.88 toward the purchase, but the freezer had a maximum retail value of only $300.

**ISSUE:** May a court refuse to enforce a contract for the sale of goods on the ground that the price term was "unconscionable"?

**HOLDING AND DECISION:** (Wachtler, J.) Yes. UCC § 2-302 allows a court to refuse enforcement of a contract containing an unconscionable price term. The sale of a freezer having a retail value of $300 for $900 ($1,439.69, including credit charges and $18 sales tax) is unconscionable as a matter of law. But UCC § 2-302 is not simply a mathematical ratio formula. Other factors in the balance include: (1) financial resources of the buyer known to the seller at the time of sale; (2) "knowing advantage" taken of the buyer; and (3) a gross inequality of bargaining power. Accordingly, the contract should be reformed by changing the payments called for therein to equal the amount already paid by Jones (P).

▎ *ANALYSIS*

It is not convincing for the court simply to assert, as it does: "There is no reason to doubt that UCC § 2-302 is intended to encompass the price term of an agreement." The court's paternalistic recognition of a kind of so-called substantive unconscionability, in which the court's valuation of the goods is substituted for that of the parties, needs further justification than it receives in this case. [See also *Williams v. Walker-Thomas*, 350 F. 2d 445 (D.C. Cir., 1965).] Most courts have stopped short of taking this step and have required some sort of procedural unconscionability ("bargaining nastiness") before refusing to enforce a contract. Further, the court's remedy of reformation of the contract to the amount already paid seems most suspect. How does this amount reflect anything other than pure fortuity?

*Quicknotes*

**REFORMATION** A correction of a written instrument ordered by a court to cause it to reflect the true intentions of the parties.

**UNCONSCIONABLE** A situation in which a contract, or a particular contract term, is unenforceable if the court determines that such term(s) are unduly oppressive or unfair to one party to the contract.

# Scott v. Cingular Wireless

Cell phone customers (P) v. Cell phone company (D)

Wash. Sup. Ct., 160 Wash. 2d 843, *en banc* (2007).

**NATURE OF CASE:** Appeal from grant of motion to compel arbitration in action challenging cell phone charges.

**FACT SUMMARY:** Scott (P) and other cellular telephone (cell phone) customers of Cingular Wireless (Cingular) (D), a cell phone company, brought a class action challenging certain cell phone charges. They contended that a mandatory arbitration clause in their contracts that prohibited class actions was substantively and procedurally unconscionable and, therefore, unenforceable so that arbitration should not have been compelled.

---

**🏛 RULE OF LAW**
A class action waiver within an arbitration clause that is embedded in a consumer contract of adhesion is substantively unconscionable as violating consumer protection laws.

---

**FACTS:** Scott (P) and other cellular telephone (cell phone) customers of Cingular Wireless (Cingular) (D), a cell phone company, brought a class action claiming that they were overcharged up to around $45 per month for unlawfully imposed long distance and/or out-of-network roaming charges. The contracts they all signed were standard preprinted agreements that included a clause requiring mandatory arbitration. This clause, in turn, contained a provision prohibiting consolidation of cases, class actions, and class arbitration. Cingular (D) amended the clause to specify that arbitration would be conducted according to American Arbitration Association (AAA) rules; that Cingular (D) would pay the filing, administrator, and arbitration fees unless the customer's claim was found to be frivolous; that Cingular (D) would reimburse the customer for reasonable attorney fees and expenses incurred for the arbitration (provided that the customer recovered at least the demand amount); and that the arbitration would take place in the county of the customer's billing address. It also removed limitations on punitive damages. Cingular (D) moved to compel individual arbitration, and Scott (P) and the other plaintiffs resisted by arguing that the class action waiver was substantively and procedurally unconscionable as against the state's Consumer Protection Act (CPA) and, therefore, unenforceable so that arbitration should not be compelled. The trial court granted Cingular's (D) motion, finding that although Cingular's (D) contract was a contract of adhesion, it was not sufficiently complex, illegible, or misleading to be deemed procedurally unconscionable. The trial court also found no substantive unconscionability. The state's highest court granted review.

**ISSUE:** Is a class action waiver within an arbitration clause that is embedded in a consumer contract of adhesion substantively unconscionable as violating consumer protection laws?

**HOLDING AND DECISION:** (Chambers, J.) Yes. A class action waiver within an arbitration clause that is embedded in a consumer contract of adhesion is substantively unconscionable as violating consumer protection laws. Although some jurisdictions have held that class action waivers are enforceable, others have held such waivers in arbitration clauses to be unconscionable, so that there is a split of authority. This case is unusual in that the arbitration clause itself is not being challenged, but only the class action waiver within it. Under the state's CPA, this action waiver is unconscionable because it is injurious to the public. Class actions are the only effective method to vindicate the public's rights when numerous small claims are involved; and state policy favors such actions to vindicate consumer claims. Such actions are critical to the enforcement of consumer protection laws. Without such actions, consumers could not act as private attorneys general to promote the public good. For these reasons, the class action waiver clause presented here is an unconscionable violation of the state's policy to protect the public, and, to the extent that this waiver prevents CPA cases, it is substantively unconscionable. Another question is whether the waiver is unconscionable because it effectively exculpates its drafters from liability for a large class of wrongful conduct. Contract provisions that exculpate the author for wrongdoing, especially intentional wrongdoing, undermine the public good. On its face, the waiver at issue does not exculpate Cingular (D) from any liability but merely channels disputes into individual arbitrations or small claims court. In effect, however, this exculpates Cingular (D) from liability where the cost of pursuing a wrong outweighs the potential recovery. As in this case, even shifting the cost of arbitration to Cingular (D) does not seem likely to make it worth the time, effort, and stress to pursue such individually small claims. This supposition is supported by the fact that no claims have been brought against Cingular (D) in this state in the past six years. Even though Cingular's (D) willingness to pay for the arbitrations is laudable, this measure alone is insufficient to ensure that a remedy for small consumer claims is practically available. First, the attorney fees are awarded only if the plaintiffs recover at least the full amount of their demand. Thus, a plaintiff could recover 99 percent of a claim and still not be awarded any attorney fees, whereas Cingular's (D) lawyers would be

*Continued on next page.*

paid regardless of result. But, if the consumer loses or achieves an award of one dollar less than sought, there is no award of fees. Even if all of the contingencies were met and attorney fees were awarded, the arbitrator could still consider the amount in controversy in awarding fees. Moreover, as a practical reality, no attorney would take a case for a trivial amount such as involved here—which, of course, is precisely why class actions were created in the first place. Thus, the waiver effectively prevents the consumer from pursuing valid claims and effectively exculpates the drafter from potential liability for small claims, no matter how numerous. The class action waiver is therefore substantively unconscionable as severely limiting the remedies of only one party to the contract. Because the waiver states that if it is found to be unenforceable, the entire arbitration clause is null and void, there remains no basis on which to compel arbitration. Reversed and remanded.

**DISSENT:** (Madsen, J.) First, the public policy that the majority finds violated is judge-made policy. If there is a public policy that disfavors class action waivers, it should come from the legislature. Second, the majority's holding disfavors arbitration, which contradicts strong federal legislative public policy that favors it and which holds that every presumption favoring arbitration must be given effect. This policy of favoring arbitration should be especially upheld regarding a contract such as the one at issue that provides significant financial protections for consumers. Finally, the majority has abandoned the case-by-case approach to determining contract unconscionability, and thereby effects a sweeping rule that potentially could invalidate thousands of arbitration clauses without regard to their specifics. Also, contrary to the majority's reasoning, consumers here will be able to obtain legal representation since attorney fees are available and Cingular (D) will pay the cost of arbitration. Thus, consumers can vindicate the public interest under the CPA by pursuing individual actions. For these reasons, the class action waiver is not unconscionable.

## ANALYSIS

The dissenting judge in this case points to the Federal Arbitration Act (FAA), Title 9 U.S.C., as requiring every presumption to be resolved in favor of arbitration. However, some (including the majority in this case) have argued that Congress simply requires states to put arbitration clauses on the same footing as other contracts, but not make them the special favorites of the law. Also, it stands to reason that class action waivers have very little to do with arbitration. Clauses that eliminate causes of action, eliminate categories of damages, or otherwise strip away a party's right to vindicate a wrong do not change their character merely because they are found within an arbitration clause. In this case, Cingular (D) could have favored arbitration by permitting class-wide arbitration as well as individual arbitration, and could have thereby avoided having its arbitration clause ruled invalid.

## Quicknotes

**ADHESION CONTRACT** A contract, usually in standardized form, that is prepared by one party and offered to another, whose terms are so disproportionately in favor of the drafting party that courts tend to question the equality of bargaining power in reaching the agreement.

**CLASS ACTION** A suit commenced by a representative on behalf of an ascertainable group that is too large to appear in court, who shares a commonality of interests and who will benefit from a successful result.

**UNCONSCIONABILITY** Rule of law whereby a court may excuse performance of a contract, or of a particular contract term, if it determines that such terms are unduly oppressive or unfair to one party to the contract as a result of disparity in bargaining power during the formation of the contract.

# Dalton v. Educational Testing Service

Test taker (P) v. Testing service (D)

N.Y. Ct. App., 87 N.Y.2d 384, 663 N.E.2d 289 (1995).

**NATURE OF CASE:** Breach of contract suit.

**FACT SUMMARY:** Dalton (P) sued Education Testing Service (ETS) (D) after ETS (D) informed him that they were canceling his second SAT score on the basis that it was taken by another individual.

> 🏛 **RULE OF LAW**
> Implicit in all contracts is a covenant of good faith and fair dealing.

**FACTS:** Dalton (P) took the SAT two times, the second time increasing his score more than 410 points. The members of Education Testing Service (ETS) (D) reviewed his exams and, upon concluding there was disparate handwriting, they were submitted to a handwriting specialist who opined they were taken by two different persons and his later score was subsequently canceled. Dalton (P) commenced suit to prevent ETS (D) from canceling the score. The trial court found that ETS (D) breached its contract to act in good faith and ordered the immediate release of the score. The appellate division affirmed.

**ISSUE:** Is a covenant of good faith and fair dealing implicit in all contracts?

**HOLDING AND DECISION:** (Kaye, C.J.) Yes. Implicit in all contracts is a covenant of good faith and fair dealing. Encompassed within that implied obligation is a pledge that neither party will interfere with the right of the other to "receive the fruits of the contract." Where the contract is discretionary, this includes a pledge not to act arbitrarily or irrationally in exercising that discretion. However, no obligation may be implied that is inconsistent with the terms of the contract. ETS (D) failed to meet its obligation in not considering relevant material provided by Dalton (P) and thus did not meet its covenant of good faith. Affirmed as modified.

---

▎ *ANALYSIS*

Note that the court states that once the relevant material information is considered by ETS (D), then it fulfills its contractual obligation and becomes the "final arbiter" of the appropriate weight to accord such information and the validity of Dalton's (P) score. Such determination is considered discretionary and is subject to the arbitrary or irrational standard.

*Quicknotes*

**SPECIFIC PERFORMANCE** An equitable remedy whereby the court requires the parties to perform their obligations pursuant to a contract.

# De La Concha of Hartford, Inc. v. Aetna Life Insurance Company

## Lessee (P) v. Lessor (D)

Conn. Sup. Ct., 269 Conn. 424, 849 A.2d 382 (2004).

**NATURE OF CASE:** Appeal from judgment for defendant in action for breach of a lease's implied covenant of good faith and fair dealing.

**FACT SUMMARY:** De La Concha of Hartford, Inc. (De La Concha) (P), a retailer that leased space in a mall owned by Aetna Life Insurance Company (Aetna) (D) at the Hartford Civic Center, contended that Aetna (D) breached the lease's implied covenant of good faith and fair dealing by, inter alia, changing its leasing and promotional practices at the Civic Center during De La Concha's (P) tenancy and by refusing to renew De La Concha's (P) lease.

## RULE OF LAW

A party to a contract does not breach the contract's implied duty of good faith and fair dealing where the party does not engage in purposeful, bad faith conduct that is inimical to the material terms of the lease.

**FACTS:** De La Concha of Hartford, Inc. (De La Concha) (P), a tobacco retailer, entered a lease in 1975 with Aetna Life Insurance Company (Aetna) (D) for space in Aetna's (D) enclosed mall at the then-new Civic Center in Hartford. The Civic Center also contained a coliseum used for events and exhibitions, and an arena for sporting contests. Interdependency of the retailers at the mall was particularly important, as consumers who came to the Civic Center to make an intended purchase at one store frequently made an impulse purchase at another store. Thus, full occupancy helped all the retailers to prosper. On the other hand, low occupancy gave the Civic Center a deserted feeling that depressed the sales of the remaining retailers. The lease contained a promotional fund provision, which required Aetna (D) to contribute not less than 25 percent of the total amount that the Civic Center tenants had paid into the promotional fund. Although the mall was full when it opened, its occupancy rate fluctuated with the Hartford economy. At no time, however, did Aetna (D) realize a profit on the venture, and instead, it lost money every year. By 1995, 20 years after opening, Aetna (D) had lost $50 million. An analysis showed that Aetna's (D) best option, financially, would be to sell the Civic Center. Eventually, the sports team (the Whalers) left, there was an expansion of shopping malls in the suburbs, and the downtown Hartford economy deteriorated. Accordingly, the Civic Center's manager undertook a policy of entering into short-term leases or leases giving Aetna (D) the right to recapture the premises in order to make the Civic Center more saleable. Aetna (D) also essentially terminated its efforts to promote the Civic Center and substantially cut its promotion budget. By 1999, when Aetna (D) entered into a contract to sell the Civic Center, De La Concha's (P) business had been declining, due in large part to a decline in cigar sales, and De La Concha (P) began defaulting on its rent. It had also failed to maintain its annual sales at a minimum of $262,500, a condition for renewing the lease (the gross sales provision). Thus, in 2000, when De La Concha (P) sought to renew its lease for five years, Aetna (D) rejected the renewal option. De La Concha (P) closed its business in 2001, and then brought suit against Aetna (D), claiming that Aetna (D) had breached the lease's implied covenant of good faith and fair dealing. In particular, De La Concha (P) claimed that Aetna (D) had an obligation, implied under its lease, to make good faith efforts to promote and to maintain the mall. In support of this contention, De La Concha (P) relied on the gross sales provision, as well as the promotional fund provision. De La Concha (P) argued that the gross sales provision of the lease impliedly obligated Aetna (D) to refrain from conduct that created any unfair or unnecessary risk of adversely affecting De La Concha's (P) sales. De La Concha (P) further claimed that the promotional fund provision imposed on Aetna (D) a duty to make reasonable efforts to promote and to maintain the Civic Center for the purpose of achieving an occupancy rate that was consistent with the economic well-being of the tenants. The trial court rejected the claims as factually unfounded and rendered judgment for Aetna (D). De La Concha (P) appealed, contending that the trial court's findings were unsupported by the evidence. The state's highest court granted review.

**ISSUE:** Does a party to a contract breach the contract's implied duty of good faith and fair dealing where the party does not engage in purposeful, bad faith conduct that is inimical to the material terms of the lease?

**HOLDING AND DECISION:** (Palmer, J.) No. A party to a contract does not breach the contract's implied duty of good faith and fair dealing where the party does not engage in purposeful, bad faith conduct that is inimical to the material terms of the lease. The duty of good faith and fair dealing is an implied duty that requires that neither party do anything that will injure the right of the other to receive the benefits of the agreement. To breach this duty, the acts by which a party allegedly impedes the other party' right to receive benefits that he or she reasonably expected to receive under the contract must have been taken in bad faith. Bad faith generally means more than negligence, and

*Continued on next page.*

it involves a dishonest purpose. Applying these principles here, it cannot be said that Aetna (D) engaged in bad faith or otherwise breached the implied duty of good faith and fair dealing. The facts show that Aetna (D) conducted itself in conformity with the express lease provisions and with De La Concha's (P) justified expectations in light of those provisions. The evidence supported the trial court's finding that Aetna's (D) decision to sell the Civic Center and the steps it took to implement that decision were undertaken reasonably and in good faith, and for the purpose of extricating itself from a well-intended but unsuccessful business venture that resulted in significant losses. The evidence established that Aetna (D) went to considerable lengths to retain existing tenants and to attract new ones, and, in fact, offered certain tenants substantial rent reductions to induce them to renew their leases. With respect to Aetna's (D) decision to enter into short-term leases with recapture provisions, a number of tenants or potential tenants themselves insisted on such terms in light of the precarious state of the Hartford economy. Moreover, some existing tenants simply refused to renew their leases, not because of the terms offered by Aetna (D) but, rather, because of the bleak retail climate in downtown Hartford. In light of the weak economy, it also was difficult, if not impossible, for Aetna (D) to attract new tenants to the Civic Center. Moreover, the trial court reasonably concluded that Aetna's (D) actions once it decided to sell the Civic Center were not the cause of De La Concha's (P) shrinking sales, which declined as a result of Hartford's economic downturn and the end of the cigar boom. Thus, Aetna's (D) elimination of direct expenditures for promotional activities had no material bearing on the De La Concha's (P) gross sales. Further, the evidence does not support the assertion that Aetna (D) undertook its policies in bad faith. Aetna (D) was free to take appropriate action to reduce the losses it had incurred for many years, and the evidence fully supported the trial court's conclusion that the ameliorative measures that it had taken were reasonably designed to achieve that end. Aetna (D), moreover, had no obligation to buy out De La Concha's (P) lease or even to relieve De La Concha (P) of its responsibilities under the lease. Aetna (D) was also not obligated to ensure De La Concha's (P) fiscal well-being. Accordingly, the trial court did not err in finding that Aetna's (D) actions were not motivated by some improper purpose or scheme but, rather, were motivated by a legitimate interest in curtailing its losses. Finally, because Aetna (D) did not breach the implied covenant of good faith and fair dealing, and was not responsible for De La Concha's (P) failure to meet the renewal conditions, it was entitled to decline De La Concha's (P) renewal of the lease. Affirmed.

## ANALYSIS

It should be noted that the implied duty of good faith and fair dealing does not create a fiduciary duty between the parties to a contract. A fiduciary is required to treat his principal as if the principal were he, and therefore he may not take advantage of the principal's incapacity, ignorance, inexperience, or even naïveté. In fact, the law contemplates that people frequently will take advantage of the ignorance of those with whom they contract, without thereby incurring liability. The duty of good faith, even expansively conceived, is not a duty of candor, since a party may make a binding contract to purchase something it knows the seller undervalues. As the *De La Concha* decision demonstrates, a party is not obliged to become an altruist toward the other party and relax the terms if the other party gets into trouble in performing his side of the bargain. Instead, a party is not permitted to engage in sharp dealing. In essence, the duty of good faith and fair dealing lies somewhere between fiduciary duty (the duty of utmost good faith) and the duty merely to refrain from active fraud.

## Quicknotes

**BAD FAITH** Conduct that is intentionally misleading or deceptive.

**IMPLIED COVENANT OF GOOD FAITH AND FAIR DEALING** An implied warranty that the parties will deal honestly in the satisfaction of their obligations and without an intent to defraud.

# Market Street Associates Limited Partnership v. Frey

Lessee's assignee (P) v. Lessor (D)

941 F.2d 588 (7th Cir. 1991).

**NATURE OF CASE:** Appeal from summary judgment dismissing action seeking specific performance.

**FACT SUMMARY:** A principal of Market Street Associates Limited Partnership (P) allegedly deliberately failed to notify General Electric Pension Trust (General Electric) (D) of a particular paragraph in a contract that could result in forfeiture of General Electric's (D) property.

## 🏛 RULE OF LAW
A party to a contract may not intentionally exploit the other party's oversight of an important fact.

**FACTS:** J.C. Penney entered into a sale-leaseback arrangement with General Electric Pension Trust (General Electric) (D) on a property. Paragraph 34 in the lease provided if General Electric (D) failed to negotiate with the lessee regarding future financing, the property could be purchased at less than market value. Years later, Market Street Associates Limited Partnership (Market Street) (P), J.C. Penney's assignee, attempted to negotiate financing with General Electric (D). General Electric (D), no longer being aware of the clause, refused to negotiate. Market Street (P) then sought to exercise its option and sued for specific performance. At his deposition, the principal of Market Street (P) primarily responsible for the property testified his counterpart at General Electric (D) might not be aware of the clause and that he had realized it during negotiations. Based on this, the district court entered summary judgment dismissing the action, holding Market Street (P) to have acted in bad faith. Market Street (P) appealed.

**ISSUE:** May a party to a contract intentionally exploit the other party's oversight of an important fact?

**HOLDING AND DECISION:** (Posner, J.) No. A party to a contract may not intentionally exploit the other party's oversight of an important fact. That parties to a contract must act in good faith does not mean, as some courts seem to believe, that the parties must act in an altruistic or fiduciary manner toward each other; they need not do so. Furthermore, it is quite legitimate for a party to use his superior knowledge to drive an advantageous bargain. However, it is one thing to have superior knowledge, but it is quite another to know that the other party is unaware of a crucial fact and take advantage of this ignorance. This constitutes sharp practice, which departs from good faith. Here, the district court held that Market Street's (P) principal had engaged in such conduct. This

may be true, but it is a factual issue, addressable only at trial, not at the summary judgment level. Reversed and remanded.

## ▶ ANALYSIS

A mutual mistake is grounds for nullifying a contract or a term thereof. Unilateral mistake may or may not be. As the court stated here, unilateral mistake combined with an opponent's overreaching may be grounds for rescission.

━━

## Quicknotes

**GOOD FAITH** An honest intention to abstain from taking advantage of another.

**MUTUAL MISTAKE** A mistake by both parties to a contract, who are in agreement as to what the contract terms should be, but the agreement as written fails to reflect that common intent; such contracts are voidable or subject to reformation.

**RESCISSION** The canceling of an agreement and the return of the parties to their positions prior to the formation of the contract.

**SPECIFIC PERFORMANCE** An equitable remedy whereby the court requires the parties to perform their obligations pursuant to a contract.

**SUMMARY JUDGMENT** Judgment rendered by a court in response to a motion made by one of the parties, claiming that the lack of a question of material fact in respect to an issue warrants disposition of the issue without consideration by the jury.

━━

# Bloor v. Falstaff Brewing Corp.

Trustee (P) v. Brewery (D)

601 F.2d 609 (2d Cir. 1979).

**NATURE OF CASE:** Action for damages for breach of contract.

**FACT SUMMARY:** Bloor (P), Reorganization Trustee of the once-successful Ballantine Brewery, brought suit alleging that Falstaff Brewing Corp. (D) had breached its contractual obligation to use its "best efforts to promote and maintain a high volume of sales" of the Ballantine brands.

---

## 🏛 RULE OF LAW
A contractual provision obligating one to use its "best efforts" to promote and maintain a high volume of sales of a certain product is breached by a policy which emphasizes profit without fair consideration of the effect on sales volume.

---

**FACTS:** Falstaff Brewing Corp. (Falstaff) (D) contracted to purchase Ballantine's brewing labels, trademarks, etc., for $4 million plus a fifty-cent royalty on each barrel of Ballantine brands sold between 1972 and 1978. The contract provided Falstaff (D) would use its best efforts to promote and maintain a high volume of sales of Ballantine products and contained a liquidated damages clause operative if Falstaff (D) ever substantially discontinued distribution of beer under the brand name "Ballantine." With policies based on profit to Falstaff (D), there was a continual decline in sales volume, and Bloor (P), the Reorganization Trustee of the company which had been Ballantine & Sons, sued to recover damages for breach of contract. The trial court found Falstaff (D) had breached the best efforts clause, for which damages were to be awarded, but that such did not trigger the liquidated damages clause.

**ISSUE:** Does one breach a contract obligating him to use best efforts to maintain a high volume of sales of an item if he makes policy based primarily on considerations of profit?

**HOLDING AND DECISION:** (Friendly, J.) Yes. Where, as in this case, a party contractually obligates itself to use its best efforts to promote and maintain a high volume of sales of a particular item, its action in making policies and decisions based primarily on considerations of profit and without fair consideration of the effect on sales volume constitutes a breach of that contractual provision, and damages may be sought. Even taking into account Falstaff's (D) right to give reasonable consideration to its own interest, including the profit interest, it breached its duty to use best efforts to maintain and promote a high sales volume with regard to Ballantine brands. It must,

therefore, pay damages based on a reasonable estimate of the royalties which would have been paid had such breach not occurred. That was the standard used by the lower court. Affirmed.

## ▶ ANALYSIS

UCC § 2-306(2) provides for the imposition of an obligation on the part of both parties to an agreement for exclusive dealing in goods to use their "best efforts." It is a codification of the judicially made rule that was formed over the years, i.e., that certain contracts carried an implied obligation to use "best efforts" because they would otherwise lack mutuality of obligation.

---

### Quicknotes

**BEST EFFORTS** In order to enforce an agreement, pursuant to which only one party appears to be furnishing consideration, the court will imply a promise on the part of the other party to use its best efforts.

**LIQUIDATED DAMAGES** An amount of money specified in a contract representing the damages owed in the event of breach.

---

*maintaing high volume ≠ high profits*

# Bovard v. American Horse Enterprises, Inc.

Seller (P) v. Manufacturer of drug paraphernalia (D)

Cal. Ct. App., 201 Cal. App. 3d 832, 247 Cal. Rptr. 340 (1988).

**NATURE OF CASE:** Appeal from dismissal of a breach of contract action.

**FACT SUMMARY:** Bovard (P) sold American Horse Enterprises (AHE) (D), a business which produced drug paraphernalia, to Ralph (D) and sought to enforce the sales contract in court.

> ### 🏛 RULE OF LAW
> Courts will not enforce contracts which violate public policy considerations.

**FACTS:** Bovard (P) contracted with Ralph (D) to sell American Horse Enterprises (AHE) (D), a company which produced drug paraphernalia. Ralph (D) defaulted on the agreement, and Bovard (P) brought a breach of contract action against AHE (D) and Ralph (D) to enforce the deal. Bovard (P) was able to recover the assets of AHE (D) but sought the remaining price due. The trial court concluded that the contract was illegal and void as contrary to public policy because AHE's (D) manufacture of drug paraphernalia violated public policy considerations. Thus, the trial court refused to enforce the contract between Bovard (P) and Ralph (D) and dismissed the complaint. Bovard (P) appealed.

**ISSUE:** Must courts enforce contracts which violate public policy considerations?

**HOLDING AND DECISION:** (Puglia, J.) No. Courts will not enforce contracts which violate public policy considerations. According to California Civil Code § 1607, the consideration of a contract must be lawful. Under § 1667, consideration is unlawful which is contrary to an express provision of law, or contrary to the policy of express laws. Whether a contract is contrary to public policy is a question of law to be determined from the circumstances of a particular case. Where a court determines that a contract is illegal, the court may not entertain an action to enforce the agreement. Generally, courts give wide latitude to parties in this matter. The Restatement (Second) of Contracts states some factors that should be considered in determining whether a contract should be unenforced as contrary to public policy: (1) the strength of the policy as manifested by the legislature; (2) the likelihood that refusing to enforce the contract would further that policy; (3) the public interest in enforcement of the deal; and (4) the possibility of forfeiture if enforcement is denied. The policy of a state against drug paraphernalia which facilitates the use of drugs is strongly implied in the statutory prohibition against possession of drugs. Refusal to enforce Bovard's (P) sale to Ralph (D) would further

this policy because it would serve notice on the manufacturers of drug paraphernalia that the judicial system will not protect their business interests. Furthermore, Bovard's (P) forfeiture was significantly mitigated by his recovery of AHE's (D) corporate assets. Therefore, the factors indicate that the trial court was correct in denying enforcement of the contract. Affirmed.

## ▶ ANALYSIS

The court also denied Ralph's (D) contention that he was entitled to attorney fees in this case. The court noted that while the attorney fees are usually available to the prevailing party even if the contract is held unenforceable, a different rule applies where the contract is illegal. In cases involving illegal contracts, neither party may recover attorney fees.

■=■

## Quicknotes

**BREACH OF CONTRACT** Unlawful failure by a party to perform its obligations pursuant to contract.

**PUBLIC POLICY** Policy administered by the state with respect to the health, safety and morals of its people in accordance with common notions of fairness and decency.

■=■

# X.L.O. Concrete Corp. v. Rivergate Corp.

Concrete subcontractor (P) v. General contractor (D)

N.Y. Ct. App. 83 N.Y.2d 513, 634 N.E.2d 158 (1994).

**NATURE OF CASE:** Certified question in action for breach of contract, account stated, and unjust enrichment.

**FACT SUMMARY:** When X.L.O. Concrete Corp. (P) completed a project allocated to it by the Mafia, Rivergate Corp. (D) refused to pay the balance due on the contract on the ground that it was part of an extortion and labor bribery operation.

## 🏛 RULE OF LAW
Antitrust defenses to a contract will be upheld where enforcement of the contract would compel the precise conduct made unlawful by the antitrust laws.

**FACTS:** The "Club" was made up of the heads of several Mafia families who controlled the subcontracting of concrete contractors in the city of New York. X.L.O. Concrete Corp. (X.L.O.) (P) was awarded a project through the Club. Rivergate Corp. (D), the general contractor, negotiated the contract in full awareness of the involvement of the Club. X.L.O. (P) fully performed the contract, but Rivergate (D) refused to pay the outstanding balance, contending that the contract violated the New York antitrust laws and was therefore per se illegal. X.L.O. (P) brought suit for breach of contract.

**ISSUE:** Will antitrust defenses to a contract be upheld if enforcement of the contract would compel the precise conduct made unlawful by the antitrust laws?

**HOLDING AND DECISION:** (Ciparick, J.) Yes. Antitrust defenses to a contract will be upheld where enforcement of the contract would compel the precise conduct made unlawful by the antitrust laws. Allowing the use of antitrust defenses often has the effect of enriching the party who has reaped the benefit of a contract and then tries to avoid paying for those benefits. Therefore, the defense should only be allowed when not enforcing the contract would prevent the activity the antitrust laws were intended to prevent. In deciding whether to permit the interposition of an antitrust defense, the court must consider whether the contract was an indivisible, effectuating component of an illegal arrangement, whether the contract price was excessive, and whether sustaining the illegality defense would render the contract void. The relative culpability, bargaining power, and knowledge of the parties should also be considered in assessing the possibility of unjust enrichment. These are all questions that require further development at trial. Affirmed.

## ◗ ANALYSIS

The court also noted that public policy favored frustrating or discouraging the sorts of schemes perpetuated by the Club. However, other remedies were available to the state attorney general, including injunctions and prosecutions, which would attack the alleged antitrust violations in a more direct fashion. In addition, state law provided that the injured party could recover treble damages and other relief for antitrust violations.

## Quicknotes

**BREACH OF CONTRACT** Unlawful failure by a party to perform its obligations pursuant to contract.

**BRIBERY** The offering, giving, receiving, or soliciting of something of value for the purpose of influencing the action of an official in the discharge of his or her public or legal duties.

**EXTORTION** The unlawful taking of property of another by threats of force.

**PUBLIC POLICY** Policy administered by the state with respect to the health, safety and morals of its people in accordance with common notions of fairness and decency.

**UNJUST ENRICHMENT** The unlawful acquisition of money or property of another for which both law and equity require restitution to be made.

# Hopper v. All Pet Animal Clinic

## Veterinarian (D) v. Former employer (P)

Wyo. Sup. Ct., 861 P.2d 531 (1993).

**NATURE OF CASE:** Appeal from grant of an injunction against the practice of veterinary medicine.

**FACT SUMMARY:** Dr. Hopper (D) competed directly with All Pet Animal Clinic (All Pet) (P), her former employer, despite a covenant not to compete contained in her employment contract with All Pet (P).

## 🏛 RULE OF LAW
A covenant not to compete is valid only if the restraint is no greater than is required for the protection of the employer, does not impose undue hardship on the employee, and is not injurious to the public.

**FACTS:** Dr. Hopper (D) worked part-time as a veterinarian for All Pet Animal Clinic (All Pet) (P). Her employment contract with All Pet (P) included a covenant not to compete by practicing small animal medicine within a five-mile radius of the city limits for a period of three years following termination. The agreement was amended and her salary increased in consideration for the noncompetition clause. After being discharged, Dr. Hopper (D) opened a small animal practice in the city and took some of All Pet's (P) clients with her. All Pet (P) sued to enjoin her practice. Nearly two years later the trial court granted the injunction but denied damages, and both parties appealed.

**ISSUE:** Is a covenant not to compete valid if the restraint is reasonable?

**HOLDING AND DECISION:** (Taylor, J.) Yes. A covenant not to compete is valid only if the restraint is no greater than is required for the protection of the employer, does not impose undue hardship on the employee, and is not injurious to the public. In this case, the increase in Dr. Hopper's (D) salary was sufficient consideration for the covenant not to compete. As to the rule of reason inquiry, All Pet (P) shared a great deal of information regarding clients, pricing, and clinic operations with Dr. Hopper (D) which she did not have prior to working there. This information had a monetary value for which All Pet (P) is entitled to protection. Secondly, the covenant not to compete was not an undue hardship for Dr. Hopper (D) because it did not prevent her from practicing large animal medicine. The geographical limitation was also reasonable. However, the three-year durational limit imposed an unreasonable restraint of trade; the term should only be for one year. The public will not be harmed by enforcing the covenant. Remanded for determination of damages.

*per P.*

**DISSENT:** (Cardine, J.) The one-year period, which the court finds reasonable, should run from the day the judgment is entered, not from the date of termination, which was two years ago.

## ▶ ANALYSIS

Although not illegal, noncompetition clauses implicate important policy considerations. Such clauses must be limited so they do not restrain competition in trade or violate an individual's right to work. In *Karpinski v. Ingrasci*, 268 N.E.2d 751 (N.Y. 1971), for example, the court refused to validate an agreement that prohibited a former employer from practicing both oral surgery and dentistry in the employer's vicinity, although it permitted an injunction as to the oral surgery. The court reasoned that public policy would not sanction the loss of a man's livelihood.

---

## Quicknotes

**INJUNCTION** A court order requiring a person to do or prohibiting that person from doing a specific act.

**PUBLIC POLICY** Policy administered by the state with respect to the health, safety and morals of its people in accordance with common notions of fairness and decency.

**RESTRICTIVE COVENANT** A promise contained in a deed to limit the uses to which the property will be made.

**RULE OF REASON** The standard for determining whether there has been a violation of § 1 of the Sherman Antitrust Act, requiring a determination of whether the activity unreasonably restrains competition as demonstrated by actual harm.

# Sheets v. Teddy's Frosted Foods

Fired employee (P) v. Employer (D)

Conn. Sup. Ct., 179 Conn. 471, 427 A.2d 385 (1980).

**NATURE OF CASE:** Appeal from dismissal of wrongful discharge lawsuit.

**FACT SUMMARY:** Sheets (P) contended that he had been terminated in violation of public policy.

## RULE OF LAW
An employee hired at-will may maintain an action for wrongful discharge if he can prove that the discharge violates public policy.

**FACTS:** Sheets (P) was hired for an indefinite term as quality control director by Teddy's Frosted Foods (Teddy's) (D). After Sheets (P) attempted to apprise management of repeated mislabeling in violation of the state food and drug law, he was terminated by Teddy's (D). He filed suit for wrongful discharge. Teddy's (D) motion to strike the complaint was granted on the grounds that there can be no liability in tort for termination of an at-will employment contract. Sheets (P) appealed.

**ISSUE:** May an employee hired at will maintain an action for wrongful discharge?

**HOLDING AND DECISION:** (Peters, J.) Yes. An employee hired at-will may maintain an action for wrongful discharge. It remains generally true that, unless the parties have provided otherwise, employment is at-will and terminable by either party. However, an employer cannot, without liability, terminate an employee for exercising some right available to him at law or from refraining to do something in violation of the law; an employee should not have to choose between a living and illegal conduct. Here, Teddy's (D) was selling mislabeled food in violation of state law; moreover, as one involved in the manufacturing process and aware of the nonconformity of the products, Sheets (P) himself would have been in violation of the law had he ignored the problem. Since Sheets (P) has stated a cause of action for intentionally tortious conduct, the motion to strike should not have been granted. Reversed and remanded.

**DISSENT:** (Cotter, C.J.) The court has created an overly broad cause of action which is sure to lead to a large number of nuisance suits by disgruntled ex-employees.

## ANALYSIS

Many states, either by decision or statute, follow the rule here. Others have stopped short of a public policy exception to at-will termination but have created a general "good cause" requirement for discharge. The leading case that first established a restriction on the employer's power to terminate involved an employee fired for refusing to submit to sexual overtures by her foreman. See *Monge v. Beebe Rubber Co.,* 316 A.2d 549 (N.H. 1974).

## Quicknotes

**AT-WILL EMPLOYMENT** The rule that an employment relationship is subject to termination at any time, or for any cause, by an employee or an employer in the absence of a specific agreement otherwise.

**CONNECTICUT UNIFORM FOOD, DRUG, AND COSMETIC ACT** Prohibits the sale of mislabeled food and imposes criminal penalties on violators.

**EMPLOYMENT-AT-WILL** The rule an employment relationship is subject to termination at any time, or for any cause, by an employee or an employer in the absence of a specific agreement otherwise.

**PUBLIC POLICY** Policy administered by the state with respect to the health, safety and morals of its people in accordance with common notions of fairness and decency.

# Balla v. Gambro, Inc.

## Former in-house counsel (P) v. Former employer (D)

Ill. Sup. Ct., 584 N.E.2d 104 (1991).

**NATURE OF CASE:** Appeal from reversal of summary judgment for defendant employer in action for retaliatory discharge.

**FACT SUMMARY:** After Balla (P) was discharged as Gambro, Inc.'s (D) in-house counsel, because he informed his employer he would stop the sale by Gambro (D) of defective dialysis equipment, Balla (P) contended that he was entitled to recover under the tort of retaliatory discharge.

### 🏛 RULE OF LAW
In-house counsel may not sue his former employer for the tort action of retaliatory discharge.

**FACTS:** Balla (P) served as Gambro, Inc.'s (D) in-house counsel and as its manager of regulatory affairs. Gambro (D) was in the business of selling kidney dialysis equipment. When Balla (P) told Gambro's (D) president to reject a shipment of equipment because it did not comply with FDA regulations, the president ignored him and sought a buyer. Upon learning this, Balla (P) told the president he would do whatever he could to stop the sale. Thereafter, Gambro (D) discharged Balla (P). Balla (P) informed the FDA of the shipment. The FDA determined the shipment was adulterated. Balla (P) sued Gambro (D) for the tort of retaliatory discharge, seeking $22 million in damages. The trial court granted summary judgment to Gambro (D), but the state's intermediate appellate court reversed and remanded. The state's highest court granted review.

**ISSUE:** May in-house counsel sue his former employer for the tort action of retaliatory discharge?

**HOLDING AND DECISION:** (Clark, J.) No. In-house counsel may not sue his former employer for the tort action of retaliatory discharge. The tort of retaliatory discharge is a limited and narrow exception to the general rule of at-will employment. Because in-house counsel are already bound by the state's rules of professional conduct, the public policy protected by the tort of retaliatory discharge—in this case, the protection of citizens' lives and property—is adequately safeguarded without extending the tort of retaliatory discharge to in-house counsel. The rules of professional conduct require an attorney, including in-house counsel, to reveal information about a client to the extent it appears necessary to prevent the client from committing an act that would result in death or serious bodily injury. Here, the adulterated equipment potentially could have caused death or bodily injury, so Balla (P) was under a duty to report the sale of the equipment. Contrary to

Balla's (P) argument, he was not faced with the choice of complying with his duties and losing his job, or not complying with his duties and keeping his job. Balla (P) had no choice in the matter: he was required to comply with his obligations as an attorney. Attorneys know or should know that at certain times in their professional career they will have to forgo economic gains in order to protect the integrity of the legal profession. Further, extending the tort of retaliatory discharge to in-house counsel would have an undesirable effect on the attorney-client relationship that exists between employers and their in-house counsel, and might have a chilling effect on attorney-client communications. Employers have the right to terminate their attorneys at any time, with or without cause. If in-house counsel were granted the right to sue their employers for retaliatory discharge, employers might be less willing to be forthright and candid with their in-house counsel, and might be hesitant to turn to their in-house counsel for advice regarding potentially questionable corporate conduct knowing that their in-house counsel could use this information in a retaliatory discharge suit. It would also be inappropriate to extend the retaliatory discharge tort to in-house counsel because doing so would force the employer to bear the cost of the attorney's compliance with the rules of professional conduct. Instead, the attorney must bear that economic burden. Finally, Balla's (P) argument that he learned of the defective equipment in his role of manager of regulatory of affairs is no supported by the evidence, since his discharge resulted from information he learned as in-house counsel, and from conduct he performed as an attorney. Reversed. The decision of the trial court is affirmed.

### ▶ ANALYSIS

Critics of the reasoning in *Balla* have observed that it appears to reflect not only an unspoken adherence to an anachronistic model of the attorney's place and role in contemporary society, but an inverted view of the consequences of the in-house attorney's essential professional role. Some critics have also commented that it seems bizarre that a lawyer employee, who has affirmative duties concerning the administration of justice, should be denied redress for discharge resulting from trying to carry out those very duties. While these critics agree with the court in *Balla* that a good beginning point for analysis may well be the employer's right to discharge the lawyer-employee, they find that that cannot be the ending point as well, given that the lawyer-client relationship exists in the

*Continued on next page.*

context of employment law as well as law regulating the lawyer's duties to third persons, the courts, and the government. Some courts have also rejected the reasoning of the court in *Balla*. For example, the California Supreme Court in *General Dynamics Corporation v. The Superior Court of San Bernardino County,* 876 P.2d 487 (Cal. 1994), reasoned that precisely because of in-house counsels' uniquely influential position they should be accorded a retaliatory discharge remedy in those instances in which mandatory ethical norms embodied in the rules of professional conduct collide with illegitimate demands of the employer and the attorney insists on adhering to his or her clear professional duty. Because it is the purpose of the retaliatory discharge tort to vindicate fundamental public policies by encouraging employees to act in ways that advance them, by providing the employee with a remedy in tort damages for resisting socially damaging organizational conduct, the courts mitigate the otherwise considerable economic and cultural pressures on the individual employee to silently conform.

■═■

## Quicknotes

**AT-WILL EMPLOYMENT** The rule that an employment relationship is subject to termination at any time, or for any cause, by an employee or an employer in the absence of a specific agreement otherwise.

**RETALIATORY DISCHARGE** The firing of an employee in retaliation for an act committed against the employer's interests.

■═■

# Simeone v. Simeone

### Wife (P) v. Husband (D)

Pa. Sup. Ct., 581 A.2d 162 (1990).

**NATURE OF CASE:** Divorce proceedings.

**FACT SUMMARY:** Catherine (P) signed a prenuptial agreement without the advice of counsel, limiting her potential recovery upon divorce to $25,000.

## 🏛 RULE OF LAW
Contracting parties are normally bound by their agreements without regard to whether the terms thereof were read and fully understood and whether the agreements embodied reasonable or good bargains.

**FACTS:** Catherine (P) and Frederick (D) entered into a prenuptial agreement on the eve of their wedding. Frederick's (D) attorney presented Catherine (P) with the document limiting her recovery upon divorce to $25,000. She signed the agreement without counsel. The couple later divorced and Catherine (P) applied for alimony. The prenuptial agreement was upheld and Catherine (P) appealed.

**ISSUE:** Are contracting parties normally bound by their agreements without regard to whether the terms thereof were read and fully understood and whether the agreements embodied reasonable or good bargains?

**HOLDING AND DECISION:** (Flaherty, J.) Yes. Contracting parties are normally bound by their agreements without regard to whether the terms thereof were read and fully understood and whether the agreements embodied reasonable or good bargains. Prenuptial agreements are subject to the same standards as other contracts. There is no merit in the contention that the agreement should be declared void because Catherine (P) failed to consult with independent counsel. Affirmed.

**CONCURRENCE:** (Papadakos, J.) I view prenuptial contracts as being in the nature of contracts of adhesion with one party generally being in a position of greater authority than the other.

**DISSENT:** (McDermott, J.) Upon divorce, a spouse should be able to avoid the operation of a prenuptial agreement with clear and convincing evidence that despite full and fair disclosure at the time of the agreement's execution it was nevertheless so inequitable and unfair that it should not be enforced.

## ▶ ANALYSIS

This decision expressly overruled the prior rule of *Estate of Geyer*, 533 A.2d 423 (1987), which held a prenuptial agreement valid "if it either made a reasonable provision for the spouse or was entered after a fair and full disclosure of the general financial positions of the parties." The court's rationale was that such a rule was based on outdated, paternalistic notions of the relationships between the sexes. The rule set forth here was intended to reflect the equal status of men and women in modern society.

---

## Quicknotes

**ADHESION CONTRACT** A contract that is not negotiated by the parties and is usually prepared by the dominant party on a "take it or leave it" basis.

**PRENUPTIAL AGREEMENT** An agreement entered into by two individuals, in contemplation of their impending marriage, in order to determine their rights and interests in property upon dissolution or death.

---

# In the Matter of Baby M

Surrogate parents (P) v. Birth mother (D)

N.J. Sup. Ct., 537 A.2d 1227 (1988).

**NATURE OF CASE:** Appeal from judgment in an action regarding a surrogacy contract.

**FACT SUMMARY:** Stern (P) sued Whitehead (D), the birth mother, to enforce a surrogacy contract and to obtain custody of Baby M.

## 🏛 RULE OF LAW
Surrogate contracts violate public policy and are unenforceable.

**FACTS:** Stern (P) and Whitehead (D) entered into a contract whereby Whitehead (D) agreed to be artificially inseminated by Stern (P) for $10,000 and to give up all parental rights to the child. Whitehead (D) carried and gave birth to Baby M. However, Whitehead (D) refused to give up Baby M, and Stern (P) sued to enforce the surrogate contract. The trial court affirmed the contract and awarded custody of Baby M to Stern (P) because that was in the best interest of the child. Whitehead (D) appealed.

**ISSUE:** Are surrogate contracts enforceable?

**HOLDING AND DECISION:** (Wilentz, C.J.) No. Surrogate contracts violate public policy and are unenforceable. The state has a strong interest in protecting children. Thus, there are laws against buying and selling children. Natural parents must not be coerced into surrendering their rights. Additionally, surrogate contracts violate a state policy that the rights of the natural parents are equal, in that the mother's right has already been contracted away. While Whitehead (D) agreed to the contract, she was not counseled as to the ramifications, nor did anyone take into consideration the rights of the child. Furthermore, the best interests of a child must remain paramount over the freedom to contract. Taking into account the best interests of Baby M, custody should still go to Stern (P), and Whitehead's (D) visitation rights should be restored. Reversed in part, affirmed in part, and remanded.

## ▌ ANALYSIS

This case highlights the evolution of the courts' involvement in the freedom to contract. Before the Great Depression, courts were highly reluctant to limit anyone's right to contract as such actions were viewed as anathema to individual liberty. More recently, courts have recognized that they have constitutional authority to regulate contracts in many ways.

## Quicknotes

**ARTIFICIAL INSEMINATION** The impregnation of a woman by the injection of semen into the uterus.

**SURROGACY CONTRACT** An agreement between parties that sets forth the parental rights and responsibilities of each party according to the role it has played in the life of the child.

■═■

## Quick Reference Rules of Law

# CHAPTER 7

# Campbell Soup Co. v. Wentz

## Soup manufacturer (P) v. Carrot farmer (D)

172 F.2d 80 (3d Cir. 1948).

**NATURE OF CASE:** Appeal from denial of equitable relief in action for specific performance.

**FACT SUMMARY:** Campbell Soup Co. (P) contended that its contract with the Wentzes (D) for delivery of a certain kind of carrot that was otherwise unavailable on the market should have been enforced through specific performance.

## 🏛 RULE OF LAW
Where a purchaser has contracted in advance for goods of a special type that are unavailable on the open market and that support the purchaser's good reputation, specific performance should be granted where the seller has breached the contract.

**FACTS:** Campbell Soup Co. (Campbell) (P) entered into a contract with the Wentzes (D) for delivery of all Chantenay red cored carrots to be grown on 15 acres of the Wentzes' (D) farm, with Campbell (P) providing the seed for the carrots. The price ranged from $23 to $30 per ton, depending on time of delivery. Campbell (P) used this particular kind of carrot in 15 of the 21 soups it manufactured, as its shape made it easy to process, and its bright color made it unique looking. The Wentzes (D) harvested around 100 tons of the carrots from the acreage covered by the contract, but they refused to deliver the carrots at the contract price because the market price had increased to $90 per ton. They sold around 62 tons to their neighbor farmer (D), who turned around and sold these on the open market, with about half going to Campbell (P). The carrots were otherwise virtually unobtainable on the open market. Campbell (P), suspecting that the neighbor (D) was selling "contract" carrots, brought suit to enjoin further sales of the contract carrots to anyone other than Campbell (P) and for specific performance. The district court denied the requested equitable relief, and the court of appeals granted review.

**ISSUE:** Where a purchaser has contracted in advance for goods of a special type that are unavailable on the open market and that support the purchaser's good reputation, should specific performance be granted where the seller has breached the contract?

**HOLDING AND DECISION:** (Goodrich, J.) Yes. Where a purchaser has contracted in advance for goods of a special type that are unavailable on the open market and that support the purchaser's good reputation, specific performance should be granted where the seller has breached the contract. The general rule, that specific performance of a contract for the sale of chattels is appropriate where the

legal remedies would be inadequate, applies here. Based on the particular facts of this case, legal remedies would be inadequate since it was virtually impossible to obtain Chantenay red cored carrots on the open market, the carrots' blunt shape makes them easier to process, and its color, being brighter than that of other carrots, makes their appearance uniform in Campbell's (P) products. This uniformity of appearance in a food article marketed throughout the country and sold under the manufacturer's name is of considerable commercial significance and one that should be considered in determining whether a substitute ingredient is just as good as the original. The district court concluded that Campbell (P) had failed to objectively establish that the carrots are not unique goods, but since that is not purely a factual conclusion but rather a legal one, and since the appropriateness of specific performance may be judged by a subjective standard, that issue must be revisited. Applying the general standards applicable to determining the adequacy of a legal remedy, specific performance should have been granted because a legal remedy here would have been inadequate given that the carrots were of a special type, were unavailable on the open market, had been contracted for in advance in anticipation of Campbell's (P) needs, and were part of the uniformity of appearance on which Campbell (P) had built its good reputation. Affirmed.

## ▶ ANALYSIS

The court in this case ultimately affirmed the district court's denial of equitable relief because it found that the contract was too one-sided in favor of Campbell (P). The court's determination that legal remedies would be inadequate is questionable. It seems that Campbell's (P) damages could have been ascertained by calculating the difference between what it had to pay the neighbor farmer (D), $90, and the contract prices. The court's conclusion that Campbell (P) could not have obtained the carrots is also questionable, since Campbell (P) was in fact able to obtain them from the neighbor (D), albeit at a price higher than specified in the contract.

▬▬▮

### Quicknotes

**BREACH OF CONTRACT** Unlawful failure by a party to perform its obligations pursuant to contract.

▬▬▮

# Klein v. PepsiCo, Inc.

Corporate jet purchaser (P) v. Seller (D)

845 F.2d 76 (4th Cir. 1988).

**NATURE OF CASE:** Appeal from an order for specific performance in an action for breach of contract.

**FACT SUMMARY:** When an agreement between Klein (P) and PepsiCo, Inc. (D) for the purchase and sale of a corporate jet fell through, Klein (P) sued for breach of contract in an effort to force PepsiCo (D) to honor the agreement.

## 🏛 RULE OF LAW
A specific performance is inappropriate where damages are recoverable and adequate.

**FACTS:** Universal Jet Sales, Inc. (UJS) negotiated with PepsiCo, Inc. (D) to purchase a Gulfstream G-II corporate jet which UJS intended to resell to Klein (P). After an inspection and some dickering, the parties arrived at a price, sending each other "offering" and "accepting" tel-exes. Klein (P) gave UJS a deposit to give to PepsiCo (D), and PepsiCo (D) agreed to pay for repairs needed on the right engine. However, PepsiCo's (D) chairman withdrew the plane from the market two days later. When Klein (P) demanded delivery, PepsiCo (D) refused, contending that discussions had not reached the point of agreement. Klein (P) filed suit. The district court found that a contract was evidenced by the confirming telex, which "accepted" Pep-siCo's (D) offer to sell the jet. The court also ordered specific performance after finding that the aircraft was unique. PepsiCo (D) appealed.

**ISSUE:** Is specific performance appropriate where damages are recoverable and adequate?

**HOLDING AND DECISION:** (Ervin, J.) No. Specific performance is inappropriate where damages are recoverable and adequate. Here, however, money damages would make Klein (P) whole. UJS bought two G-IIs which they offered to Klein (P) after this deal fell through, and Klein (P) made bids on two other G-IIs after PepsiCo (D) withdrew its aircraft from the market. Thus, it is very difficult to support a ruling that the aircraft was so unique it merited an order of specific performance. Affirmed in part, reversed in part and remanded.

## ▌ ANALYSIS

Under the UCC, Klein (P) had two alternative remedies from which to choose once he realized that the G-II he wanted was no longer for sale. Under UCC § 2-713, it is assumed that he could have mitigated his loss by purchasing a substitute aircraft. His damages would then have been the difference between the market price and the contract price. Alternatively, had he actually "covered" by purchasing another G-II, his damages would have been the difference between the cost of "cover" and the contract price.

■━■

## Quicknotes

**BREACH OF CONTRACT** Unlawful failure by a party to perform its obligations pursuant to contract.

**COVER** The purchase of an alternate supply of goods by a buyer, after a seller has breached a contract for sale, for which the buyer may recover the difference between the cost of the substituted goods and the price of the original goods pursuant to the contract, so long as the buyer puchased the alternate goods in good faith and without unreasonable delay.

**SPECIFIC PERFORMANCE** An equitable remedy whereby the court requires the parties to perform their obligations pursuant to a contract.

■━■

# Morris v. Sparrow

Ranch owner (D) v. Cowboy (P)

Ark. Sup. Ct., 225 Ark. 1019, 287 S.W.2d 583 (1956).

**NATURE OF CASE:** Appeal from order requiring delivery of personal property in action for specific performance.

**FACT SUMMARY:** Morris (D) contended that Sparrow (P) could not enforce through equity, by an action for specific performance, an agreement to deliver to Sparrow (P) a horse in exchange for work performed by Sparrow (P) on Morris's (D) ranch.

## RULE OF LAW
An action for specific performance for the delivery of personal property may be maintained in equity where the personal property is unique.

**FACTS:** Morris (D) owned a ranch and participated in rodeos, as did Sparrow (P), a cowboy who was adept at training horses. The men met at a rodeo and then both went to Morris's (D) ranch. They agreed that while Morris (D) left the ranch for 16 weeks, Sparrow (P) would take care of it for $400. Sparrow (P) claimed that in addition to the money consideration, Morris (D) promised him a horse named Keno. At the time Sparrow (P) arrived at Morris's (D) ranch, Keno was unbroken, but during his spare time, Sparrow (P) trained the horse to the point where, with very little extra training, Keno would be a first class roping horse. Although Morris (D) paid Sparrow (P) the money, he refused to give him Keno, contending that Sparrow (P) was to get Keno only if he did a good job, which Morris (D) contended Sparrow (P) failed to do. Sparrow (P) brought suit in equity for specific performance of the alleged agreement, and the trial court ordered that Morris (D) deliver Keno to him. The state's highest court granted review.

**ISSUE:** May an action for specific performance for the delivery of personal property be maintained in equity where the personal property is unique?

**HOLDING AND DECISION:** (Robinson, J.) Yes. An action for specific performance for the delivery of personal property may be maintained in equity where the personal property is unique. Ordinarily, equity will not enforce through specific performance a contract for the sale of chattels. However, it will do so where special and peculiar reasons exist that make it impossible for the injured party to obtain relief through a suit at law for damages. Here, Sparrow's (P) turning Keno from an unbroken horse into a roping horse would have a peculiar and unique value, so that if Sparrow (P) were otherwise entitled to prevail, he should get the horse and not its monetary market value. As to whether the contract was conditional (i.e., depending on

how Sparrow (P) performed), that is a fact question that was determined by the trial court, and that court's determination was not against the preponderance of the evidence. Affirmed.

## ANALYSIS

The court here assumes that Sparrow (P) could not have obtained sufficient relief from money damages, but theoretically, expectation damages may have made him whole. Expectation damages are based on the particular promisee (here, Sparrow (P)) and, as noted in Restatement § 347, look to the loss in value to the promisee plus any other loss, including incidental or consequential loss, less any costs avoided by not having to perform. Here, the loss in value to Sparrow (P) through Morris's (D) breach could be measured by market value. The "other loss" potentially could have been measured by the value to Sparrow (P) of training an unbroken horse and turning it into a roping horse and of owning such a horse. While it is difficult to place a value on these "other losses" it is not impossible. Often when performance might provide a peculiar and unique value, courts express the view that money damages are too speculative or uncertain, but in essence they are ruling that it might be too difficult, or a drain on court resources, to make such a determination.

━■━■

## Quicknotes

**EXPECTATION DAMAGES** Damages awarded in actions for non-performance of a contract, which are calculated by subtracting the injured party's actual dollar position as a result of the breach from that party's expected dollar position had the breach not occurred.

**SPECIFIC PERFORMANCE** An equitable remedy whereby the court requires the parties to perform their obligations pursuant to a contract.

━■━■

# Laclede Gas Co. v. Amoco Oil Co.

Distributing utility (P) v. Propane supplier (D)

522 F.2d 33 (8th Cir. 1975).

**NATURE OF CASE:** Appeal from denial of damages or specific performance for breach of contract.

**FACT SUMMARY:** After Amoco Oil Co. (D) breached a long-term propane supply contract, Laclede Gas Co. (P) sought specific performance of the contract.

## 🏛 RULE OF LAW
Specific performance is available as a remedy for breach of a long-term supply contract.

**FACTS:** A contract existed between Laclede Gas Co. (Laclede) (P) and Amoco Oil Co. (Amoco) (D) for the latter to supply the former with propane on a long-term basis. Laclede (P) had no other long-term propane supply contracts. A dispute arose between Laclede (P) and Amoco (D) as to Amoco's (D) obligations. Amoco (D) eventually abrogated the contract. Laclede (P) sued for specific performance or, in the alternative, damages. The trial court found the contract void and dismissed the suit. Laclede (P) appealed.

**ISSUE:** Is specific performance available as a remedy for breach of a long-term supply contract?

**HOLDING AND DECISION:** (Ross, J.) Yes. Specific performance is available as a remedy for breach of a long-term supply contract. The court first held the contract enforceable and then discussed damages. While ordering specific performance is within a trial court's discretion, that discretion is limited. When a litigant can show that damages will not make him whole, and that no policy considerations militate against specific performance, it shall be granted. Here, Laclede (P) had no other long-term supply contracts, so no amount of damages could guarantee it a supply of propane. This court does not believe that such a remedy would require onerous court supervision, nor does it believe the contract to be so uncertain as to make specific performance unworkable. This being so, Laclede (P) is entitled to specific performance as a matter of law. Reversed and remanded.

## ▶ ANALYSIS

Amoco (D) made one additional argument, to which the court gave no consideration. It argued that mutuality of remedy did not exist, and this barred specific performance. At common law in England, authority existed for the proposition that specific performance had to be available to both parties for any party to obtain it. This rule has long since been abandoned.

## Quicknotes

**MUTUALITY OF REMEDY** An equitable doctrine that one party to a contract may not have available an equitable remedy if the other party does not have such remedy available.

**SPECIFIC PERFORMANCE** An equitable remedy whereby the court requires the parties to perform their obligations pursuant to a contract.

# Northern Delaware Industrial Development Corp. v. E.W. Bliss Co.

## Property owner (P) v. Contractor (D)

Del. Ct. Ch., 245 A.2d 431 (1968).

**NATURE OF CASE:** Action seeking an order of specific performance of a term in a construction contract.

**FACT SUMMARY:** Northern Delaware Industrial Development Corp. and Phoenix Steel Corp. (Phoenix) (collectively "plaintiffs") (P) contended that the court should exercise its equitable jurisdiction to order E.W. Bliss Co. (Bliss) (D), a general contractor modernizing Phoenix's (P) steel plant, to hire and put more workers on the job so Bliss (D) could stay on schedule as called for in the construction contract.

---

> ### 🏛 RULE OF LAW
> Absent special circumstances or public policy concerns, specific performance of a term of a construction contract will not be ordered where it would be impractical to carry out such an order.

---

**FACTS:** E.W. Bliss Co. (Bliss) (D), a general contractor, contracted to modernize the steel plant owned by Phoenix Steel Corp. (Phoenix) (P), which was spread out over 60 acres, for $27,500,000. When Bliss (D) fell behind schedule, Phoenix (P), along with the Northern Delaware Industrial Development Corp. (collectively "plaintiffs") (P) sought to have the court exercise its equitable jurisdiction and issue an order compelling Bliss (D) to requisition 300 more workmen for a night shift, thus requiring Bliss (D) to put on the job, as it contracted to do, the number of men required to make up a full second shift at the Phoenix (P) plant site during the period when one of the Phoenix (P) mills had to be shut down in order that its modernization could be carried out under the contract.

**ISSUE:** Absent special circumstances or public policy concerns, will specific performance of a term of a construction contract be ordered where it would be impractical to carry out such an order?

**HOLDING AND DECISION:** (Marvel, V.C.) No. Absent special circumstances or public policy concerns, specific performance of a term of a construction contract will not be ordered where it would be impractical to carry out such an order. A court of equity has jurisdiction to order specific performance of construction contract, especially where the construction is tied to a contract for the sale of land and the construction in question is largely finished. However, a court exercising its discretion should not order specific performance of a construction contract where it would be impractical to carry out the order, unless there are special circumstances or the public interest is directly involved. Here, the contract provision relied on by the plaintiffs (P) is insufficiently precise, and it would be im-

practical for the court to supervise the requested order. The plaintiffs (P), instead of seeking specific performance, should pursue their remedies at law for any damages they have sustained as a result of Bliss's (D) delays. [Subsequently, on a motion for reargument, the court denied the plaintiffs' (P) motion on the ground performance of a personal services contract, even one of a unique nature, will not be enforced through specific performance.]

## ▶ ANALYSIS

This case illustrates the principle that, generally, construction contracts will not be enforced through an order for specific performance. Some exceptions to this general arise where: the contract is defined and certain; the defendant has contracted to construct a defined project on his own land; the defendant has agreed to build on lands acquired from the plaintiff; or there has been a part performance so that the defendant is enjoying the benefits in kind.

■=■

## Quicknotes

**PERSONAL SERVICES CONTRACT** A contract whose bargained-for performance includes specific conduct or activity that must be performed by one party.

**SPECIFIC PERFORMANCE** An equitable remedy whereby the court requires the parties to perform their obligations pursuant to a contract.

■=■

# Walgreen Co. v. Sara Creek Property Co.

Tenant (P) v. Landlord (D)

966 F.2d 273 (7th Cir. 1992).

**NATURE OF CASE:** Appeal from a grant of permanent injunctive relief in suit for breach of contract.

**FACT SUMMARY:** Walgreen Co. (P) filed suit to enforce a clause contained in its lease agreement that provided that no space in the mall would be rented to a competing pharmacy.

## 🏛 RULE OF LAW
Where the costs of injunctive relief are less than the costs of a damages remedy, injunctive relief is an appropriate remedy, even when the damages remedy is not shown to be inadequate.

**FACTS:** Walgreen Co. (P) operated a pharmacy in a mall under a lease that provided that the landlord, Sara Creek Property Co. (Sara Creek) (D), would not lease space to anyone else who wanted to operate a pharmacy or store containing a pharmacy in the mall. After losing its primary tenant, Sara Creek (D) informed Walgreen (P) that it intended to lease space to Phar-Mor, a "deep discount" chain. The Phar-Mor store would include a pharmacy. Walgreen (P) filed a diversity suit for breach of contract and asked for injunctive relief mandating compliance with the nonrental clause. Evidence was offered by Sara Creek (D) that Walgreen's (P) damages were readily ascertainable. The injunction was granted and Sara Creek (D) appealed.

**ISSUE:** Where the costs of injunctive relief are less than the costs of a damages remedy, is injunctive relief an appropriate remedy even when the damages remedy is not shown to be inadequate?

**HOLDING AND DECISION:** (Posner, J.) Yes. Where the costs of injunctive relief are less than the costs of a damages remedy, injunctive relief is an appropriate remedy, even when the damages remedy is not shown to be inadequate. Generally, the plaintiff seeking an injunction has the burden of persuasion. In the case of a permanent injunction, it must be shown that damages are inadequate. If it is likely that the costs of the damages remedy would exceed the costs of the injunction, then for the sake of efficiency, the injunction is the proper remedy. In this case, despite testimony by Sara Creek (D) to the contrary, the damages remedy would have been difficult to compute. It would have required calculation of lost profits for at least ten years into the future. An injunction, on the other hand, removes the evidentiary issue from the court. And since supervision of the injunction would rest with Walgreen (P), the future cost to the court is likewise minimal. By imposing the injunction on Sara Creek (D), the issue becomes one of private bargaining. The parties are free to

negotiate a fee for the removal of the injunction. The trial court properly weighed the costs and benefits of injunctive relief. Affirmed.

## ▶ ANALYSIS

Certain categories of contracts will regularly win equitable remedies. When subject matter is unique, such as with real estate, specific performance will usually be granted. The rationale is that money damages cannot adequately compensate for the loss of a unique item. This is, however, something of a fallacy since most individuals would be willing to bargain away rights to a specific item for some price. The problem, however, rests with the trier of fact, as it is next to impossible to determine the appropriate premium to pay for the loss of a unique item.

■=■

### Quicknotes

**BURDEN OF PERSUASION** The duty of a party to introduce evidence to support a fact that is in dispute in an action.

**INJUNCTIVE RELIEF** A court order issued as a remedy, requiring a person to do, or prohibiting that person from doing, a specific act.

**PERMANENT INJUNCTION** A remedy imposed by the court ordering a party to cease the conduct of a specific activity until the final disposition of the cause of action.

■=■

# Vitex Manufacturing. Corp. v. Caribtex Corp.

## Cloth processor (P) v. Importer (D)

377 F.2d 795 (3d Cir. 1967).

**NATURE OF CASE:** Appeal from award of damages for breach of a contract for services.

**FACT SUMMARY:** Caribtex Corp. (D) contracted with Vitex Manufacturing Co. (Vitex) (P) for the latter to process a large quantity of wool in its factory. Vitex (P) reopened a factory in order to fulfill its side of the bargain, but Caribtex (D) never sent the wool to be processed.

### 🏛 RULE OF LAW
In a claim for lost profits, overhead should be treated as part of the gross profits and recoverable as damages and should not be considered as part of the seller's (or processor's) costs.

**FACTS:** At the time of this suit, there were high tariffs on imported woolens, but if such goods were imported into the Virgin Islands and were processed so that their finished value exceeded importation value by at least 50 percent, then high tariffs to importation into the continental United States could be avoided. This enabled Virgin Island-processed wool to enjoy a price advantage. So that Congress would not be moved to change the situation, the island government imposed quotas on processors, limiting their output. Vitex Manufacturing Corp. (Vitex) (P) had not yet fulfilled its quota and so contracted to process 125,000 yards of woolen material at $0.26 a yard with Caribtex Corp. (D). Vitex (P) reopened a closed plant to begin processing, but because Caribtex (D) was unsure as to whether the wool could enter duty-free after processing, it did not send any wool to Vitex (P) for processing. Vitex (P) received an award of $21,114 for lost profits, and Caribtex (D) appealed, arguing that overhead should have been included in the calculation.

**ISSUE:** In a claim for lost profits, should overhead be treated as part of the gross profits and recoverable as damages, and should it not be considered as part of the seller's (or processor's) costs?

**HOLDING AND DECISION:** (Staley, C.J.) Yes. In a claim for lost profits, overhead should be treated as part of the gross profits and recoverable as damages and should not be considered as part of the seller's (or processor's) costs. Because of the uncertainty in exactly setting Vitex's (P) costs due to Caribtex's (D) wrongful conduct in repudiating its contract before Vitex (P) could perform, Caribtex (D) was not permitted to benefit by the uncertainty it caused. Overhead includes the continuous expenses of the business irrespective of the outlay on a particular contract. While Vitex (P) did not expressly seek recovery for overhead, if a portion of that expense was allocated as costs to the Caribtex (D) contract, the damages should be reduced accordingly.

However, the court believed it was the better rule to treat overhead as part of the gross profits rather than as part of the seller's costs in a claim for lost profits. If Vitex (P) had not entered into any contracts including the Caribtex (D) contract for the rest of the year, Vitex's (P) profits would have been found by deducting its production costs and overhead from gross receipts yielded in previous transactions. Its overhead would have remained constant whether or not it entered into the Caribtex (D) contract. Its additional expenses were incurred in reopening the plant, recalling employees, buying fuel oil, and buying chemicals. Since overhead remained constant, it could not be attributable to or affected by the Caribtex (D) contract and cannot be considered as a cost of Vitex's (P) performance deductible from the gross proceeds from the Caribtex (D) contract. Affirmed.

### ▶ ANALYSIS

First, the breach here was straightforward and complete. Vitex (P) relied on the contract by reopening its plant, recalling employees, and taking other necessary steps to begin processing. For this, Vitex (P) received reliance damages. Generally, most damages prayed for are awarded upon a willful breach. The general formula, "damages = loss in value cost avoided + other loss," came into play here. Vitex's (P) loss on the bargain was the difference between loss in value and cost avoided. The loss in value to the injured party is the difference in the value of what the other party was to have done and of what he did. The cost avoided arises when the breach is total, which is the money saved by being excused from completing performance. Therefore, the loss on the bargain plus any other loss resulting from the breach equals the damages. Other loss may be any physical harm to the injured party's property or person and any expenses incurred by him in an attempt to salvage the transaction after the breach.

---

### Quicknotes

**BREACH OF CONTRACT** Unlawful failure by a party to perform its obligations pursuant to contract.

**OVERHEAD** The necessary costs associated with the operation of a business that are constant and are unrelated to the costs of production.

*Sale of goods*

# Laredo Hides Co., Inc. v. H&H Meat Products Co., Inc.

## Leather purchaser (P) v. Seller (D)

Tex. Civ. App. Ct., 513 S.W.2d 210 (1974).

**NATURE OF CASE:** Action for damages for breach of contract.

**FACT SUMMARY:** When H&H Meat Products Co., Inc. (D) refused to continue to deliver hides under its contract with Laredo Hides Co. (Laredo) (P), Laredo (P) purchased them from other sources and sued to recover the price difference.

🏛 **RULE OF LAW**
When a seller wrongfully repudiates a contract or fails to make delivery of the goods thereunder, the buyer may "cover" by obtaining such goods elsewhere and sue the seller for the difference between the cost of cover and the contract price plus any incidental or consequential damages.

**FACTS:** Laredo Hides Co., Inc. (Laredo) (P) contracted with H&H Meat Products Co., Inc. (H&H) (D) to buy its entire production of hides during the period March through December 1972. When a check Laredo (P) sent was delayed in the mail, H&H (D) issued an ultimatum for immediate payment and stated it considered the contract breached and canceled when such was not forthcoming. Thus, H&H (D) stopped delivering hides to Laredo (P), which had already contracted with a tannery for sale of all the hides it expected to receive under its contract with H&H (D). Laredo (P) then proceeded to purchase substitute hides from other dealers and sued H&H (D) for damages. It had to pay $142,254.48 more for the hides than it would have under the contract with H&H (D) and incurred additional transportation and handling costs of $3,448.95. The trial court rendered judgment for H&H (D), and Laredo (P) appealed.

**ISSUE:** Upon wrongful repudiation by the seller, can the buyer "cover" by buying substitute goods elsewhere and sue the seller for the difference between the cost of cover and the contract price plus any incidental or consequential damages?

**HOLDING AND DECISION:** (Bissett, J.) Yes. The Texas Business and Commerce Code, like the Uniform Commercial Code, allows a buyer faced with a seller's wrongful repudiation of a contract or his failure to make delivery of the goods thereunder to "cover" by making a good-faith reasonable purchase of substitute goods elsewhere without unreasonable delay. The buyer can then recover from the seller as damages the difference between the cost of "cover" and the contract price together with any incidental or consequential damages or he can have damages measured by the difference between the market price at the time when the buyer learned of the breach and the contract price together with any incidental and consequential damages. In this case, H&H (D) wrongfully repudiated the contract. Laredo (P) acted properly to "cover" and is thus entitled to recover the difference between the "cover" price and the contract price plus the additional expenses thus engendered. Reversed.

▶ *ANALYSIS*

The rule on "cover" is found in UCC § 2-712, in that article of the Code which covers contracts for the sale of goods only. Under this very innovative rule, when a buyer complies with the requirements of § 2-712, his purchase of substitute goods is presumed proper and the seller has the burden of proving that "cover" was not properly obtained.

■━■

## Quicknotes

**BREACH OF CONTRACT** Unlawful failure by a party to perform its obligations pursuant to contract.

**COVER** The purchase of an alternate supply of goods by a buyer, after a seller has breached a contract for sale, for which the buyer may recover the difference between the cost of the substituted goods and the price of the original goods pursuant to the contract, so long as the buyer purchases the alternate goods in good faith and without unreasonable delay.

**REPUDIATION** The actions or statements of a party to a contract that evidence his intent not to perform, or to continue performance, of his duties or obligations thereunder.

■━■

- can you recover b/c it's close

- it has to be a reasonable purchase.

Contract price – cost avoided = to put me at the same place

Sale dgoods.

# R.E. Davis Chemical Corp. v. Diasonics, Inc.

### Medical facility operator (P) v. Equipment manufacturer (D)

826 F.2d 678 (7th Cir. 1987).

**NATURE OF CASE:** Appeal of summary judgment awarding damages as restitution.

**FACT SUMMARY:** Diasonics, Inc. (D) claimed it lost a "volume sale" when R.E. Davis Chemical Corp. (P) breached a contract of sale.

> 🏛 **RULE OF LAW**
> An aggrieved seller may recover, after resale, lost profits from the original sale if he can show that the subsequent sale would have occurred absent the breach and would have been profitable.

**FACTS:** R.E. Davis Chemical Corp. (Davis) (P) contracted to purchase certain diagnostic equipment from Diasonics, Inc. (D). Davis (P) placed a $300,000 deposit. Davis (P) later reneged, and Diasonics (D) resold the equipment at a comparable price. Diasonics (D) contended it was entitled to keep the deposit as lost profits from the sale. Davis (P) sued for restitution. The district court granted summary judgment in favor of Davis (P), and Diasonics (D) appealed.

**ISSUE:** May an aggrieved seller recover, after resale, lost profits from the original sale if he can show that the subsequent sale would have occurred absent the breach and would have been profitable?

**HOLDING AND DECISION:** (Cudahy, J.) Yes. An aggrieved seller may recover, after resale, lost profits from the original sale if he can show that the subsequent sale would have occurred absent the breach and would have been profitable. UCC § 2-708 concerns itself with damages from lost profits. Section 2-706 measures damages in the traditional contract price less market price manner. The UCC does not give much guidance as to when any particular measure is applicable. The district court apparently concluded that when § 2-706 is available, § 2-708 should not be used. This approach is supported neither by law nor by good reasoning. Simply because a seller has availed himself of the chance to resell an item is no reason to deny him lost profits, so long as he can show the subsequent sale would have occurred anyway, as in the case of a volume seller. The seller must show, however, that the subsequent sale would have occurred even if the original breach had not and would have generated a profit. This matter must be resolved at trial. Reversed and remanded.

## ▶ ANALYSIS

"Lost volume" sales are as legitimate as more traditional types. However, courts vary as to the level of proof required. Some have required proof involving economic/ market condition analysis, such as the existence of a "seller's market." Others have been more lenient.

■■■

## Quicknotes

**LOST PROFITS** The potential value of income earned or goods which are the subject of the contract; may be used in calculating damages where the contract has been breached.

**LOST-VOLUME SELLER** A seller who can accommodate more than one buyer and for whom a buyer's breach does not release the goods for sale to another customer; in such a case, the appropriate measure of damages is the net profit the seller would have earned pursuant to the sale.

**RESTITUTION** The return or restoration of what the defendant has gained in a transaction to prevent the unjust enrichment of the defendant.

**SUMMARY JUDGMENT** A judgment rendered by a court in response to a motion by one of the parties, claiming that the lack of a question of material fact in respect to an issue warrants disposition of the issue without consideration by the jury.

**UCC § 2-706** Provides that where resale by the seller is made in good faith and in a commercially reasonable manner, the seller may recover the difference between the resale price and the contract price.

**UCC § 2-708** The measure of damages for non-acceptance or repudiation by the buyer is the difference between the market price at the time and place for tender and the unpaid contract price, plus incidental damages, minus expenses saved due to the breach.

■■■

# United States v. Algernon Blair, Inc.

Federal government (P) v. Prime contractor (D)

479 F.2d 638 (4th Cir. 1973).

**NATURE OF CASE:** Action to recover in quantum meruit the value of labor and equipment furnished.

**FACT SUMMARY:** Coastal Steel Erectors, a subcontractor, brought suit in the name of the United States (P) against Algernon Blair, Inc. (D), the prime contractor on a government project, to recover in quantum meruit the value of the labor and materials it had furnished up to the point at which it justifiably ceased work.

## 🏛 RULE OF LAW
A promisee is allowed to recover in quantum meruit the value of services he gave to a defendant who breached the contract irrespective of whether he would have lost money had the contract been fully performed and would thus be precluded from recovering in a suit on the contract.

**FACTS:** Algernon Blair, Inc. (Algernon) (D) was the prime contractor on a U.S. government project. Coastal Steel Erectors (Coastal), a subcontractor on the project, furnished materials and labor up to the point that Algernon (D) breached its contract with Coastal. At that point, Coastal ceased work and brought an action under the Miller Act, in the name of the United States (P), to recover in quantum meruit the value of the equipment and labor it had theretofore supplied. The district court found Algernon (D) had breached the contract, but held that Coastal would have lost money on the contract had it been fully performed. For this reason, it denied recovery, and Coastal appealed.

**ISSUE:** Even if a promisee would have lost money had he completed the contract, can he nonetheless recover in quantum meruit the value of services he gave to a defendant who breached the contract?

**HOLDING AND DECISION:** (Craven, J.) Yes. Regardless of whether or not the promisee would have lost money had he completed the contract, he can recover in quantum meruit the value of the services he gave to a defendant who breached the contract. It is an accepted principle of contract law, often applied in the case of construction contracts, that the promisee upon breach has the option to forgo any suit on the contract and claim only the reasonable value of his performance. Thus, Coastal can recover for the equipment and labor it supplied despite the fact that it would have lost money on the contract and would thus have been unable to recover in a suit on the contract. Recovery in quantum meruit is measured by the reasonable value of the performance and is undiminished by any loss which would have been incurred by complete performance. Reversed and remanded for findings as to the reasonable value of the equipment and labor supplied by Coastal.

## ▶ ANALYSIS

The applicable standard in determining the "reasonable value" of services rendered is the amount for which such services could have been purchased from one in the plaintiff's position at the time and place the services were rendered. Some courts have held that the contract price is not only evidence of the reasonable value but is a ceiling on recovery, but others disagree. The rationale is that one should not recover more for part performance than he would have upon full performance.

■■■

## Quicknotes

**QUANTUM MERUIT** Equitable doctrine allowing recovery for labor and materials provided by one party, even though no contract was entered into, in order to avoid unjust enrichment by the benefited party.

■■■

# Jacob & Youngs v. Kent

## Contractor (P) v. Customer (D)

N.Y. Ct. App., 230 N.Y. 239, 129 N.E. 889 (1921).

**NATURE OF CASE:** Appeal from grant of new trial in action for damages for breach of a construction contract.

**FACT SUMMARY:** Jacob & Youngs (P) was hired to build a $77,000 country home for Kent (D). When the dwelling was completed, it was discovered that through an oversight, pipe, not of Reading manufacture (though of comparable quality and price), which had been specified in the contract, was used. Kent (D) refused to make final payment of $3,483.46 upon learning of this.

### 🏛 RULE OF LAW
An omission, both trivial and innocent, will sometimes be atoned for by allowance of the remitting damage and will not always be the breach of a condition to be followed by forfeiture. For damages in construction contracts, the owner is entitled merely to the difference between the value of the structure if built to specifications and the value it has as constructed.

**FACTS:** Jacob & Youngs (Jacob) (P) built a country home for $77,000 for Kent (D) and sued for $3,483.46 which remained unpaid. Almost a year after completion, Kent (D) discovered that not all pipe in the home was of Reading manufacture as specified in the contract. Kent (D) ordered the plumbing replaced, but as it was encased in the walls, except in those spots where it must necessarily remain exposed, Jacob (P) refused to replace the pipe, stating that the pipe used was of comparable price and quality. It appears that the omission was neither fraudulent nor willful and was due to oversight. Kent (D) refused to pay the balance of the construction cost still due. The trial court directed a verdict for Kent (D), but the appellate division reversed, and granted a new trial.

**ISSUE:** Was the omission by Jacob (P) so trivial and innocent so as not to be a breach of the condition?

**HOLDING AND DECISION:** (Cardozo, J.) Yes. Where the significance of the default or omission is grievously out of proportion to the oppression of the forfeiture, the breach is considered to be trivial and innocent. A change will not be tolerated if it is so dominant and pervasive so as to frustrate the purpose of the contract. The contractor cannot install anything he believes to be just as good. It is a matter of degree judged by the purpose to be served, the desire to be gratified, the excuse for deviation from the letter, and the cruelty of enforced adherence. Under the circumstances, the measure of damages should not be the cost of replacing the pipe which would be great. Instead, the difference in value between the dwelling as specified and the dwelling as constructed should be the measure, even though it may be nominal or nothing. Usually, the owner is entitled to the cost of completion, but not where it is grossly unfair and out of proportion to the good to be obtained. This simply is a rule to promote justice when there is substantial performance with trivial deviation. Affirmed.

## ▶ ANALYSIS

Substantial performance cannot occur where the breach is intentional, as it is the antithesis of material breach. The part unperformed must not destroy the purpose or value of the contract. Because here there is a dissatisfied land owner who stands to retain the defective structure built on his land, there arises the problem of unjust enrichment. Usually, it would appear that the owner would pocket the damages he collected rather than remedying the defect by tearing out the wrong pipe and replacing it with the specified pipe. The owner would have a home substantially in compliance and a sum of money greatly in excess of the harm suffered by him. Note that under the doctrine of de minimis non curat lex, which means "the law is not concerned with trifles" (*Black's Law Dictionary*, Ninth Edition), trivial defects, even if willful, will be ignored. The party who claims substantial performance has still breached the contract and is liable for damages but in a lesser amount than for a willful breach.

■=■

## Quicknotes

**DE MINIMIS NON CURAT LEX** Not of sufficient significance to invoke legal action. Shortened to "de minimis."

**FORFEITURE** The loss of a right or interest as a penalty for failing to fulfill an obligation.

**SUBSTANTIAL PERFORMANCE** Performance of all the essential obligations pursuant to an agreement.

■=■

# Plante v. Jacobs

## Contractor (P) v. Customer (D)

Wis. Sup. Ct., 10 Wis. 2d 567, 103 N.W.2d 296 (1960).

**NATURE OF CASE:** Action to establish a lien upon property for breach of a construction contract.

**FACT SUMMARY:** When the Jacobses (D) believed that Plante (P), whom they had contracted to build a home on their lot for $26,765, used faulty workmanship and incomplete construction, they stopped further payments to him after having paid $20,000. Plante (P) then refused to complete and sued to establish a lien on the property.

## 🏛 RULE OF LAW
There can be no recovery on a contract as distinguished from quantum meruit unless there is substantial performance which is defined as where the performance meets the essential purpose of the contract.

**FACTS:** Plante (P) contracted with Frank and Carol Jacobs (D) to furnish materials and construct a house on their lot in accordance with plans and specifications for $26,765. Plante (P) received $20,000 during the course of construction when a dispute arose between the parties as to faulty workmanship and incomplete construction. The Jacobses (D) refused to continue payments, and Plante (P) refused to complete construction. Plante (P) then sued to establish a lien on the property so as to recover the unpaid balance plus extras. The Jacobses (D) alleged that faulty workmanship on at least 20 items plus decreasing the width of the living room by one foot did not amount to substantial performance.

**ISSUE:** Can there be recovery on a contract without there having been substantial performance?

**HOLDING AND DECISION:** (Hallows, J.) No. There can be no recovery on a contract as distinguished from quantum meruit unless there is substantial performance which is defined as where the performance meets the essential purpose of the contract. When applied to house construction, this does not mean that every detail must be in strict compliance with specifications and plans. Here, the specifications were standard printed forms, and the plan was a "stock floor plan." While the Jacobses (D) received a house with which they were dissatisfied, the contract was substantially performed. The misplacing of a wall by one foot so as to narrow the living room did not affect the value of the home. Gutters and rainspouts, kitchen cabinets, and clothes closet poles were omitted. As the measure of damages for substantial, but incomplete, performance, Plante (P) should receive the contract price less the damages caused the Jacobses (D) by incomplete perfor-

mance. For faulty construction, the "diminished value" rule pertains which is the difference between the value of the house as it would stand complete and as it stands faulty but substantially complete. The trial court applied the "cost of repair" rule which allows the cost to repair a number of small defects and omissions. If the separation of defects would lead to confusion, the diminished value rule can be applied to all defects. There was no confusion here in separating the defects. Whether a defect comes under the diminished value or cost of repair rule depends upon the magnitude of defect. However, the trial court was not in error in applying the cost of repair rule (usually applied to small items) to repairing a patio floor, plaster cracks in ceiling, and repair of a nonstructural patio wall. The misplaced wall in the living room was of a magnitude sufficient as to place it under the diminished value rule, but as misplacing the wall was of no effect to the value of the house and as it would have been economical waste to move it, no legal damage was suffered. Affirmed.

## ▌ ANALYSIS

The doctrine of substantial performance is applied when the unperformed portion does not destroy the purpose or value of the contract. Of course, this is like saying that the breach must not be material. Here, when the Jacobses (D) occupied the house, they showed that it served its purpose and thereby assumed the burden to show performance was not substantial to the terms of the contract. The primary application of the doctrine of substantial performance is with building contracts where fairly large defaults have been treated as immaterial, while a small default is often sufficient to breach a sales contract due to practical considerations. The unhappy buyer can return the goods or refuse delivery. The unhappy landowner keeps the incomplete structure; hence, greater are the possibilities for unjust enrichment.

━■

## Quicknotes

**COST OF REPAIR RULE** A measure of computing damages pursuant to a breach of contract, representing the cost to the non-breaching party to place himself in the same position he would have been in had the contract not been breached.

**DIMINISHED VALUE RULE** A measure of computing damages pursuant to a breach of contract, representing the decrease in the value of the subject matter of the

*Continued on next page.*

contract as a result of the breach, as measured by the difference in the value of the realty before and after the breach.

**LIEN** A claim against the property of another in order to secure the payment of a debt.

**QUANTUM MERUIT** Equitable doctrine allowing recovery for labor and materials provided by one party, even though no contract was entered into, in order to avoid unjust enrichment by the benefited party.

**SUBSTANTIAL PERFORMANCE** Performance of all the essential obligations pursuant to an agreement.

■══■

# Groves v. John Wunder Co.

Gravel pit lessor (P) v. Lessee (D)

Minn. Sup. Ct., 205 Minn. 163, 286 N.W. 235 (1939).

**NATURE OF CASE:** Appeal from award of damages for breach of a contract for the lease of land.

**FACT SUMMARY:** When John Wunder Co. (D) surrendered the gravel pit it leased from Groves (P), it was found to have deliberately breached the contract by removing the best and richest gravel without having restored the land to its existing grade.

## RULE OF LAW

Value of the land as distinguished from the value of the intended product of the contract, which ordinarily will be equivalent to its reasonable cost, is no proper part of any measure of damages for willful breach of a building contract.

**FACTS:** In August 1927, S. J. Groves & Sons Co. (Groves) (P) and John Wunder Co. (Wonder) (D) contracted for the latter to lease from the former Groves's (P) gravel pit and gravel screening plant (besides getting rid of Groves [P] as a competitor) for a period of seven years for $105,000. A condition of the contract was that Wunder (D) agreed to remove sand and gravel while leaving the land "at a uniform grade, substantially the same as the grade now existing." Wunder (D) deliberately breached by removing the best and richest gravel without having restored the grade and leaving the land broken and uneven. The trial court found that 288,495 cubic yards of soil would need to be excavated and deposited elsewhere at a cost of $60,000 in order to restore the grade, but if Wunder (D) had left the land at the end of the lease at the correct grade, the land's value would have been $12,160, and gave judgment in that lesser amount. Groves (P) appealed the amount of damages awarded him as too low.

**ISSUE:** Is value of the land as distinguished from the value of the intended product of the contract, which will ordinarily be equivalent to its reasonable cost, a proper part of any measure of damages for willful breach of a building contract?

**HOLDING AND DECISION:** (Stone, J.) No. Value of the land as distinguished from the value of the intended product of the contract, which ordinarily will be equivalent to its reasonable cost, is no proper part of any measure of damages for willful breach of a building contract. Where a contractor willfully and fraudulently breaches a construction contract, he cannot sue upon it nor can he have the benefit of the doctrine of substantial performance. As a willful transgressor, Wunder (D) must accept the penalty of his transgression. Nowhere will change be tolerated if it is so dominant or pervasive as in

any real or substantial measure to frustrate the purpose of the contract. Damages for a breach of a construction contract should give the injured party, as far as money is concerned, what he was promised. Therefore, Groves (P) was entitled to recover what it would cost to complete the grading as contemplated by the contract. No past decision has suggested that lack of value in the land furnished to the contractor who has bound himself to improve it is any escape from the ordinary consequences of a breach of contract. The level from which to figure damages is the hypothetical point of accomplishment rather than value which would have been reached had the work been done as contracted. An owner's right to improve his property is not limited by its small value. To lessen damages recoverable by the low value landholder would be to favor the faithless contractor. Reversed and a new trial ordered.

**DISSENT:** (Olson, J.) The diminished value rule should be applied in absence of evidence showing that the completed product was to satisfy the personal taste of the promisee. The willfulness of the breach should not affect the measure of damages.

## ▶ ANALYSIS

Where on the surface the contract appears to be for the lease of land, the provision for improvement brings it within the rules governing construction contracts. If the court in determining damages considered the low value of the land, the owner would be greatly limited in what he could do with the land. It has been said that a landowner can submit to any caprice or folly in the control of his own land, but if in dealing with contractors in amounts greater than the value of the land, it would be unfair to limit recovery to the value of the land only should the contractor breach. This would place the low value landowner at the mercy of unethical contractors. As has been seen, if there would be economic waste in approving a large amount of damages, such as in tearing out one manufacture of plumbing for the same quality but originally specified plumbing, such an order would not be declared. But if it is shown that the owner's purpose was to satisfy some personal taste or fancy, damages equal to the cost of completion will be awarded even if it involves economic waste.

---

## Quicknotes

**BREACH OF CONTRACT** Unlawful failure by a party to perform its obligations pursuant to contract.

*Continued on next page.*

**MEASURE OF DAMAGES** Monetary compensation that may be awarded by the court to a party who has sustained injury or loss to his person, property or rights due to another party's unlawful act, omission or negligence.

■━■

# Peevyhouse v. Garland Coal & Mining Co.

## Farm owner (P) v. Coal mining lessee (D)

Okla. Sup. Ct., 1962 Okla. 267, 382 P.2d 109 (1962).

**NATURE OF CASE:** Cross-appeals from award of damages for breach of contract.

**FACT SUMMARY:** Garland Coal Mining & Mining Co. (D) promised it would perform restorative and remedial work on the Peevyhouses' (P) farm at the end of the lease period, but then argued that the cost of the repair work would far exceed the total value of the farm.

## 🏛 RULE OF LAW
Where a contract provision breached is merely incidental to the main purpose, and where the economic benefit which would result to lessor by full performance of the work is grossly disproportionate to the cost of performance, the damages which lessor may recover are limited to the diminution in value resulting to the premises because of the nonperformance.

**FACTS:** The Peevyhouses (P) owned a farm with coal deposits on it. This land was leased in November 1954 to Garland Coal & Mining Co. (Garland) (D) for five years for coal mining purposes. Garland (D) also agreed to perform restorative and remedial work at the end of the lease period at a cost estimated at about $29,000. After Garland (D) failed to restore the land, the Peevyhouses (P) sued for $25,000. Garland (D) introduced testimony at trial as to the diminution of value of the farm due to Garland's (D) failure to perform under the contract. The jury awarded the Peevyhouses (P) $5,000, which was more than the total value of the farm even after the remedial work was done, but only a fraction of the cost of performance. The Peevyhouses (P) appealed, arguing that damages should be the cost to obtain performance of the work not done due to Garland's (D) default.

**ISSUE:** Where a contract provision breached was merely incidental to the main purpose, and where the economic benefit which would result to lessor by full performance of the work is grossly disproportionate to the cost of performance, are the damages which lessor may recover limited to the diminution in value resulting to the premises because of the nonperformance?

**HOLDING AND DECISION:** (Jackson, J.) Yes. Where a contract provision breached was merely incidental to the main purpose, and where the economic benefit which would result to lessor by full performance of the work is grossly disproportionate to the cost of performance, the damages which lessor may recover are limited to the diminution in value resulting to the premises be-

cause of the nonperformance. The damages recoverable are to be a reasonable amount that is not contrary to substantial justice and that prevents the Peevyhouses (P) from recovering a greater amount for breach of an obligation than would have been gained by full performance. The judgment was excessive and should be reduced to $300. Affirmed as modified.

**DISSENT:** (Irwin, J.) Garland (D) knew that the cost of performance would be disproportionate to the value or benefits received by the Peevyhouses (P) when it entered into the contract. The function of a court is to enforce a contract as it is written. The Peevyhouses (P) were entitled to specific performance, or failing that, the cost of that performance.

## ▶ ANALYSIS

The Restatement (Second) of Contracts § 348 reflects this court's decision. Section 348(2)(a) states that "if a breach results in defective or unfinished construction and the loss in value to the injured party is not proved with sufficient certainty, he may recover damages based on the diminution in the market price of the property caused by the breach." Under § 348(2)(b), he may, in the alternative, recover damages based on "the reasonable cost of completing performance or of remedying the defects if that cost is not clearly disproportionate to the probable loss of value."

---

## Quicknotes

**BREACH OF CONTRACT** Unlawful failure by a party to perform its obligations pursuant to contract.

**DIMINUTION IN VALUE** A measure of computing damages pursuant to a breach of contract representing the decrease in the value of the subject matter of the contract as a result of the breach.

**NONPERFORMANCE** Failure to perform a duty.

# Rockingham County v. Luten Bridge Co.

County commissioners (D) v. Bridge builder (P)

35 F.2d 301 (4th Cir. 1929).

**NATURE OF CASE:** Appeal from award damages for breach of a construction contract.

**FACT SUMMARY:** Rockingham County (the County) (D) had contracted to have Luten Bridge Co. (Luten) (P) build a bridge upon which the latter began construction. Due to public opposition to the bridge, the County (D) notified Luten (P) to stop work under the contract, but Luten (P) refused, having already expended $1,900, and completed the bridge for $18,000.

## RULE OF LAW
After an absolute repudiation or refusal to perform by one party to a contract, the other party cannot continue to perform and recover damages based on full performance.

**FACTS:** On January 7, 1924, the Board of Commissioners of Rockingham County (the County) (D) contracted to have Luten Bridge Co. (Luten) (P) build a bridge. After Luten (P) had expended $1,900 for labor and material, the County (D) decided not to go ahead with the contract due to great public opposition to the proposed bridge. The County (D) so notified Luten (P), which refused to stop the project and built the bridge in accordance with the contract. Luten (P) sued successfully for $18,301.07 due on the construction cost, and the County (D) appealed.

**ISSUE:** After an absolute repudiation or refusal to perform by one party to a contract, can the other party continue to perform and recover damages based on full performance?

**HOLDING AND DECISION:** (Parker, J.) No. After an absolute repudiation or refusal to perform by one party to a contract, the other party cannot continue to perform and recover damages based on full performance. Even though the County (D) had no right to rescind the contract, and notice of such amounted to a breach, after receiving notice, Luten (P) had the duty not to increase the amount of damages flowing from the breach. Luten's (P) remedy was to treat the contract as broken when it received notice and sue to recover such damages as it may have sustained from the breach, including any profit it may have realized upon performance, as well as any losses that it may have suffered. The completed bridge, standing alone in the forest without connecting roads, is now without value. As Luten (P) was obviously interested only in its profit, it would have been wiser to sue for that and use the time spent on bridge construction in a more worthwhile manner. Reversed.

## ANALYSIS

The rule of mitigation of damages basically states that one cannot sue for a loss he could have avoided. Obviously, then, Luten (P) should not have increased the damages by going ahead with the project. On the other hand, if Luten (P) had repudiated the contract, County (D) would have had to mitigate damages by securing another contractor. In line with this is UCC § 2-610(a), but, remember, the UCC does not apply to construction contracts. Only reasonable efforts to mitigate damages are required; there is no penalty for failing to mitigate successfully. In cases where the defendant who repudiates still receives a benefit from the plaintiff who fails to mitigate, the defendant may then have to pay for the completed work. In this case, the bridge, lacking connecting roads, was useless. The County (D) clearly received no benefit and did not have to pay damages, which could have been mitigated.

## Quicknotes

**MITIGATION** Reduction in penalty.

**REPUDIATION** The actions or statements of a party to a contract that evidence his intent not to perform, or to continue performance, of his duties or obligations thereunder.

**RESCISSION** The canceling of an agreement and the return of the parties to their positions prior to the formation of the contract.

# Tongish v. Thomas

Farmer (D) v. Sunflower seed purchaser (P)

Kan. Sup. Ct., 840 P.2d 471 (1992).

**NATURE OF CASE:** Review of order awarding damages for breach of contract.

**FACT SUMMARY:** After the Decatur Coop Association (P) lost money on a resale contract due to Tongish's (D) breach, it contended that the market price measure of damages should be used instead of its actual loss.

---

**🏛 RULE OF LAW**
When a seller breaches, market damages should be awarded even though in excess of the buyer's actual loss.

---

**FACTS:** Tongish (D), a farmer, agreed to sell sunflower seeds to the Decatur Coop Association (Coop) (P) at a specified price. Coop (P) planned to resell the seeds for the same price it paid Tongish (D) and pocket a small handling fee. The price of sunflower seeds increased substantially prior to delivery. Tongish (D) refused to honor the contract and sold to another at a higher price. Coop (P) sued Tongish (D). The trial court awarded $455 in handling charges based on Coop's (P) actual loss. The court of appeals reversed, holding that the proper measure of damages was market price under UCC § 2-713. Tongish (D) appealed.

**ISSUE:** When a seller breaches, should market damages be awarded?

**HOLDING AND DECISION:** (McFarland, J.) Yes. When a seller breaches, market damages should be awarded. Tongish (D) contends that market price damages in the situation of a seller's failing to honor a sales contract conflict with the general principle embodied in § 1-106, i.e., that contract remedies are designed to put parties in the position they would have attained absent the breach. Damages awarded under § 2-713 often, as in this case, greatly exceed actual damages, resulting in a windfall for the nonbreaching party. However, § 2-713 encourages parties to honor contracts by preventing a breaching party from being able to take advantage of market fluctuations. Therefore, more contracts are honored, resulting in a more efficient and stable market. Affirmed.

---

**▶ ANALYSIS**

Section 1-106 is a general, axiom-like statute. Section 2-713 deals with a specific situation. The usual role of statutory construction is that a specific rule will prevail over a general rule. This, in fact, was the result here.

---

## Quicknotes

**BREACH OF CONTRACT** Unlawful failure by a party to perform its obligations pursuant to contract.

**UCC § 2-713** Provides that the measure of damages for non-delivery by the seller is the difference between the market price at the time the buyer learned of the breach and the contract price.

# Parker v. Twentieth Century-Fox Film Corp.

Actress (P) v. Film studio (D)

Cal. Sup. Ct., 3 Cal. 3d 176, 474 P.2d 689 (1970).

**NATURE OF CASE:** Appeal from award of damages for breach of a contract for employment.

**FACT SUMMARY:** Parker (P), an actress, was to have the lead role in the motion picture "Bloomer Girl," but Twentieth Century-Fox Film Corp. (D) decided not to make the movie and offered her the leading role in a film, "Big Country, Big Man," instead.

## 🏛 RULE OF LAW
The general measure of recovery by a wrongfully discharged employee is the amount of salary agreed upon for the period of service, less the amount which the employer affirmatively proves the employee has earned or with reasonable effort might have earned from other employment.

**FACTS:** Parker (P), an actress professionally known as Shirley MacLaine, was hired for the lead role in the film "Bloomer Girl," to be produced by Twentieth Century-Fox Film Corp. (Fox) (D). She was to receive a salary of $750,000 for 14 weeks. Under the contract, Parker (P) was to have approval over the director or any substitute, the dance director, and the screenplay. Fox (D) decided not to make the film and offered Parker (P) the lead in "Big Country, Big Man," which, unlike the other film, was not a musical but a western. Also, Fox (D) did not offer Parker (P) approval of the director or screenplay (and there was no need for a dance director). "Bloomer Girl" was to have been filmed in Los Angeles; "Big Country, Big Man" was to be made in Australia. Parker (P) rejected the second film offer and successfully sued for her salary and resulting damages.

**ISSUE:** Is the general measure of recovery by a wrongfully discharged employee the amount of salary agreed upon for the period of service, less the amount which the employer affirmatively proves the employee has earned or with reasonable effort might have earned from other employment?

**HOLDING AND DECISION:** (Burke, J.) Yes. The general measure of recovery by a wrongfully discharged employee is the amount of salary agreed upon for the period of service, less the amount which the employer affirmatively proves the employee has earned or with reasonable effort might have earned from other employment. Fox (D), in claiming that Parker (P) unreasonably refused the second film offer, must show that the other employment was comparable to the first or, at least, substantially similar to that which their employee has been deprived. The employee's rejection of or failure to seek other available employment of a different or inferior kind may not be used to mitigate

damages. If the western film offer were found different or inferior to the musical film offer, it makes no difference whether Parker (P) reasonably or unreasonably refused the second offer. The western was a different and inferior film where Parker (P) could not use her singing and dancing talents as in the musical. The western required travel to Australia for extensive outdoor filming rather than the use of sound stages in Los Angeles. The "Big Country" offer impaired or eliminated several rights of approval. Accordingly, as the second offer was different and inferior to the first, Parker (P) is awarded $750,000. Affirmed.

**DISSENT:** (Sullivan, C.J.) Employment which is different in kind should not be required to be accepted by the employee, but the mere existence of differences between two jobs in the same field should not be sufficient to release the employee and would effectively eliminate any obligation to attempt to minimize damage arising from a wrongful discharge.

## ▶ *ANALYSIS*

The court points out that if the other offer of employment is of a different or inferior kind, it does not matter whether the employee acts reasonably or unreasonably in rejecting the offer. The person with the duty to mitigate need not expose himself to undue risk, expense, or humiliation. It may be possible that, considering the kinds of movies Parker (P) had made in the past, which included no westerns, in the management of an actress's career, such a film may have been considered a risk or, even possibly, a humiliation. Also, many cases have held that the employee is not required to accept employment unreasonably distant from the original location. The court apparently thought that Australia was unreasonably distant when Parker (P) was regularly working in Los Angeles and had intended to work on "Bloomer Girl" there. Note that in mitigating, the employee also does not have to accept a position of lesser rank or at a lower salary. Also, Parker (P) asked for damages in addition to her salary, but such special damages are rarely awarded in cases of wrongful discharge. Damages for injury to the reputation of the employee are considered to be too remote and not within the contemplation of the parties. There is authority for damages when the denied employment would have enhanced the employee's reputation, such as a motion picture credit, but this has only been applied once in the United States, although it is common in England. The dissent would apparently foist an unacceptable film role

*Continued on next page.*

upon an actress. Due to the nature of the industry and its regularly accepted business practices, the majority probably kept in mind the actor's need "to feel right" about a role and script before accepting it.

■═■

## Quicknotes

**MITIGATION** Reduction in penalty.

■═■

# Hadley v. Baxendale

## Mill operator (P) v. Shipping company (D)

Ct. of Exchequer, 9 Ex. 341, 156 Eng. Rep. 145 (1854).

**NATURE OF CASE:** Action for damages for breach of a carrier contract.

**FACT SUMMARY:** Hadley (P), a mill operator in Gloucester, arranged to have Baxendale's (D) company, a carrier, ship his broken mill shaft to the engineer in Greenwich for a copy to be made. Hadley (P) suffered a £300 loss when Baxendale (D) unreasonably delayed shipping the mill shaft, causing the mill to be shut down longer than anticipated.

### 🏛 RULE OF LAW
The injured party may recover those damages as may reasonably be considered arising naturally from the breach itself and, second, may recover those damages as may reasonably be supposed to have been in contemplation of the parties, at the time they made the contract, as the probable result of a breach of it.

**FACTS:** Hadley (P), a mill operator in Gloucester, arranged to have Baxendale's (D) shipping company return his broken mill shaft to the engineer in Greenwich who was to make a duplicate. Hadley (P) delivered the broken shaft to Baxendale (D) who, in consideration for his fee, promised to deliver the shaft to Greenwich in a reasonable time. Baxendale (D) did not know that the mill was shut down while awaiting the new shaft. Baxendale (D) was negligent in delivering the shaft within a reasonable time. Reopening of the mill was delayed five days, costing Hadley (P) lost profits and paid-out wages of £300. Hadley (P) had paid Baxendale (D) 2£ 4s to ship the mill shaft. Baxendale (D) paid into court £25 in satisfaction of Hadley's (P) claim. The jury awarded an additional £25 for a total £50 award. [Note: The headnote taken from the English reporter and reprinted in the casebook is in error when it states that Hadley's (P) servant told Baxendale (D) the mill was stopped and the shaft must be sent immediately.]

**ISSUE:** Shall damages to be awarded be left to the discretion of the jury?

**HOLDING AND DECISION:** (Alderson, B.) No. Damages to be awarded shall not beleft to the discretion of the jury. The jury requires a rule for its guidance in awarding damages justly. When a party breaches his contract, the damages he pays ought to be those arising naturally from the breach itself and, in addition, those as may reasonably be supposed to have been in contemplation of the parties, at the time they made the contract, as the probable result of the breach of it. Therefore, if the special circumstances under which the contract was made were known to both parties, the resulting damages upon breach would be those reasonably contemplated as arising under those communicated and known circumstances. But if the special circumstances were unknown, then damages can only be those expected to arise generally from the breach. Hadley's (P) telling Baxendale (D) that he ran a mill and his mill shaft which he wanted shipped was broken did not notify Baxendale (D) that the mill was shut down. Baxendale (D) could have believed reasonably that Hadley (P) had a spare shaft or that the shaft to be shipped was not the only defective machinery at the mill. Here, it does not follow that a loss of profits could fairly or reasonably have been contemplated by both parties in case of breach. Such a loss would not have flowed naturally from the breach without the special circumstances having been communicated to Baxendale (D). New trial ordered.

### ▶ ANALYSIS

This case lays down two rules guiding damages. First, only those damages as may fairly and reasonably be considered arising from the breach itself may be awarded. Second are those damages which may reasonably be supposed to have been in contemplation of the parties at the time they made the contract as the probable result of a breach of it. The second is distinguished from the first because with the latter, both parties are aware of the special circumstances under which the contract is made. Usually those special circumstances are communicated by the plaintiff to the defendant before the making of the contract. But that is not an absolute condition. If the consequences of the breach are foreseeable, the party which breaches will be liable for the lost profits or expectation damages. Foreseeability and assumption of the risk are ways of describing the bargain. If there is an assumption of the risk, the seller or carrier must necessarily be aware of the consequences. A later English case held that there would be a lesser foreseeability for a common carrier than for a seller as a seller would tend to know the purpose and use of the item sold while the common carrier probably would not know the use of all items it carried. If all loss went on to the seller, this would obviously be an incentive not to enter into contracts. Courts balance what has become a "seller beware" attitude by placing limitations on full recovery. The loss must be foreseeable when the contract is entered into. It cannot be overly speculative. The seller's breach must be judged by willingness, negligence, bad faith, and availability of replacement items. Restatement (First) § 331(2) would allow recovery in the

*Continued on next page.*

situation in this case under an alternative theory. If the breach were one preventing the use and operation of property from which profits would have been made, damages can be measured by the rental value of the property or by interest on the value of the property. UCC § 2-715(2) allows the buyer consequential damages for any loss which results from general or particular needs of which the seller had reason to know.

◼▬◼

## Quicknotes

**ASSUMPTION OF RISK DOCTRINE** An affirmative defense to a negligence suit contending that the plaintiff knowingly and voluntarily subjected himself to a hazardous condition absolving the defendant of liability for injuries incurred.

**NOLLE PROSEQUI** A formal entry on the record by either a prosecutor or a plaintiff that he will discontinue prosecution of an action.

**RULE NISI** Motion by one party to make a final ruling against the opponent, unless the opponent can show cause as to why such ruling should not be ordered.

◼▬◼

# Delchi Carrier Spa v. Rotorex Corp.

## Buyer (P) v. Seller (D)

71 F.3d 1024 (2d Cir. 1995).

**NATURE OF CASE:** Appeal from judgment for plaintiff for contract damages.

**FACT SUMMARY:** Delchi Carrier Spa (P) was awarded damages for lost profits and other consequential damages when Rotorex Corp. (D) shipped nonconforming compressors for air conditioners.

🏛️ **RULE OF LAW**
A contract plaintiff may collect damages to compensate for the full loss, which includes, but is not limited to, foreseeable lost profits.

**FACTS:** Rotorex Corp. (D), a New York corporation, contracted to sell compressors to Delchi Carrier Spa (Delchi) (P), an Italian manufacturer of air conditioners. Prior to execution of the contract, Rotorex (D) sent a sample compressor and written performance specifications. When the compressors arrived in Italy, they were rejected in quality control checks because they had lower cooling capacity and consumed more power than the sample model and specifications. Rotorex (D) refused to supply new, conforming compressors, claiming the performance specifications were inadvertently communicated to Delchi (P). Delchi (P) then cancelled the contract and suffered a loss in its sales volume because it could not obtain substitute compressors in time. Delchi (P) filed suit under the United Nations Convention on Contracts for the International Sale of Goods (CISG) for breach of contract and failure to deliver conforming goods. The court granted Delchi's (P) motion for summary judgment and awarded damages that included lost profits. Delchi (P) appealed, claiming the judge erroneously denied damages for various consequential and incidental damages because they would allegedly constitute a double recovery.

**ISSUE:** May a contract plaintiff collect damages to compensate for the full loss, which includes, but is not limited to, foreseeable lost profits?

**HOLDING AND DECISION:** (Winter, J.) Yes. A contract plaintiff may collect damages to compensate for the full loss, which includes, but is not limited to, foreseeable lost profits. The award for lost profits did not compensate Delchi (P) for costs actually incurred that led to no sales. Awarding damages for costs actually incurred in no way creates a double recovery. Affirmed in part, reversed in part and remanded.

▶ **ANALYSIS**

The CISG did not expressly provide for calculating lost profits. The district court applied the standard formula most American courts use and deducted only variable costs from sales revenue. On appeal, the district court's decision in that regard was upheld as correct.

■=■

## Quicknotes

**BREACH OF CONTRACT** Unlawful failure by a party to perform its obligations pursuant to contract.

**CONSEQUENTIAL DAMAGES** Monetary compensation that may be recovered in order to compensate for injuries or losses sustained as a result of damages that are not the direct or foreseeable result of the act of a party, but that nevertheless are the consequence of such act and which must be specifically pled and demonstrated.

**LOST PROFITS** The potential value of income earned or goods which are the subject of the contract; may be used in calculating damages where the contract has been breached.

■=■

# Kenford Co. v. County of Erie

## Land owner (P) v. County (D)

N.Y. Ct. App., 73 N.Y.2d 312, 537 N.E.2d 176 (1989).

**NATURE OF CASE:** Breach of contract suit.

**FACT SUMMARY:** Kenford Co. (P) sued Erie County (the County) (D) for loss of anticipated increase in value of peripheral lands as a result of the County's (D) breach of a contract to build a stadium on such property.

### 🏛 RULE OF LAW
In order to impose extraordinary damages on a breaching party, such damages must have been brought within the contemplation of the parties as the probable result of a breach at or prior to the time of contracting.

**FACTS:** The County of Erie (the County) (D) adopted enabling legislation authorizing it to finance and contract a domed sports stadium. When the County (D) learned that the project would cost $22 million in excess of its bond resolution it terminated the contract. Kenford Co. (P), owner of the proposed site, brought suit for breach of contract and specific enforcement of the agreement, or for damages of $90 million. The jury awarded $18 million in lost appreciation, $6 million in out-of-pocket, and $25.6 million in lost profits. The appellate division reversed the breach of contract claim and DSI, the management company, sought review. On retrial the jury awarded $6.5 million for loss of anticipated land appreciation. The appellate division affirmed and the County (D) appealed.

**ISSUE:** In order to impose extraordinary damages on a breaching party, must such damages have been brought within the contemplation of the parties as the probable result of a breach at or prior to the time of contracting?

**HOLDING AND DECISION:** (Mollen, J.) Yes. In order to impose extraordinary damages on a breaching party, such damages must have been brought within the contemplation of the parties as the probable result of a breach at or prior to the time of contracting. In the absence of a provision regarding entitlement to recover damages for lost anticipated appreciation in the value of peripheral lands, the applicable rule is to consider what the parties would have concluded had they considered the subject. Here there was no provision in the contract, nor evidence in the record, to demonstrate that the parties reasonably contemplated that the County (D) would be liable for lack of appreciation in the value of Kenford's (P) peripheral lands in the event the stadium was not built. Kenford (P) is not entitled to recovery for lost appreciation in the value of peripheral lands cause by the breach. Reversed.

## ▶ ANALYSIS

The general rule is that a nonbreaching party may recover damages for the natural and probable consequences of a breach. Anything more must be within the "reasonable contemplation" of the parties taking into account the circumstances surrounding the contract. The court must also consider "what liability the defendant fairly may be supposed to have assumed consciously, or to have warranted the plaintiff reasonably to suppose that it assumed, when the contract was made." *Globe Ref. Co. v. Landa Cotton Oil Co.*, 190 U.S. 540, 544.

## Quicknotes

**ANTICIPATORY REPUDIATION** Breach of a contract subsequent to formation but prior to the time performance is due.

**BREACH OF CONTRACT** Unlawful failure by a party to perform its obligations pursuant to contract.

**COVER** The purchase of an alternate supply of goods by a buyer, after a seller has breached a contract for sale, for which the buyer may recover the difference between the cost of the substituted goods and the price of the original goods pursuant to the contract, so long as the buyer purchases the alternate goods in good faith and without unreasonable delay.

**SPECIFIC PERFORMANCE** An equitable remedy whereby the court requires the parties to perform their obligations pursuant to a contract.

# Fera v. Village Plaza, Inc.

Prospective lessee (P) v. Lessor (D)

Mich. Sup. Ct., 396 Mich. 639, 242 N.W.2d 372 (1976).

**NATURE OF CASE:** Appeal from reversal of award of damages for breach of contract.

**FACT SUMMARY:** A portion of damages awarded to Fera (P) involving a new business consisted of lost profits.

## 🏛 RULE OF LAW
A new business may recover lost profit damages for breach of a lease, if the profits are not excessively speculative.

**FACTS:** Fera (P), intending to open a liquor-related business in a shopping center operated by Village Plaza, Inc. (D), leased retail space. However, Village Plaza (D) misplaced its copy of the lease and subsequently let to another. Fera (P) brought an action to recover his deposit and lost profits. At trial, extensive evidence regarding Fera's (P) qualifications and the market conditions was presented. The jury awarded $200,000. The court of appeals reversed, holding that new business lost profit damages were inherently speculative. Fera (P) appealed.

**ISSUE:** May a new business recover lost profit damages for breach of a lease, if the profits are not excessively speculative?

**HOLDING AND DECISION:** (Kavanagh, C.J.) Yes. A new business may recover lost profit damages for breach of a lease, if the profits are not excessively speculative. It is the general rule that lost profit damages may be awarded, provided that they can be proven. From this axiom had developed a dichotomy allowing lost profits to be awarded to an ongoing business but denied to a new business. New businesses were denied lost profit damages not because they were new but because it was thought that the damages could not be proven. If such damages could be proven, it was not per se improper to allow such damages. Here, a good deal of testimony was presented at trial concerning market conditions and other economic factors, and the trial court was satisfied that this was sufficient to allow the issue to go to a jury. The trial court was within its rights in doing this and the reversal was improper. Reversed.

**CONCURRENCE AND DISSENT:** (Coleman, J.) While agreeing with the principle enunciated here, the plaintiff in this case did not meet his burden of proof.

## ▶ ANALYSIS

Lost profit damages were once universally frowned upon. This was due to the inherent uncertainty surrounding them. However, as time passed, advances in economics and related social sciences have increased the predictability of lost profits sufficiently to convince a majority of jurisdictions that they are proper.

━■━■

## Quicknotes

**LOST PROFITS** The potential value of income earned or goods which are the subject of the contract; may be used in calculating damages where the contract has been breached.

━■━■

# Dave Gustafson & Co. v. State

General contractor (P) v. State (D)

S.D. Sup. Ct., 156 N.W.2d 185 (1968).

**NATURE OF CASE:** Appeal from judgment for defendant in action for payment on a construction contract.

**FACT SUMMARY:** When the State (D) withheld a portion of the contract payment for Dave Gustafson & Co.'s (Gustafson's) (P) highway paving work, pursuant to a contract provision that provided for "liquidated damages" arising from delays, Gustafson (P) brought suit, contending the amount withheld was in the nature of an unenforceable penalty.

## 🏛 RULE OF LAW
A provision for payment of a stipulated sum as a liquidation of damages will ordinarily be sustained if it appears that: at the time the contract was made the damages in the event of a breach will be incapable or very difficult of accurate estimation; there was a reasonable attempt by the parties to fix fair compensation; and the amount stipulated bears a reasonable relation to probable damages and is not disproportionate to any damages reasonably to be anticipated.

**FACTS:** Dave Gustafson & Co. (Gustafson) (P) entered into a contract with the State (D) for paving a highway. The contract provided a graduated scale of per diem liquidated damages that depended on the size of the contract. For Gustafson's (P) contract, the per diem amount was $210 for every day's delay. Based on a delay of 67 days, the State (D) withheld $14,070 from what it paid Gustafson (P). Gustafson (P) brought suit, claiming that the amount withheld was an unenforceable penalty. The trial court held that the amount was valid liquidated damages, and the state's highest court granted review.

**ISSUE:** Will a provision for payment of a stipulated sum as a liquidation of damages ordinarily be sustained if it appears that: at the time the contract was made the damages in the event of a breach will be incapable or very difficult of accurate estimation; there was a reasonable attempt by the parties to fix fair compensation; and the amount stipulated bears a reasonable relation to probable damages and is not disproportionate to any damages reasonably to be anticipated?

**HOLDING AND DECISION:** (Hanson, J.) Yes. A provision for payment of a stipulated sum as a liquidation of damages will ordinarily be sustained if it appears that: at the time the contract was made the damages in the event of a breach will be incapable or very difficult of accurate estimation; there was a reasonable attempt by the parties to fix fair compensation; and the amount stipulated bears a

reasonable relation to probable damages and is not disproportionate to any damages reasonably to be anticipated. Judged by this standard, the provision at issue is one for liquidated damages rather than a penalty. First, damages for delay in constructing a new highway are impossible of measurement. Second, the amount stated in the contract as liquidated damages indicates an effort by the parties to fix fair compensation for the loss, inconvenience, added costs, and deprivation of use caused by delay. Daily damage is graduated according to total amount of work to be performed, and it may properly be assumed that a large project involves more loss than a small one, and that each day of delay adds to the loss, inconvenience, cost and deprivation of use. Third, for these reasons, the amount stipulated in the contract bears a reasonable relation to probable damages and is not, as a matter of law, disproportionate to any and all damage reasonably to be anticipated from the unexcused delay in performance. Affirmed.

## ▶ ANALYSIS

This case reflects the modern tendency not to look with disfavor on liquidated damages provisions in contracts. When they are fair and reasonable attempts to fix just compensation for anticipated loss caused by breach of contract, liquidated damages provisions are enforced because they serve a particularly useful function when damages are uncertain in nature or amount or are unmeasurable, as is the case in many government contracts. Provisions requiring liquidated damages for delay are not against public policy and are an appropriate means of inducing due performance, or of giving compensation, in case of failure to perform.

■═■

## Quicknotes

**LIQUIDATED DAMAGES** An amount of money specified in a contract representing the damages owed in the event of breach.

■═■

# Lake River Corp. v. Carborundum Co.

## Distributor (P) v. Powder manufacturer (D)

769 F.2d 1284 (7th Cir. 1985).

**NATURE OF CASE:** Appeal from judgments in diversity suit for liquidated damages and counterclaim for conversion.

**FACT SUMMARY:** Lake River Corp. (P) sued Carborundum Co. (D) for liquidated damages resulting from breach of a distributorship agreement. Carborundum Co. (D) counterclaimed under the theory of conversion. The district judge entered judgment for both parties. Both parties appealed.

### 🏛 RULE OF LAW
A minimum-guarantee provision is an unenforceable penalty, rather than an enforceable liquidated damages clause, where it is designed always to assure the promisee more than its actual damages.

**FACTS:** Carborundum Co. (D) manufactures "Ferro Carbo," an abrasive powder used in making steel. Carborundum (D) entered into a distributorship contract with Lake River Co. (P) to better serve its Midwestern clients. Lake River Co. (P) had a warehouse in Illinois and agreed to receive Ferro Carbo in bulk from Carborundum (D), "bag" it, and ship the bagged product to Carborundum's (D) customers. To honor this agreement, Carborundum (D) insisted that Lake River (P) install a new bagging system. Lake River (P) sought to ensure that it would be able to recover the cost of this new system ($89,000) and make a profit of 20 percent. Thus, Lake River (P) insisted on a minimum-quantity guarantee that in consideration of the new bagging system, Carborundum (D) would ship to Lake River (P) for bagging, a minimum of 22,500 tons of Ferro Carbo. If this minimum was not met, Lake River (P) would invoice Carborundum at the then-prevailing rates for the difference between the quantity bagged and the minimum guaranteed. Shortly after the contract between Carborundum (D) and Lake River (P) was signed, the demand for domestic steel fell dramatically and Carborundum (D) failed to ship the guaranteed amount. Lake River (P) demanded payment for the difference and Carborundum (D) refused. At this time, Lake River (P) had 500 tons of bagged Ferro Carbo in its warehouse, having a market value of $269,000, which it refused to release unless Carborundum (D) paid the $241,000 difference due under the formula. Carborundum (D) trucked in bagged Ferro Carbo from the East to serve its customers in Illinois at an additional cost of $31,000. Lake River (P) brought suit for $241,000 and Carborundum (D) counterclaimed for the value of the bagged Ferro Carbo which Lake River (P) had impounded. The district judge entered judgment for both parties. Both parties appealed, and the court of appeals granted review. [The court affirmed the district court's ruling that Lake River (P) did not have a valid lien on the bagged powder.]

**ISSUE:** Is a minimum-guarantee provision an unenforceable penalty, rather than an enforceable liquidated damages clause, where it is designed always to assure the promisee more than its actual damages?

**HOLDING AND DECISION:** (Posner, C.J.) Yes. A minimum-guarantee provision is an unenforceable penalty, rather than an enforceable liquidated damages clause, where it is designed always to assure the promisee more than its actual damages. Leaving aside the theoretical question of whether courts should (paternalistically) refuse to enforce a contract provision that acts as a penalty against a large, sophisticated company—given that it can be argued on the one hand that there are some benefits to having penalties in contracts, but on the other hand that penalties also may discourage efficient as well as inefficient breaches of contract—the court must apply state law. Here, applicable state law requires that a liquidated damages clause, in order to be enforceable, must be a reasonable estimation at the time of contracting of the probable damages from breach, and the need for estimation must be based on the likely difficulty of assessing the actual damages suffered in the event of breach; otherwise, such clause is void as a penalty. Here, the damage formula is a penalty because it is designed always to assure Lake River (P) more than its actual damages. The formula—full contract price minus the amount already invoiced to Carborundum (D)—is invariant to the gravity of the breach. It also indicates a failure to reasonably estimate actual damages. Regardless of when a breach occurs, Lake River (P) will recover more than its expected profit at that point. If the breach occurs early, Lake River (P) will receive a windfall; if it occurs late, Lake River (P) still would get more than the profits it could reasonably anticipate if there had not been a breach. Despite the fact that the damage formula is invalid, Lake River (P) is still entitled to its common-law damages (the unpaid contract price of $241,000 minus the costs that Lake River (P) saved by not having to complete the contract (the variable costs on the other 45 percent of the Ferro Carbo that it never had to bag). Remanded to the district court to fix these damages.

### ▶ ANALYSIS

Although the court here sustains the distinction between penalty clauses and liquidated damages provisions, Judge

*Continued on next page.*

Posner expressly states his disagreement with such a distinction. While he admits that penalty clauses impute a sense of exigency into the contract's terms, this advantage is heavily outweighed by countervailing concerns. First, the presence of the penalty clause increases the costs of contracting. Second, penalty clauses may discourage efficient breaches of contract. Nevertheless, he concludes that such a distinction is to be determined by the state courts in accordance with the common law, and may not be dictated by federal judges.

■══■

## Quicknotes

**LIQUIDATED DAMAGES** An amount of money specified in a contract representing the damages owed in the event of breach.

**PENALTY CLAUSE** A provision in a contract imposing penalties for failure to comply with its terms and which is usually unenforceable.

■══■

# Wasserman's, Inc. v. Township of Middletown

## Lessee (P) v. Municipality lessor (D)

N.J. Sup. Ct., 137 N.J. 238, 645 A.2d 100 (1994).

**NATURE OF CASE:** Appeal from judgment awarding stipulated damages in breach of contract action.

**FACT SUMMARY:** A lease between Wasserman's, Inc. (P) and the Township of Middletown (D) contained a stipulated damages provision based on Wasserman's (P) gross receipts.

## 🏛 RULE OF LAW
Provisions for liquidated damages are enforceable only if they are a reasonable forecast of just compensation for the harm caused by the breach.

**FACTS:** The Township of Middletown, N.J. (the Township) (D) leased a commercial property to Wasserman's, Inc. (P). The lease contained a provision fixing damages in the event of a breach by the Township (D) as follows: a pro rata reimbursement of any improvement costs, plus 25 percent of Wasserman's (P) gross receipts for one year. Wasserman's (P) subsequently sublet the premises to Jo-Ro, Inc. (P). Years later, the Township (D) canceled the lease and sold the property. Wasserman's (P) and Jo-Ro (P) sued to enforce the stipulated damages provision. The trial court upheld the clause and, applying it, awarded $346,058.45. The appellate division affirmed, and the New Jersey Supreme Court granted review.

**ISSUE:** Are provisions for liquidated damages enforceable if they are a reasonable forecast of just compensation for the breach?

**HOLDING AND DECISION:** (Pollock, J.) Yes. Provisions for liquidated damages are enforceable if they are a reasonable forecast of just compensation for the breach. At common law, courts generally looked with suspicion on such clauses. This was because such provisions often constituted a penalty and were more or less forced upon the party having lesser bargaining power. Also, they often did not reflect actual loss, as contractual remedies are designed to do. Finally, courts felt that allowing parties to set their own measure of damages usurped a judicial function. Today, this early unfavorable attitude has relaxed somewhat. Stipulated damage provisions that constitute a legitimate attempt to predict actual damages are valid liquidated damages provisions; those that do not are considered penalty provisions which do not advance the aims of contract law and thus are not enforceable. In general, gross receipts do not reflect actual losses incurred when a lease is canceled. It is not possible to determine from the record here whether the stipulated damages are arbitrary or would be likely to flow from the breach. The court should consider the parties' reasoning behind the damages calculation, the duty to mitigate, and the market value of replacement space. Therefore, this matter must be remanded to the trial court for a determination of whether the stipulated damages clause based on gross receipts is a valid liquidated damages clause. Affirmed in part and remanded.

## ▶ ANALYSIS

A subissue that can arise when the reasonableness of a damages provision is challenged is that of timing. Some courts set the time for considering damages as of the time the contract is executed. Others look to the time of the breach. The modern trend is to assess reasonableness at either time. The UCC reflects this trend in § 2-718 with a reference to "anticipated or actual harm."

---

## Quicknotes

**LIQUIDATED DAMAGES** An amount of money specified in a contract representing the damages owed in the event of breach.

**STIPULATION** An agreement by the parties regarding an issue before the court not in dispute so as to avoid unnecessary expense and delay.

# Performance and Breach

## Quick Reference Rules of Law

# Luttinger v. Rosen

## Sellers (D) v. Purchasers (P)

Conn. Sup. Ct., 164 Conn. 45, 316 A.2d 757 (1972).

**NATURE OF CASE:** Action to recover a deposit on real property.

**FACT SUMMARY:** The Rosens (P) signed a contract to purchase the Luttingers' (D) premises and put down a deposit "subject to and conditional upon" their obtaining specified mortgage financing. *[handwritten: no financing → no K]*

🏛 **RULE OF LAW**
A condition precedent is a fact or event which the parties intend must exist or take place before there is a right to performance, and if the condition precedent is not fulfilled the contract is not enforceable.

**FACTS:** The contract by which the Rosens (P) agreed to purchase the Luttingers' (D) premises for $85,000 was "subject to and conditional upon" their obtaining "first mortgage financing on said premises from a bank or other lending institution" of $45,000 for no less than 20 years at an interest rate not exceeding 8½ percent per annum. They agreed to use due diligence in seeking such financing but put in only one application because only one bank was then lending as much as $45,000 on single-family dwellings. It would not commit to an interest rate any lower than 8¾ percent. However, the Luttingers' (D) attorney offered to make up the difference between the interest rate offered by the bank and the 8½ percent rate provided in the contract. The Rosens (P) refused and sued for a refund of their deposit. The trial court rendered judgment in their favor, and the Luttingers (D) appealed.

**ISSUE:** Is a contract enforceable if a condition precedent is not fulfilled?

**HOLDING AND DECISION:** (Loiselle, J.) No. If a condition precedent is not fulfilled, a contract is unenforceable. A condition precedent is a fact or event which the parties intend must exist or take place before there is a right to performance. Looking at the contract in this case, it is clear that the parties conditioned the purchase by the Rosens (P) on their obtaining a mortgage as specified therein. Since this condition precedent was not fulfilled, the contract is unenforceable. Affirmed.

▸ **ANALYSIS**

The use of "subject to financing" clauses is widespread, although many are not as specific as this one and speak of the buyer obtaining "reasonable financing" or "proper financing." Since the plaintiff attempting to enforce the agreement has the burden of proof as to conditions prece-dent, failure to clearly delineate what will constitute satisfaction of the financing condition can prove treacherous.

*Quicknotes*

**CONDITION PRECEDENT** The happening of an uncertain occurrence, which is necessary before a particular right or interest may be obtained or an action performed.

*[handwritten: • Condition was put in there to protect the buyer]*

# Internatio-Rotterdam, Inc. v. River Brand Rice Mills, Inc.

Exporter (P) v. Rice processor (D)

259 F.2d 137 (2d Cir. 1958).

**NATURE OF CASE:** Action for damages for breach of a contract for sale of goods.

**FACT SUMMARY:** Internatio-Rotterdam, Inc. (Internatio) (P) ordered 95,600 pockets of rice from River Brand Rice Mills, Inc. (River Brand) (D) under a contract requiring at least two weeks' notice for December delivery at either Houston or Lake Charles. When Internatio (P) did not give notice by December 17 so delivery could be on December 31, River Brand (D) rescinded the contract.

## 🏛 RULE OF LAW

A condition, which is an act or event, other than a lapse of time, must be literally complied with.

**FACTS:** Internatio-Rotterdam, Inc. (Internatio) (P), a rice exporter, contracted to buy 95,600 pockets of rice from River Brand Rice Mills, Inc. (River Brand) (D), a rice processor, at $8.25 to be delivered alongside ship at Lake Charles or Houston, Texas. Shipment was to be made in December 1952, with two weeks' notice from Internatio (P). Internatio (P) elected to have 50,000 pockets delivered at Lake Charles and so notified River Brand (D) December 10. River Brand (D) made delivery. By December 17, the last day an order could be made for delivery within the month, River Brand (D) received no instructions for delivery of the other 45,600 pockets as Internatio (P) was having difficulty finding a ship and dock space at Houston. On December 18, River Brand (D) rescinded the contract for the remaining rice. Internatio (P) sued for breach. The trial court dismissed the complaint.

**ISSUE:** Must a condition, which is an act or event, other than a lapse of time, be literally complied with?

**HOLDING AND DECISION:** (Hincks, J.) Yes. A condition, which is an act or event, other than a lapse of time, must be literally complied with. Notice was a condition precedent to shipment. Shipment could not be made until the ship and location to which River Brand (D) was to deliver was identified. If shipment within December was of the essence of the contract, then failure to notify by December 17 was a breach as that was the last day notice could be given in order to allow River Brand (D) two weeks to ship by December 31. December delivery went to the essence of the contract as December was the peak rice month and both sides wanted the protection of a specified delivery period. A postponement of notice could damage River Brand (D) in light of fluctuating rice prices. The letter of credit guaranteed payment only for December deliveries. The mere establishment of the letter of credit

was not an act of performance but was made in preparation thereof and was of no benefit to River Brand (D). As there was an option on delivery sites, the contract was divisible, and by continuing Lake Charles deliveries, River Brand (D) did not waive its right to cancel the Houston deliveries. Duties of the parties to the Lake Charles shipment were in no way dependent on the Houston deliveries. Affirmed.

## ▶ ANALYSIS

A condition precedent is an act or event, other than a lapse of time, which must exist or occur before a duty of immediate performance of a promise arises. However, the term "condition" ordinarily describes acts or events which must occur before a duty of performance under an existing contract becomes absolute. Here, the court looked for intent. By starting with a promise to sell for a promise to buy, the promise to sell was contingent upon notice by December 17, that is, timely instruction. In this way, time was of the essence. Unless the condition is met, the promise to perform will be excused. Note that the buyer, Internatio (P), took the risk that the price after contracting would go down, and the seller, River Brand (D), took the risk prices would go up. The price did, in fact, go up. But after December 17, River Brand (D) assumed the risk both ways. Hence, Internatio (P) could not wait to give notice up to the end of December for January delivery.

■=■

## Quicknotes

**CONDITION PRECEDENT** The happening of an uncertain occurrence, which is necessary before a particular right or interest may be obtained or an action performed.

**LETTER OF CREDIT** An agreement by a bank or other party that it will honor a customer's demand for payment upon the satisfaction of specified conditions.

**RESCISSION** The canceling of an agreement and the return of the parties to their positions prior to the formation of the contract.

■=■

# Peacock Construction Co. v. Modern Air Conditioning, Inc.

## Builder (D) v. Subcontractor (P)

Fla. Sup. Ct., 353 So. 2d 840 (1977).

**NATURE OF CASE:** Consolidation on appeal of action for breaches of identical contractual provisions.

**FACT SUMMARY:** Modern Air Conditioning, Inc. (P) had subcontracted to do work for Peacock Construction Co. (D) under a contract calling for final payment of subcontractors "within 30 days after the completion of the work ... and full payment therefore by the Owner."

## 🏛 RULE OF LAW
Ambiguous provisions in subcontracts, which do not expressly shift the risk of payment failure by the owner to the subcontractor, will be interpreted as constituting absolute promises to pay and not as setting payment by the owner as a condition precedent to payment.

**FACTS:** As builder of a condominium project, Peacock Construction Co. (Peacock) (D) subcontracted the heating and air conditioning work to Modern Air Conditioning, Inc. (Modern Air) (P) and the "rooftop swimming pool" work to Overly Manufacturing (Overly) (P). Both subcontractors signed agreements providing that they would receive final payment "within 30 days after the completion of the work included in this subcontract, written acceptance by the Architect and full payment therefore by the Owner." When the work was completed, both subcontractors requested final payment, which Peacock (D) withheld because it had not received full payment from the owner. Although Peacock (D) urged that payment by the owner was a condition precedent to its duty to pay the subcontractors, the trial court disagreed and granted summary judgments to the subcontractors (P) when they sued for damages for breach of contract. The decisions were affirmed on appeal.

**ISSUE:** Will a subcontract be interpreted as making the owner's payment a condition precedent to payment of the subcontractors only if such is unambiguously provided for in the contract?

**HOLDING AND DECISION:** (Boyd, C.J.) Yes. This case will be decided under the rule adopted in the majority of jurisdictions, that a subcontract will not be interpreted as making the owner's payment a condition precedent to payment of the subcontractors unless such is unambiguously provided for in the contract. In the typical subcontracting situation, it is not intended that the subcontractor will assume the risk of the owner's failure to pay the general contractor. That is the reason for this majority rule. Of course, the parties can, by express and unambigu-

ous contractual language, shift the risk of payment failure by the owner to the subcontractor. In this case, there was no such express provision. Thus, payment by the owner is not a condition precedent to paying the subcontractors. Affirmed.

## ▶ ANALYSIS

Restatement (Second) § 224 defines a "condition" as "an event, not certain to occur, which must occur, unless its nonoccurrence is excused, before performance under a contract becomes due." Conditions can be express, implied in fact (inferred from the contract's express provisions), or "constructive" (created by operation of law).

◼▬◼

## Quicknotes

**CONDITION PRECEDENT** The happening of an uncertain occurrence, which is necessary before a particular right or interest may be obtained or an action performed.

**SUMMARY JUDGMENT** Judgment rendered by a court in response to a motion by one of the parties, claiming that the lack of a question of material fact in respect to an issue warrants disposition of the issue without consideration by the jury.

◼▬◼

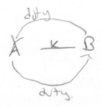

- promises are independent: if A doesn't do duty, B has to do duty but can seek damages for breach.
- promises are

an owner's payment is not a condition precedent, unless it says so in the contract.

# Gibson v. Cranage

## Artist (P) v. Client (D)

Mich. Sup. Ct., 39 Mich. 49 (1878).

**NATURE OF CASE:** Appeal from defense verdict in action to recover damages for breach of contract.

**FACT SUMMARY:** Cranage's (D) liability to Gibson (P) was conditioned on Cranage's (D) personal satisfaction with a portrait.

## 🏛 RULE OF LAW
Where two parties agree that one of them must be "personally satisfied" before liability will arise, that party may insist on his right to personal satisfaction.

**FACTS:** Gibson (P) contracted to make a portrait for Cranage (D). It was further agreed that if the portrait failed to satisfy Cranage (D), Cranage (D) need not accept or pay for it. The portrait failed to satisfy Cranage (D), and Gibson (P) sued for the contract price. The trial court ruled in favor of Cranage (D), and Gibson (P) appealed.

**ISSUE:** May two parties make a contract wherein personal satisfaction of one of the parties is necessary for contractual liability to arise?

**HOLDING AND DECISION:** (Marston, J.) Yes. Where two parties agree that one of them must be "personally satisfied" before liability will arise, that party may insist on his right to personal satisfaction. That which is an excellent portrait in the eyes of one, may certainly prove very unsatisfactory to another. Affirmed.

## ▌ANALYSIS

Note that the condition precedent to liability in this well-known case was a completely subjective test of personal satisfaction. The parties might have made the test objective by including such a clause as: "and acceptance and payment shall not be unreasonably withheld." However, they did not do so, and since a subjective test does not violate public policy in this situation, the court decided in favor of freedom of contract. Note further that the court expresses some doubt as to whether there was even a contract at all (since the subjective test may render Cranage's (D) promise illusory and, therefore, not consideration for a return promise) but does not pursue the matter. It would seem, however, that where personal satisfaction is called for, a minimum "good faith" requirement must be imposed to remove such a "contract" from the class of illusory agreements. (Often where satisfaction is a matter of "mechanical fitness, utility, or marketability" an objective, "reasonable person" test is presumed by the courts.)

## Quicknotes

**ASSUMPSIT** An oral or written promise by one party to perform or pay another.

**CONDITION PRECEDENT** The happening of an uncertain occurrence, which is necessary before a particular right or interest may be obtained or an action performed.

**ILLUSORY AGREEMENT** An agreement that is not legally enforceable because performance of the obligation by the promisor is completely within his discretion.

**PLAINTIFF IN ERROR** Appellant; a party that appeals from a lower court judgment.

# McKenna v. Vernon

### Contractor (P) v. Property owner (D)

Penn. Sup. Ct., 101 A. 919 (1917).

**NATURE OF CASE:** Appeal from judgment for plaintiff in action for payment of balance due on a construction contract.

**FACT SUMMARY:** Vernon (D) contended that McKenna (P) was not entitled to payment of the balance due on a construction contract because the contract specified that an architect's certificate of work done was a condition of payment, and no such certificate was secured. McKenna (P) argued that this condition was waived because prior payments had been made in the absence of the architect's certificate.

## 🏛 RULE OF LAW
A contract condition will be waived where it has previously and repeatedly been waived in the course of performance.

**FACTS:** McKenna (P), a general contractor, entered into an agreement with Vernon (D) to build a movie theater. The contract provided that the contract price of $8,750 was to be paid in installments, and that the work was to be done under the direction of an architect, whose certificate of work done was a condition of each installment payment by Vernon (D). With one exception, Vernon (D) paid seven of the installments, amounting to $6,000, without having secured the architect's certificate. McKenna (P) brought suit for the remainder owing after Vernon (D) failed to pay him the balance, claiming the work was defective. The architect testified that the work complied with the building specifications, and judgment was rendered for McKenna (P). Vernon (D) appealed, claiming there was no right of action absent the architect's certificate of completion. McKenna (P) asserted this condition had been waived. The state's highest court granted review.

**ISSUE:** Will a contract condition be waived where it has previously and repeatedly been waived in the course of performance?

**HOLDING AND DECISION:** (Stewart, J.) Yes. A contract condition will be waived where it has previously and repeatedly been waived in the course of performance. Having consistently and repeatedly waived the condition before, it is too late now for Vernon (D) to assert the condition as a bar to McKenna's (P) recovery. Given that Vernon (D) waived the condition during the progress of the work, which was shown to have been satisfactorily completed, there are no grounds for him to assert that he did not also waive the final payment. [Affirmed.]

## ▶ ANALYSIS

"Waiver" is often inexactly defined as "the voluntary relinquishment of a known right." When the waiver is reinforced by reliance, enforcement is often said to rest on "estoppel." Since the more common definition of estoppel is limited to reliance on a misrepresentation of an existing fact, reliance on a waiver or promise as to the future is sometimes said to create a "promissory estoppel." The common definition of waiver may lead to the incorrect inference that the promisor must know his legal rights and must intend the legal effect of the promise, but, at least under the approach in Restatement § 93, it is sufficient if he has reason to know the essential facts. That section provides that a waiver is not binding unless the promisor knew or had reason to know the essential facts of the previous transaction to which the promise relates, but his knowledge of the legal effect of the facts is immaterial.

---

## Quicknotes

**PROMISSORY ESTOPPEL** A promise that is enforceable if the promisor should reasonably expect that it will induce action or forbearance on the part of the promisee, and does in fact cause such action or forbearance, and it is the only means of avoiding injustice.

**WAIVER** The intentional or voluntary forfeiture of a recognized right.

---

# Hicks v. Bush

## Shareholder in corporation (P) v. Shareholder in a different corporation (D)

### N.Y. Ct. App., 180 N.E.2d 425 (1962).

**NATURE OF CASE:** Appeal in action for specific performance of a merger agreement.

**FACT SUMMARY:** Hicks (P) contended that parol evidence of a purported oral understanding he had with shareholders (D) in the Clinton G. Bush Company, that a fully integrated written merger agreement was subject to the raising of certain equity expansion funds, was inadmissible.

## 🏛 RULE OF LAW
Parol evidence is admissible to prove an oral condition precedent to the legal effectiveness of a written agreement if the condition does not contradict the express terms of such written agreement.

**FACTS:** Hicks (P), an owner of certain corporate interests, entered into a completely integrated agreement with the shareholders (D) of the Clinton G. Bush Company (Bush Company), whereby the parties were to merge their various corporate interests into a single holding company, to be known as Bush-Hick Enterprises. Each party was to subscribe to a certain number of shares in the new entity, and the consideration was to be each party's exiting shares in the parties' respective existing corporate entities. Hicks (P) transferred his shares, but the shareholders (D) of the Bush Company did not, and the merger fell through. Hicks (P) brought suit for specific performance. As a defense, the Bush Company shareholders (D) asserted that an oral condition to the contract was that certain equity expansion funds be raised, and that such funds were not raised. The trial court determined that these funds were essential to the successful operation of the new venture, and that the parties had an oral understanding that the entire merger was subject to the condition that these funds be secured. Hicks (P) denied the oral condition, claiming no such condition had been placed on the written agreement. The trial court rendered judgment for the Bush Company shareholders (D), and the state's highest court granted review.

**ISSUE:** Is parol evidence admissible to prove an oral condition precedent to the legal effectiveness of a written agreement if the condition does not contradict the express terms of such written agreement?

**HOLDING AND DECISION:** (Fuld, J.) Yes. Parol evidence is admissible to prove an oral condition precedent to the legal effectiveness of a written agreement if the condition does not contradict the express terms of such written agreement. This parol evidence rule does not bar proof of every orally established condition precedent, but only of those that in a real sense contradict the terms of the written agreement. Here, there is no such contradiction. The merger agreement was silent as to the equity expansion funding, and, although the contract contained another condition precedent to the merger, the condition requiring the equity expansion funding did not contradict that other condition. The two conditions can stand side by side, and the equity funding condition is a condition in addition to the other. Moreover, evidence of an oral condition is not to be excluded as contradictory or inconsistent merely because the written agreement contains other conditions precedent. Accordingly, the trial court could properly conclude that the parties intended and understood that the merger was to be one of proposal only and that, even though the formal preliminary steps were to be taken, the writing was not to become operative as a contract or the merger effective until the equity expansion funding was raised, especially given that such a condition was not unreasonable under the circumstances. Therefore, the trial court did not err in admitting the parol evidence, and in holding that there was no operative merger contract that could be enforced. [Affirmed.]

## ▶ ANALYSIS

The Uniform Commercial Code (UCC) provides in § 2-202 that terms with respect to which the confirmatory memoranda of the parties agree or which are otherwise set forth in a writing intended by the parties as a final expression of their agreement with respect to such terms as are included therein may not be contradicted by evidence of any prior agreement or of a contemporaneous oral agreement but may be explained or supplemented by course of dealing or usage of trade, or by course of performance, and by evidence of consistent additional terms unless the court finds the writing to have been intended also as a complete and exclusive statement of the terms of the agreement. As with the result reached in this case, the UCC provides that consistent additional terms, not reduced to writing, may be proved. However, under the UCC approach, the additional terms may not be proved if the court finds that the writing was intended by both parties as a complete and exclusive statement of all the terms. If the additional terms are such that, if agreed upon, they would certainly have been included in the document in the view of the court, then evidence of their alleged making must be kept from the trier of fact.

Continued on next page.

## *Quicknotes*

**PAROL EVIDENCE**  Evidence given verbally; extraneous evidence.

**PAROL EVIDENCE RULE**  Doctrine precluding parties to an agreement from introducing evidence of prior or contemporaneous agreements in order to repudiate or alter the terms of a written contract.

**SPECIFIC PERFORMANCE**  An equitable remedy whereby the court requires the parties to perform their obligations pursuant to a contract.

# Kingston v. Preston

Business owner (P) v. Purchaser (D)

K.B., Lofft 194, 2 Doug. 689, 99 Eng. Rep. 437 (1773).

**NATURE OF CASE:** Action to recover damages for breach of contract.

**FACT SUMMARY:** Preston (D) agreed to sell his business to Kingston (P), and Kingston (P) agreed to, but did not, give security for the payments.

## 🏛 RULE OF LAW
Breach of a covenant by one party to a contract relieves the other party's obligation to perform another covenant which is dependent thereon, the performance of the first covenant being an implied condition precedent to the duty to perform the second covenant.

**FACTS:** Preston (D) agreed (among other things) to sell his business to Kingston (P). Kingston (P) agreed (among other things) to give sufficient security for his payments. Kingston's (P) personal worth was negligible. Kingston (P) failed to provide sufficient security, and thereafter Preston (D) refused to sell.

**ISSUE:** When one party agrees to sell and a second party agrees to give sufficient security for his payments, are those covenants mutual and independent so that it is no excuse for nonperformance by the first party for him to allege breach of covenant by the second party?

**HOLDING AND DECISION:** (Lord Mansfield, J.) No. When one party covenants to sell and a second party covenants in return to give sufficient security for his payments, those covenants are dependent. Therefore, Kingston (P) must show that he has provided or is ready and willing to provide sufficient security as a condition precedent to Preston's (D) duty to sell. The dependence or independence of covenants is to be determined from the intention of the parties which in turn will normally be determined by the "order of time in which the intent of the transaction requires their performance." Here, the security was to be given "at and before the sealing and delivery of the deeds" conveying the business. Thus, according to the "temporal sequence" test, Preston's (D) duty to convey his business was dependent on Kingston's (P) giving of sufficient security. Furthermore, it would be the greatest injustice if Kingston (P) should prevail. The giving of sufficient security was the essence of this agreement and, therefore, must necessarily be a condition precedent.

## ▶ ANALYSIS

Although Lord Mansfield in this famous decision focused on the time sequence of the contract provisions (e.g., a

provision to be performed after another provision is dependent on that other provision), he was very likely reacting primarily to the personal poverty of Kingston (P) and the "injustice" that would be done by making Preston (D) go through with his performance and then sue poor Kingston (P) for damages. (Kingston (P), presumably, might run the business into the ground very quickly, leaving Preston's (D) court victory a purely theoretical one.) Note that Lord Mansfield, in determining the time sequence (which he felt was so important), apparently looked not only to the contract itself but also to what he thought must have been the reasonable intentions of the parties.

## Quicknotes

**CONDITION PRECEDENT** The happening of an uncertain occurrence, which is necessary before a particular right or interest may be obtained or an action performed.

# Stewart v. Newbury

Builder (P) v. Foundry owner (D)

N.Y. Ct. App., 220 N.Y. 379, 115 N.E. 984 (1917).

**NATURE OF CASE:** Appeal from award of damages for breach of a construction contract.

**FACT SUMMARY:** Stewart (P), who was contracted to do excavating for Newbury (D), alleged that he was to be paid in the "usual manner," i.e., 85 percent every 30 days, 15 percent being retained until work was completed, even though this was not written into the contract. When Newbury (D) failed to pay, Stewart (P) stopped work.

## 🏛 RULE OF LAW

Where a contract is made to perform work and no agreement is made as to payment, the work must be substantially performed before payment can be demanded.

**FACTS:** Stewart (P) was contracted by Newbury (D) to do excavating work and claimed that over the telephone Newbury (D) promised to pay in the "usual manner." That is to say, 85 percent each 30 days or end of the month, 15 percent being retained until completion of the work. Newbury (D) denied so promising. Excavation began in July and continued until the end of September when Newbury (D) refused to pay the first bill. Stewart (P) claimed that Newbury (D) would not permit him to continue work because there were alleged variations from specifications. The trial judge charged the jury that if no agreement for payment was made, the builder could expect payment at reasonable intervals, if it were not understood that payments were due monthly, and if payments were not made, builder could abandon the work. The jury found for Stewart (P), and Newbury (D) appealed.

**ISSUE:** Where a contract is made to perform work and no agreement is made as to payment, must the work be substantially performed before payment can be demanded?

**HOLDING AND DECISION:** (Crane, J.) Yes. Where a contract is made to perform work and no agreement is made as to payment, the work must be substantially performed before payment can be demanded. It is settled that where a contract is made to perform work and no agreement is made as to payment, the work must be substantially performed before payment can be demanded. As the case was submitted also upon the ground that variation from specifications may have constituted breach, and since it is impossible to tell under which theory the jury arrived at its conclusion, the judgment must be reversed and a new trial ordered.

## ▶ ANALYSIS

It is not unusual in a bilateral contract that the parties will neglect to state in what order their promises will be performed. First, a party must perform before he is entitled to payment. That is to say, performance is a constructive condition precedent to payment. Periodic payments, as herein illustrated, are not implied. If periodic payments are agreed to, performance is a constructive condition precedent to first payment which is a constructive condition precedent to the next stage of performance, etc. These rules are ordinary business practice and have been said to be the "practice of centuries."

## Quicknotes

**CONSTRUCTIVE CONDITION** A condition that is not expressly stated in, or implied by, the terms of an agreement, but is imposed by law.

*P must perform substantially to be paid*

# Jacob & Youngs v. Kent

## Contractor (P) v. Customer (D)

N.Y. Ct. App., 230 N.Y. 239, 129 N.E. 889 (1921).

**NATURE OF CASE:** Appeal from grant of new trial in action for damages for breach of a construction contract.

**FACT SUMMARY:** Jacob & Youngs (P) was hired to build a $77,000 country home for Kent (D). When the dwelling was completed, it was discovered that through an oversight, pipe, not of Reading manufacture (though of comparable quality and price), which had been specified in the contract, was used. Kent (D) refused to make final payment of $3,483.46 upon learning of this.

### 🏛 RULE OF LAW
An omission, both trivial and innocent, will sometimes be atoned for by allowance of the remitting damage and will not always be the breach of a condition to be followed by forfeiture. For damages in construction contracts, the owner is entitled merely to the difference between the value of the structure if built to specifications and the value it has as constructed.

**FACTS:** Jacob & Youngs (Jacob) (P) built a country home for $77,000 for Kent (D) and sued for $3,483.46 which remained unpaid. Almost a year after completion, Kent (D) discovered that not all pipe in the home was of Reading manufacture as specified in the contract. Kent (D) ordered the plumbing replaced, but as it was encased in the walls, except in those spots where it must necessarily remain exposed, Jacob (P) refused to replace the pipe, stating that the pipe used was of comparable price and quality. It appears that the omission was neither fraudulent nor willful and was due to oversight. Kent (D) refused to pay the balance of the construction cost still due. The trial court directed a verdict for Kent (D), but the appellate division reversed, and granted a new trial.

**ISSUE:** Was the omission by Jacob (P) so trivial and innocent so as not to be a breach of the condition?

**HOLDING AND DECISION:** (Cardozo, J.) Yes. Where the significance of the default or omission is grievously out of proportion to the oppression of the forfeiture, the breach is considered to be trivial and innocent. A change will not be tolerated if it is so dominant and pervasive so as to frustrate the purpose of the contract. The contractor cannot install anything he believes to be just as good. It is a matter of degree judged by the purpose to be served, the desire to be gratified, the excuse for deviation from the letter, and the cruelty of enforced adherence. Under the circumstances, the measure of damages should not be the cost of replacing the pipe which would be great.

Instead, the difference in value between the dwelling as specified and the dwelling as constructed should be the measure, even though it may be nominal or nothing. Usually, the owner is entitled to the cost of completion, but not where it is grossly unfair and out of proportion to the good to be obtained. This simply is a rule to promote justice when there is substantial performance with trivial deviation. Affirmed. *for P.*

**DISSENT:** (McLaughlin, J.) Jacob (P) failed to perform as specified. It makes no difference why Kent (D) wanted a particular kind of pipe. Failure to use the kind of pipe specified was either intentional or due to gross neglect which amounted to the same thing.

## ▶ ANALYSIS

Substantial performance cannot occur where the breach is intentional, as it is the antithesis of material breach. The part unperformed must not destroy the purpose or value of the contract. Because, here, there is a dissatisfied-landowner who stands to retain the defective structure built on his land, there arises the problem of unjust enrichment. Usually, it would appear that the owner would pocket the damages he collected rather than remedying the defect by tearing out the wrong pipe and replacing it with the specified pipe. The owner would have a home substantially in compliance and a sum of money greatly in excess of the harm suffered by him. Note that under the doctrine of de minimis non curat lex, which means "the law is not concerned with trifles" (*Black's Law Dictionary*, Ninth Edition), trivial defects, even if willful, will be ignored. The party who claims substantial performance has still breached the contract and is liable for damages but in a lesser amount than for a willful breach.

*P still liable for damages.*

## Quicknotes

**DE MINIMIS NON CURAT LEX** Not of sufficient significance to invoke legal action. Shortened to "de minimis."

**FORFEITURE** The loss of a right or interest as a penalty for failing to fulfill an obligation.

**SUBSTANTIAL PERFORMANCE** Performance of all the essential obligations pursuant to an agreement.

# Bartus v. Riccardi

Hearing aid seller (P) v. Buyer (D)

N.Y. City Ct., 284 N.Y.S.2d 222, 55 Misc. 2d 3 (1967).

**NATURE OF CASE:** Action for breach of contract.

**FACT SUMMARY:** Bartus (P) gave Riccardi (D) an Acousticon hearing aid, Model A-665, which was supposedly the improved model of the A-660 hearing aid ordered by Riccardi (D).

## 🏛 RULE OF LAW
A seller may offer to cure a nonconforming tender even though the buyer has previously revoked his acceptance and it is beyond the contract time if there are reasonable grounds to believe that the nonconforming goods would be accepted and there is reasonable notice of intent to cure.

**FACTS:** Riccardi (D) was informed by a hearing clinic that he needed a hearing aid. The Model A-660 Acousticon was recommended for his needs. Riccardi (D) was informed by Bartus (P), who sold hearing aids, that the A-660 had been improved, and Riccardi (D) purchased the improved model, the A-665. After using the model for several days, Riccardi (D) returned it. Bartus (P) subsequently informed Riccardi (D) that he would get him the A-660 or any other model he wished. Riccardi (D) refused to accept a replacement, and Bartus (P) brought suit on the unpaid balance of the contract price of the A-665. Bartus (P) alleged that he had the right to cure even after the rejection of the model as nonconforming.

**ISSUE:** Does the failure to tender strict performance and the subsequent rejection and revocation by the buyer prevent the seller from attempting a cure?

**HOLDING AND DECISION:** (Hymes, J.) No. UCC § 2-508 has altered the concept of strict performance. A seller is permitted to cure a nonconforming delivery before the expiration of the contract time by notifying the buyer of his intention and by delivery before the contract has expired. UCC § 2-508(2) would allow a cure beyond the contract time even if acceptance has been revoked if the seller had reasonable grounds to believe the nonconforming goods would be accepted and he reasonably notifies the buyer of his intent to promptly deliver conforming goods. Bartus (P) had reason to believe that the A-665 would be accepted, and he reasonably notified Riccardi (D) of his offer to cure. Riccardi (D) had not altered his position at that time by purchasing a hearing aid elsewhere. Judgment for Bartus (P).

## ▶ ANALYSIS

If the buyer, after rejecting the nonconforming goods, alters his position before notice of an attempted cure,

and this was commercially reasonable under the circumstances, the buyer will not be liable where the seller subsequently attempts to cure. Whether the action is commercially reasonable depends on whether the contract has expired; the buyer's needs for prompt delivery; the seller's apparent ability to perform; prior conduct of the parties; etc.

## Quicknotes

**CURE** In a commercial transaction, the seller has a right to correct a delivery of defective goods within the time originally provided for performance as specified in the contract.

**MATERIAL BREACH** Breach of a contract's terms by one party that is so substantial as to relieve the other party from its obligations pursuant thereto.

**SUBSTANTIAL PERFORMANCE** Performance of all the essential obligations pursuant to an agreement.

# Gill v. Johnstown Lumber Co.

## Log driver (P) v. Sawmill (D)

Pa. Sup. Ct., 151 Pa. 534, 25 A. 120 (1892).

**NATURE OF CASE:** Appeal from directed verdict for the defense action to recover damages for breach of contract.

**FACT SUMMARY:** Gill (P) contracted to drive and deliver four million feet of logs but had delivered only a part of that amount when a flood swept away the rest of the logs.

### 🏛 RULE OF LAW
When consideration for work done is apportionable or apportioned in the contract, that contract will be interpreted as divisible (severable) in case of part performance.

**FACTS:** Gill (P) contracted to drive four million feet of logs to Johnstown Lumber Co's (Johnstown's) (D) boom. The work undertaken by Gill (P) consisted of driving logs of oak and other kinds of timber and also driving cross ties. Gill (P) was to be paid $1 per thousand feet for the oak logs, $0.75 per thousand feet for all other logs, and $0.03 each for cross ties. Gill (P) did deliver some of the logs as promised, but a flood swept other logs past Johnstown's (D) boom after Gill (P) had driven them part of the way. Gill (P) sued for payment, but the court directed a verdict for Johnstown (D) based on Gill's (P) default. Gill (P) appealed.

**ISSUE:** When consideration for work done is apportionable or apportioned in the contract, will that contract be interpreted as divisible (severable) in case of part performance?

**HOLDING AND DECISION:** (Heydrick, J.) Yes. If the part to be performed by one party consists of several and distinct items, and the price to be paid by the other is (1) apportioned to each item to be performed or (2) is left to be implied by law, such a contract will generally be held to be severable. The consideration to be paid for Gill's (P) work was not an entire sum but was apportioned among the several items at the rate of $1 per thousand feet for the oak logs, $0.75 per thousand feet for all other logs, $0.03 each for cross ties, etc. Applying the test of an apportionable or apportioned consideration to the contract in question, it will be seen at once that it is severable. Thus, Gill (P) may recover at the contract rate for the logs delivered as promised. If the consideration to be paid is single and entire, the contract must be held to be entire. With respect to each log (or bunch of logs), the consideration to be paid is an entire sum for the whole distance and is not apportionable to parts of the drive. The contract in this respect is "like a contract of common carriage which is dependent upon the delivery of the goods at the designated place." Thus, Gill (P) may not recover for any part-way shipment which took place before the flood. Reversed.

### ▶ ANALYSIS

A more general test of divisibility is whether, had the parties thought of it, they would have been willing to exchange the part performances irrespective of what transpired subsequently. It is rare that the parties express an intention on this question so that whether a contract is "divisible" (separable) or "entire" is usually a matter of interpretation. Thus, the "apportionable consideration" test which the court uses in the present case is a bit facile and cannot always be counted on as the appropriate manifestation of the parties' intention to enter a divisible contract.

---

### Quicknotes

**BREACH OF CONTRACT** Unlawful failure by a party to perform its obligations pursuant to contract.

**CONSIDERATION** Value given by one party in exchange for performance, or a promise to perform, by another party.

**PART PERFORMANCE** Partial performance of a contract, promise or obligation.

# Britton v. Turner

Laborer (P) v. Employer (D)

N.H. Sup. Ct., 6 N.H. 481 (1834).

**NATURE OF CASE:** Appeal from recovery in quantum meruit for work done.

**FACT SUMMARY:** Britton (P) contracted to work for Turner (D) for an entire year but left without cause before the year was up.

## RULE OF LAW
A defaulting party, although unable to recover on his contract, may recover under a quasi-contractual theory the reasonable value of his services less any damages to the other party arising out of the default.

**FACTS:** Britton (P) was under contract to labor for Turner (D) for one year and was to be paid $120 for the work. Britton (P), without cause, left Turner's (D) employ after nine and one half months and sought to recover the reasonable value of his labor. A jury awarded Britton (P) a verdict for $95. Turner (D) appealed.

**ISSUE:** Can one who performs work under an entire contract but leaves without cause before the expiration of the term of the contract, recover in quantum meruit the reasonable value of the work he has performed?

**HOLDING AND DECISION:** (Parker, J.) Yes. Although it is clear that one who has labored for only a portion of the contract term may not recover on the contract, he may recover in quantum meruit the reasonable value of his services to the extent that the other party has received a benefit in excess of damages arising from the breach. A contrary result would be unjust and unequal in its operation. By that result, the party who attempts performance may be placed in a much worse situation than he who wholly disregards his contract, and the other party may receive much more, by the breach of the contract, than the injury, which he sustained by such breach, and more than he could be entitled to if he was seeking to recover damages by an action. In the present case, Turner (D) has been receiving benefit from day to day which he cannot now reject, and the circumstance is not distinguishable from those circumstances surrounding contracts to build houses where quantum meruit recoveries have been allowed despite deviations from the building contracts. Since Turner (D) has alleged no damages arising from Britton's (P) breach, the jury's verdict should be affirmed.

## ANALYSIS

The court here acknowledges the contrary rule which will not allow a breaching party any recovery after only part performance (subject to the doctrine of substantial performance). Even today the present case still represents the minority view although the trend is in its direction. The court emphasizes the injustice of the prevailing role that one who attempts performance is in a worse position than one who totally ignores the contract. Although there is a temptation to respond, "So what?" courts following Britton's (P) lead have pointed to the arbitrary forfeitures which breachers would suffer and the pure windfalls to the breachees. Further, the current trend in contract law is not to treat a breach as an inherently evil thing; the effect of allowing an unabashed forfeiture would be to sanction a kind of punitive damage.

## Quicknotes

**ASSUMPSIT** An oral or written promise by one party to perform or pay another.

**QUANTUM MERUIT** Equitable doctrine allowing recovery for labor and materials provided by one party, even though no contract was entered into, in order to avoid unjust enrichment by the benefited party.

**QUASI-CONTRACT** An implied contract created by law to prevent unjust enrichment.

# Kirkland v. Archbold

## General contractor (P) v. Property owner (D)

Ohio Ct. App., 113 N.E.2d 496 (1953).

**NATURE OF CASE:** Action to recover in quantum meruit for work done.

**FACT SUMMARY:** Kirkland (P) contracted to repair and improve Archbold's (D) property but defaulted after partial performance.

## RULE OF LAW
A defaulting party may recover for partial performance, on a quasi-contractual theory, the benefit received by the other party diminished by the damages to that other party arising from the default.

**FACTS:** Kirkland (P) agreed, for $6,000, to be paid in scheduled progress payments, to make certain repairs and improvements on Archbold's (D) property. (The court held that the contract was not severable.) Kirkland (P) defaulted after partial performance and sought to recover in quantum meruit for the reasonable value of his services.

**ISSUE:** May a defaulting builder who has enriched the estate of another recover, on a quasi-contractual theory, for the reasonable value of his partial performance?

**HOLDING AND DECISION:** (Skeel, J.) Yes. Although earlier case law would not allow a defaulting plaintiff to recover for partial performance (subject to the doctrine of "substantial performance"), the modern trend is to relax the severity of this rule and to permit defaulting contractors to recover in quantum meruit where their work has contributed a substantial value to the other contracting party's property. The result of the older decisions was to penalize a defaulting contractor to the extent of the value of all benefit conferred by his work and materials upon the property of the other party. That result came from unduly emphasizing the technical unity and entirety of contracts. Some decisions permit such result only when the defaulting contractor's conduct was willful or malicious. The modern trend, following the lead of *Britton v. Turner*, 6 N.H. 481 (1834), is based on the theory of unjust enrichment and an abhorrence of forfeiture. The action is not founded on the broken contract, but on a quasi-contract to pay for the benefits received, which cannot be returned, diminished by the damages sustained because of the contractor's breach of his contract. Reversed and Remanded.

## ▌ ANALYSIS

Allowing quasi-contractual recovery is a court's way of attempting to do what is "justice" in its eyes when traditional contract theory leads to an "unjust" result. Note the present court's citation or use of such phrases as "natural justice" and "[lack of] conscious moral fault." Although the present case probably still represents the minority view, the modern trend of the law is indeed in its direction. See *Britton v. Turner*, 6 N.H. 481 (1834).

## Quicknotes

**FORFEITURE** The loss of a right or interest as a penalty for failing to fulfill an obligation.

**PART PERFORMANCE** Partial performance of a contract, promise or obligation.

**QUANTUM MERUIT** Equitable doctrine allowing recovery for labor and materials provided by one party, even though no contract was entered into, in order to avoid unjust enrichment by the benefited party.

**QUASI-CONTRACT** An implied contract created by law to prevent unjust enrichment.

**UNJUST ENRICHMENT** The unlawful acquisition of money or property of another for which both law and equity require restitution to be made.

# Walker & Co. v. Harrison

## Sign servicer (P) v. Dry cleaner (D)

Mich. Sup. Ct., 347 Mich. 630, 81 N.W.2d 352 (1957).

**NATURE OF CASE:** Appeal from award of damages for breach of contract.

**FACT SUMMARY:** Harrison (D) rented a neon sign and sought to repudiate the rental agreement when Walker & Co. (Walker) (P) delayed in repairing the sign.

---

**RULE OF LAW**
A party attempting to repudiate a contract must convince the court that the other party has materially breached the contract.

---

**FACTS:** Walker & Co. (Walker) (P) contracted to rent a neon sign to Harrison (D). The rental agreement included repair service "as deemed necessary by Walker (P) to keep sign in first class advertising condition." Shortly after the sign was installed, someone hit it with a tomato. Rust was allegedly visible on the chrome, and cobwebs had collected in the corners. Harrison (D) made several calls to Walker (P) complaining of the sign's condition, but maintenance was not forthcoming. Harrison (D) repudiated the contract and Walker (P) sued for the rent. [Walker (P) subsequently repaired the sign.] From a judgment for Walker (P), Harrison (D) appealed.

**ISSUE:** May one party to a contract, repudiate that contract under circumstances which do not amount to a "material breach" by the other party?

**HOLDING AND DECISION:** (Smith, J.) No. It is essential to one party's repudiation of a contract that he demonstrates a "material breach" by the other party. As to the criterion for "materiality," there is no single touchstone. Here, although Walker's (P) delay in rendering service was certainly irritating, it cannot be said as a matter of law that the delay was a material breach. There was no valid ground for Harrison's (D) repudiation and failure to comply with the terms of the contract was itself a material breach, entitling Walker (P) to judgment. Affirmed.

---

**⦿ ANALYSIS**

The primary advantage in alleging "material breach" is that the alleging party, if successful, may rescind the whole contract. If a breach is not material, the breachee may recover damages flowing therefrom but may not cancel the contract. In the present case, for example, it would not be surprising to find that Harrison (D) wanted out of his contract for reasons other than the breach and alleged "materiality" as a means to that end. As the court indicates, there is no simple test for materiality (which is unfortunate since so much can hinge on the characterization). Among the factors often considered are: (1) To what extent has the contract been performed prior to the breach? (2) Was the breach willful? (3) Was the breach "quantitatively" serious? and (4) What will be the consequences of the determination (e.g., will it work extreme hardship on one of the parties)? Some of the above factors should undoubtedly be given more weight than others, and arguably some of them overlap. Perhaps the most important factor is the last one which openly acknowledges "materiality" as a conclusory label to be applied insofar as a sense of "justice" requires it.

---

## Quicknotes

**ASSUMPSIT** An oral or written promise by one party to perform or pay another.

**MATERIALITY** Importance; the degree of relevance or necessity to the particular matter.

**RECOUPMENT** The right of a defendant to have the plaintiff's award of damages reduced because of either prior payment tendered or some unlawful action on the part of the plaintiff.

**REPUDIATION** The actions or statements of a party to a contract that evidence his intent not to perform, or to continue performance, of his duties or obligations thereunder.

# K&G Construction Co. v. Harris

General contractor (P) v. Subcontractor (D)

Md. Ct. App., 223 Md. 305, 164 A.2d 451 (1960).

**NATURE OF CASE:** Action to recover damages for breach of contract

**FACT SUMMARY:** Harris (D) breached his covenant to perform in a workmanlike manner, and K&G Construction Co. (P) thereafter declined to make good its return covenant to pay. Harris (D) refused to perform further, causing damage to K&G (P).

### ▥ RULE OF LAW
Whenever possible, according to the intentions of the parties and the good sense of the case, mutual promises in a contract will be regarded as dependent covenants.

**FACTS:** Harris (D) subcontracted to do excavating for K&G Construction Co. (K&G) (P), all work to be performed in a "workmanlike manner." Harris (D) was to be paid each month after submission of a requisition of the prior month's work. In the course of excavating, Harris's (D) bulldozer operator drove his machine too close to K&G's (P) house, causing the collapse of a wall and other damage to the house. [The court held this to be a breach of Harris's (D) promise to perform in a "workmanlike manner."] When Harris (D) thereafter would not pay for the bulldozer damage, K&G (P) withheld payment for some prior work. Harris (D) in turn refused to continue working after K&G's (P) withholding of payment. K&G (P) subsequently hired someone else to complete the job at a higher cost and sued Harris (D) for damages.

**ISSUE:** Are a covenant to perform in a "workmanlike manner" and a return covenant to pay independent of each other?

**HOLDING AND DECISION:** (Prescott, J.) No. The modern rule is a presumption that mutual promises in a contract are dependent and should be so regarded when possible. *Kingston v. Preston*, 2 Doug. 689 (1773), created the modern rule by deciding against the ancient presumption of independence of covenants (absent an express provision to the contrary). The present test for dependency is the intention of the parties and the good sense of the case. In the present case, the most reasonable conclusion as to the parties' intention is in accordance with the natural presumption of dependence. If the covenant were not held dependent here, subcontractors would have a much greater tendency to become insolvent before completing their contracts. Since K&G's (P) duty to pay was dependent on Harris's (D) performance according to contract, K&G (P) was entitled to withhold payment following Harris's (D) breach of his covenant to perform in a "workmanlike

manner." Further, Harris's (D) refusal to continue work was an additional breach for which K&G (P) may recover its cost to complete. Reversed.

### ▶ ANALYSIS
The present case demonstrates the basic modern rule that a party who is to perform work must perform (according to the contract) before he is entitled to payment. In other words, performance of work is a constructive condition precedent to payment. The present case, which concerns periodic payments, involves a series of alternating constructive conditions precedent (e.g., performance by Harris (D) is a constructive condition precedent to K&G's (P) duty to make the first payment, which is in turn a constructive condition precedent to Harris's (D) duty to perform the next stage of work, etc.). Thus, K&G's (P) refusal to pay was justified and not a "breach" since the payment was conditioned on the prior "workmanlike" performance by Harris (D) which was not forthcoming.

---

### Quicknotes

**CONDITION PRECEDENT** The happening of an uncertain occurrence, which is necessary before a particular right or interest may be obtained or an action performed.

**DEPENDENT COVENANTS** An obligation of one party to perform pursuant to an agreement, which is dependent upon the performance of the other.

**MUTUAL PROMISES** Promises that bind both parties.

# Iron Trade Products Co. v. Wilkoff Co.

## Rail purchaser (P) v. Supplier (D)

Pa. Sup. Ct., 272 Pa. 172, 116 A. 150 (1922).

**NATURE OF CASE:** Action to recover damages for breach of contract.

**FACT SUMMARY:** Wilkoff Co. (D) contracted to deliver rails to Iron Trade Products Co. (Iron Trade) (P) but refused to do so after Iron Trade (P) reduced the available supply and made Wilkoff's (D) performance more difficult.

### 🏛 RULE OF LAW
Mere difficulty of performance will not excuse a breach of contract even though that difficulty was created by the other contracting party.

**FACTS:** Iron Trade Products Co. (Iron Trade) (P) contracted to purchase 2,600 tons of rails from Wilkoff Co. (D) at the rate of $41 per ton. Iron Trade (P) thereafter purchased additional rails from one of the very few rail suppliers, thereby reducing the overall rail supply and driving up the market price. Because of the reduced supply and increased price of rails, it became difficult and unprofitable for Wilkoff (D) to procure rails for Iron Trade (P). Wilkoff (D) failed to deliver. Iron Trade (P) subsequently covered at a higher price and sued for damages. The trial court entered judgment for Iron Trade (P), and Wilkoff (D) appealed.

**ISSUE:** Does one party's conduct, which renders performance by the second party more difficult, excuse that second party's refusal to perform?

**HOLDING AND DECISION:** (Walling, J.) No. If a party seeking to secure all the merchandise which he could, entered into a contract for a quantity of the required goods, and subsequently made performance of the contract by the seller more difficult by making other purchases which increased the scarcity of the available supply, his conduct would furnish no excuse for refusal to perform the prior contract. Here, Iron Trade's (P) conduct did not render performance by Wilkoff (D) impossible but only more difficult. Mere difficulty of performance will not excuse a breach of contract. (The case of *U.S. v. Peck*, 102 U.S. 64 (1880), in which one party cut off the other party's only available source of supply, thus rendering performance impossible, is not parallel.) Finally, there was no restriction in the contract on subsequent purchases by Iron Trade (P). Affirmed.

### ▶ ANALYSIS

Although there is no straightforward rule which explains the result in all the cases similar to the present one, perhaps the connecting thread is an assumption-of-risk notion. The court here undoubtedly felt that a deflated supply (and the resulting inflated market price) was a foreseeable commercial risk which Wilkoff (D) undertook when he entered the contract. However, if Iron Trade (P) had interfered with what it knew to be Wilkoff's (D) only source of supply, Wilkoff's (D) duty might have been discharged since Wilkoff (D) would not be held to have assumed the risk of Iron Trade's (P) knowing interference. See *Patterson v. Meyerhofer*, 204 N.Y. 96 (1912). A court will use its instinct for "justice" in each case.

---

## Quicknotes

**BREACH OF CONTRACT** Unlawful failure by a party to perform its obligations pursuant to contract.

# New England Structures, Inc. v. Loranger

Subcontractor (D) v. General contractor (P)

Mass. Sup. Jud. Ct., 354 Mass. 62, 234 N.E.2d 888 (1968).

**NATURE OF CASE:** Action for damages for breach of a construction contract.

**FACT SUMMARY:** Loranger (P), which contracted with New England Structures, Inc. (Structures) (D) for the latter to construct a gypsum roof on a school, terminated the deal, contending that Structures (D) failed to provide enough skilled workmen as required by the contract.

---

### 🏛 RULE OF LAW
In stating his reasons for rejecting performance or his objections to a performance which he has accepted, a promisee has not excused other grounds upon which he may have rejected the defective performance unless the promisor shows that it has relied to its detriment upon the particular ground stated.

---

**FACTS:** Loranger (P), general contractor on a school project, contracted on July 11, 1961, with New England Structures, Inc. (Structures) (D), a subcontractor, to install a gypsum roof deck in the school. Structures (D) began work on November 24, 1961. On December 18, 1961, Loranger (P) sent a telegram to Structures (D) terminating the agreement on the ground that Structures (D) had failed to provide a sufficient number of skilled workmen as required by article 5 of the contracts. Loranger (P) stated its intention of obtaining other workers and charging any higher costs to Structures (D). As five days' notice was required, Structures (D) was told to remove itself from the project by December 26, 1961. Loranger (P) claimed that all the work was not properly done, while Structures (D) claimed that it was not allowed to complete its five days and had it been it could have completed the work. The trial judge ruled as a matter of law that Loranger's (P) justification of termination as being Structures' (D) failure to supply enough skilled workers confined Loranger (P) to that ground only, which, if so found, would have been sufficient for the jury to find Structures (D) in breach. The judge also instructed that Structures (D) could not be found in breach if it had supplied a sufficient number of skilled workers even though it may have done improper work as Loranger (P) limited grounds for breach by its telegram. But if Structures (D) was found to have breached, these other allegations could be considered for the purposes of setting damages.

**ISSUE:** In stating his reasons for rejecting performance or his objections to a performance which he has accepted, has a promisee excused other grounds upon which he may have rejected the defective performance unless the promi-

sor shows that it has relied to its detriment upon the particular ground stated?

**HOLDING AND DECISION:** (Cutter, J.) No. In stating his reasons for rejecting performance or his objections to a performance which he has accepted, a promisee has not excused other grounds upon which he may have rejected the defective performance unless the promisor shows that it has relied to its detriment upon the particular ground stated. The grounds for breach would not be limited unless Structures (D) showed it has detrimentally relied on the justification given. When one has several reasons for acting the way he did, he is not prevented from relying upon them simply because he put forth only one originally, unless the other party has been misled to its harm or he is estopped on some other ground. When a period of notice is required, the contract remains in force and must continue to be performed during the established period set after notice of termination, here, five days. "Strong practical considerations" make it appear that a five-day period was intended to permit the subcontractor to remove his workers and equipment rather than give time to permit an attempt to cure the defect in performance. Nothing suggests that had Structures (D) cured the defect within five days, Loranger (P) would have had to withdraw termination. But if Loranger (P) was not justified in terminating, it would be liable for breach. Accordingly, exceptions are sustained.

---

### ▶ ANALYSIS

The view of this case is a more modern view and is typical of a growing trend away from cases which had limited termination to the stated grounds rather than the general grounds of the contract. Basically, one can change his defense unless the other party has relied on it. In Restatement (First) § 305, this is dealt with where performance of the condition or promise requires the tender of money. If the tender is not made with tender legal for that purpose, but it is rejected without reason, the party making tender cannot have a defense on the ground no reason was given.

━═▪

### Quicknotes

**DETRIMENTAL RELIANCE** Action by one party, resulting in loss, which is based on the conduct or promises of another.

━═▪

# Hochster v. De La Tour

Prospective employee (P) v. Employer (D)

Q.B., 2 E. & B. 678, 118 Eng. Rep. 922 (1853).

**NATURE OF CASE:** Action to recover damages for breach of contract.

**FACT SUMMARY:** Before Hochster (P) was due to perform his contract of employment for De La Tour (D), De La Tour (D) announced his intention to repudiate the contract, whereupon Hochster (P) immediately commenced an action for breach of contract.

## 🏛 RULE OF LAW
A party to a contract who renounces his intention to perform may not complain if the other party, instead of waiting until performance is due, elects to sue immediately for breach of contract.

**FACTS:** In April, Hochster (P) contracted to serve as De La Tour's (D) employee beginning on June 1. On May 11, De La Tour (D) wrote to Hochster (P) that he had changed his mind and declined Hochster's (P) services. On May 22, Hochster (P) brought this action for breach of contract.

**ISSUE:** When the time for performance has not arrived, but one party nevertheless indicates his intention not to perform, must the other party wait until the performance should have occurred before bringing action for breach of contract?

**HOLDING AND DECISION:** (Lord Campbell, C.J.) No. "The man who wrongfully renounces a contract into which he has deliberately entered cannot justly complain if he is immediately sued for a compensation in damages by the man whom he has injured; and it seems reasonable to allow an option to the injured party, either to sue immediately, or to wait till the time when the act was to be done." If Hochster (P) had to wait until June 1 to sue, he would not be able to enter any employment which would interfere with his promise to begin work at that time. But it is surely more rational that after renunciation by De La Tour (D), Hochster (P) should be at liberty to consider himself absolved from any future performance. Thus, he would be free to seek other employment in mitigation of damages. De La Tour's (D) renunciation may be treated as a breach of contract. Judgment for Hochster (P).

## ▶ ANALYSIS

This is the leading case on the so-called doctrine of "anticipatory breach." The court's reasoning is erroneous insofar as it felt that Hochster (P) would otherwise be caught in a dilemma: to remain idle and hope for a favorable future judgment or to obtain other employment and thereby forfeit his rights against De La Tour (D). The court overlooked the rule that where a party manifests prospective unwillingness to perform the other party may suspend his performance and change his position without surrendering his right to sue after the breach occurs. In other words, the court could have considered the repudiation as (1) a defense to an action brought by De La Tour (D) and (2) an excuse of the constructive condition that Hochster (P) be ready, willing, and able to perform on June 1. The fact that the leading case is based on erroneous premises has caused hostility by some commentators toward the doctrine of "anticipatory breach." The doctrine, however, has been widely accepted both in England and the United States. (There is much, from a practical viewpoint, to support the doctrine, and it could, perhaps, rest more cleanly on a constructive duty not to repudiate. Compare other constructive conditions and duties of cooperation imposed on contracting parties.)

---

## Quicknotes

**ACTION IN ASSUMPSIT** Action to recover damages for breach of an oral or written promise to perform or pay pursuant to a contract.

**ANTICIPATORY BREACH** Breach of a contract subsequent to formation but prior to the time performance is due.

**REPUDIATION** The actions or statements of a party to a contract that evidence his intent not to perform, or to continue performance, of his duties or obligations thereunder.

# Kanavos v. Hancock Bank & Trust Co.

Option holder (P) v. Stock holder (D)

Mass. Sup. Jud. Ct., 395 Mass. 199, 479 N.E.2d 168 (1985).

**NATURE OF CASE:** Appeal of reversal of directed verdict in action for damages for breach of contract.

**FACT SUMMARY:** Hancock Bank & Trust Co. (D) sold certain stock to which Kanavos (P) had earlier been given a contractual right of first refusal.

> ## 🏛 RULE OF LAW
> A party's ability to recover for breach of a contract giving a right of first refusal depends on his having had the financial resources to exercise the option.

**FACTS:** Kanavos (P) contracted with Hancock Bank & Trust Co. (the Bank) (D) for the right of first refusal in the purchase of a limited partnership controlling certain real estate. The Bank (D) eventually sold the shares without notifying Kanavos (P), who sued for breach. At trial, the Bank (D) was granted a nonsuit. This was reversed by the court of appeals. On remand, the trial court held that Kanavos's (P) right to recover was not dependent on his ability to have exercised the right at the time of sale.

**ISSUE:** Does a party's ability to recover for breach of a contract giving a right of first refusal depend on his having had the financial resources to exercise the option?

**HOLDING AND DECISION:** (Wilkins, J.) Yes. A party's ability to recover for breach of a contract giving a right of first refusal depends on his having had the financial resources to exercise the option. It is the general rule that when performance under a contract is concurrent, one party cannot put another in default unless he is able to perform his obligation. From this general rule it has been held that the financial ability of a prospective buyer of property is a material issue in his action for damages against a repudiating seller. The situation here falls squarely within this rule, and the trial court therefore erred. Remanded for retrial.

## ▶ ANALYSIS

A sub-issue here was who had the burden of proof regarding Kanavos's (P) ability to pay. The court held that Kanavos (P) had to prove he was able to pay. The court admitted that the rulings on this issue vary from state to state but believed Kanavos (P) was in a better position to give evidence on this issue.

■■■

## Quicknotes

**DIRECTED VERDICT** A verdict ordered by the court in a jury trial.

**NONSUIT** Judgment against a party who fails to make out a case.

■■■

# Cosden Oil & Chemical Co. v. Karl O. Helm Aktiengesellschaft

Oil supplier (P) v. International trading company (D)

736 F.2d 1064 (5th Cir. 1984).

**NATURE OF CASE:** Appeal from award of damages for breach of contract.

**FACT SUMMARY:** Cosden Oil & Chemical Co. (P) contended Karl O. Helm Aktiengesellschaft (D) failed to pay for delivered goods, and this constituted a repudiation of the balance of the contract.

## 🏛 RULE OF LAW
Damages for a seller's anticipatory repudiation are measured at a commercially reasonable time after the repudiation.

**FACTS:** Cosden Oil & Chemical Co. (Cosden) (P) contracted to supply petroleum products to Karl O. Helm Aktiengesellschaft (Helm) (D). Due to problems in supply, only part of the order could be filled. Helm (D) refused to pay for the goods delivered, and Cosden (P) sued. Helm (D) contended that Cosden (P) had anticipatorily repudiated the contract. The trial court found for Helm (D) on its counterclaim and affixed damages at a commercially reasonable time after the repudiation. Both parties appealed.

**ISSUE:** Are damages for a seller's anticipatory repudiation measured at a commercially reasonable time after the repudiation?

**HOLDING AND DECISION:** (Reavley, J.) Yes. Damages for a seller's anticipatory repudiation are measured at a commercially reasonable time after the repudiation. This allows the buyer sufficient time to choose his remedies and to consider mitigation. Affirmed in part, reversed in part, and remanded.

## ▶ ANALYSIS

The court rejected Cosden's (P) argument that products purchased by Helm (D) as cover provide a ceiling for the damages assessed. The jury found such purchases were not covered. Thus, the court could not apply the suggested standard.

■■■

## Quicknotes

**ANTICIPATORY REPUDIATION** Breach of a contract subsequent to formation but prior to the time performance is due.

**MITIGATION** Reduction in penalty.

**REPUDIATION** The actions or statements of a party to a contract that evidence his intent not to perform, or to continue performance, of his duties or obligations thereunder.

■■■

# McCloskey & Co. v. Minweld Steel Co.

## Contractor (P) v. Subcontractor (D)

220 F.2d 101 (3d Cir. 1955).

**NATURE OF CASE:** Appeal from dismissal of action for damages for breach of a construction contract.

**FACT SUMMARY:** Minweld Steel Co. (Minweld) (D), a subcontractor, had contracted to supply and erect certain steel portions for McCloskey & Co. (McCloskey) (P), the general contractor, on a state hospital project for Pennsylvania. When, because of the outbreak of the Korean War, Minweld (D) had difficulty procuring steel and requested, by letter, McCloskey's (P) aid, McCloskey (P) treated Minweld's (D) letter as an admission of breach and terminated the agreement.

> ## 🏛 RULE OF LAW
> In order to give rise to a renunciation amounting to a breach of contract, there must be an absolute and unequivocal refusal to perform or a distinct and positive statement of an inability to do so.

**FACTS:** McCloskey & Co. (McCloskey) (P), a contractor on a Pennsylvania state hospital project, made three contracts with Minweld Steel Co. (Minweld) (D) for the latter to furnish and erect all structural steel for two of the hospital buildings. If Minweld (D) failed or refused to supply sufficient materials of proper quality, McCloskey (P) would have the right to terminate on two days' notice. When Minweld (D) had difficulty procuring steel due to the outbreak of the Korean War, it wrote McCloskey (P), requesting its help or the state's help in finding steel. McCloskey (P) treated this letter as notice of Minweld's (D) alleged positive intention not to perform the contracts, hence, a breach. At trial, Minweld's (D) motion for judgment on the ground McCloskey (P) had failed to state a cause of action was granted.

**ISSUE:** In order to give rise to a renunciation amounting to a breach of contract, must there be an absolute and unequivocal refusal to perform or a distinct and positive statement of an inability to do so?

**HOLDING AND DECISION:** (McLaughlin, J.) Yes. In order to give rise to a renunciation amounting to a breach of contract, there must be an absolute and unequivocal refusal to perform or a distinct and positive statement of an inability to do so. The letter conveyed no idea of contract repudiation by Minweld (D). While it was in a desperate situation, Minweld (D) realistically faced its problem and did not indicate definite abandonment or loss of all hope of finishing the project. Minweld (D) did not absolutely or unequivocally refuse to perform. Moreover, failure to take preparatory action before the time when any performance is promised is not anticipatory breach, even though such failure made it impossible for performance to take place, though the promisor at the time of failure does not intend to perform his promise. Minweld (D) was no more than unable to give assurances as to preparatory arrangements. Affirmed.

## ▶ ANALYSIS

A statement such as "I will not perform" is an anticipatory breach if it is made before performance is due. Under the doctrine of prospective unwillingness to perform, the other party may suspend his performance and change his position. As the repudiation was an anticipatory breach, the other party may sue immediately. But if the statement is basically "I doubt that I will be able to perform," as occurred in this case, there is not repudiation. Accordingly, suit cannot be brought immediately under the doctrine of anticipatory repudiation. However, under the doctrine of prospective unwillingness to perform, the other party could suspend his performance and demand assurances and take any other steps allowable under the doctrine. This is the same for the circumstance where a party says "I will not perform unless X occurs." It is very possible that the unforeseen circumstance, the tightening up of the steel industry resulting from the outbreak of the Korean War and subsequent presidential directive, moved the court to excuse Minweld's (D) words, which basically did have the effect of a repudiation.

■━■

## Quicknotes

**ANTICIPATORY BREACH** Breach of a contract subsequent to formation but prior to the time performance is due.

**RENUNCIATION** The abandonment of a right or interest.

**REPUDIATION** The actions or statements of a party to a contract that evidence his intent not to perform, or to continue performance, of his duties or obligations thereunder.

■━■

# By-Lo Oil Co. v. ParTech, Inc.

Software consumer (P) v. Software company (D)

11 Fed. Appx. 538 (6th Cir. 2001).

**NATURE OF CASE:** Appeal from grant of summary judgment to defendant in action for anticipatory breach of contract.

**FACT SUMMARY:** By-Lo Oil Co. (By-Lo) (P) claimed that it had reasonable grounds for insecurity in early 1998 based on the software support contract it had with ParTech, Inc. (D) where ParTech (D) informed By-Lo (P) that it had not at that point made a decision how to ensure that its software would by Y2K-compliant, and By-Lo (P) further claimed that ParTech's (D) assurance that it would let By-Lo (D) know its decision in time to avert Y2K-related software problems was inadequate. By-Lo (D) also contended that these were factual issues that should not have been decided judicially as a matter of law.

🏛 **RULE OF LAW**
Under the UCC, a court may determine, as a matter of law, whether a party to a contract has reasonable grounds for insecurity, and whether a party has given adequate assurance.

**FACTS:** ParTech, Inc. (D) supplied By-Lo Oil Co. (By-Lo) (P) software for By-Lo's (P) operations. Their contract provided that ParTech (D) would provide continuing support to By-Lo (P) for a fixed monthly fee. This included making the software Y2K-compliant. By-Lo (P) wrote to ParTech (D) in 1997 expressing its concern that the software continue to function properly after December 31, 1999. By-Lo (P) again wrote to ParTech (D) in early 1998, this time requesting a response and assurance that the software would be Y2K-compliant. The letter also threatened a lawsuit if no response was forthcoming, and warned that By-Lo (P) would replace the software and seek the replacement cost from ParTech (D). A few weeks later, ParTech (D) responded, stating that ParTech (D) had not as of that time made a decision as to how to deal with the Y2K problem, and that it would notify By-Lo (P) as soon as the decision was made. After By-Lo's (P) representative travelled to ParTech's (D) headquarters and received essentially the same response—i.e., that By-Lo (P) would be notified once a decision had been made—By-Lo (P) filed suit against a different ParTech entity on May 1, 1998, but later realized that it was not the entity with which it had the software contract. Then, in June 1998, By-Lo (P) purchased new software and hardware from a different computer systems supplier for over $175,000. Unaware of these events, ParTech (D), on November 20, 1998, gave By-Lo (P) the definitive answer for which it had been looking. ParTech (D) stated it would supply the needed software at no cost and that the software needed to be installed prior to

January 1, 1999. On December 18, 1998, ParTech (D), as promised, sent By-Lo (P) the necessary software with detailed instructions for loading it. Because By-Lo (P) was now operating on a different system, it did not install the software. Instead, By-Lo (P) sued ParTech (D) in May 1999 in state court, and the action was removed to federal district court. By-Lo (P) claimed it had a right to obtain new computer equipment because of ParTech's (D) actions, which it characterized as an anticipatory breach under the state's UCC §§ 2-609 and 2-610. ParTech (D) moved for summary judgment on the grounds that (1) it had not made an overt communication of intent to repudiate the contract and therefore there was not a breach under § 2-610; and (2) By-Lo (P) did not have the reasonable grounds for insecurity necessary to seek assurance, and the assurance ParTech (D) gave was adequate, and therefore there was no basis to find a breach under § 2-609. The district court granted ParTech's (D) motion. The court of appeals granted review.

**ISSUE:** Under the UCC, may a court determine, as a matter of law, whether a party to a contract has reasonable grounds for insecurity, and whether a party has given adequate assurance?

**HOLDING AND DECISION:** (Kennedy, J.) Yes. Under the UCC, a court may determine, as a matter of law, whether a party to a contract has reasonable grounds for insecurity, and whether a party has given adequate assurance. The district court did not improperly decide questions of fact in analyzing the anticipatory repudiation claim. Generally, the question of whether a party has reasonable grounds for insecurity, and whether a party has given adequate assurance, are factual questions left to the trier of fact. However, in certain cases—this being one of them—the court has the power to determine these issues as a matter of law. As to the reasonableness of By-Lo's (P) insecurity, that is to be determined by commercial standards. The issue thus becomes whether it was commercially reasonable for By-Lo (P) to be insecure two years before the Y2K fix (if any) was necessary. In other words, would a reasonable merchant in By-Lo's (P) position "feel that his expectation of receiving full performance was threatened?" The fact that performance was to come due at some point is not sufficient under § 2-609. Merely becoming aware of the Y2K problem (of which the parties were not aware when they entered the contract) also is by itself an insufficient ground for insecurity. ParTech's (D) failure to return calls might have given rise to reasonable grounds for insecurity at some point before Y2K, but not in

*Continued on next page.*

January 1998. That is because By-Lo (P) did not complain about ParTech's (D) previous service, nor was there any indication that it was under a time constraint to obtain a new system if ParTech (D) did not respond quickly. There also was no indication that By-Lo (P) had reason to believe it would take a lengthy period of time to make any corrections ParTech (D) required. Further, evidence presented by By-Lo (P), in an attempt to show that as of May 1998 it had little time to obtain new software and implement it or to install any software sent by ParTech (D), is unconvincing. For all these reasons, there was little reason for By-Lo (P) to be concerned at such an early date—so little that no reasonable jury could have found for By-Lo (P). A similar analysis applies to the issue of adequate assurance. The question is: what are the minimum kinds of promises or acts on the part of the promisor that would satisfy a reasonable merchant in the position of the promisee that his expectation of receiving due performance will be fulfilled? In evaluating the assurance, the court should keep in mind the reputation of the promisor, the grounds for insecurity, and the kinds of assurance available. As already determined By-Lo (P) did not have reasonable grounds for insecurity in January 1998, given that the Y2K problem was almost two years away. There was no indication that ParTech (D) had failed to fulfill its obligations in the past, nor was there any evidence that ParTech's (D) reputation should have given By-Lo (P) cause for concern. Because it is not clear what else ParTech (D) could have done, other than what it did, the district court was correct to hold that, as a matter of law, ParTech's (D) assurance that it was evaluating the matter was adequate despite the fact that it was less than requested. Affirmed.

## ▶ *ANALYSIS*

UCC § 2-609 provides that when reasonable grounds for insecurity arise with respect to the performance of either party, the other may in writing demand adequate assurance of due performance, and, until he receives such assurance, may, if commercially reasonable, suspend any performance for which he has not already received the agreed return. While this section imposes a written demand requirement, some courts have held that an oral demand for assurance may suffice provided as it communicates a clear understanding of the insecure party's intent to suspend performance until receipt of adequate assurance from the other party.

■══■

## *Quicknotes*

**ANTICIPATORY BREACH** Breach of a contract subsequent to formation but prior to the time performance is due.

**ANTICIPATORY REPUDIATION** Breach of a contract subsequent to formation but prior to the time performance is due.

■══■

# Rocheux Int'l. of N.J. v. U.S. Merchants Fin. Group

Plastic distributor (P) v. Plastic purchaser (D)

741 F. Supp. 2d 651 (2010).

**NATURE OF CASE:** Appeal from cross-motions for summary judgment in action, and countersuit, for breach of contract.

**FACT SUMMARY:** After U.S. Merchants Fin. Group, Inc. (U.S. Merchants) (D) failed to pay over $2 million of past-due invoices for shipments of plastics made by Rocheux Int'l. of N.J. (Rocheux) (P), Rocheux (P) informed U.S. Merchants (D) that it would sell plastics delivered to a warehouse for U.S. Merchants' (D) convenience (the "warehouse goods") worth over $1.5 million and recover any deficiency from U.S. Merchants (D) if U.S. Merchants (D) did not make payment on all open invoices. U.S. Merchants (D) did not pay the open invoices, and Rocheux (P) sold the warehouse goods at a loss, and sought to recover the deficiency from U.S. Merchants (D), which contended that, as a matter of law, Rocheux (P) could not recover the deficiency because Rocheux (P) improperly repudiated its contracts with U.S. Merchants (D) under UCC § 2-609 without demanding adequate assurance and despite receiving such assurance from U.S. Merchants (D).

## RULE OF LAW

(1) A party's demand for adequate assurances is not insufficient as a matter of law where, although it conditions its own future performance on the other party's performance of other contracts, its insecurity arises from the other party's nonperformance of all contracts, and, despite not using the exact term "adequate assurance," the party provides a clear understanding of its intent to suspend performance until receipt of adequate assurances from the other party.

(2) Where a party has repeatedly failed to pay open invoices, the party does not provide adequate assurances as a matter of law by offering to either pay on a C.O.D. basis or extend a letter of credit.

**FACTS:** U.S. Merchants Fin. Group, Inc. (U.S. Merchants) (D) ordered large quantities of raw PVC and APET plastic from Rocheux Int'l. of N.J. (Rocheux) (P) in 2005 and 2006, and Rocheux (P) delivered some of the plastics. U.S. Merchants (D), however, did not pay for most if not all of the 2006 deliveries, for which it owed Rocheux (P) over $2 million. In addition, Rocheux (P) delivered some of the plastics to a local warehouse so that U.S. Merchants (D) would be able to access the goods as needed on short notice. These "warehouse goods," were

worth over $1.5 million. On August 2, 2006, Rocheux (P) President Steed emailed U.S. Merchants (D) President and Chief Executive Officer (CEO) Green with a proposal to remedy U.S. Merchants' (D) non-payment on the purchase orders that comprised both the 2006 deliveries and the warehouse goods. Steed recognized that U.S. Merchants (D) had recently sent a check on an invoice, and proposed that Rocheux (P) ship on a two to one payment ration; i.e. for every two truckload invoices paid by U.S. Merchants (D), Rocheux (P) would release one truckload. On September 21, 2006, Steed sent a letter to Green stating that unless payment of past-due invoices was received by September 29, 2006, Rocheux (P) would have no alternative but to commence an action and seek all appropriate remedies to recover the amounts plus other damages available to Rocheux (P). The letter indicated that it constituted notice of Rocheux's (P) intent, in the event payment was not forthcoming, to sell or otherwise dispose of the warehouse goods and recover any deficiency from U.S. Merchants (D). On September 24, 2006, Steed sent an email to Green requesting the delinquent payments for the 2006 deliveries and the warehouse goods by September 29, 2006, and notifying U.S. Merchants (D) that failure to pay would result in Rocheux (P) selling the warehouse goods and seeking any deficiency from U.S. Merchants (D) pursuant to UCC § 2-706. On October 4, 2006, Green wrote to Steed, generally disputing U.S. Merchant's (D) liability for Rocheux's (P) invoices, but nevertheless indicating that U.S. Merchants (D) was willing to purchase certain undelivered plastics at quantities and prices seemingly adopted from the parties' 2005-2006 purchase orders. Green offered to pay either on a C.O.D. (cash on delivery) basis or to extend a letter of credit for each delivery. On October 6, 2006, Steed responded, stating in her letter that U.S. Merchants' (D) "continuing failure to pay Rocheux's outstanding invoices ... relieved [Rocheux] of any obligation to ship any material to [U.S. Mercants]," but proposed that withheld materials would be released to U.S. Merchants (D) "only on the condition that, prior to shipment, [U.S Merchants] open an irrevocable letter of credit in favor of Rocheux ... for an amount not less than the total amount of the open invoices. ..." The letter concluded "[t]he aforesaid letter of credit need be your only reply." Rocheux (P) eventually sold the warehouse goods to third parties for $1,194,582.68, resulting in a deficiency of $387,699.70 compared to the original purchase price for the warehouse goods. U.S. Merchants (D) claimed that the 2006 deliveries contained substantial

*Continued on next page.*

amounts of unusable and/or nonconforming materials. The defects were not immediately detectable, since the plastics were delivered in rolled up sheets, and the defects only became apparent when used in production assembly lines, sometimes long after U.S. Merchants (D) had received the goods. Because it could not use the defective plastics, and because Rocheux (P) did not want the defective goods back, U.S. Merchants (D) sold it as scrap. For its part, Rocheux (P) claimed that it was not notified of problems with the 2006 deliveries until Steed received an email from Green on September 6, 2006, prior to which, Rocheux (P) claimed that U.S. Merchants (D) had generally acknowledged that it owed payments for the 2006 deliveries. Rocheux (P) also claimed that U.S. Merchants (D) never complained about the quality of goods delivered by Rocheux (P) during the course of the parties' relationship, and that U.S. Merchants (D) never rejected or otherwise indicated that it did not want to keep the 2006 deliveries, noting that, if it had, Rocheux (P) would have requested an opportunity to inspect the goods, and that Rocheux (P) would have returned any defective goods to the original manufacturer for credits. To support this claim, Rocheux (P) noted that its representatives met with Green on three occasions: April 1, 2006, May 31, 2006, and July 17, 2006. According to Rocheux (P), U.S. Merchants (D) never expressed any concerns with the 2006 deliveries at these meetings, and Green acknowledged that U.S. Merchants (D) owed the amounts listed in Rocheux's (P) invoices, but that the delay in payments for the 2006 deliveries was attributable to problems with U.S. Merchants' (D) new accounting software. On September 7, 2006, Steed replied to Green's email, requesting that Green provide full details regarding his assertion of defects with delivered goods, and asserting that Rocheux (P) stood behind the goods it sold, that it would send a team to investigate, and that any defective product should be returned for full credit. Steed asserted that U.S. Merchants (D) never responded to her request for inspection or return of defective goods, and U.S. Merchants (D) conceded that the vast majority of the 2006 deliveries had been discarded as scrap when they received Steed's September 7 email. Rocheux (P) sued U.S. Merchants (D) for breach of contract, and U.S. Merchants (D) countersued. Rocheux (P) moved for summary judgment, seeking $4,635,761.18 in damages, interest, attorneys' fees, and costs. U.S. Merchants (D) claimed that, with regard to the warehouse goods, Rocheux (P) could not recover as a matter of law, because Rocheux (P) improperly repudiated its contracts without demanding adequate assurance and despite receiving such assurance from U.S. Merchants (D).

## ISSUE:

(1) Is a party's demand for adequate assurances insufficient as a matter of law where, although it conditions its own future performance on the other party's performance of other contracts, its insecurity arises from the other party's nonperformance of all contracts, and, despite

not using the exact term "adequate assurance," the party provides a clear understanding of its intent to suspend performance until receipt of adequate assurances from the other party?

(2) Where a party has repeatedly failed to pay open invoices, does the party provide adequate assurances as a matter of law by offering to either pay on a C.O.D. basis or extend a letter of credit?

## HOLDING AND DECISION: (Brown, C.J.)

(1) No. A party's demand for adequate assurances is not insufficient as a matter of law where, although it conditions its own future performance on the other party's performance of other contracts, its insecurity arises from the other party's nonperformance of all contracts, and, despite not using the exact term "adequate assurance," the party provides a clear understanding of its intent to suspend performance until receipt of adequate assurances from the other party. U.S. Merchants (D) argues that Rocheux (P) did not demand adequate assurance, as was required by § 2-609 prior to repudiating the parties' contracts, because Rocheux (P) conditioned its own future performance on U.S. Merchants' (D) payment of prior contracts. U.S. Merchants (D) bases this argument on Steed's September 21, 2006 letter, wherein she stated that if payment of past-due invoices was not received, Rocheux (P) would sell the warehouse goods and seek recovery of any deficiency from U.S. Merchants (D). Although U.S. Merchants (D) is correct that a party's breach of a collateral contract does not authorize the aggrieved party to refuse performance under a separate and distinct contract, a ground for insecurity need not arise from or be directly related to the contract in question. Steed's September 21 letter indicates that Rocheux's (P) insecurity arose from U.S. Merchants' (D) failure to pay for both the 2006 deliveries and the warehouse goods. Thus, U.S. Merchants (D) overlooks the fact that Rocheux's (P) September 21 letter, as well as Steed's prior email of August 2, 2006, sought to remedy non-payment on the purchase orders that comprised both the 2006 deliveries and the warehouse goods. Rocheux's (P) correspondence indicates that it sought nothing more than the performance due under all the parties' contracts. Given that the parties' course of dealings included U.S. Merchants' (D) failure to pay more than $2 million of the purchase price for the 2006 deliveries and the warehouse goods, Rocheux's (P) insecurity was not unreasonable as a matter of law. Further, Rocheux's (P) correspondence, which did not use the exact terms "adequate assurances," nevertheless clearly conveyed its reasons for insecurity, i.e., U.S. Merchants' (D) failure to pay substantial sums related to invoices for the 2006

*Continued on next page.*

deliveries and the warehouse goods, and clearly indicated that it intended to suspend its own performance. Although neither message included the exact term "adequate assurance," courts have generally eschewed applying formalistic requirements for the demand of adequate assurances, instead opting for a case-specific approach that considers a party's demands in the context of its course of dealings with the adverse party. Considering the parties' course of dealings, which included multiple in-person meetings between the parties concerning U.S. Merchants' (D) failure to pay Rocheux's (P) invoices on time, it cannot be said, as a matter of law, that Rocheux's (P) correspondence of August 2 and September 21, 2006 did not constitute a demand for adequate assurance.

(2) No. Where a party has repeatedly failed to pay open invoices, the party does not provide adequate assurances as a matter of law by offering to either pay on a C.O.D. basis or extend a letter of credit. U.S. Merchants (D) contends that it provided adequate assurances in Green's October 4, 2006 letter, where it offered to pay on a C.O.D. basis or extend a letter of credit. Although it is generally recognized that letters of credit provide adequate assurance of performance due, here U.S. Merchants (D) did not provide a letter of credit for the warehouse goods, even after Rocheux's (P) October 6 response indicated that the "letter of credit need be [U.S. Merchants'] only reply." The reasonableness of U.S. Merchants' (D) offer must be determined according to commercial standards. There is no authority that an insecure party must accept assurance of C.O.D. payment as adequate assurances where the delinquent party has fallen in arrears more than $2 million on delivered goods. Given U.S. Merchants' (D) continued failure to pay outstanding invoices regarding the 2006 deliveries and warehouse goods, it cannot be said as a matter of law that Rocheux's (P) demand for a letter of credit covering these goods was unreasonable—especially given that U.S. Merchants' (D) October 4 letter sought to change the terms of delivery of the warehouse goods (by extending the delivery period for the retained goods; by extending the payment period; or by obtaining a discount for C.O.D. payments). While this might be seen as repudiation by U.S. Merchants (D), that is a matter of fact, and it cannot be said as a matter of law that Green's letter of October 4 constituted repudiation or provided inadequate assurance. A reasonable jury could conclude that the October 4 letter provided adequate assurance and did not repudiate the parties' contracts. Accordingly, both parties' cross-motions for summary judgment with regard to the warehouse goods are denied.

assurances," whether the merchant has requested, or given, such assurances, must usually be determined on a case-by-case basis by a trier of fact, rather than by the court as a matter of law. This determination must be made, per § 2-609(2), according to commercial standards. The determination must also be made in light of the parties' course of conduct. Thus, as illustrated by comment 4 to this section, as well as the court's decision in *Rocheux*, repeated delinquencies must be viewed as cumulative, and, for example, where a buyer can make use of a defective delivery, a mere promise by a seller of good repute that he is giving the matter his attention and that the defect will not be repeated, is normally sufficient. Under the same circumstances, however, a similar statement by a known corner-cutter might well be considered insufficient without the posting of a guaranty or, if so demanded by the buyer, a speedy replacement of the delivery involved.

---

## Quicknotes

**ASSURANCES** Guarantees; security.

**REPUDIATION** The actions or statements of a party to a contract that evidence his intent not to perform, or to continue performance, of his duties or obligations thereunder.

---

 **ANALYSIS**

As this case demonstrates, given that UCC § 2-609 does not require a merchant to use the exact words "adequate

# Basic Assumptions: Mistake, Impracticability and Frustration

## Quick Reference Rules of Law

# Sumerel v. Goodyear Tire & Rubber Co.

Consumer (P) v. Rubber products manufacturer (D)

Colo. Ct. App., 232 P.3d 128 (2009).

**NATURE OF CASE:** Appeal from judgment to enforce a purported settlement agreement.

**FACT SUMMARY:** Goodyear Tire & Rubber Co. (Goodyear) (D), which had been adjudged liable to various consumers (P) for various damages, contended that, in an attempt to come to agreement on the prejudgment interest owed on a portion of the damages, an email and erroneous charts that Goodyear's (D) counsel sent to the consumers' (P) counsel—which contained a $550,000 windfall for the consumers (P)—did not constitute an offer capable of acceptance because it did not invite acceptance and was, on its face, too good to be true. Goodyear (D) also contended that even if an offer had been made, any agreement based on it would be unenforceable under the doctrine of unilateral mistake.

## 🏛 RULE OF LAW

(1) An offer is not made where communications do not invite acceptance and on their face are "too good to be true."

(2) Where a party to a contract has made a unilateral mistake, that party will be able to avoid the contract where the other party knew of or had reason to know of the mistake and, even if the other party did not know of or have reason to know of the mistake, enforcement of the contract would be oppressive to the mistaken party, and relief from the contract would impose no substantial hardship on the other party.

**FACTS:** In a products liability action brought by consumers (P) against Goodyear Tire & Rubber Co. (Goodyear) (D), a jury awarded the consumers (P) approximately $1.3 million against Goodyear (D), including repair and replacement costs, diminution in value damages, and "other costs and losses." In addition, the jury found that Goodyear (D) was responsible for 36 percent of such "other costs and losses" suffered by two consumers (P) and 48 percent of those incurred by two other consumers (P). Goodyear (D) was ordered to pay prejudgment interest on these various damages, and, at some point in the proceedings, counsel for Goodyear (D) and counsel for the consumers (P) entered discussions as to the proper accrual dates for prejudgment interest on "other costs and losses." Goodyear's (D) lead attorney, Thomasch, discussed with the consumers' (P) lead attorney, Maywhort, a potential compromise on the applicable accrual dates. Thomasch proposed certain accrual dates and advised Maywhort of the amount of prejudgment interest that would result from

using these proposed dates. Thomasch's calculation of these amounts took into account the jury's 36 percent and 48 percent allocations of fault, and Thomasch expressly conveyed that fact to Maywhort. Following up on the discussion between Thomasch and Maywhort, co-counsel for the consumers (P), Gray, called Brooks, co-counsel for Goodyear (D). Although the parties came to agreement on the applicable accrual dates with little difficulty, they had trouble getting their calculations of prejudgment interest based on these dates to match. Brooks advised Gray that his calculations showed a total amount owed by Goodyear (D) of approximately $2.7 million. At some point within the following few days, Gray responded that this amount appeared to be larger than his own estimates by "about six figures," but did not elaborate. Brooks then called Gray to speculate about the discrepancy, but without Gray's calculations, Brooks could not be sure whether he had, in fact, resolved the discrepancy. A few days later, believing that he may have discovered the source of the discrepancy, Brooks sent Gray an e-mail, stating, "Here are our charts providing the numers [sic] that Goodyear believes are appropriate. . . . Please review these, then let's discuss." Attached to this e-mail were charts that reflected Goodyear's (D) then existing calculations as to the total amounts due to each consumer (P). When Maywhort reviewed the charts, he realized that Goodyear's (D) calculations had failed to reduce the damages for "other costs and losses" according to the jury's finding that Goodyear (D) was only liable for 36 percent of the some of the consumers' (P) and 48 percent of the other consumers' (P) "other costs and losses." This was in contrast to other categories of damages set forth in Goodyear's (D) charts, in which Goodyear (D) had correctly applied the jury's fault allocations. This error resulted in an overstatement of the damages due by more than $550,000. Maywhort, however, did not call this error to Brooks's attention, or to the attention of any other Goodyear (D) counsel. Instead, he and Gray took the position that Goodyear (D) had intended this result, notwithstanding that the parties were not negotiating the amounts due but rather were attempting to determine why there was a discrepancy in their mathematical calculations. Ultimately, no consumer representative called Brooks to discuss his charts, as Brooks had requested. Rather, Maywhort, who had not been directly involved in the more recent discussions regarding the calculations, left a voicemail message for Thomasch, who also had not been directly involved, stating that the consumers (P) accepted Goodyear's (D) "offer." Maywhort then followed his voice-

*Continued on next page.*

mail with a fax confirming the acceptance of that purported "offer." Notably, neither Maywhort nor Gray informed Brooks of this "acceptance," nor was Brooks copied on Maywhort's fax to Thomasch. Thereafter, Brooks prepared a form of satisfaction of judgment that he sent to Gray, with a notation that the document was a draft for discussion purposes only. That same day, before anyone had signed the satisfaction of judgment, Brooks realized the error in his earlier calculations. He immediately called the error to Gray's attention and sent Gray corrected versions of the charts and a revised satisfaction of judgment with corrected numbers. Instead of acknowledging the error and signing the satisfaction, counsel for the consumers (P) insisted that Goodyear (D) adhere to the parties' alleged agreement, which would have resulted in the consumers (P) receiving over $550,000 more than what was due them. When Goodyear (D) refused to do so, the consumer (P) filed a motion to enforce the purported "settlement agreement," which the trial court granted. Goodyear (D) paid the amounts that the parties agreed were due and owing, and appealed, contending that it had not made an offer that could have been accepted, and that even if it had, the resulting agreement was not enforceable. The state's intermediate court of appeals granted review.

## ISSUE:

(1) Is an offer made where communications do not invite acceptance and on their face are "too good to be true"?

(2) Where a party to a contract has made a unilateral mistake, will that party be able to avoid the contract where the other party knew of or had reason to know of the mistake and, even if the other party did not know of or have reason to know of the mistake, enforcement of the contract would be oppressive to the mistaken party, and relief from the contract would impose no substantial hardship on the other party?

## HOLDING AND DECISION: (Gabriel, J.)

(1) No. An offer is not made where communications do not invite acceptance and on their face are "too good to be true." Goodyear's (D) e-mail and attached erroneous charts, sent by Brooks, did not constitute an offer that was properly capable of acceptance. The parties were not negotiating dollar amounts, but were merely attempting to resolve a discrepancy in their mathematical computations. Thus, Brooks's e-mail used qualifying and indefinite language, noting that the calculations were what "Goodyear believes are appropriate." This indefinite language alone is an indication of a lack of a definite offer. In addition, Brooks's e-mail did not solicit an acceptance but rather solicited a return call—it ended with: "Please review these, then let's discuss." Thus, the email could not justify the consumers' (P) counsel in understanding that their assent was invited and would conclude a bargain. Based on these factors alone, there was no offer. In this case, this conclusion is bolstered by the rule that "an offeree may not

snap up an offer that is on its face manifestly too good to be true." If a purported offer is "too good to be true," the offeree should know that an offer was not intended. The facts here present just such a case. Liability had been adjudged and apportioned, the parties agreed on the accrual dates, and all that was left to be done was a simple mathematical calculation. When the consumers' (P) counsel received Brooks's charts, they immediately recognized that the calculations assumed that Goodyear (D) was 100 percent liable for the "other costs and losses," rather than the 36 percent and 48 percent allocation of fault that the jury had found, resulting in an error in their clients' favor of over $550,000. Therefore, Brooks's e-mail and erroneous charts raised a presumption of error because they were inconsistent with (1) the jury's award; (2) Thomasch's prior discussion with Maywhort, in which Thomasch specifically pointed out that the calculations that he had provided were based on the percentages of fault that the jury had allocated to Goodyear (D); and (3) other calculations in the same charts, in which Goodyear (D) consistently used the jury's allocations of fault. At a minimum, these obvious inconsistencies gave rise to a duty on the part of the consumers' (P) counsel to inquire before attempting to accept the purported "offer." Without such an inquiry, there was no offer capable of acceptance. Reversed as to this issue.

(2) Yes. Where a party to a contract has made a unilateral mistake, that party will be able to avoid the contract where the other party knew of or had reason to know of the mistake and, even if the other party did not know of or have reason to know of the mistake, enforcement of the contract would be oppressive to the mistaken party, and relief from the contract would impose no substantial hardship on the other party. Here, even if Brooks's email and charts constituted an offer, Goodyear (D) could avoid any agreement based on that offer. The principles regarding unilateral mistake are well-established and almost universally followed. Where the offeror has acted in good faith and where the offeree knew of the mistake before accepting the offer, it would contravene fundamental principles of fairness to allow the offeree to take advantage of offeror's mistake and gain a windfall. The Restatement permits the mistaken party to avoid the contract where that party did not bear the risk of mistake. However, it is unusual for a party to bear the risk of a mistake that the other party had reason to know of. Here, Goodyear's (D) calculations were in error, and it is undisputed that the consumers (P) knew or had reason to know of the error. Enforcement of the purported agreement would be oppressive to Goodyear (D) and unconscionable, because the consumers (P) would be exploiting Goodyear's (D) mistake to gain a windfall of over $550,000 more than

*Continued on next page.*

the jury awarded to them, and relief from such an agreement would pose no substantial hardship on the consumers (P), since they would receive the amount to which they were entitled. Finally, Goodyear (D) did not bear the risk of mistake here. Goodyear (D) acted in good faith, and the evidence does not show that that Brooks chose to charge ahead in conscious ignorance, believing that his limited knowledge was sufficient. Instead, his email clearly shows that he was continuing to try to resolve the discrepancy and was seeking further discussion with Gray. Ultimately, this phase of the litigation should have never arisen. As soon as the consumers' (P) counsel recognized Brooks's (D) error, they should have immediately called Brooks, identified the discrepancy, and concluded the matter without further delay—thus sparing both parties the substantial expense of this needless litigation. Reversed as to this issue. Reversed and remanded for the sole purpose of allowing the parties to file a satisfaction of judgment for the amounts already paid by Goodyear (D).

## ▌ANALYSIS

Under Restatement § 154, A party bears the risk of a mistake when (a) the risk is allocated to him by agreement of the parties, or (b) he is aware, at the time the contract is made, that he has only limited knowledge with respect to the facts to which the mistake relates but treats his limited knowledge as sufficient, or (c) the risk is allocated to him by the court on the ground that it is reasonable in the circumstances to do so. Here, the consumers (P) argued that Goodyear (D) bore the risk of mistake under subsection (b), contending that Brooks chose to charge ahead in conscious ignorance, believing that his limited knowledge was sufficient, but the court rejected this argument as unsupported by the record.

■══■

## Quicknotes

**OFFER** A proposed promise to undertake performance of an action, or to refrain from acting, that is to become binding upon acceptance by the offeree.

■══■

# Stees v. Leonard

Property owner (P) v. Builder (D)

Minn. Sup. Ct., 20 Minn. 494, 20 Gil. 448 (1874).

**NATURE OF CASE:** Appeal from plaintiff's judgment in action for damages for breach of a construction contract.

**FACT SUMMARY:** Stees (P) alleged that Leonard (D) had breached a contract to build a structure on a St. Paul lot when the structure collapsed upon reaching three stories, as did a subsequent structure upon a second attempt. Leonard (D) claimed subsoil conditions were aggravated by quicksand, making it impossible for the land to support a structure.

## RULE OF LAW
If one binds oneself by a positive, express contract to do an act in itself possible, one must perform unless prevented by act of God, the law, or the other party to the contract and will not be excused by hardship, unforeseen hindrance, or difficulty short of absolute impossibility.

**FACTS:** Stees (P) sought damages for Leonard's (D) failure to erect a structure as contracted on a lot owned by Stees (P) in St. Paul. Two attempts were made to build the building, but both times when the building reached the height of three stories it collapsed. Leonard (D) claimed that the soil under the foundation was quicksand and was incapable of supporting a structure whenever water flowed in. Leonard (D) had fulfilled Stees's (P) specifications for construction of the foundation. Stees (P) had judgment for $5,214.80 plus interest ($3,745.80 paid during progress of construction, $1,000 damages for loss of use of the lot, and $469 damage to an adjacent structure of Stees [P] injured by the collapse).

**ISSUE:** If one binds oneself by a positive, express contract to do an act in itself possible, must one perform unless prevented by act of God, the law, or the other party to the contract and not be excused by hardship, unforeseen hindrance, or difficulty short of absolute impossibility?

**HOLDING AND DECISION:** (Young, J.) Yes. When one has bound oneself to a contract, one must perform unless prevented by act of God, law, or other party to the contract. Performance will not be excused by hardship, unforeseen hindrance, or difficulty short of absolute impossibility. The apparent hardship is attributable to the contractor himself who has accepted an absolute as opposed to a qualified liability. The law only enforces the contract as the party has made it. Cases have held that latent defects in the soil and unexpected impediments must fall on the contractor, as a party must do what he

agreed to do. Leonard (D) contracted to "erect and complete a building" and was required to do so even if it required going beyond Stees's (P) specifications. Affirmed.

## ANALYSIS

Early cases as illustrated here held that if the building is destroyed or rendered less valuable because of defective plans and specifications supplied by the owner, the builder by accepting the owner's plans promised to produce the structure called for and accepted the risks attendant upon using the owner's specifications. It was thought that the owner relied upon the technical knowledge of the builder. The modern cases have held that where the owner has hired professionals who have prepared the plans and specifications, the owner has warranted the plans to be adequate unless the builder has reason to know of inadequacy or unless the parties have contracted otherwise. The parties can allocate risks by agreement. Note that the rules for contracts to repair or alter existing structures are different than the rules for the construction of new buildings. Also, Restatement, Restitution, § 9 is authority for avoiding a construction contract made without sufficient information about soil conditions on the ground of mutual mistake.

---

## Quicknotes

**LATENT DEFECTS** A defect that cannot be discovered upon ordinary examination.

# Renner v. Kehl

Purchaser (P) v. Seller (D)

Ariz. Sup. Ct., 150 Ariz. 94, 722 P.2d 262 (1986).

**NATURE OF CASE:** Action for rescission.

**FACT SUMMARY:** Renner (P) sought to rescind a contract entered into with Kehl (D) for the purchase of land when several test wells failed to produce sufficient water to cultivate jojoba.

 **RULE OF LAW**
Mutual mistake of fact is a basis for rescission.

**FACTS:** The Kehls and the Moyles (D) decided to sell their interest in undeveloped land. Renner (P) agreed to pay $100 an acre for the leases for the purpose of cultivating jojoba. Renner (P) abandoned the project when test wells failed to produce water of a sufficient quality for cultivating jojoba. The trial court directed the sellers to reimburse the purchasers and the court of appeals affirmed.

**ISSUE:** Is mutual mistake of fact a basis for rescission?

**HOLDING AND DECISION:** (Gordon, V.C.J.) Yes. Mutual mistake of fact is a basis for rescission. A contract may be rescinded where such mistake of material fact constitutes an essential part and condition of the contract. Here, the basis of the contract was for the purchaser to cultivate jojoba; thus, the belief that adequate water supplies existed was a basic assumption of the bargain. Upon finding that such belief was erroneous, the contract was voidable and the respondents entitled to rescission. However, absent proof of breach for fraud or misrepresentation, a party who rescinds a contract may not recover consequential damages. This means that Renner (P) may not recover the costs of developing the land in the form of consequential damages, but is entitled to restitution of the down payment and any amount to which the land was enhanced. Kehl (D) is entitled to fair rental value of the property. Affirmed in part, reversed in part, and remanded.

▶ **ANALYSIS**

If a party rescinds a contract on the basis of mutual mistake, the proper measure of damages is restitution for any benefit conferred through either part performance or reliance. Such recoveries are intended to avoid unjust enrichment and are not intended to be compensatory. In determining proper restitution, the rescinding party must also return any value received.

■■■

## Quicknotes

**CONSEQUENTIAL DAMAGES** Monetary compensation that may be recovered in order to compensate for injuries or losses sustained as a result of damages that are not the direct or foreseeable result of the act of a party, but that nevertheless are the consequence of such act and which must be specifically pleaded and demonstrated.

**MISTAKE OF FACT** An unintentional mistake in knowing or recalling a fact without the will to deceive.

**RESCISSION** The canceling of an agreement and the return of the parties to their positions prior to the formation of the contract.

**RESTITUTION** The return or restoration of what the defendant has gained in a transaction to prevent the unjust enrichment of the defendant.

■■■

# Mineral Park Land Co. v. Howard

## Builder (D) v. Landowner (P)

Cal. Sup. Ct., 172 Cal. 289, 156 P. 458 (1916).

**NATURE OF CASE:** Appeal from award of damages for breach of contract.

**FACT SUMMARY:** Mineral Park Land Co. (D) contended it was not bound to remove gravel from Howard's (P) land that would be commercially impracticable to haul away.

## RULE OF LAW
A party is excused from performing under a contract where such performance is so much more expensive than contemplated that it would be impracticable to complete.

**FACTS:** Mineral Park Land Co. (Mineral Park) (D) agreed to obtain its gravel requirements for building a bridge from Howard's (P) land and to pay for it at 5 cents per yard. It hauled away all the gravel above the water level but refused to go below that because to do so would cost 10 to 12 times the usual cost of hauling gravel. Howard (P) sued to require Mineral Park (D) to perform fully. The trial court held that because it was merely commercially disadvantageous to remove the gravel, and not physically impossible, Mineral Park (D) was bound to perform and had breached the contract. Mineral Park (D) appealed, contending it was excused from performing due to impracticability.

**ISSUE:** May a party be excused from performing under a contract on the basis of impracticability?

**HOLDING AND DECISION:** (Sloss, J.) Yes. A party may be excused from performing under a contract where such performance has become impracticable because its cost would greatly exceed that contemplated. In this case, although it would have been physically possible to remove gravel below the water level, for practical purposes no further gravel was available due to the severe increased cost. Therefore, Mineral Park (D) must be excused from further performance due to the nonexistence of the contractual subject matter for practical purposes. Affirmed as modified.

## ANALYSIS

With this case, California led the way toward relaxation of the strict common law rule which required virtual physical impossibility to excuse performance. Today, modern courts equate extreme impracticability with impossibility, and this was the approach adopted in the First Restatement in § 454. UCC § 2-615 defines "impracticable" as including impossibility, and the Restatement (Second) adopts a similar approach.

# Taylor v. Caldwell

## Lessee (P) v. Music hall owner (D)

K.B., 3 B. & S. 826, 122 Eng. Rep. 309 (1863).

**NATURE OF CASE:** Action for damages for breach of a contract for letting of premises.

**FACT SUMMARY:** Taylor (P) contracted to let Caldwell's (D) hall and gardens for four fetes and concerts, for four days, for £100 per day. Taylor (P) expended money in preparation and for advertising, but Caldwell (D) could not perform when the hall burned down without his fault.

> ### 🏛 RULE OF LAW
> In contracts in which the performance depends on the continued existence of a given person or thing, a condition is implied that the impossibility of performance arising from the perishing of the person or thing shall excuse the performance.

**FACTS:** By written agreement, Caldwell (D) agreed to let the Surrey Gardens and Musical Hall at Newington, Surrey, for four days for giving four "Grand Concerts" and "Day and Night Fetes." Taylor (P) was to pay £100 at the end of each day. Before any concerts were held, the hall was completely destroyed by fire without any fault of either of the parties. Taylor (P) alleged that the fire and destruction of the hall was a breach and that it resulted in his losing large sums in preparation and advertising for the concerts and fetes.

**ISSUE:** In contracts in which the performance depends on the continued existence of a given person or thing, is a condition implied that the impossibility of performance arising from the perishing of the person or thing shall excuse the performance?

**HOLDING AND DECISION:** (Lord Blackburn, J.) Yes. In contracts in which the performance depends on the continued existence of a given person or thing, a condition is implied that the impossibility of performance arising from the perishing of the person or thing shall excuse the performance. Caldwell (D) was excused from performance. First, the agreement was not a lease but a contract to "let." The entertainments that were planned could not be made without the existence of the hall. Ordinarily, when there is a positive contract to do something that is not unlawful, the contractor must perform or pay damages for not doing it even if an unforeseen accident makes performance unduly burdensome or even impossible. This is so when the contract is absolute and positive and not subject to either express or implied conditions and that if it appears that the parties must have known from the beginning that the contract could not be fulfilled unless a particular, specified thing continued to exist and there is no

express or implied warranty that the thing shall exist, the contract is not positive and absolute. It is subject to the implied condition that the parties shall be excused in case, before breach, performance becomes impossible from the perishing of the thing without fault of the contractor. This appears to be within the intention of the parties when they enter into a contract. The excuse from the contract's performance is implied in law because from the nature of the contract it is apparent it was made on the basis of the continued existence of the particular, specified thing. Judgment for the defendants.

## ▶ ANALYSIS

It was important for Lord Blackburn not to find the agreement to be a lease; otherwise the decision would come within direct conflict of *Paradine v. Jane*, K.B., 82 Eng. Rep. 897 (1647), which held that a lease must be performed to the letter despite unforeseen hardship or good fortune. Next, performance is excused only if the destruction of the specified thing is without fault. Had Caldwell (D) been shown to be guilty of arson in the destruction of the hall, he would not have been excused. If there is impossibility of performance due to no one's fault, the one seeking to enforce performance takes the risk. It might be said that the court was actually apportioning the loss if the contract was, in effect, a joint venture with Taylor (P) paying Caldwell (D) £100 out of each day's admission fees to the concerts (Caldwell (D) was supplying the band). The view of this case is found in UCC § 2-613 where for total destruction of the specified thing, the contract is avoided, or if the specified thing is goods which have so deteriorated as to no longer conform, the contract can be avoided or the goods can be accepted with an allowance for their lesser value. Note that there is not a satisfactory distinction between a contract to let and a lease.

■▬■

## Quicknotes

**IMPOSSIBILITY** A doctrine relieving the parties to a contract from liability for nonperformance of their duties thereunder, if the subject matter of the contract ceases to exist, a person essential to the performance of the contract is deceased, or the service or goods contracted for has become illegal.

■▬■

# Transatlantic Financing Corporation v. United States

Wheat exporter (P) v. Federal government (D)

363 F.2d 312 (D.C. Cir. 1966).

**NATURE OF CASE:** Appeal from dismissal of action for unforeseen costs in execution of a contract for carriage.

**FACT SUMMARY:** Transatlantic Financing Corporation (Transatlantic) (P), under charter of the United States (D), contracted to ship a full cargo of wheat from Galveston, Texas, to Iran. Shipment was contemplated on Transatlantic's (P) SS Christos through the Suez Canal, but war broke out between Egypt and Israel, forcing the closure of the canal. The SS Christos had to steam an extra 3,000 miles around the Cape of Good Hope.

## 🏛 RULE OF LAW
When the issue of impossibility is raised, the court must construct a condition of performance based on changed circumstances involving the following: (1) a contingency, something unexpected, must have occurred, (2) the risk of unexpected occurrence must not have been allocated either by agreement or custom, and (3) occurrence of the contingency must have rendered performance commercially impracticable.

**FACTS:** Transatlantic Financing Corporation (Transatlantic) (P), under charter to the United States (D), contracted to carry a full cargo of wheat on its SS Christos from Galveston, Texas, to a safe port in Iran. On July 26, 1956, Egypt nationalized the Suez Canal. During the international crisis resulting from this, the parties contracted on October 2, 1956, for Transatlantic (P) to ship the wheat as described. The charter stated the termini of the voyage but not the route. The SS Christos sailed October 27, 1956, on a planned route through the Suez Canal. On October 29, 1956, war between Egypt and Israel broke out. On October 31, 1956, Great Britain and France invaded the Suez Canal Zone. On November 2, 1956, Egypt obstructed the canal with sunken vessels, closing it to traffic. Transatlantic (P) sought an agreement for additional compensation for a voyage around the Cape of Good Hope from a concededly unauthorized department of agriculture employee who advised Transatlantic (P) that it had to perform the charter according to its terms but could always file a claim. The SS Christos changed course for the Cape of Good Hope, arriving in Bandar Shapur, Iran, on December 30, 1956. The planned 10,000-mile voyage was increased by 3,000 miles. Transatlantic (P) sought the added expense of $43,972 over the $305,842 contract price. The district court dismissed the libel (an action in admiralty).

**ISSUE:** Was the contract legally impossible, that is, only able to be done at an excessive and unreasonable cost?

**HOLDING AND DECISION:** (Wright, J.) No. While it was reasonable to assume that when no route was mentioned in the charter, the usual and customary route (through the Suez Canal) would be taken. But just because this means of performance was impossible, the court must find whether the risk of the contingency (the closure of the canal) was allocated and, if not, whether performance by alternate routes was rendered impracticable. Allocation of risk of the contingency's occurrence may be expressed or implied in the agreement or found in the surrounding circumstances, including custom and usages of the trade. Nothing in the charter specified the Suez route or implied continued availability of that route for performance. Nothing in custom or trade usage, or in the surrounding circumstances, supported such a condition of performance. An implied expectation of the Suez route was hardly adequate proof of an allocation to the promises of the risk of closure. Circumstances instead seemed to place the risk on Transatlantic (P), as the parties knew or should have known of the crisis. Freight rates were most likely affected by the increased risk of voyage in the Suez area. While one might not have foreseen that nationalization of the canal would have brought about a subsequent closure, the circumstances did indicate Transatlantic's (P) willingness to assume abnormal risks. That legitimately causes the court to judge impracticability of performance by alternative route in stricter terms. Impracticability did not appear as the goods could be shipped in the less temperate climate. The ship and crew were fit for the longer voyage, and Transatlantic (P) was no less able than the Government (D) to purchase insurance. In fact, the ship's operator would be more reasonably expected to cover the hazards of war. To justify relief there must be more of a variation between expected cost and the cost of performing by alternative means than was present here as the promisor can be presumed to have accepted greater than normal risk and impracticability is argued on the basis of expense alone. Affirmed.

## ▶ ANALYSIS
In determining impossibility, the court will look first to see which party assumed the risk of unforeseen circumstances. If that cannot be determined, then it looks to see whether performance was legally impossible. Legally impossible means impracticable, that is, at excessive and unreasonable cost. Knowledge of the crisis would tend to show assumption of the risk. The court, with respect to

*Continued on next page.*

unreasonable cost, examined Transatlantic's (P) theory of relief. If the contract was impossible, it was a nullity from the start. Transatlantic (P) asked for quantum meruit not for the total performance as it should have. The court believed that Transatlantic (P) wanted to avoid losing any of what appeared to be an advantageous contract price. The court would not place a burden on one party to preserve the other's profit. Note that when the court discussed foreseeability of the risk, that foreseeability is as much a fiction as implied conditions, and the parties might honestly have not foreseen the canal closure. Foreseeability is used as a tool in considering where the risk was to be allocated.

## Quicknotes

**CHANGE OF CONDITIONS**  A defense to a claim of ameliorative waste, based on the theory that a change in the surrounding area warranted the alterations to the property.

**IMPOSSIBILITY**  A doctrine relieving the parties to a contract from liability for nonperformance of their duties thereunder, if the subject matter of the contract ceases to exist, a person essential to the performance of the contract is deceased, or the service or goods contracted for has become illegal.

# Selland Pontiac-GMC, Inc. v. King

Buyer (P) v. Seller (D)

Minn. Ct. App., 384 N.W.2d 490 (1986).

**NATURE OF CASE:** Breach of contract.

**FACT SUMMARY:** Selland Pontiac-GMC, Inc. (P) sued King (D) for failure to deliver four school bus bodies.

> ## 🏛 RULE OF LAW
> A partial failure of a seller's source of supply generally has been treated as a foreseeable contingency, the risk of which is allocated to the seller absent a specific provision to the contrary in the contract.

**FACTS:** Selland Pontiac-GMC, Inc. (Seeland) (P) sued King (D), doing business as Superior, for breach of its contract to buy four school buses. In reliance on the contract Selland (P) ordered four bus chassis from General Motors. Superior later went into receivership and never manufactured the buses.

**ISSUE:** Is partial failure of a seller's source of supply generally treated as a foreseeable contingency, the risk of which is allocated to the seller absent a specific provision to the contrary in the contract?

**HOLDING AND DECISION:** (Randall, J.) Yes. A partial failure of a seller's source of supply generally has been treated as a foreseeable contingency, the risk of which is allocated to the seller absent a specific provision to the contrary in the contract. The trial court's holding of no breach of contract is consistent with this rule. Affirmed.

---

## ▶ *ANALYSIS*

The court rests its decision on a rule set forth in *Barbarossa & Sons v. Iten Chevrolet, Inc.*, 265 N.W.2d 655 (1978), in which the manufacturer was not indicated as the source of supply as Superior was here. Furthermore, there the supplier did not cease operations, but merely failed to fulfill the contract.

■━■

### *Quicknotes*

**BREACH OF CONTRACT** Unlawful failure by a party to perform its obligations pursuant to contract.

■━■

# Canadian Industrial Alcohol Co. v. Dunbar Molasses Co.

Molasses purchaser (P) v. Molasses seller (D)

N.Y. Ct. App., 258 N.Y. 194, 179 N.E. 383 (1932).

**NATURE OF CASE:** Appeal from judgment for plaintiff in action for damages for breach of a contract for the sale of goods.

**FACT SUMMARY:** Canadian Industrial Alcohol Co. (P) contracted to buy Dunbar Molasses Co.'s (Dunbar) (D) usual allotment of refined blackstrap molasses, about 1,500,000 wine gallons, Dunbar (D) received from a sugar refinery. That year, Dunbar (D) received much less than the amount contracted, less than 500,000 gallons in all, and could not fulfill its contracted quantity.

---

### 🏛 RULE OF LAW
If the promisor is in some respects responsible for the event which makes performance of his promise impossible, and takes no steps to alleviate the impossibility, his duty of performance is not excused.

---

**FACTS:** At the end of 1927, Canadian Industrial Alcohol Co. (Alcohol Co.) (P) contracted to buy from Dunbar Molasses Co. (Dunbar) (D) about 1,500,000 wine gallons of refined blackstrap molasses, about 60 percent sugar, of the usual run from the National Sugar Refinery, Yonkers, New York. Delivery was to begin April 1, 1928, "to be spread out during the warm weather." The refinery that year produced far less than its capacity, less than a half-million gallons. Dunbar (D), which had no contract with the refinery, shipped its entire allotment, 344,083 gallons, to Alcohol Co. (P). Dunbar (D) did not attempt to enter into a contract which would have assured it would get a sufficient supply of molasses, nor did it inform Alcohol Co. (P) that it did not have such a contract. Alcohol Co. (P) sued for damages, but Dunbar (D) contended that its duty was conditioned by an implied term: the refinery's producing enough molasses to fill Alcohol Co.'s (P) order. Judgment was rendered for Alcohol Co (P), and the state's highest court granted review.

**ISSUE:** If the promisor is in some respects responsible for the event which makes performance of his promise impossible, and takes no steps to alleviate the impossibility, is his duty of performance excused?

**HOLDING AND DECISION:** (Cardozo, C.J.) No. If the promisor is in some respects responsible for the event which makes performance of his promise impossible, and takes no steps to alleviate the impossibility, his duty of performance is not excused. Performance here was not implicitly conditioned by the refinery's producing enough molasses to fill Alcohol Co.'s (P) order. The contract as read in the light of circumstances did not keep Dunbar's (D) duty within such narrow boundaries. Dunbar (D) never even attempted to get a contract with the refinery between the time of acceptance and the start of shipments. Accordingly, contributory fault is implied to Dunbar (D), which put its faith in the mere chance that the refinery's output would remain as in past years. Dunbar's (D) customer did not take that chance; only Dunbar (D) did. Affirmed.

---

### ▶ ANALYSIS

There is no one rule for allowing the unforeseen risk, but the basis of all existing rules is the attempt to place the risk where the parties would have if they had foreseen it. If it is reasonably foreseeable, the promisor will have been deemed to have accepted it. Excuse of performance on grounds of impossibility involves, in the interests of justice, the creation of a condition. If the promisor is in some respects responsible for the event making performance impossible, that is, if he is guilty of contributory fault, performance will not be excused. Had the refinery in this case been destroyed without the fault of Dunbar (D), Dunbar (D) would have been excused from performance. The destruction of the refinery would not have been a risk assumed by the promisor, Dunbar (D). Even had Dunbar (D) made a contract with the refinery, it would still appear that Alcohol Co. (P) would have a cause of action and that Dunbar (D) would still not be excused, as Dunbar (D) would have a cause of action against the refinery. The refinery would then have been liable for Dunbar's (D) loss.

---

### Quicknotes

**BREACH OF CONTRACT** Unlawful failure by a party to perform its obligations pursuant to contract.

**DAMAGES** Monetary compensation that may be awarded by the court to a party who has sustained injury or loss to his person, property or rights due to another party's unlawful act, omission or negligence.

**IMPOSSIBILITY** A doctrine relieving the parties to a contract from liability for nonperformance of their duties thereunder, if the subject matter of the contract ceases to exist, a person essential to the performance of the contract is deceased, or the service or goods contracted for has become illegal.

# Eastern Air Lines, Inc. v. Gulf Oil Corporation

Fuel purchaser (P) v. Supplier (D)

415 F. Supp. 429 (S.D. Fla. 1975).

**NATURE OF CASE:** Action for damages and specific performance for breach of contract.

**FACT SUMMARY:** Gulf Oil Corporation (D) contracted with Eastern Air Lines, Inc. (Eastern) (P) to supply Eastern's (P) fuel requirements.

## 🏛 RULE OF LAW
A requirements contract entered into in good faith is not void for want of mutuality.

**FACTS:** Eastern Air Lines, Inc. (Eastern) (P) contracted with Gulf Oil Corporation (Gulf) (D) for the latter to supply the former's fuel needs on a long-term basis. Price increases were tied to an index of posted prices for a certain oil grade. In response to the fuel crisis of 1974, the federal government created a two-tier price regulation system, wherein prices were regulated up to a certain per-well output, and left unregulated the output beyond the specified amount. Only regulated prices were posted, which had the effect of tying the cost of Eastern's (P) fuel to an amount much less than the going market value. Gulf (D) refused to continue performance, and Eastern (P) sued for damages and specific performance.

**ISSUE:** Is a requirements contract entered into in good faith void for want of mutuality?

**HOLDING AND DECISION:** (King, J.) No. A requirements contract entered into in good faith is not void for want of mutuality. At common law, requirements contracts, while at first thought to be invalid because the buyer had not obligated himself to purchase in a theoretical sense, gradually gained acceptance where the buyer had an ongoing business and could demonstrate a real need for the product in question. Now, the UCC, in § 2-306, specifically authorizes requirements contracts, provided that the requirements are not grossly disproportionate to stated estimates made in good faith. Here, the amount of fuel is not in issue, and there is no evidence of any bad faith. For this reason, the contract is binding and enforceable. [The court awarded specific performance of the contract.]

## ▶ *ANALYSIS*

A supplier can proceed against a buyer in a requirements contract. If, for instance, a buyer shuts down merely to avoid a high-priced requirements contract, the seller would be entitled to some form of relief. However, if the buyer were to shut down for normal business reasons, his requirements would legitimately cease, and the seller would have no cause of action.

## *Quicknotes*

**BREACH OF CONTRACT** Unlawful failure by a party to perform its obligations pursuant to contract.

**MUTUALITY** Reciprocal actions of two parties; in a contract context, refers to mutual promises between two parties to perform an action in exchange for performance on the part of the other party.

**REQUIREMENTS CONTRACT** An agreement pursuant to which one party agrees to purchase all his required goods or services from the other party exclusively for a specified time period.

**SPECIFIC PERFORMANCE** An equitable remedy whereby the court requires the parties to perform their obligations pursuant to a contract.

# Krell v. Henry

Flat owner (P) v. Coronation spectator (D)

K.B. Ct. App., 2 K.B. 740 (1903).

**NATURE OF CASE:** Action for damages for breach of a contract for a license for use.

**FACT SUMMARY:** Henry (D) paid a deposit of £25 to Krell (P) for the use of his apartment in Pall Mall, London, for the purpose of a viewing sight for King Edward VII's coronation procession. The King became ill, causing a delay of the coronation upon which Henry (D) refused to pay a £50 balance, for which Krell (P) sued.

## RULE OF LAW
Where the object of one of the parties is the basis upon which both parties contract, the duties of performance are constructively conditioned upon the attainment of that object.

**FACTS:** In two letters of June 20, 1902, Henry (D) contracted through Krell's (P) agent, Bisgood, to use Krell's (P) flat in Pall Mall, London, to view the coronation procession of King Edward VII, which had been advertised to pass along Pall Mall. The contract made no mention of this purpose. The period of use of the flat was the daytime only of June 26 and 27, 1902, for £75, £25 paid in deposit with the £50 remainder due on June 24, 1902. Henry (D) became aware of the availability of Krell's (P) flat as an announcement to that effect had been made which was reiterated by Krell's (P) housekeeper when she showed Henry (D) the rooms. When the King became very ill, the coronation was delayed, and Henry (D) refused to pay the £50 balance, for which Krell (P) brought suit.

**ISSUE:** Where the object of one of the parties is the basis upon which both parties contract, are the duties of performance constructively conditioned upon the attainment of that object?

**HOLDING AND DECISION:** (Lord Williams, J.) Yes. Where the object of one of the parties is the basis upon which both parties contract, the duties of performance are constructively conditioned upon the attainment of that object. It can be inferred from the surrounding circumstances that the rooms were taken for the purpose of viewing the processions, and that was the foundation of the contract. It was not a lease of the rooms—they could not be used at night—but a license for use for a particular purpose. With the defeat of the purpose of the contract, the performance is excused. Appeal dismissed.

## ▌ ANALYSIS

This case is an extension of *Taylor v. Caldwell*, 122 Eng. Rep. 309 (K.B. 1863), and as in that case it was necessary to remove the roadblock of a lease in order to avoid a

conflict with *Paradine v. Jane*, 82 Eng. Rep. 897 (K.B. 1647). The rule explained here is "frustration of purpose" or "commercial frustration." It has not been made clear whether this doctrine rests upon the failure of consideration or the allocation of the risks. While there is a frustration, performance is not impossible. No constructive condition of performance has failed as Krell (P) made no promise that the condition would occur. Rather, a constructive condition based upon the attainment of the purpose or object has arisen. Note that the frustration should be total or nearly total, though that is a matter of degree.

---

## Quicknotes

**CONSTRUCTIVE CONDITION** A condition that is not expressly stated in or implied by the terms of an agreement, but is imposed by law.

**FRUSTRATION OF PURPOSE** A doctrine relieving the parties to a contract from liability for nonperformance of their duties thereunder when the purpose of the agreement ceases to exist, due to circumstances not subject to either party's control.

# Swift Canadian Co. v. Banet

Pelt seller (P) v. Buyer (D)

224 F.2d 36 (3d Cir. 1955).

**NATURE OF CASE:** Appeal from summary judgment for the defense in action for damages for breach of a contract for the sale of goods.

**FACT SUMMARY:** After Banet (D) contracted to purchase lamb pelts from Swift Canadian Co. (P), the U.S. Bureau of Animal Industry, after partial shipment was made, issued stricter regulations for the importation of lamb pelts, and, thus, Banet (D) refused to accept further deliveries.

## 🏛 RULE OF LAW
Assuming a party is ready to perform, he is not obligated to perform in vain where the other party has given notice of refusal to accept performance.

**FACTS:** Banet (D) contracted to purchase lamb pelts from Swift Canadian Co. (Swift) (P), a Canadian corporation located in Toronto, Canada. Part of the order was shipped F.O.B. Toronto to Philadelphia. On March 12, 1952, Swift (P) notified Banet (D) of its readiness to ship the remainder from Toronto to Philadelphia. On or about that day, the U.S. Bureau of Animal Industry issued stricter regulations for importation of lamb pelts into the United States. For this reason, Banet (D) refused to accept further shipments. The parties agreed that the price of the pelts would be U.S. $3.80 each, F.O.B. Toronto, that neither party was to be liable for orders or acts of any government or governmental agency, and that as pelts were sold F.O.B. seller's plant title and risk of loss passed to Banet (D) when the pelts were loaded on cars at Swift's (P) plant. The trial court granted Banet's (D) motion for summary judgment, and Swift (P) appealed.

**ISSUE:** Assuming a party is ready to perform, is he obligated to perform in vain where the other party has given notice of refusal to accept performance?

**HOLDING AND DECISION:** (Goodrich, J.) No. Assuming a party is ready to perform, he is not obligated to perform in vain where the other party has given notice of refusal to accept performance. If Swift (P) fulfilled its obligation when it did deliver, it is clear that when it failed to load the pelts because Banet (D) had signified his refusal to accept them, Swift (P) can assert the same rights as if it had loaded them. Generally, when goods are sold F.O.B., free on board, pursuant to contract, the goods pass at the point where they are loaded. Though this is merely a presumption, nothing was shown to counteract that presumption. When Swift (P) made its delivery, it was to send a bill of lading through a Philadelphia bank, Banet's (D) location. The seller's (P) performance was fully complete

when the goods were delivered F.O.B. Toronto. The risk of loss and possibility of profit if the market advanced moved to the buyer (D) at that point. Despite the fact that the pelts could not be imported into the United States, they could be delivered to most anywhere else in the world. Reversed with instructions.

## ▶ ANALYSIS

In this case the buyer was allocated the risk. The court looks to the purpose of the contract. Remember that in *Krell v. Henry*, 2 K.B. 740 (1903), the contract had one purpose: to view the coronation procession; here, the purpose was to buy pelts and resell them for a profit in Philadelphia. The buyer, Banet (D), knew he would need insurance on the pelts during shipment. F.O.B. means that seller's responsibility terminates at the location specified, here Toronto. But if the purpose of F.O.B. is to allocate the risk, the rule of this case would not be in line with that as the court looks mainly to readiness and willingness to perform. If the court placed a responsibility on each party to be aware of its respective government's possible new regulations and to be held to them, then there is a stronger basis for the rule of the case.

◼▬◼

## Quicknotes

**BILL OF LADING** A receipt or other documentation given to a shipper by a carrier evidencing the contract to transport such goods and that the shipper possessed title to the goods shipped.

**F.O.B.** "Free on board"; agreement between a seller and buyer pursuant to which the seller agrees to deliver the subject matter of the contract to a particular destination at his own expense and until which time he assumes all liability therefore.

**SUMMARY JUDGMENT** Judgment rendered by a court in response to a motion by one of the parties, claiming that the lack of a question of material fact in respect to an issue warrants disposition of the issue without consideration by the jury.

◼▬◼

# Chase Precast Corp. v. John J. Paonessa Co.

## Barrier supplier (P) v. Contractor (D)

Mass. Sup. Jud. Ct., 409 Mass. 371, 566 N.E.2d 603 (1991).

**NATURE OF CASE:** Appeal from denial of damages for breach of contract.

**FACT SUMMARY:** When a highway reconstruction project was halted due to citizen protests, John J. Paonessa Co. (D), the contractor, canceled the contract with its supplier, Chase Precast Corp. (Chase) (P), after Chase (P) had already produced one-half of the concrete median barriers required by the project.

### 🏛 RULE OF LAW
A defendant may rely on frustration of purpose as a defense to a breach of contract claim if the risk of the occurrence of the frustrating event is not allocated by the contract to the defendant.

**FACTS:** In 1982, Massachusetts entered into two contracts with John J. Paonessa Co. (Paonessa) (D) to replace a highway grass median strip with precast concrete barriers. Paonessa (D) subsequently contracted with Chase Precast Corp. (Chase) (P) to supply the concrete median barriers. After Chase (P) had produced about one-half of the barriers, angry residents brought a halt to the project. On June 7, 1983, Paonessa (D) notified Chase (P) by letter to stop producing the barriers, which Chase (P) did as soon as it received the letter on June 8. Paonessa (D) paid Chase (P) for all the barriers it had produced at the contract price. Chase (P) then brought an action against Paonessa (D) to recover its anticipated profit on the barriers called for in the contract but not produced. The trial court ruled in favor of Paonessa (D) based on impossibility of performance. The appeals court affirmed, but noted that the doctrine of frustration of purpose was a more accurate description of the basis of the trial judge's decision than the doctrine of impossibility. Chase (P) appealed.

**ISSUE:** May a defendant rely on frustration of purpose as a defense to a breach of contract claim if the risk of the occurrence of the frustrating event is not allocated by the contract to the defendant?

**HOLDING AND DECISION:** (Lynch, J.) Yes. A defendant may rely on frustration of purpose as a defense to a breach of contract claim if the risk of the occurrence of the frustrating event is not allocated by the contract to the defendant. Frustration of purpose is defined by the Restatement (Second) of Contracts § 265 (1981) as follows: "Where, after a contract is made, a party's principal purpose is substantially frustrated without his fault by the occurrence of an event the nonoccurrence of which was a basic assumption on which the contract was made, his remaining duties to render performance are discharged,

unless the language or the circumstances indicate the contrary." Since Paonessa (D) was in no way responsible for the state's elimination of the median barriers from the project, whether it can rely on the defense of frustration turns on whether elimination of the barriers was a reasonably foreseeable risk allocated by the contracts to Paonessa (D). Because Chase (P) had supplied barriers to the state before, it was aware of the state's power to eliminate items from its contracts, paying only the contract unit price for items actually accepted. Chase (P) was also aware that lost profits were not an element of damage, giving further credence to the state's power to decrease quantities. But even if the parties were aware generally of the state's power to eliminate contract items, they did not contemplate the cancellation of a major portion of the project of such a widely used item as concrete median barriers and did not allocate the risk of such cancellation. Affirmed.

### ▶ ANALYSIS

Note the difference between impossibility and frustration as defenses to a breach of contract. The supplier of goods or services who finds himself unable to perform will use the impossibility defense. The buyer of the goods and services will typically use the defense of frustration. This is because it is always possible for the buyer to fulfill his promise to pay, even if he is no longer in need of the service or product and will essentially gain nothing for his money. To further add to the confusion, the Restatement (Second) of Contracts employs the same four criteria for both frustration and impossibility.

■═■

### Quicknotes

**DOCTRINE OF IMPOSSIBILITY** A doctrine relieving the parties to a contract from liability for nonperformance of their duties thereunder, if the subject matter of the contract ceases to exist, a person essential to the performance of the contract is deceased, or the service or goods contracted for has become illegal.

**FRUSTRATION OF PURPOSE** A doctrine relieving the parties to a contract from liability for nonperformance of their duties thereunder when the purpose of the agreement ceases to exist, due to circumstances not subject to either party's control.

■═■

# Northern Indiana Public Service Co. v. Carbon County Coal Co.

## Public power utility (P) v. Coal supplier (D)

799 F.2d 265 (7th Cir. 1986).

**NATURE OF CASE:** Appeal from award of damages for breach of contract.

**FACT SUMMARY:** Northern Indiana Public Service Co. (P) contended that it was excused from performance of its contract to purchase coal from Carbon County Coal Co. (D) because governmental restrictions rendered performance impossible or impracticable.

## 🏛 RULE OF LAW
A party cannot avoid performance of a contract on the basis of impracticability or impossibility where the contract specifically shifts the risk of such to that party.

**FACTS:** Northern Indiana Public Service Co. (NIPSCO) (P), a public power utility, contracted with Carbon County Coal Co. (Carbon County) (D) to purchase a set amount of coal over a period of time. The contract was not a requirements contract; it obligated NIPSCO (P) to purchase a set amount of coal over a twenty-year period. Subsequently, the Public Service Commission ordered NIPSCO (P) to use good-faith efforts to purchase power from other utilities if such alternatives were more economical than producing it. If such was available, NIPSCO (P) could not pass on the increased costs of creating power to customers. NIPSCO (P) could in fact purchase power more economically and decided to refuse performance on the coal contracts. It sued for a declaration that the governmental restrictions rendered its performance impossible or impracticable. Carbon County (D) counterclaimed for breach and specific performance. A damage award for Carbon County (D) was appealed by NIPSCO (P) and a denial of specific performance was appealed by Carbon County (D).

**ISSUE:** Can a party avoid performance of a contract on the basis of impossibility or impracticability where the risk of such was allocated to it in the contract?

**HOLDING AND DECISION:** (Posner, J.) No. A party cannot avoid performance of a contract on the basis of impossibility or impracticability where the risk of such is allocated to it in the contract. The risk of impracticability was placed on NIPSCO (P) by the governmental orders. Also, the contract being a fixed price contract is an explicit assignment of the risk of market price decreases to the buyer. Thus, performance could not be avoided. Specific performance was unavailable because continued production would be uneconomical. Affirmed.

## ▶ ANALYSIS

The court rejected NIPSCO's (P) argument that a force majeure clause excused performance. That clause excused performance where a governmental act prevents utilization of the coal. The act in this case rendered use uneconomical but not illegal; thus, the court affirmed the trial court's refusal to instruct the jury on this issue.

## Quicknotes

**FORCE MAJEURE CLAUSE** A clause pursuant to an oil and gas lease, relieving the lessee from liability for breach of the lease if the party's performance is impeded as the result of a natural cause that could not have been prevented.

**PRELIMINARY INJUNCTION** An order issued by the court at the commencement of an action, requiring a party to refrain from conducting a specified activity that is the subject of the controversy, until the matter is determined.

**UCC § 2-615** Provides that a delay in delivery by a seller is not a breach of his duty under a contract for sale if performance has been made impracticable by the occurrence of a contingency the non-occurrence of which was a basic assumption on which the contract was made.

# Young v. City of Chicopee

## Contractor (P) v. Municipality (D)

Mass. Sup. Jud. Ct., 186 Mass. 518, 72 N.E. 63 (1904).

**NATURE OF CASE:** Action for damages for breach of a repair contract.

**FACT SUMMARY:** Young (P) contracted with the City of Chicopee (D) to repair a bridge. After part of the work was done, the bridge was destroyed by fire without fault of either party. Young (P) sued for the value of the work done and for his lumber destroyed in the fire.

## RULE OF LAW
There is an implied condition that a thing upon which work is to be done shall continue to exist, and if it is destroyed without fault, the owner is liable for the value of the work done.

**FACTS:** Young (P) contracted to repair a bridge belonging to City of Chicopee (D). Young's (P) compensation was to be measured by the number of feet of new lumber wrought into the bridge. So that public travel would not be unnecessarily inconvenienced, the contract provided that at least one-half the materials were to be on the job before work could begin. Lumber, not yet being used, was spread about the bridge and upon the river banks. The bridge was destroyed by fire without fault of the parties. Part of the yet unused lumber was destroyed. Chicopee (D) did not dispute its liability for the work done but refused liability for the destroyed unused lumber.

**ISSUE:** Is there an implied condition that a thing upon which work is to be done shall continue to exist, and if it is destroyed without fault, is the owner liable for the value of the work done?

**HOLDING AND DECISION:** (Hammond, J.) Yes. There is an implied condition that a thing upon which work is to be done shall continue to exist, and if it is destroyed without fault, the owner is liable for the value of the work done. While it was required to be on the job, title to the lumber remained in Young (P). Chicopee (D) had no care or control over it. The purpose of the requirement for the lumber to be on the job was to ensure rapid progress of the work and not to affect the parties' rights to the lumber. The contract was entire as the total compensation was to be fixed by the amount of lumber wrought into the bridge. Chicopee's (D) liability is measured by the amount of the contract work done that, at the time of the destruction of the bridge, had become so identified with the bridge that it would have inured to Chicopee (D) as contemplated by the contract. However, Chicopee (D) will not be liable for the loss of the lumber owned by Young (P) at the time of the fire which had not yet been incorporated into the bridge. Reversed. Judgment for the plaintiff.

## ANALYSIS

Note that repair contracts are treated differently than construction contracts. Under a construction contract, the contractor would not be compensated upon loss for destruction. Under a repair contract, the contractor is excused from further performance and is compensated for that which he has done. The continued existence of the structure being repaired is deemed to be a basic assumption of the parties. This same rule has been applied to subcontractors working under a general contractor when a building under construction is destroyed. Therefore, the lumber here that was destroyed had not yet been placed into the repair work. While there may have been a minor benefit to Chicopee (D) in that travelers were not inconvenienced, it was not enough to transfer title.

## Quicknotes

**IMPLIED CONDITION** A condition that is not expressly stated in the terms of an agreement, but which is inferred from the parties' conduct or the type of dealings involved.

# Third Parties: Rights and Responsibilities

## *Quick Reference Rules of Law*

# Lawrence v. Fox

Third-party beneficiary (P) v. Promisor in breach (D)

N.Y. Ct. App., 20 N.Y. 268 (1859).

**NATURE OF CASE:** Appeal from judgment for third party in action to recover damages for breach of contract.

**FACT SUMMARY:** Fox (D) promised Holly for consideration that he would pay Holly's debt to Lawrence (P).

## RULE OF LAW
A third party for whose benefit a contract is made may bring an action for its breach.

**FACTS:** Holly owed Lawrence (P) $300. Holly loaned $300 to Fox (D) in consideration of Fox's (D) promise to pay the same amount to Lawrence (P), thereby erasing Holly's debts to Lawrence (P). Fox (D) did not pay Lawrence (P), and Lawrence (P) brought this action for breach of Fox's (D) promise to Holly. The jury returned a verdict for Lawrence (P) for the amount of the loan plus interest, and Fox (D) appealed.

**ISSUE:** Is a third party precluded for want of privity of contract from maintaining an action on a contract made for his benefit?

**HOLDING AND DECISION:** (Gray, J.) No. In the case of a promise made to one for the benefit of another, he for whose benefit it is made may bring an action for its breach. This principle, which has been long applied in trust cases, is in fact a general principle of law. Affirmed.

**CONCURRENCE:** (Johnson, J.) The promise was made to Lawrence (P) through his agent. Lawrence (P) could have ratified the action when it came to his knowledge, although he had not been privy to the action.

**DISSENT:** (Comstock, J.) In general, there must be privity of contract. Here Lawrence (P) had nothing to do with the promise on which he brought the action. It was not made to him, nor did the consideration proceed from him. If Lawrence (P) can maintain the suit, it is because an anomaly has found its way into the law on this subject.

## ANALYSIS

This is the leading case which started the general doctrine of "third-party beneficiaries." In the parlance of the original Restatement of Contracts, Lawrence (P) was a "creditor" beneficiary. Restatement (Second) § 133 has eliminated the creditor/donee distinction which the original Restatement fostered and has lumped both under the label of "intended" beneficiary. Although the court in the present case went to some effort to discuss trusts and agency,

ultimately the court allowed Lawrence (P) to recover because it was manifestly "just" that he should recover. Such has been the creation of many a new legal doctrine. The dissenting justices were primarily worried about freedom of contract and the continuing ability of promisor and promisee to rescind or modify their contract. As the doctrine has developed, various rules have arisen to handle these situations.

---

## Quicknotes

**NONSUIT** Judgment against a party who fails to make out a case.

**PRIVITY** Commonality of rights or interests between parties.

**THIRD-PARTY BENEFICIARY** A party who benefits from a promise made pursuant to a contract although he is not a party to the agreement.

# Seaver v. Ransom

Decedent's niece (P) v. Estate executor (D)

N.Y. Ct. App., 224 N.Y. 233, 120 N.E. 639 (1918).

**NATURE OF CASE:** Action by a third party to recover damages for breach of a contract.

**FACT SUMMARY:** Berman made a promise to his wife for the benefit of their niece, Seaver (P), who sued Berman's executor (D) for breach of that promise.

## 🏛 RULE OF LAW
A niece for whose benefit a promise was made to her aunt may successfully bring an action for breach of that promise.

**FACTS:** Mrs. Berman, on her deathbed, wished to leave some property to her niece, Seaver (P). Her husband induced his dying wife to sign a will leaving all property to him by promising that he would leave a certain amount in his own will to Seaver (P). Mr. Berman died without making such a provision for Seaver (P). Seaver (P) successfully brought suit against Ransom (D), as executor of Berman's estate, for Berman's breach of his promise to his dying wife, and Ransom (D) appealed.

**ISSUE:** Does a niece for whose benefit a promise was made to her aunt have an action for breach of that promise?

**HOLDING AND DECISION:** (Pound, J.) Yes. Although a general rule requires privity between a plaintiff and a defendant as necessary to the maintenance of an action on the contract, one of several exceptions to the rule is the case where a contract is made for the benefit of another member of the family. Here, Mrs. Berman was childless, and Seaver (P) was a beloved niece. However, the constraining power of conscience is not regulated by the degree of relationship alone. The dependent or faithful niece may have a stronger claim than the affluent or unworthy son. No sensible theory of moral obligation denies arbitrarily to the former what would be conceded to the latter. The reason for this "family" exception (and other exceptions) to the rule is that it is just and practical to permit the person for whose benefit a contract is made to enforce it against one whose duty it is to pay. The doctrine of *Lawrence v. Fox*, 20 N.Y. 2008 (1859), is progressive, not retrograde. Finally, in this particular case, the "equities" are with Seaver (P). Affirmed.

## ▶ ANALYSIS

In this case, the court (as does the original Restatement of Contracts) uses the term "donee beneficiary" to describe Seaver (P). The Restatement (Second) erases the creditor/donee distinction and labels both types of beneficiaries as "intended." Although the court here is very insistent on the close family relationship, subsequent New York cases have erased that requirement for donee beneficiaries as the doctrine governing third-party beneficiaries has expanded. These subsequent cases represent the now-prevailing view in the country.

## Quicknotes

**DONEE BENEFICIARY** A third party, not a party to a contract, but for whose benefit the contract is entered with the intention that the benefits derived therefrom be bestowed upon the person as a gift.

**PRIVITY** The commonality of rights or interests between parties.

**RESIDUARY LEGATEE** The recipient of the residuary estate of a testator.

# Sisney v. State

Kosher-observant prisoner (P) v. State (D)

S.D. Sup. Ct., 754 N.W.2d 639 (2008).

**NATURE OF CASE:** Appeal from dismissal of action for breach of contract on grounds that the plaintiff lacked standing to bring the action as a third-party beneficiary.

**FACT SUMMARY:** Sisney (P), a kosher-observant prisoner, contended that he was a third-party beneficiary of a contract between the State (D) and CBM Inc. (D) pursuant to which CBM (D) provided food services to the State's (D) prisons, and contended that CBM (D) breached the contract by failing to provide him with a sufficiently caloric or kosher diet.

## 🏛 RULE OF LAW
One who benefits only incidentally from a public contract and who is not expressly intended to be benefitted by the contract does not have standing to bring suit to challenge a breach of the contract that allegedly affects him directly.

**FACTS:** CBM, Inc. (D) provided food services to the State's (D) prisons pursuant to a contract. The contract specified the number of daily calories that each prisoner would get and that the meals provided would accommodate prisoners' religious beliefs. Sisney (P), a Jewish prisoner who was kosher-observant, claimed that the kosher diet CBM (D) provided to him did not meet the contract's calorie requirements and also did not meet the dictates of his religious beliefs. After filing the appropriate administrative grievances, Sisney (P) was informed by Weber (D), the state's director of prison operations, that no further action would be taken on his grievance. Sisney (P) then filed suit alleging the State (D), Weber (D), and CBM (D) had conspired to allow a breach of contract to his detriment because of his religious beliefs and that that this breach resulted in financial gain to the defendants. Sisney (P) asserted standing to sue on the grounds that he was a third-party beneficiary of the contract and that the breach of the contract directly affected him and his well-being. The trial court granted the defendants' motion to dismiss for failure to state a claim on the grounds that Sisney's (P) claims were barred by statutory immunity and a lack of standing to assert a breach of a public contract. The state's highest court granted review.

**ISSUE:** Does one who benefits only incidentally from a public contract and who is not expressly intended to be benefitted by the contract have standing to bring suit to challenge a breach of the contract that allegedly affects him directly?

**HOLDING AND DECISION:** (Zinter, J.) No. One who benefits only incidentally from a public contract and who is not expressly intended to be benefitted by the contract does not have standing to bring suit to challenge a breach of the contract that allegedly affects him directly. By statute in this state a contract made expressly for the benefit of a third person may be enforced by him at any time before the parties thereto rescind it. However, not everyone who receives a benefit from the contract is entitled to enforce it. For the third party to have standing to enforce the contract, at the time the contract was executed, it must have been the contracting parties' intent to expressly benefit the third party more than just incidentally. This is especially true with government contracts, and absent plain and clear language of the contract to the contrary, a private third-party right of enforcement will not be inferred because of the potential burden that expanded liability would impose. Consequently, when a public contract is involved, private citizens—as well as inmates—are presumed not to be third-party beneficiaries. Because public contracts are intended to benefit everyone, the inmate's benefit is presumed to be only incidental to the contract. Here, there was no language in the contract expressly indicating that it was intended for Sisney's (P) direct benefit or enforcement. To the contrary, the contract was expressly for the State's (D) benefit. Whatever collective benefit that inmates may have received was only incidental to that of the State (D). Sisney's (P) argument, that because the contract provided that CBM would describe the complaint resolution process in place for addressing complaints, he possessed a right of enforcement, is unpersuasive. That process, however, was a general institutional process provided to all inmates independently of the CBM contract. Therefore, the contract's reference to that policy did not confer contractual third-party beneficiary status on Sisney (P) to enforce the contract. Affirmed.

## ▶ ANALYSIS

As this case suggests, government contracts pose unique difficulties in the area of third-party beneficiary rights because, to some extent, every member of the public is directly or indirectly intended to benefit from such a contract. Thus the presumption applied in this case, i.e., that private citizens are presumed not to be third-party beneficiaries, operates, as a general rule, to insulate private parties who contract with the government from liability at the hands of the public. Restatement § 302, which distinguishes between intended and incidental beneficiaries, supports this approach.

⬛▬⬛

*Continued on next page.*

## Quicknotes

**STANDING** The right to commence suit against another party because of a personal stake in the resolution of the controversy.

**THIRD-PARTY BENEFICIARY** A party who benefits from a promise made pursuant to a contract although he is not a party to the agreement.

■━■

# Sisney v. Reisch

## Kosher-observant prisoner (P) v. State official (D)

S.D. Sup. Ct., 754 N.W.2d 813 (2008).

**NATURE OF CASE:** Appeal from dismissal of action for breach of a settlement agreement on grounds that the plaintiff lacked standing to bring the action as a third-party beneficiary.

**FACT SUMMARY:** Sisney (P), a kosher-observant prisoner, contended that he was a third-party beneficiary of a settlement agreement between the state's Department of Corrections (DOC) (D) and a former inmate, Heftel, and that the DOC (D) breached the agreement by failing to provide him with pre-packaged, certified kosher meals.

## 🏛 RULE OF LAW

Where a contract is made expressly for the benefit of a class of individuals, a member of that class has standing to enforce the agreement.

**FACTS:** Heftel, a former inmate who was Jewish and kosher-observant, entered into a settlement agreement with the state's Department of Corrections (DOC), pursuant to which the DOC agreed to provide a kosher diet to all Jewish inmates who requested it, and that the kosher diet would include prepackaged meals which were certified kosher for noon and evening meals. Several years later, the provider of food services to the state's prisons quit serving prepackaged kosher meals and began serving a new kosher diet. Sisney (P), a current inmate who was also Jewish and kosher-observant, alleged that this change violated the Heftel agreement and his religious beliefs. Sisney (P) subsequently submitted a grievance through DOC administrative procedures. When this was denied, he brought suit against state prison officials (D), claiming they had breached the Heftel agreement. The trial court dismissed on several grounds including the ground that the complaint failed to state a claim because it contained no factual assertions supporting an inference that it was the prison officials' (D) responsibility to carry out the Heftel agreement. However, the trial court did not reach Sisney's (P) argument that he had standing to bring his suit as a third-party beneficiary of the Heftel agreement. The state's highest court granted review.

**ISSUE:** Where a contract is made expressly for the benefit of a class of individuals, does a member of that class have standing to enforce the agreement?

**HOLDING AND DECISION:** (Zinter, J.) Yes. Where a contract is made expressly for the benefit of a class of individuals, a member of that class has standing to enforce the agreement. As a threshold matter, the settlement agreement's history and content gives rise to the inference that the prison officials (D) had the responsibility

to enforce the Heftel agreement. State statute provides that a contract made expressly for the benefit of a third person may be enforced by him at any time before the parties thereto rescind it. Standing to enforce an agreement as a third-party beneficiary may also be conferred upon a class of individuals. As with standing for individuals, the contract must clearly express the intent to benefit the identifiable class. Here, the Heftel agreement clearly expressed that the DOC agreed to provide a kosher diet to an identifiable class of which Sisney (P) was a member, i.e., "to all Jewish inmates who request it." The agreement also expressly reflected an intent to benefit all members of that class. The explicit contractual language reflected the signatories' intent to provide more than an incidental benefit: the contractual language raised the inference that the Heftel agreement was intended to expressly benefit all Jewish inmates who requested a kosher diet. Because Sisney (P) alleged that he was a member of that class, he sufficiently stated a claim that he was a third-party beneficiary with standing to enforce the Heftel agreement. Reversed and remanded.

## ▶ ANALYSIS

The decision in *Reisch* is distinguishable from the same court's decision in *Sisney v. State*, 754 N.W.2d 639 (S.D. 2008), which rejected Sisney's (P) argument that he had standing to enforce a contract between the state and a contractor that provided food services for the state's prisons, because the contract in *Sisney v. State* was a public contract that did not expressly indicate it was made for the benefit of Sisney (P) or a class of individuals of which Sisney (P) was a member. The key difference was that in *Reisch*, the court found that the contract at issue, the Heftel agreement, had been made with the express intent of benefitting the class of which Sisney (P) was a member.

■━■

## Quicknotes

**STANDING** The right to commence suit against another party because of a personal stake in the resolution of the controversy.

**THIRD-PARTY BENEFICIARY** A party who benefits from a promise made pursuant to a contract although he is not a party to the agreement.

■━■

# Verni v. Cleveland Chiropractic College

## Student (P) v. College (D)

Mo. Sup. Ct., 212 S.W.3d 150 (2007).

**NATURE OF CASE:** Appeal from verdict and judgment in breach of contract action.

**FACT SUMMARY:** Makarov (D), a teacher at the Cleveland Chiropractic College (Cleveland), contended that Verni (P), his student, did not have standing as an intended third-party beneficiary of the contract between Makarov (D) and Cleveland, even if the faculty handbook was a part of that contract, to bring a suit for breach of contract.

### 🏛 RULE OF LAW
A third party is not an intended beneficiary of a contract where the terms of the contract do not directly and clearly express the intent to benefit the third party or any class to which the party belongs, even if the third party is incidentally benefited by the contract.

**FACTS:** Verni (P) was Makarov's (D) student at the Cleveland Chiropractic College (Cleveland). The faculty handbook required that faculty members treat students with courtesy, respect, fairness, and professionalism, and also provided that students were entitled to expect such treatment. The contract between Makarov (D) and Cleveland was a one-page document that provided that Makarov (D) would be a full-time faculty member of Cleveland for one year. The contract required him to be on campus a certain amount of time each week and outlined his teaching duties. In return, the contract provided Makarov's (D) salary and employment benefits. The contract required Makarov (D) to comply with the policies in the faculty handbook. Claiming that he was an intended third-party beneficiary of the contract between Makarov (D) and Cleveland, on the basis that the faculty handbook was a part of that contract, Verni (P) brought suit against Makarov (D) for breach of contract for having treated Verni (P) in a manner inconsistent with the handbook requirements. Verni (P) won a verdict and judgment against Makarov (D) for $10,000. The state's highest court granted review.

**ISSUE:** Is a third party an intended beneficiary of a contract where the terms of the contract do not directly and clearly express the intent to benefit the third party or any class to which the party belongs, even if the third party is incidentally benefited by the contract?

**HOLDING AND DECISION:** (Wolff, C.J.) No. A third party is not an intended beneficiary of a contract where the terms of the contract do not directly and clearly express the intent to benefit the third party or any class to which the party belongs, even if the third party is inciden-

tally benefited by the contract. Where a contract does not express such intent, there is a strong presumption that the third party is not a beneficiary and that the parties contracted to benefit only themselves. Even if the third party is incidentally benefited by the contract, as Verni (P) and all students were benefited here, this incidental benefit does not rebut the presumption that the party was intended to be benefited. Here, although the contract might have incidentally provided a benefit to Cleveland students, it did not contain a clear expression of intent that Makarov (D) was undertaking a duty to benefit Verni (P) or any students. Even if, arguendo, the faculty handbook was a binding part of the contract, the language in the handbook does not overcome the strong presumption that Cleveland and Makarov (D) executed the contract for their own benefit. Because only intended, rather than incidental, beneficiaries of a contract have standing to bring a claim under that contract, Verni (P) did not have standing to bring his breach of contract claim. Reversed.

## ▸ ANALYSIS

Here, the court focused on "intent" of the parties, and finding the contract lacked language to support such intent, ruled that Verni (P) was not an intended beneficiary. However, some notable commentators on contracts law, such as Corbin, view the focus on "intent" or "purpose" or "motive" to be misplaced since those terms tend to be subjective and obscure. They propose that the focus should instead be on whether the purported beneficiary's benefit is so direct and substantial and so closely connected with that of the promisee, that it makes economic sense to permit such a beneficiary to enforce the contract, whereas if the purported beneficiary's benefit is so indirect and incidental it would not make economic sense to permit them to enforce the contract. Under such an analysis, it would seem that Verni (P) might very well have prevailed because the students in this case greatly benefited from the policies in the faculty handbook.

▰▭▰

### Quicknotes

**ARGUENDO** Hypothetical argument.

**BENEFICIARY** A third party who is the recipient of the benefit of a transaction undertaken by another.

**BREACH OF CONTRACT** An unlawful failure by a party to perform its obligations pursuant to contract.

▰▭▰

# Grigerik v. Sharpe

Buyer (P) v. Engineer (D)

Conn. Sup. Ct., 247 Conn. 293, 721 A.2d 526 (1998).

**NATURE OF CASE:** Negligence suit.

**FACT SUMMARY:** Grigerik (P) contracted to purchase property based on Sharpe's (D) site plans.

## 🏛 RULE OF LAW
The intent of both parties to a contract determines whether a third party has contract rights as a third-party beneficiary.

**FACTS:** Grigerik (P) contracted to purchase land from Lang, subject to the town's approval of the tract as a building lot. Lang contracted with an engineer, Sharpe (D), to prepare a site plan for drainage. The site plan was prepared and the sale executed. When Grigerik (P) later applied for a building permit, it was denied. Grigerik (P) brought suit against Sharpe (D) alleging negligence and an entitlement as a third-party beneficiary. Judgment was entered for Grigerik (P), but was reversed on appeal.

**ISSUE:** Does the intent of both parties to a contract determine whether a third party has contract rights as a third-party beneficiary?

**HOLDING AND DECISION:** (Borden, J.) Yes. The intent of both parties to a contract determines whether a third party has contract rights as a third-party beneficiary. The right to performance in a third-party beneficiary is determined both by the intention of the contracting parties and by the intention of one of the parties to benefit the third party. Grigerik (P) cannot prevail on the breach of contract claim since the jury specifically found that he failed to prove he was an intended beneficiary of the contact between Lang and Sharpe (D). Reversed and remanded.

## ▶ ANALYSIS

Note that although the jury found that Grigerik (P) was a foreseeable beneficiary of the contract, the court states that foreseeability is a tort concept and not sufficient to sustain a claim of rights for a third-party beneficiary in a contract.

■═■

## *Quicknotes*

**FORESEEABILITY** Reasonable expectation that an act or omission would result in injury.

**THIRD-PARTY BENEFICIARY** A party who benefits from a promise made pursuant to a contract although he is not a party to the agreement.

■═■

# Sally Beauty Co. v. Nexxus Products Co.

Beauty products distributor (P) v. Product manufacturer (D)

801 F.2d 1001 (7th Cir. 1986).

**NATURE OF CASE:** Appeal from a grant of defendant's motion for summary judgment in an action for breach of contract.

**FACT SUMMARY:** After Sally Beauty Co. (P) acquired a company with which Nexxus Products Co. (Nexxus) (D) had an exclusive distribution agreement, Nexxus (D) refused to continue complying with the agreement, since Sally Beauty (P) was a wholly owned subsidiary of a Nexxus (D) competitor in the hair care market.

> ## RULE OF LAW
> The duty of performance under an exclusive distributorship may not be delegated to a competitor in the marketplace or to the wholly owned subsidiary of a competitor without the obligee's consent.

**FACTS:** Sally Beauty Co. (P) acquired Best Barber Beauty & Supply Company, which had an exclusive "best efforts" agreement to distribute and promote Nexxus Products Co. (Nexxus) (D) hair care products in the Texas market, in a merger and acquisition. Because Sally Beauty (P) was a wholly owned subsidiary of Alberto-Culver, one of Nexxus's (D) competitors in the marketplace, Nexxus (D) refused to continue its agreement with Best. Sally Beauty (P) sued Nexxus (D) for breach of contract and violation of antitrust laws. Nexxus (D) moved for summary judgment on the breach of contract claim. The trial court granted the motion, finding that the contract was not simply an ordinary commercial contract, but one based upon a relationship of personal trust and confidence between the parties. Sally Beauty (P) appealed.

**ISSUE:** May the duty of performance under an exclusive distributorship be delegated to a competitor in the marketplace or to the wholly owned subsidiary of a competitor without the obligee's consent?

**HOLDING AND DECISION:** (Cudahy, J.) No. The duty of performance under an exclusive distributorship may not be delegated to a competitor in the marketplace or to the wholly owned subsidiary of a competitor without the obligee's consent. Nexxus (D) should not be required to accept the "best efforts" of Sally Beauty (P) when those efforts are subject to the control of Alberto-Culver. It is entirely reasonable that Nexxus (D) conclude that this performance would be other than what it had bargained for. When performance of personal services is delegated, the duty is per se nondelegable. There is no inquiry into whether the delegation is as skilled or worthy of trust and confidence as the original obligor. The delegate was not bargained for, and the obligee need not consent to the substitution. Nexxus (D) has a substantial interest in not seeing this contract performed by Sally Beauty (P); thus, the contract was not assignable without Nexxus's (D) consent. Affirmed.

**DISSENT:** (Posner, J.) Sally Beauty (P) distributes hair care supplies made by many different companies, which appear to compete with Alberto-Culver as vigorously as Nexxus (D) does. At most, so far as the record shows, Nexxus (D) may have had grounds for "insecurity" regarding the performance by Sally Beauty (P) of its obligation to use its best efforts to promote Nexxus (D) products. Since this is the case, its remedy was not to cancel the contract but to demand assurances of due performance. No such demand was made.

## ANALYSIS

The majority noted that, if the assignee were only a partially owned subsidiary, there presumably would have to be fact-finding about the degree of control the competitor-parent had over the subsidiary's business decisions. While the court of appeals affirmed the decision of the district court, it did so, on a different ground. The court found instead that Sally Beauty's (P) position as a wholly owned subsidiary of a competing company was sufficient to bar the delegation of Best's duties under its agreement with Nexxus (D).

■═■

### Quicknotes

**SUMMARY JUDGMENT** Judgment rendered by a court in response to a motion by one of the parties, claiming that the lack of a question of material fact in respect to an issue warrants disposition of the issue without consideration by the jury.

**UCC § 2-210** A party may perform his duty through a delegate unless otherwise agreed or unless the other party has a substantial interest in having his original promisor perform or control the acts required by the contract.

■═■

# Herzog v. Irace

## Assignee (P) v. Attorney (D)

Me. Sup. Jud. Ct., 594 A.2d 1106 (1991).

**NATURE OF CASE:** Appeal of an award of damages for breach of assignment.

**FACT SUMMARY:** Although Jones assigned a personal injury claim to Herzog (P) and so notified his attorneys, Irace (D) and Lowry (D), they failed to pay the settlement to Herzog (P).

---

### 🏛 RULE OF LAW
An assignment is binding upon the obligor where the assignor has intended to relinquish his rights and the obligor is notified of the intent to relinquish his rights to the assignee.

---

**FACTS:** Jones, who was injured in a motorcycle accident, hired attorneys Irace (D) and Lowry (D) to represent him in a personal injury action. Jones required surgery for his injuries, which was performed by Herzog (P), a physician. Since Jones was unable to pay for this treatment, he signed a letter stating that he requested "that payment be made directly . . . to John Herzog [P]" from money received in settlement for his claim. Herzog (P) notified Irace (D) and Lowry (D) of the assignment in 1988. The following year, Jones received a $20,000 settlement for his claim. Jones instructed Irace (D) and Lowry (D) to pay the money to him rather than to Herzog (P). Irace (D) and Lowry (D) followed this instruction, and Jones failed to pay Herzog (P) for the medical treatment. Herzog (P) brought a breach of assignment action against Irace (D) and Lowry (D), and the trial court ruled in favor of Herzog (P). The appellate court affirmed, and Irace (D) and Lowry (D) appealed to the state supreme court.

**ISSUE:** Is an assignment binding upon the obligor where the assignor has intended to relinquish his rights and the obligor has been notified?

**HOLDING AND DECISION:** (Brody, J.) Yes. An assignment is binding upon an obligor where the assignor has intended to relinquish his rights and the obligor has been notified. The letter directing payment to be made directly to Herzog (P) clearly and unequivocally showed Jones's intent to relinquish his control over any money received for his personal injury claim. Irace (D) and Lowry (D) were duly notified of this assignment, and therefore the settlement money should have been paid to Herzog (P). Although the assignment interfered with the ethical obligations that Irace (D) and Lowry (D) owed to Jones, the rules of professional conduct do not override the client's right to assign the proceeds of a lawsuit to a third party. Affirmed.

---

### ▶ ANALYSIS

Limitations on the right of assignment exist in many situations. Most states have a statute which restricts the assignment of wages. Also, public policy considerations protect assignors who attempt to assign future rights. The Restatement (Second) of Contracts § 317(2) does not allow assignment where the duty to the obligor would be materially changed.

---

### Quicknotes

**ASSIGNEE** A party to whom another party assigns his interest or rights.

**ASSIGNMENT** A transaction in which a party conveys his or her entire interest in property to another.

**ASSIGNOR** A party who assigns his interest or rights to another.

**OBLIGOR** Promisor; a party who has promised or is obligated to perform.

**PUBLIC POLICY** Policy administered by the state with respect to the health, safety and morals of its people in accordance with common notions of fairness and decency.

# Bel-Ray Company v. Chemrite (Pty) Ltd.

Seller (P) v. Buyer (D)

181 F.3d 435 (3d Cir. 1999).

**NATURE OF CASE:** Breach of contract.

**FACT SUMMARY:** Bel-Rey Company (P) sued Lubritene (D) for breach of an agreement assigned to it by Chemrite (Pty) Ltd. (D)

### 🏛 RULE OF LAW
Contractual provisions limiting or prohibiting assignments operate only to limit the parties' right to assign the contract, but not their power to do so, unless the parties manifest an intention to the contrary with specificity.

**FACTS:** Bel-Ray Company (P), a New Jersey corporation, entered into agreements with a South African corporation, Chemrite (Pty) Ltd. (D), for the distribution of its products in South Africa. Later, Lubritene (D) acquired Chemrite's (D) business, including rights under the agreements with Bel-Rey (P). Bel-Rey (P) brought suit against Lubritene charging it with fraud and violation of the agreements. The district court granted Bel-Rey (P) an order to arbitrate and Lubritene (D) appealed.

**ISSUE:** Do contractual provisions limiting or prohibiting assignments operate only to limit the parties' right to assign the contract, but not their power to do so, unless the parties manifest an intention to the contrary with specificity?

**HOLDING AND DECISION:** (Stapleton, J.) Yes. Contractual provisions limiting or prohibiting assignments operate only to limit the parties' right to assign the contract, but not their power to do so, unless the parties manifest an intention to the contrary with specificity. None of the agreements here contain language specifically stating that an assignment without Bel-Rey's (P) written consent would be void or invalid. Such language is not requisitely clear to limit Chemrite's (D) power to assign the agreements, thus the order to compel Lubritene (D) to arbitrate is enforceable. Affirmed.

### ▌ANALYSIS

Under the Federal Arbitration Act (FAA), a court may compel arbitration only if the parties have entered into a written agreement to arbitrate that covers the particular dispute.

**ASSIGNMENT** A transaction in which a party conveys his or her entire interest in property to another.

### Quicknotes

**ARBITRATION** An agreement to have a dispute heard and decided by a neutral third party, rather than through legal proceedings.

# Delacy Investments, Inc. v. Thurman & Re/Max Real Estate Guide, Inc.

Commissions factoring company (P) v. Real estate brokerage firm (D)

Minn. Ct. App., 693 N.W.2d 479 (2005).

**NATURE OF CASE:** Appeal from summary judgment for defendant in action for payment of account receivable.

**FACT SUMMARY:** Delacy Investments, Inc. d/b/a Commission Express (CE) (P), a commissions factoring company, contended that commissions generated by Thurman on the sale of real estate that Thurman had assigned to CE (P) belonged to CE (P) because Re/Max Real Estate Guide, Inc. (Re/Max) (D), the real estate broker through which Thurman generated the commissions on the basis of an independent-contractor agreement, was on notice of the previously executed assignment agreement between CE (P) and Thurman.

> ### 🏛 RULE OF LAW
> Under UCC § 9-404, a secured assignee is not entitled to payment of an account receivable where the assignor is not entitled to the account, but an account debtor is entitled to it, even where the account debtor has notice of a previously executed assignment agreement between the assignor and assignee.

**FACTS:** Thurman, a real estate agent, entered into an agreement with Delacy Investments, Inc. d/b/a Commission Express (CE) (P), a commissions factoring company, whereby he assigned his future commissions, or accounts receivable, to CE (P). CE (P) had a security interest in the accounts receivable and perfected this interest by filing a Uniform Commercial Code (UCC) financing statement with the state. Over a year later, Thurman entered a standard independent-contractor agreement with Re/Max Real Estate Guide, Inc. (Re/Max) (D), a real estate broker. Under the agreement with Re/Max (D), Thurman agreed to pay certain overhead expenses and the agreement provided that Thurman would be entitled to commissions only to the extent that they exceeded Thurman's past-due financial obligations to Re/Max (D). Thus, under the agreement with CE (P), Thurman was the assignee, CE (P) was the assignor, and Re/Max (D) was an "account debtor," meaning that Re/Max had the potential right to receive that which Thurman assigned to CE (P). A couple of months later, Re/Max (D) executed an acknowledgment of CE's (P) security interest in Thurman's account receivable from the sale of certain real estate. Accordingly, Re/Max (D) directed that the commission be paid directly to CE (P). Subsequently, Thurman and CE (P) entered an agreement whereby Thurman assigned to CE (P) $10,000 of a commission he anticipated earning on the sale of a different

property. Less than a couple of months later, Re/Max (D) terminated Thurman for poor performance and other performance-related issues. At the time of his termination Thurman owed Re/Max (D) over $11,000. Consequently, Re/Max (D) refused to pay the assigned receivable to CE (P) and, as per the independent-contractor agreement, applied the commission to Thurman's balance. CE (P) brought suit for payment of $10,000 of Thurman's account receivable. The trial court granted summary judgment to Re/Max (D), finding that because Thurman was not entitled to the commission, neither was CE (P). The state's intermediate appellate court granted review.

**ISSUE:** Under UCC § 9-404, is a secured assignee entitled to payment of an account receivable where the assignor is not entitled to the account, but an account debtor is entitled to it, even where the account debtor has notice of a previously executed assignment agreement between the assignor and assignee?

**HOLDING AND DECISION:** (Halbrooks, J.) No. Under UCC § 9-404, a secured assignee is not entitled to payment of an account receivable where the assignor is not entitled to the account, but an account debtor is entitled to it, even where the account debtor has notice of a previously executed assignment agreement between the assignor and assignee. This is a case of first impression in this jurisdiction. However, under UCC § 9-404, an assignee's rights are subject to all terms of the agreement between the account debtor and the assignor. Therefore, so long as Thurman was not entitled to collect a commission while his fees were in arrears, CE (P) was not entitled to the commission because it did not have a greater right to the commission than Thurman did. Or, as the official comment to the UCC indicates, an assignee generally takes an assignment subject to the defenses and claims of an account debtor. Moreover, it makes no difference whether the defense or claim accrues before or after the account debtor is notified of the assignment. Thus, under UCC § 9-404(a)(1), the rights of CE (P) are subject to all the terms of the independent-contractor agreement between Thurman and Re/Max (D). This conclusion is supported by black-letter law that an assignee can take no greater rights than the assignor, and cannot be in a better position than the assignor, and is also supported by case law from other jurisdictions. For all these reasons, CE (P) is bound by the independent-contractor agreement and is not entitled to the commission. Nonetheless, CE (P) contends that

*Continued on next page.*

under UCC § 9-404(a)(2), Re/Max (D), as an account debtor, was not permitted to contract away the rights of Thurman as assignee after having received notice of the previously executed assignment agreement. Although CE (P) is correct in asserting that Re/Max (D) had notice of the agreement, a perfected security interest is generally effective against creditors except as otherwise provided in the UCC Uniform Commercial Code § 9-404(a)(1) provides otherwise, so UCC § 9-404(a)(2) is inapplicable here. UCC § 9-404(a)(1) makes it clear that CE's (P) rights "are subject to . . . all terms of the agreement between the account debtor and assignor." Therefore, the trial court did not err by granting summary judgment to Re/Max (D). Affirmed.

## ▶ ANALYSIS

In keeping with the holding of this case, the Restatement (Second) of Contracts § 336, ct. b (1981) explains that an assignor can assign "only what he has" and "is subject to limitations imposed by the terms of that contract [creating the right] and to defenses which would have been available against the [account debtor] had there been no assignment."

## Quicknotes

**ASSIGNEE** A party to whom another party assigns his interest or rights.

**ASSIGNOR** A party who assigns his interest or rights to another.

**SUMMARY JUDGMENT** A judgment rendered by a court in response to a motion made by one of the parties, claiming that the lack of a question of material fact in respect to an issue warrants disposition of the issue without consideration by the jury.

# Chemical Bank v. Rinden Professional Association

## Assignee (P) v. Lessee (D)

N.H. Sup. Ct., 126 N.H. 688, 498 A.2d 706 (1985).

**NATURE OF CASE:** Appeal from award of damages for breach of contract.

**FACT SUMMARY:** Rinden Professional Association (Rinden) (D) contended it did not waive its defenses to performance of a lease agreement because such waiver was unconscionable.

> **RULE OF LAW**
> A valid waiver is accomplished where an agreement to waive is made for value, in good faith, and without notice of a claim or defense.

**FACTS:** Rinden Professional Association (Rinden) (D) leased phone equipment from Intertel, making monthly payments. Intertel assigned its rights in the lease to Chemical Bank (P) after Rinden (D) signed a document waiving any defenses assertable against Intertel. The phones malfunctioned, and Rinden (D) ceased payments. Chemical Bank (P) sued for breach. Rinden (D) contended no valid waiver occurred because such would be unconscionable. Rinden (D) appealed judgment for Chemical Bank (P).

**ISSUE:** Is a valid waiver accomplished after an agreement to waive is entered for value, in good faith, and without notice of claim or defense?

**HOLDING AND DECISION:** (Douglas, J.) Yes. A valid waiver is attained upon an agreement to waive for value, in good faith, and without notice of claim or defense. Here, Rinden (D) voluntarily and knowingly waived the defenses, and Chemical Bank (P) acted in good faith in giving full disclosure of its intentions. It paid value for the lease and lacked knowledge of any problems with the system. Thus, the waiver was effective. Affirmed.

> **ANALYSIS**
>
> This case is analogous to the bona fide purchaser situation where value is paid for a negotiable instrument or parcel of property without knowledge of any defenses thereto. The lessee here, however, clearly waived any defenses assertable against Intertel, and thus it could not assert such defenses against Chemical Bank (P).

## Quicknotes

**UCC 2-209 (1)** An agreement modifying a contract within this article needs no consideration to be binding.

**WAIVER** The intentional or voluntary forfeiture of a recognized right.

# Glossary

*Common Latin Words and Phrases Encountered in the Law*

**A FORTIORI:** Because one fact exists or has been proven, therefore a second fact that is related to the first fact must also exist.

**A PRIORI:** From the cause to the effect. A term of logic used to denote that when one generally accepted truth is shown to be a cause, another particular effect must necessarily follow.

**AB INITIO:** From the beginning; a condition which has existed throughout, as in a marriage which was void ab initio.

**ACTUS REUS:** The wrongful act; in criminal law, such action sufficient to trigger criminal liability.

**AD VALOREM:** According to value; an ad valorem tax is imposed upon an item located within the taxing jurisdiction calculated by the value of such item.

**AMICUS CURIAE:** Friend of the court. Its most common usage takes the form of an amicus curiae brief, filed by a person who is not a party to an action but is nonetheless allowed to offer an argument supporting his legal interests.

**ARGUENDO:** In arguing. A statement, possibly hypothetical, made for the purpose of argument, is one made arguendo.

**BILL QUIA TIMET:** A bill to quiet title (establish ownership) to real property.

**BONA FIDE:** True, honest, or genuine. May refer to a person's legal position based on good faith or lacking notice of fraud (such as a bona fide purchaser for value) or to the authenticity of a particular document (such as a bona fide last will and testament).

**CAUSA MORTIS:** With approaching death in mind. A gift causa mortis is a gift given by a party who feels certain that death is imminent.

**CAVEAT EMPTOR:** Let the buyer beware. This maxim is reflected in the rule of law that a buyer purchases at his own risk because it is his responsibility to examine, judge, test, and otherwise inspect what he is buying.

**CERTIORARI:** A writ of review. Petitions for review of a case by the United States Supreme Court are most often done by means of a writ of certiorari.

**CONTRA:** On the other hand. Opposite. Contrary to.

**CORAM NOBIS:** Before us; writs of error directed to the court that originally rendered the judgment.

**CORAM VOBIS:** Before you; writs of error directed by an appellate court to a lower court to correct a factual error.

**CORPUS DELICTI:** The body of the crime; the requisite elements of a crime amounting to objective proof that a crime has been committed.

**CUM TESTAMENTO ANNEXO, ADMINISTRATOR (ADMINISTRATOR C.T.A.):** With will annexed; an administrator c.t.a. settles an estate pursuant to a will in which he is not appointed.

**DE BONIS NON, ADMINISTRATOR (ADMINISTRATOR D.B.N.):** Of goods not administered; an administrator d.b.n. settles a partially settled estate.

**DE FACTO:** In fact; in reality; actually. Existing in fact but not officially approved or engendered.

**DE JURE:** By right; lawful. Describes a condition that is legitimate "as a matter of law," in contrast to the term "de facto," which connotes something existing in fact but not legally sanctioned or authorized. For example, de facto segregation refers to segregation brought about by housing patterns, etc., whereas de jure segregation refers to segregation created by law.

**DE MINIMIS:** Of minimal importance; insignificant; a trifle; not worth bothering about.

**DE NOVO:** Anew; a second time; afresh. A trial de novo is a new trial held at the appellate level as if the case originated there and the trial at a lower level had not taken place.

**DICTA:** Generally used as an abbreviated form of obiter dicta, a term describing those portions of a judicial opinion incidental or not necessary to resolution of the specific question before the court. Such nonessential statements and remarks are not considered to be binding precedent.

**DUCES TECUM:** Refers to a particular type of writ or subpoena requesting a party or organization to produce certain documents in their possession.

**EN BANC:** Full bench. Where a court sits with all justices present rather than the usual quorum.

**EX PARTE:** For one side or one party only. An ex parte proceeding is one undertaken for the benefit of only one party, without notice to, or an appearance by, an adverse party.

**EX POST FACTO:** After the fact. An ex post facto law is a law that retroactively changes the consequences of a prior act.

**EX REL.:** Abbreviated form of the term "ex relatione," meaning upon relation or information. When the state brings an action in which it has no interest against an individual at the instigation of one who has a private interest in the matter.

**FORUM NON CONVENIENS:** Inconvenient forum. Although a court may have jurisdiction over the case, the action should be tried in a more conveniently located court, one to which parties and witnesses may more easily travel, for example.

**GUARDIAN AD LITEM:** A guardian of an infant as to litigation, appointed to represent the infant and pursue his/her rights.

**HABEAS CORPUS:** You have the body. The modern writ of habeas corpus is a writ directing that a person (body) being detained (such as a prisoner) be brought before the court so that the legality of his detention can be judicially ascertained.

**IN CAMERA:** In private, in chambers. When a hearing is held before a judge in his chambers or when all spectators are excluded from the courtroom.

**IN FORMA PAUPERIS:** In the manner of a pauper. A party who proceeds in forma pauperis because of his poverty is one who is allowed to bring suit without liability for costs.

**INFRA:** Below, under. A word referring the reader to a later part of a book. (The opposite of supra.)

**IN LOCO PARENTIS:** In the place of a parent.

**IN PARI DELICTO:** Equally wrong; a court of equity will not grant requested relief to an applicant who is in pari delicto, or as much at fault in the transactions giving rise to the controversy as is the opponent of the applicant.

**IN PARI MATERIA:** On like subject matter or upon the same matter. Statutes relating to the same person or things are said to be in pari materia. It is a general rule of statutory construction that such statutes should be construed together, i.e., looked at as if they together constituted one law.

**IN PERSONAM:** Against the person. Jurisdiction over the person of an individual.

**IN RE:** In the matter of. Used to designate a proceeding involving an estate or other property.

**IN REM:** A term that signifies an action against the res, or thing. An action in rem is basically one that is taken directly against property, as distinguished from an action in personam, i.e., against the person.

**INTER ALIA:** Among other things. Used to show that the whole of a statement, pleading, list, statute, etc., has not been set forth in its entirety.

**INTER PARTES:** Between the parties. May refer to contracts, conveyances or other transactions having legal significance.

**INTER VIVOS:** Between the living. An inter vivos gift is a gift made by a living grantor, as distinguished from bequests contained in a will, which pass upon the death of the testator.

**IPSO FACTO:** By the mere fact itself.

**JUS:** Law or the entire body of law.

**LEX LOCI:** The law of the place; the notion that the rights of parties to a legal proceeding are governed by the law of the place where those rights arose.

**MALUM IN SE:** Evil or wrong in and of itself; inherently wrong. This term describes an act that is wrong by its very nature, as opposed to one which would not be wrong but for the fact that there is a specific legal prohibition against it (malum prohibitum).

**MALUM PROHIBITUM:** Wrong because prohibited, but not inherently evil. Used to describe something that is wrong because it is expressly forbidden by law but that is not in and of itself evil, e.g., speeding.

**MANDAMUS:** We command. A writ directing an official to take a certain action.

**MENS REA:** A guilty mind; a criminal intent. A term used to signify the mental state that accompanies a crime or other prohibited act. Some crimes require only a general mens rea (general intent to do the prohibited act), but others, like assault with intent to murder, require the existence of a specific mens rea.

**MODUS OPERANDI:** Method of operating; generally refers to the manner or style of a criminal in committing crimes, admissible in appropriate cases as evidence of the identity of a defendant.

**NEXUS:** A connection to.

**NISI PRIUS:** A court of first impression. A nisi prius court is one where issues of fact are tried before a judge or jury.

**N.O.V. (NON OBSTANTE VEREDICTO):** Notwithstanding the verdict. A judgment n.o.v. is a judgment given in favor of one party despite the fact that a verdict was returned in favor of the other party, the justification being that the verdict either had no reasonable support in fact or was contrary to law.

**NUNC PRO TUNC:** Now for then. This phrase refers to actions that may be taken and will then have full retroactive effect.

**PENDENTE LITE:** Pending the suit; pending litigation under way.

**PER CAPITA:** By head; beneficiaries of an estate, if they take in equal shares, take per capita.

**PER CURIAM:** By the court; signifies an opinion ostensibly written "by the whole court" and with no identified author.

**PER SE:** By itself, in itself; inherently.

**PER STIRPES:** By representation. Used primarily in the law of wills to describe the method of distribution where a person, generally because of death, is unable to take that which is left to him by the will of another, and therefore his heirs divide such property between them rather than take under the will individually.

**PRIMA FACIE:** On its face, at first sight. A prima facie case is one that is sufficient on its face, meaning that the evidence supporting it is adequate to establish the case until contradicted or overcome by other evidence.

**PRO TANTO:** For so much; as far as it goes. Often used in eminent domain cases when a property owner receives partial payment for his land without prejudice to his right to bring suit for the full amount he claims his land to be worth.

**QUANTUM MERUIT:** As much as he deserves. Refers to recovery based on the doctrine of unjust enrichment in those cases in which a party has rendered valuable services or furnished materials that were accepted and enjoyed by another under circumstances that would reasonably notify the recipient that the rendering party expected to be paid. In essence, the law implies a contract to pay the reasonable value of the services or materials furnished.

**QUASI:** Almost like; as if; nearly. This term is essentially used to signify that one subject or thing is almost analogous to another but that material differences between them do exist. For example, a quasi-criminal proceeding is one that is not strictly criminal but shares enough of the same characteristics to require some of the same safeguards (e.g., procedural due process must be followed in a parole hearing).

**QUID PRO QUO:** Something for something. In contract law, the consideration, something of value, passed between the parties to render the contract binding.

**RES GESTAE:** Things done; in evidence law, this principle justifies the admission of a statement that would otherwise be hearsay when it is made so closely to the event in question as to be said to be a part of it, or with such spontaneity as not to have the possibility of falsehood.

**RES IPSA LOQUITUR:** The thing speaks for itself. This doctrine gives rise to a rebuttable presumption of negligence when the instrumentality causing the injury was within the exclusive control of the defendant, and the injury was one that does not normally occur unless a person has been negligent.

**RES JUDICATA:** A matter adjudged. Doctrine which provides that once a court of competent jurisdiction has rendered a final judgment or decree on the merits, that judgment or decree is conclusive upon the parties to the case and prevents them from engaging in any other litigation on the points and issues determined therein.

**RESPONDEAT SUPERIOR:** Let the master reply. This doctrine holds the master liable for the wrongful acts of his servant (or the principal for his agent) in those cases in which the servant (or agent) was acting within the scope of his authority at the time of the injury.

**STARE DECISIS:** To stand by or adhere to that which has been decided. The common law doctrine of stare decisis attempts to give security and certainty to the law by following the policy that once a principle of law as applicable to a certain set of facts has been set forth in a decision, it forms a precedent which will subsequently be followed, even though a different decision might be made were it the first time the question had arisen. Of course, stare decisis is not an inviolable principle and is departed from in instances where there is good cause (e.g., considerations of public policy led the Supreme Court to disregard prior decisions sanctioning segregation).

**SUPRA:** Above. A word referring a reader to an earlier part of a book.

**ULTRA VIRES:** Beyond the power. This phrase is most commonly used to refer to actions taken by a corporation that are beyond the power or legal authority of the corporation.

## Addendum of French Derivatives

**IN PAIS:** Not pursuant to legal proceedings.

**CHATTEL:** Tangible personal property.

**CY PRES:** Doctrine permitting courts to apply trust funds to purposes not expressed in the trust but necessary to carry out the settlor's intent.

**PER AUTRE VIE:** For another's life; during another's life. In property law, an estate may be granted that will terminate upon the death of someone other than the grantee.

**PROFIT A PRENDRE:** A license to remove minerals or other produce from land.

**VOIR DIRE:** Process of questioning jurors as to their predispositions about the case or parties to a proceeding in order to identify those jurors displaying bias or prejudice.

# Casenote® Legal Briefs

Common law

Breach (generally)

material — not material

material:
- treat as partial (damages, but do not suspend performance)
- Suspend
  - Cure?
  - treat as total (terminate)

not material:
- treat as partial

K price = $100,000
B spent so far = $20,000
would cost $85,000 to build the, 15,000 profit
(Can add. $65,000)

reliance + profit
$35,000

loss in value        100,000
- cost avoided        65,000
                      =$35,000

K price $1,000,000.
Spent so far $600,000.
Cost & complete $500,000.

expectation damages: 500,000 (loss in value - cost saved)
Quantum meruit: $600,000
⤷ but if the other party is sharp they will deduct what you would have lost.